Tourism Planning
Policies, Processes and Relationships

Second Edition

C. MICHAEL HALL

An imprint of **Pearson Education**
Harlow, England • London • New York • Boston • San Francisco • Toronto • Sydney • Tokyo • Singapore • Hong Kong
Seoul • Taipei • New Delhi • Cape Town • Madrid • Mexico City • Amsterdam • Munich • Paris • Milan

Pearson Education Limited
Edinburgh Gate
Harlow
Essex CM20 2JE
England

and Associated Companies throughout the world

Visit us on the World Wide Web at:
www.pearsoned.co.uk

First published 2000
Second edition 2008

© Pearson Education 2000, 2008

ISBN 978-0-13-204652-7

British Library Cataloguing-in-Publication Data
A catalogue record for this book is available from the British Library

Library of Congress Cataloging-in-Publication Data

Hall, Colin Michael, 1961–
    Tourism planning : policies, processes and relationships / C. Michael Hall.— 2nd ed.
        p.   cm.
    Includes bibliographical references and index.
    ISBN-13: 978-0-13-204652-7 (pbk.)
    1. Tourism—Planning.   I. Title.
    G155.A1H349 2008
    338.4'791—dc22

                                                                        2007035893

ARP Impression 98

Typeset in 10.25/12.25 Sabon by 73
Printed in Great Britain by Clays Ltd, St Ives plc

The publisher's policy is to use paper manufactured from sustainable forests.

Tourism Planning

To the Wandering Islands

Contents

List of figures   viii
List of tables   ix
List of planning insights   xi
List of plates   xii
Preface   xiii
Acknowledgements   xv
List of abbreviations   xvi

1 Inside the 'black box' of tourism planning and policy:
setting a context   1

2 Tourism planning and policy: responding to change –
the sustainable imperative   19

3 The changing dimensions of tourism planning   44

4 Tourism planning systems: theory, thinking and exorcism   69

5 The integrated and strategic tourism planning process:
dealing with interdependence   101

6 Tourism planning and policy at the international
and supranational level   134

7 Tourism planning and policy at the national and
sub-national level   163

8 Planning destinations: competition and cooperation   191

9 Planning sites: sustainable design   227

10 Implementation and instruments: policy and implementation
as two sides of the same coin   244

11 Conclusions and reflections: thinking sustainable planning   262

Bibliography   269
Index   299

List of figures

1.1 Classifications of temporary mobility in space and time   6

1.2 Extent of temporary mobility in space and time   7

1.3 Positioning tourism planning and policy studies   14

1.4 Opening the black box of tourism planning and policy systems   15

2.1 Sustainable tourism and sustainable development   27

2.2 Dimensions of the impacts of tourism   28

2.3 Understanding the consequences and meanings of tourism   31

2.4 The influence of scale of temporal and spatial resolution on assessing tourism-related change   32

2.5 Scale in tourism analysis: primary foci in socio-economic systems, biodiversity and climate research in terms of research outputs   33

2.6 A matrix of the consequences of tourism by dimension and environment   34

2.7 Tourism and changes to ecosystem services and human well-being   38

2.8 Outline of ecological footprint analysis   40

3.1 The issue attention cycle   46

4.1 Geographical elements of a tourist system and associated psychological and industrial elements   77

4.2 The tourism system   78

4.3 Formal destination production elements of a tourism system   79

4.4 Types of tourism planning and policy analysis   83

4.5 The 4-D model of appreciative inquiry   87

5.1 A regional planning process for tourism   103

5.2 The environments of tourism planning   108

5.3 Multi-level governance fields: the case of ecotourism   109

5.4 Strategic tourism planning process   115

5.5 Categorisation of stakeholder attitudes towards tourism   123

6.1 Multi-layered tourism governance   137

6.2 The 'traditional' realm of international relations (pre-mid-nineteenth century)   138

6.3 Growth in the international scale of governance (late nineteenth century)   139

6.4 Growth in international and supranational bodies (1945–1960s)   140

6.5 Growth in transnational relations at all levels (1970s)   141

6.6 Contemporary multi-level governance   142

7.1 Factors leading to the design of government tourism institutions, their authority and tasks   176

8.1 Interrelationships of different forms of network relationships at a destination and relationship to tourist consumption   213

9.1 Metaphors of adaptive cycles   231

9.2 Design panarchy   232

9.3 Life cycle assessment   236

11.1 Planning orientations and the planning problem   266

List of tables

1.1 International tourism arrivals and forecasts 2

1.2 Range of tourism policy roles in tourism agencies 11

2.1 International milestones in sustainable development 21

2.2 Millennium development goals 22

2.3 Actions required to promote the shift towards sustainable consumption and production 23

2.4 Key messages of the Millennium Ecosystem Assessment 24

2.5 Main findings of the Millennium Ecosystem Assessment 25

2.6 Positive and negative dimensions of tourism 29

3.1 International tourism policies from 1945 to the present 45

3.2 Timelines for traditions of tourism planning 51

3.3 Tourism planning approaches: assumptions, problem definition, methods, models and literature 52

3.4 Key readings/influences in tourism planning and policy as assessed by number of citations 66

4.1 Scales of analysis in tourism 82

4.2 Comparison of action-research and appreciative inquiry 86

4.3 Inquiry strategy 89

4.4 The appreciative inquiry interview process 90

5.1 Elements of a synergistic tourism planning approach 102

5.2 Steps and outcomes in a regional planning process for tourism 104

5.3 Tourism and related organisations from the international to the local scale 111

5.4 Multiple scales of institutional arrangements for ecotourism policy and planning in the Nordic countries: the case of Finland, Norway, and Sweden 112

5.5 The collaborative process 120

5.6 Steps in the stakeholder audit 121

5.7 Roles of evaluation and monitoring in the tourism planning and policy-making process 127

5.8 Characteristics and purposes of audit and evaluation 128

6.1 World Heritage List sites by status, 1998–2006 152

7.1 'Hard' and executive survey data used to derive scores for the WEF (2007) Travel and Tourism Competitiveness Index 172

7.2 Relationships between international tourism arrivals for countries by rank and WEF competitiveness rankings 174

7.3 Institutional arrangements for government involvement for tourism in New Zealand 177

7.4 Tourism responsibilities of local government agencies in New Zealand 182

7.5 The importance of factors related to the formation of sister city relationships to New Zealand cities 187

8.1 Outline of regional factors of competitiveness 200

8.2 Low-, middle- and high-road regional competitiveness strategies 201

8.3 Key factors in the success of regional tourism development (measured in terms of numbers of visitors) 201

8.4 Examples of community management-based indicators of tourism impact in resort communities   205

8.5 Characteristics of local growth controls and management techniques   207

8.6 Potential tourism development specific growth management strategy options   209

8.7 Organisational and personal dimensions of the network construct in tourism   211

8.8 Network categorisations – using wine tourism examples   212

8.9 Classification of policy types   223

9.1 Lessons of flagship developments   238

10.1 General principles for the management of natural and cultural heritage in Australia's World Heritage properties   247

10.2 Legally required elements of management plans for a declared Australian World Heritage property   248

10.3 Tourism planning and policy instruments   250

10.4 Approaches to implementation   255

11.1 The four characteristics of a sustainable community   265

List of planning insights

1.1 The role of planning theory   12
2.1 Ecological footprint analysis   39
3.1 The issue attention cycle   46
4.1 Prescriptive and descriptive approaches to tourism planning and policy   71
4.2 Appreciative inquiry   85
5.1 Stakeholder audit   121
6.1 The transboundary air pollution calendar of East Asia   148

7.1 National travel and tourism competitiveness   171
7.2 Sister city relationships as a sub-national tourism policy tool   185
8.1 Classifying policy   223
9.1 Authenticity   230
9.2 Life cycle analysis   236
10.1 Tourism and the 'rules of the game' for First Nations in British Columbia   253

List of plates

1.1 Waterfront development at Noosa, Queensland, Australia 2

1.2 Canal estate development at Noosa 3

1.3 Rock wall at Noosa Beach 3

1.4 Severe gully erosion, Noosa, Queensland 4

1.5 Replacement of wetlands and coastal heath with a golf course 4

3.1 Bristol City Treasury, England 45

3.2 Canterbury, Kent, England 57

3.3 Canterbury Cathedral, Kent, England 58

6.1 Franklin Dam site, Tasmania, Australia 150

6.2 Mount Cook National Park, New Zealand 153

6.3 Cliff Palace World Heritage Site, Mesa Verde National Park, Colorado, USA 154

6.4 Acropolis, Athens, Greece 155

6.5 Smelter turned museum, Roros, Norway 155

8.1 Darling Harbour redevelopment, Sydney, Australia 194

8.2 Docklands redevelopment, London, England 195

8.3 Crown Casino, Melbourne, Australia 196

8.4 Waterfront redevelopment, Dublin, Ireland 197

8.5 New opera house and waterfront development, Copenhagen, Denmark 198

8.6 Clarke Quay, waterfront redevelopment, Singapore 199

8.7 Whistler, British Columbia, Canada 202

9.1 Granville Island, Vancouver, British Columbia, Canada 234

9.2 Cement works, Granville Island 235

9.3 Development of post Expo derelict land, Vancouver 235

9.4 Adaptive use of vernacular design for a hotel complex, near Lillehammer, Norway 240

9.5 Leisure, culture and tourism adaptive reuse, Christchurch, New Zealand 240

Preface

This particular book on tourism planning seeks to outline a broad approach to the problem of tourism planning that attempts to encourage the reader to conceptualise the highly complex arena within which tourism planning and policy operates. It stresses that conceptualisation and the analysis and application of planning tools need to go hand in hand. It also stresses that planning is difficult – it is irrational, complex, political, value laden and, often, frustratingly incomplete. Moreover, by stressing the search for sustainability as the vision for tourism planning it perhaps becomes even more difficult, yet maybe all the more important given the present state of the world and tourism.

This being said, I make no apologies for stating it at the outset. This book is suggesting that rather than seeing the 'irrationality' of the real world as a problem, particularly in the way tourism planning experiences often fail to match up to what the texts say should happen, we should be trying to embrace such supposed 'irrationality' and use it creatively and positively, especially as this is how the world actually works. Therefore this book aims to provide both planning tools in terms of what you need to do and encourages you to think and reflect on the nature of the tourism planning and policy process so that you can understand why the planning process works the way it does.

Some of these concerns are of course not new either in tourism studies or in some of my own previous work. My concern for the political found in my writing on tourism politics and policy making (e.g. Hall 1994; Hall and Jenkins 1995), including some of my early work on events, and the America's Cup in particular, led me into tourism research in the first place, although I was originally more interested in environmental history and natural resource management and policy. Tourism planning and development issues have also long been an interest and have found their way into a number of works I have written or co-edited on tourism, while issues of relevance, critical analysis and counter-institutional thinking have long been a somewhat 'dirty' undercurrent in some of my work (Hall 2004c, 2005a). To mention these things is important for what is to come. The book notes the significance of relational approaches to tourism planning, it talks of values, one's position in the planning process, and the importance of trust as the glue that actually makes collaboration work. In short, it highlights the personal and the dialectical. This therefore makes it important, for me at least, to note some of the influences which have affected how the book has evolved and to try to convey to the reader that the book is part of a power, interest and value-laden process and not an end in itself. It is imperfect, it will develop and change over time, but hopefully it is a useful means by which a staging post for planning dialogue, process and debate can be opened. Therefore I am seeking to try to acknowledge, albeit usually unsuccessfully, the various influences and inspirations that cannot normally be noted just by the referencing of a publication.

As the reader might then guess, this book has had a long gestation period, with some of the ideas within it dating back to when I was undertaking my graduate studies in geography, public policy and resource management. Therefore several of the ideas in this book have something approaching genesis in my experiences with my graduate supervisors Michael Wood, Bruce Mitchell and Geoff McBoyle; indeed parts of my

Master's thesis found themselves in this manuscript after a number of years lying on the back of a shelf at home unread by anyone except John Jenkins. Similarly, a number of ideas have been generated from encountering the insights of Stuart Brand, David Harvey, Giandominico Majone and John Ralston Saul. Work with a number of colleagues has also provided sources for several of the ideas used in this book. Writing in the policy areas with John Jenkins (e.g. Hall and Jenkins 1995, 2004; Hall *et al.* 1997; Butler *et al.* 1998) has proved invaluable for stimulating ideas and material on the nature of the tourism policy-making process and the role of government in tourism. Similarly, work in the field of heritage management with Simon McArthur (e.g. Hall and McArthur 1996, 1998) has proven invaluable for focusing on how the planning process can be shaped and the reasons why it should be approached in certain ways. More recently I have been fortunate to have worked with Alan Lew, Allan Williams and Stephen Page on various geographical dimensions of tourism (e.g. Hall and Lew 1998; Hall and Page 2006); Dieter Müller, Tim Coles and David Duval in relation to contemporary mobility; Stefan Gössling and Daniel Scott in the arena of global environmental change; and Dieter Müller and Jarkko Saarinen with respect to tourism in peripheral areas, with all of these projects strongly influencing my thoughts on the effects of tourism, issues of relevance in academic work, and the central role of values in tourism planning and policy making.

At times my own ideas cannot be separated from some of my colleagues', given that we have worked so closely together – even though they may at times wish so and despite the fact they don't get any of the royalties directly! In addition, I would also specifically like to thank Craig Millar for his generosity in sharing his excellent insights into the role of trust in resource management with me many years ago; Steve Selin for his excellent work on collaboration; Eliza Raymond for being willing to share her experiences in Appreciative Inquiry and Fiona McKay for her work on sister cities.

Time spent at Lund University Helsingborg, Umeå University, Oulu University, and Joensuu University at Savonlinna in recent years has also been extremely helpful and stimulating. In addition to colleagues noted above, Carmen Aitken, Bill Bramwell, Dick Butler, Dave Crag, Petrina Dodd, Ross Dowling, Thor Flognfeldt, Alison Gill, Monica Graham, Tom Hinch, Michael James, Linda Kell, Nicolette Le Cren, Jim MacBeth, Ewen Michael, Meiko Muramaya, Peter Murphy, Kati Pitkänen, Anna Dora Saethorsdottir, Nicola van Tiel, Sarah Wall, Brian Wheeller and Peter Williams have all contributed to the development of this book in various ways, although my interpretation of their thoughts is of course my own. Fiona Apple, Gavin Bryars, Nick Cave, Bruce Cockburn, ee cummings, Neil and Tim Finn, Fountains of Wayne, Pearl Jam, Ed Kuepper, Glenn Tilbrook, Chris Wilson and Rachel Yamagata have all assisted in providing an appropriate context within which the book was written. The administrative staff in the Department of Management at the University of Canterbury kindly helped with the printing and posting of the manuscript. I would also like to gratefully thank Andrew Taylor and all at Pearson for supporting the book and for being such a good team to work with. Finally, I would like to thank my friends and significant others (JC × 2), for their love, support and understanding; hopefully one day we will all look back at what we do and why and laugh.

C. Michael Hall
April 2007

Acknowledgements

We are grateful to the following for permission to reproduce copyright material:

Figures 3.1, 4.1, 4.2, 6.1, 6.2, 6.3, 6.4, 6.5, 6.6 8.1 and Table 8.7: Hall, C.M. (2005a) *Tourism: Rethinking the Social Science of Mobility,* Prentice Hall, Harlow. Reproduced with permission.

Table 2.2: United Nations (2006) *The Millennium Development Goals Report 2006.* United Nations, New York; Reproduced with permission; Table 2.3: United Nations (1992b) *Report of The United Nations Conference on Environment and Development,* (Rio de Janeiro, 3–14 June 1992) Annex I, Rio Declaration on Environment and Development, A/CONF.151/26 (Vol. I), United Nations, New York. Reproduced with permission; Table 2.4: Board of the Millenium Ecosystem Assessment (2005) Living Beyond Our Means: Natural Assets and Human Well-being, Statement from the Board. World Resources Institute and the UN Environmental Programme, Washington, D.C. and Nairobi. Reproduced with permission; Table 2.5: Millennium Ecosystem Assessment (MIA) (2005) Ecosystems and Human Well-Being: Synthesis, Island Press, Washington D.C. Reproduced with permission; Table 5.5: Gray, B. (1989) Collaborating: Finding Common Ground for Multiparty Problems, Jossey-Bass, San Francisco. Reproduced with permission; Table 6.1: World Heritage List sites by status, 1998–2006 © UNESCO used by permission of UNESCO; Table 7.1: Blanke, J. and Chiesa, T. (2007) 'The travel & tourism competitiveness index: Assessing key factors driving the sector's development', in World Economic Forum, The Travel and Tourism Competitiveness Report 2007: Furthering the Process of Economic Development, World Economic Forum, Geneva, 3–26. Reproduced with permission.

In some instances we have been unable to trace the owners of copyright material, and we would appreciate any information that would enable us to do so.

List of abbreviations

AI	appreciative inquiry
ANTO	Austrian National Tourism Organization
APEC	Asia Pacific Economic Cooperation
APPA	Appreciative Participatory Planning and Action
ASEAN	Association of South East Nations
ATM	automatic teller machine
BACIP	before, after, control, impact, paired sampling (environmental impact assessment design)
BIE	Bureau of Industry Economics
CEO	chief executive officer
DG	Directorate-Generals
DOC	Department of Conservation (New Zealand)
EF	ecological footprint
EIAs	environmental impact assessments
EC	European Community
EU	European Union
EYT	European Year of Tourism
GATS	General Agreement on Trade in Services
GEC	global environmental change
GRDO	Global Relief and Development Organisation
HMSO	Her Majesty's Stationery Office
IA	integrated assessment
IATA	International Air Transport Association
ICAO	International Civil Aviation Organization
ICCROM	International Center for Conservation in Rome
ICOMOS	International Council for Monuments and Sites
ICT	information and communications technology
IUCN	International Union for Conservation of Nature and Natural Resources
IUOTO	International Union of Travel Organizations
LAC	limits of acceptable change
LCA	life cycle assessment
NGOs	non-governmental organisations
NZTB	New Zealand Tourist Board
MEA	Millennium Ecosystem Assessment
OAS	Organization of American States
OECD	Organization for Economic Co-operation and Development
PLA	Participatory Learning and Action
RTO	regional tourism organisation
SMTEs	small and medium-sized tourism enterprises
SWOT	strengths, weaknesses, opportunities, threats
T&T	travel and tourism
TTCI	The WEF Travel and Tourism Competitiveness Index
UN	United Nations
UNCED	United Nations Conference on Environment and Development

UNESCO	United Nations Educational, Scientific and Cultural Organization	WEF	World Economic Forum
		WHC	Convention for the Protection of the World's Cultural and Natural Heritage
UNWTO	United Nations World Tourism Organization		
		WHL	World Heritage List
VAT	value-added tax	WHO	World Health Organization
WCED	World Commission on Environment and Development	WTO	World Trade Organization
		WTTC	World Travel and Tourism Council
WCS	World Conservation Strategy		

1 Inside the 'black box' of tourism planning and policy: setting a context

Chapter objectives

After reading this chapter you will:

- Have developed working definitions of tourism, planning and policy
- Appreciate some of the key questions with respect to planning theory
- Understand the relationship between the concepts of policy and planning
- Understand the scope of the field of tourism planning.

Tourism is now a major area of academic, government, industry and public concern. While it is now an oft-cited truism that tourism is the world's largest industry, tourism is significant not just because of its size in terms of the number of people travelling, how many people it employs, or how much money it brings into a destination. Tourism is significant also because of the enormous impact it has on people's lives and on the places in which they live, and because of the way in which tourism is itself substantially affected by the world around it.

The World Tourism Organization's (1997, 2001, 2006a) forecasts predict that by 2020 international arrivals will reach nearly 1.6 billion. Of these worldwide arrivals in 2020, 1.2 billion will be intraregional and 378 million will be long-haul travellers. By 2020 the top three receiving regions will be Europe (717 million tourists), East Asia and the Pacific (397 million) and the Americas (282 million), followed by Africa, the Middle East and South Asia (Table 1.1).

International tourism flows and patterns do not occur randomly. They are the result of a number of factors including economic growth, cultural factors and access to transport. However, most importantly for the purposes of this book, they are also the result of the activities of states and their policies and planning strategies and behaviours. For example, at the most basic level international travel requires a policy decision with respect to the agreement of a state to allow entry. Nowhere in international law is there enshrined a right to enter foreign spaces. Even the non-binding Universal Declaration of Human Rights only postulates a right of exit and entry to one's own country (article 13) (Hall 2006c). Indeed, the right to control and restrict entry into state territory – as well as to determine where people can travel within a country – has 'historically been viewed as inherent in the very nature of sovereignty' (Collinson 1996: 77).

This chapter will set part of the context for the book by overviewing some of the key concepts of 'planning' and 'policy' and the relationships between them, as well as discussing the concept of tourism utilised in this book. The chapter will then go on to sketch the scope of tourism planning before briefly outlining the remainder of the book.

Tourism

An understanding of the definition of tourism is important at a variety of practical and theoretical levels. However, with respect to tourism policy

Table 1.1 International tourism arrivals and forecasts

Year	World	Africa	Americas	Asia & Pacific	Europe	Middle East
1950	25.3	0.5	7.5	0.2	16.8	0.2
1960	69.3	0.8	16.7	0.9	50.4	0.6
1965	112.9	1.4	23.2	2.1	83.7	2.4
1970	165.8	2.4	42.3	6.2	113.0	1.9
1975	222.3	4.7	50.0	10.2	153.9	3.5
1980	278.1	7.2	62.3	23.0	178.5	7.1
1985	320.1	9.7	65.1	32.9	204.3	8.1
1990	439.5	15.2	92.8	56.2	265.8	9.6
1995	540.6	20.4	109.0	82.4	315.0	13.7
2000	687.0	28.3	128.1	110.5	395.9	24.2
2005	806.8	37.3	133.5	155.4	441.5	39.0
Forecast						
2010	1006	47	190	195	527	36
2020	1561	77	282	397	717	69

Sources: WTO (1997, 2006a,b).

Plate 1.1 Waterfront development at Noosa, Queensland, Australia. Tourism development at this popular resort town has been controversial for many years. Issues include engineering works on the river mouth, replacement of cheap accommodation on the peninsula by more upmarket accommodation and resorts, proposals to build resorts in natural areas, and inappropriate siting of tourism facilities.

Plate 1.2 Canal estate development at Noosa. The canal estate development replaced existing wetlands.

Plate 1.3 Rock wall at Noosa Beach. Because the beach area and the spit is geomorphologically unstable, engineering works have been required to protect the valuable real estate on the spit.

Plate 1.4 Severe gully erosion, Noosa, Queensland. Inadequate consideration of drainage needs following estate development lead to severe erosion.

Plate 1.5 Replacement of wetlands and coastal heath with a golf course. Hyatt Coolum, Queensland.

and planning the definition of tourism helps distinguish not only what we study but also how we analyse and govern it. For example, how can government develop policy for tourism unless they have a clear understanding of what it is?

According to Gunn with Var (2002: 4), 'tourism itself is an abstraction. It doesn't exist, at least not in the same sense as a residence. Tourism is not even a discipline, such as chemistry and geography'. I completely disagree! (See Hall 2005a.)

Of significance to all definitions of tourism are concepts of space (i.e. travel away from a 'home' location or region) and time (i.e. the time spent away from a home location). Yet because of the capacities of people to travel further and faster as a result of improvements in technology, changes in accessibility and increases in personal wealth, the boundaries that are selected as determinants of what constitutes short-term travel are increasingly fluid. For example, in order to improve the collection of statistics and improve understanding of tourism, the United Nations and the World Tourism Organization (WTO) recommended differentiating between visitors, tourists and excursionists (daytrippers). The WTO (1991) recommended that an international tourist be defined as:

> a visitor who travels to a country other than that in which he/she has his/her usual residence for at least one night but not more than one year, and whose main purpose of visit is other than the exercise of an activity remunerated from within the country visited

and that an international excursionist (e.g. cruise ship visitors) is defined as

> a visitor residing in a country who travels the same day to a country other than that in which he/she has his/her usual environment for less than 24 hours without spending the night in the country visited and whose main purpose of visit is other than the exercise of an activity remunerated from within the country visited.

Similar definitions were also developed for domestic tourists, with these having a time limit of 'not more than six months' (WTO 1991; United Nations 1994). As Hall and Page (2006) noted, the inclusion of a same-day travel, 'excursionist' category in technical definitions of tourism makes the division between such categories as recreation and tourism, or daytrips and tourism, even more arbitrary, and they observed that there is increasing international agreement that 'tourism' refers to all activities of visitors, including both overnight and same-day visitors.

Figure 1.1 highlights the way in which boundaries in time and space are used to delineate tourism from other forms of human mobility. As noted above, such boundaries are useful, in fact necessary from a statistical perspective, but they do not necessarily contribute very easily to a 'common-sense' perspective towards tourism, particularly as categories of tourism are scattered throughout the various statistical fields of daytrips, tourism and migration. Nevertheless, even a statistical approach to tourism can generate awareness of some of the policy dimensions of tourism as, clearly, one needs to be able to cross a border in order to become a statistic in the first place.

Perhaps more importantly in policy and planning terms, in response to the deficiencies of a statistical or technical approach to tourism in policy terms, tourism is increasingly being interpreted as but one, albeit highly significant, dimension of temporary mobility and circulation (Coles *et al.* 2004; Hall 2005a). Figure 1.2 presents a model for describing different forms of temporary mobility, such as those noted above, in terms of three dimensions of space, time and number of trips. Figure 1.2 therefore illustrates the decline in the overall number of trips or movements, time and distance away from a central generating point that would often be termed 'home'. The number of movements declines the further one travels in time and space away from the point of origin. The relationship represented in Figure 1.2 holds whether one is describing the totality of movements of individuals over their life spans from a central point (home) or for an extended period of time, or whether one is describing the total characteristics of a population. In addition, the figure illustrates the relationship between tourism and other forms of temporary mobility, including various forms of what is often regarded as migration or temporary migration.

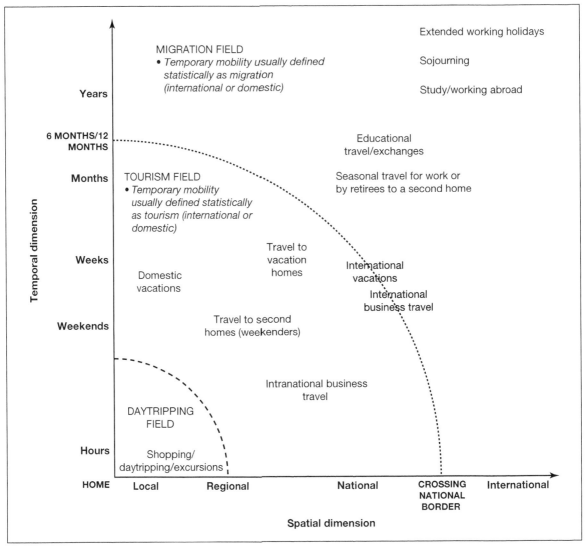

Figure 1.1 Classifications of temporary mobility in space and time
Source: From Hall (2003b).

Along with more traditional categories such as leisure travel, visiting friends and relations (VFR), and business and convention travel, such activities have increasingly come to be incorporated into contemporary understandings of tourism and tourism policy, including the following:

- travel for career, work and international experiences
- educational tourism
- health and medical tourism
- travel to second homes
- return migration.

Importantly, Figure 1.2 has an implicit political dimension in that the categories it identifies are forms of voluntary travel as opposed to the involuntary nature of forced migration and movement. In fact, it is perhaps revealing of the extent to which tourism is the domain of the relatively wealthy in society that while we can read

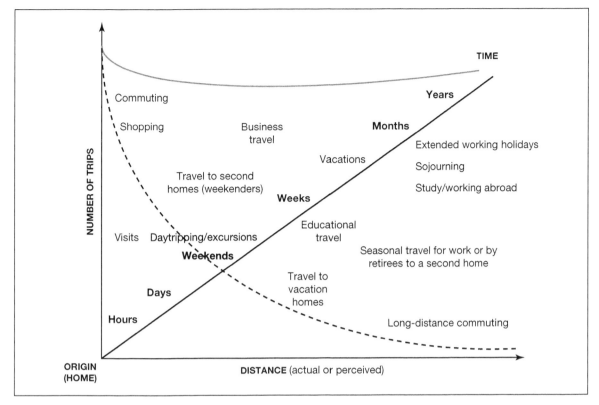

Figure 1.2 Extent of temporary mobility in space and time

Source: From Hall (2003b).

of forced migration or displaced persons the category of forced tourism does not exist.

From the perspective illustrated in Figure 1.2, tourism can therefore be interpreted as an expression of lifestyle identified either through voluntary travel or a voluntary temporary short-term change of residence. However, Figure 1.2 also highlights that there are a number of different components of such travel behaviour which, as noted above, are increasingly studied under the rubric of tourism, including travelling for education both in the short and long term, business travel, health tourism, leisure shopping, second home travel, daytrips, the combining of work and travel, and amenity-oriented migration, because of their leisure mobility orientation. Indeed, the term tourism increasingly seems to be applied in the popular press to almost every type of voluntary tourism imaginable, e.g. 'medical tourism' with respect to travel for medical treatment and cosmetic surgery, 'abortion tourism' with respect to international travel by pregnant women in order to have an abortion, and 'welfare' tourism in the case of some EU countries' concerns over visitors from accession countries seeking employment. In the case of the separation between migration and tourism it should be noted that migration is often not permanent and individuals may return to their original home many years after they left on either a permanent basis (e.g. for retirement) or a temporary basis (e.g. to a second home). Furthermore, for many migrants relationships to the country of origin may be maintained through visits that are invariably described as tourism. Therefore, as Coles *et al.* (2004) emphasised, the study of tourism must be willing to formulate a coherent approach to understanding the meaning behind the range of mobilities undertaken by individuals, not just tourists (Coles *et al.* 2004).

In policy terms these various categories of temporary mobility are vital as they serve as the focus for much of tourism policy and planning in that, with very few exceptions, countries, regions and destinations are seeking to attract and retain the voluntary mobile – as these are the people with the greatest economic and social capital and therefore capacity to contribute to regional development. Importantly, such a goal has both short- and longer-term dimensions and further indicates the fluidity of mobility in contemporary globalisation. In the short term the mobile are encouraged to stay as tourists, business travellers or convention attendees. Yet the longer the mobile stay the more they contribute economically as well as culturally. Therefore, in the mid-term, we see people staying on working holidays, short-term contracts, vacation or second home stays, medical tourism or for educational purposes. In the long term the short- and mid-term visitors may be encouraged to move 'permanently' and be categorised as migrants, therefore further contributing their bundle of economic, social, intellectual and cultural capital to the original destination, although their own mobility to other places will likely remain integral to their lifestyle and their relation to their new 'home'. The attraction of 'temporary mobility' therefore lies at the heart of tourism policy. When destination organisations state that they want their destination to be competitive what they are really saying is that they want to maintain, or more likely increase, the number of temporary mobile people they are attracting and the amount of expenditure they are generating, usually on a per person per period of visit basis.

Policy and planning

The terms planning and policy are intimately related. Planning is an extremely ambiguous and difficult word to define:

> The trouble arises because, although people realize that planning has a more general meaning, they tend to remember the idea of the plan as a physical representation or design. Thus they imagine that planning must include the preparation of such a design. (P. Hall 1992: 1)

In a seminal work on planning Dror (1973: 330) argues that 'Planning is the process of preparing a set of decisions for action in the future, directed at achieving goals by preferable means.' However, the tourism planning process is not just about *deciding* what is to be provided in the future for a given area of land or a community. It is far more complex than that. Chadwick's (1971) response to 'What is planning?' is extremely relevant. Chadwick states

> that planning is a process, a process of human thought and action based upon that thought – in point of fact, forethought, thought for the future – nothing more or less than this is planning, which is a very general human activity. (24)

Planning is a kind of decision making and policy making; however, it deals with a set of interdependent and systematically related decisions rather than individual decisions. Therefore, planning is only one part of an overall 'planning–decision–action' process. Furthermore, various activities in that process may be difficult to isolate as the planning process and other activities involve such things as bargaining and negotiation, compromise, coercion, values, choice and politics. Planning as a process must therefore be distinguished from a 'plan', which is 'a set of decisions for action in the future' (Dror 1973) and, in the case of much tourism planning, is related to land use planning in particular (e.g. Gunn 1988, 1994). As P. Hall (1992: 2) noted, there are many types of planning,

> though they will almost certainly require the production of many symbols on pieces of paper, in the form of words or diagrams, may never involve the production of a single exact physical representation of the entity which is being produced.

Although planning is a tool used by both the public and private sectors in this book we are primarily concerned with public planning. Planning is primarily a public (state) activity that may be done in concert with private and other bodies but for which the original rationale lies within the broader issue of the role of the state. There are several ways in which some of the different types of public planning may be identified. For example, Friedmann (1973) conceived of two different types of planning that lay at opposite ends of an autonomy–dependency continuum depending on where the planner or the planning agency was within the planning system:

1. *developmental planning,* which has a high degree of autonomy with respect to the setting of ends and the choice of means, and that tends to merge into what is usually described as policy making; and
2. *adaptive planning,* in that most decisions are heavily contingent on the actions of others external to the planning system and that tends to merge into programming.

Healey (1997) also recognised several strands of planning:

- *economic planning,* which aims to manage the productive forces of a country or region;
- the management of the *physical development* of towns and regions; and
- the management of *public administration* and *policy analysis,* which aims to manage the efficiency and effectiveness of public agencies.

Indeed Healey noted that most who criticise 'planning' often have the old state socialist 'command and control' model of centralised economic planning in mind, rather than other forms of planning, such as strategic planning, which are commonly used by both the public and private sectors in western democratic societies.

The most important characteristic of planning is that it is directed toward the future. Friedmann (1959: 334) provides an interesting list of planning characteristics that arise out of the future orientation of planning. Planning

- places a limit upon the time period over which projections into the future can be made without loss of practical significance for present decisions;
- establishes the necessity for continuing planning analysis and assessment throughout the planning period and the constant re-evaluation and adjustment of means to ends;
- suggests the use of expectational calculus in connection with statements about the future;
- argues for the adoption of a system of framework or structural planning;

- forces the careful consideration of flexibility in planning where the degree of flexibility introduced into a solution must be proportionate to the degree of uncertainty over future events.

As already noted, planning and policy are terms that are intimately related. According to Cullingsworth (1997: 5), 'Planning is the purposive process in which goals are set and policies elaborated to implement them.' In contrast, policy analysis is 'concerned with understanding and explaining the substance of policy content and policy decisions and the way in which policy decisions are made' (Barrett and Fudge 1981: 6), where public policy is 'the structure or confluence of values and behaviour involving a governmental prescription' (Kroll 1969: 9). Public policy is therefore the focal point of government activity. Public policy making is first and foremost a political activity. Public policy is influenced by the economic, social and cultural characteristics of society, as well as by the formal structures of government and other features of the political system. Policy should therefore be seen as a consequence of the political environment, values and ideologies, the distribution of power, institutional frameworks, and of decision-making processes (Simeon 1976; Hall and Jenkins 1995; Elliot 1997; Dredge and Jenkins 2007).

Public policy 'is whatever governments choose to do or not to do' (Dye 1992: 2). This definition covers government action, inaction, decisions and non-decisions as it implies a deliberate choice between alternatives. For a policy to be regarded as public policy, at the very least it must have been processed, even if only authorised or ratified, by public agencies (Hall and Jenkins 1995). This is an important caveat because it means that the 'policy may not have been significantly developed within the framework of government' (Hogwood and Gunn 1984: 23). Pressure/interest groups (e.g. tourism industry associations, conservation groups, community groups), significant individuals (e.g. local government councillors, business leaders), members of the bureaucracy (e.g. employees within tourism organisations or economic development agencies) and others (e.g. academics and consultants), all influence and perceive public policies in significant and often markedly different ways.

Tourism public policy is whatever governments choose to do or not to do with respect to tourism (Jenkins 1993; Hall 1994; Hall and Jenkins 1995). However, there is increasing scepticism about the effectiveness of government, particularly central government, and the intended consequences and impacts of much government policy, including with respect to tourism (Jenkins 1997; Jenkins *et al.* 1998). Nevertheless, even given demands for 'smaller government' in much of the western world, market failure still provides a number of rationales for state economic intervention, including:

- improving economic competitiveness;
- amending property rights;
- enabling state decision makers to take account of externalities;
- providing widely available public benefits;
- reducing risk and uncertainty;
- supporting projects with high capital costs and involving new technologies;
- educating and providing information (Haughton and Hunter 1994).

Policy should therefore be an important area of concern to the student of tourism. One of the most interesting studies of policy in the context of tourism was a survey of the range of tourism policy roles of agencies in Canada and the United States with respect to ecotourism (Edwards *et al.* 1998). Respondents' comments as to the nature of their roles indicate that there are tremendous variations in government tourism agency involvement in tourism policy, ranging from a more reactive, passive role in which agencies provide input and react to policies established by other agencies, to a proactive role in which government tourism agencies are researching, writing, lobbying for and implementing tourism policy. Such a situation was also indicated in a special issue on tourism policy making in *Current Issues in Tourism* (2001) and by Dredge and Jenkins (2007) in an Australasian context (Table 1.2).

One of the most detailed explanations as to why greater attention should be devoted to the study of public policy was presented by Dye (1992) who argued that public policy can be studied for three primary reasons:

1. Public policy can be studied so as to gain an understanding of the causes and consequences of policy decisions, and to improve our knowledge about society. In this instance, public policy can be viewed as either a dependent variable *or* as an independent variable. If policy is viewed as a dependent variable, the critical question becomes 'what socioeconomic [or environmental forces] and political system characteristics operate to shape the content of policy' (Dye 1992: 4). If tourism public policy is viewed as an independent variable, then the central question becomes *what impact does public policy (including tourism) have on society [the environment] and on the political system?*
2. Public policy can also be studied for professional reasons in order to understand the causes and consequences of policy. Thus, *we might seek solutions of practical problems with respect to tourism, and feed that knowledge into the political process.*
3. Public policy can be studied for political purposes so as to ensure that the 'right' policies are adopted 'to achieve the "right" goals' (Dye 1992: 5). This latter focus raises the critical issues of defining *what is 'right', and identifying by whom 'right' is determined.* These issues reflect the play of interests and values in the influence and determination of the tourism planning and policy processes (Hall and Jenkins 1995; Dredge and Jenkins 2007).

Planning for tourism

Demands for tourism planning and government intervention in the development process are typically a response to the unwanted effects of tourism development, particularly at the local level, as well as to make destinations more attractive or competitive. However, the rapid pace of tourism growth and development, the nature of

Table 1.2 Range of tourism policy roles in tourism agencies

actively involved	adapt/change agency structure
administer	advise/consult
advocate policies	answer to a commission
assist in writing	collaborate
coordinate	issue dependent
develop legislation	facilitate
find solutions to tourism issues	follow policy settings
write and formulate policy	involved in land use planning
fund policy	get people involved
implement policy	official agency for tourism policy
initiate tourism policy	serve as mediator
committee work	strategic/tourism planning
monitor policy	no role/not involved
lobby	persuade decision/policy acceptance
participate in policy process	promotions and marketing writing
play lead/key role in policy	propose policy
provide input on policy	react to policy
recommend/suggest policy	represent tourism in policy issues
research policy	licensing
form/attend councils/taskforce	follow policies set by other agencies
partner/work with others in the private and public sector	provide information and technical assistance

Sources: Derived from Edwards *et al.* (1998); also see *Current Issues in Tourism* (2001), Dredge and Jenkins (2007).

tourism itself and the corresponding absence of single agency responsibility for tourism-related development has often meant that public sector responses to the impacts of tourism on destinations have been ad hoc, rather than predetermined strategies oriented toward development objectives. Ironically, such an approach is the antithesis of planning.

Although planning is not a cure-all, in its fullest process-oriented sense planning *may* be able to minimise potential negative impacts and maximise economic returns to the destination (Benckendorff and Pearce 2003; Evans *et al.* 2003). As Murphy (1985: 156) argued in his seminal work on a community-based approach to tourism, 'Planning is concerned with anticipating

and regulating change in a system, to promote orderly development so as to increase the social, economic, and environmental benefits of the development process.' More recently Gunn with Var (2002: 1) opened their book on tourism planning by noting that 'if tourism is to reach toward better economic impact, it must be planned as well towards goals of enhanced visitor satisfaction, community integration, and above all, greater resource protection'. Therefore, planning should likely be regarded as a critical element in ensuring the sustainable development of tourist destinations. Nevertheless, as Gunn observed, tourism planning can be categorised as either 'a contradiction ... tourism implies non-directed, voluntary and personal goal-oriented travel and

The role of planning theory

Campbell and Fainstein (2003a) identified five questions with respect to planning theory, all of which are of relevance to tourism planning:

1. What are the historical roots of planning?

This first question is one of history and deals with the issue of the identity of tourism planning and how the field has developed to the present day. Reflecting on the history of a field not only helps answers of how did we get to where we are now in terms of theory and focus but also to planning and policy practice and the application of planning tools.

2. What is the justification for planning?

The issue of justification raises the key question of why and when should intervention occur in order to change or modify an existing course of events? Given that the focus of this book is on tourism planning rather than business planning by tourism firms we are therefore primarily concerned with the issue of state or government intervention. However, the reasons for government intervention have gradually changed over time.

From the late 1920s planning in terms of state intervention was often seen by government as a means to counter the undesirable effects of the market. This notion of a duality between planning and the market (i.e. that they are opposites) continued until the 1980s when, following changes in political and economic philosophy at the time of the Reagan administration in the United States and the Thatcher administration in the United Kingdom, the market came to be championed as a resource allocation mechanism to replace planning activities. However, the impact of such philosophies, often referred to as 'neoliberal' (see Peck 2001; Peck and Tickell 2002), has had a substantial impact on perceptions of the role of government throughout the developed world at all scales of governance, as well as on particular sectors such as tourism. For example, in countries such as Australia, Canada and New Zealand and in the transition economies of eastern Europe, governments' development function in tourism as an owner of tourism plant and infrastructure, such as airlines, came to be replaced with

. . . a far stronger marketing focus by government;
. . . privatisation or corporatisation of plant, facilities and infrastructure; and
. . . the development of new cooperative structures with the private sector (Hall and Jenkins 1995; Dredge and Jenkins 2007).

As a result of changes in political and economic philosophy and the accompanying structural changes to government institutions there has also been a re-evaluation of the planning–market dualism. Instead, the necessity of development of hybrid public–private relationships as well as the growth of non-government, non-profit, 'third sector' organisations, such as charities, trusts and public interest groups, has meant that there has been a significant reinterpretation of the relationship between planning and the market which is focused on the 'steering' of the many organisations that have interests in planning processes and decisions in a common direction.

3. What are the 'rules of the game' for planning with respect to ethics and values?

The breakdown of the duality between planning and the market and the development of extensive public–private relationships raises substantial questions with respect to the values of planning. When planning was regarded as being in 'the public interest' then ethical issues were clearer even though debate did occur over what the public interest was. However, the reinterpretation of government's role and the developments of new forms of public–private relations means that present-day interpretations of the public interest are now often equated with economic or sectoral interests. In addition, there are now different understandings of knowledge in the planning process which means that various knowledge and values, such

▶

as those of different groups and cultures in society, need to be acknowledged in planning processes. Such a situation therefore provides a substantial challenge to the expert or technical knowledge of the planner, and the capacity to accommodate different value positions in decision making. The changed 'rules of the game' therefore mean that students of tourism planning need to consider not only what their ethics and values are but what are the broader ethics of tourism and tourism development (Hall and Brown 2006).

4. How can planning be effective in a mixed economy?

The notion of planning as intervention raises questions as to the authority and power of those who seek to intervene and therefore their effectiveness. The authority of the planner is constrained by the economic and political power of various stakeholders and interests as well as the institutional arrangements, such as elections and legislative processes, that serve to both enable and restrain planning action over time.

5. What do planners do?

Comprehensiveness of approach has often been a main justification for undertaking planning (Campbell and Fainstein 2003b). Yet such a justification has suffered substantial criticism on three related fronts. First, the inherent complexity of many planning issues in terms of the numbers of stakeholders as well as the interrelationships between social, economic, political and environmental (physical) factors. Second, with respect to the extent that planners actually have the requisite capacities of analysis, coordination and knowledge to effectively develop comprehensive approaches to complex situations. Third, ideas of comprehensiveness often assume a common public interest whereas in reality planning may give voice to more powerful political and economic interests if other interests are unable or unwilling to participate. As Campbell and Fainstein (2003a: 9) commented:

> Planners often argued about the proper role of planning based simply on the merits of the concepts themselves (e.g. large- versus small-scale; top-down versus bottom-up), while ignoring the vaster political and economic forces that shaped and constrained planning. The articulation and eventual challenge to comprehensive planning was thus part of a broader expansion of planning theory beyond land-use planning into social and economic policy.

its corollary of free-enterprise development' (1979: 1), or more recently, as 'almost an oxymoron . . . Planning tourism, therefore, seems contrary to such an unplanned phenomenon' (Gunn with Var 2002: 4).

As a general field of research, tourism planning has mirrored broader trends within the urban and regional planning traditions (e.g. Getz 1986, 1987; Inskeep 1991; Gunn with Var 2002; Dredge and Jenkins 2007), primarily because it has tended to be focused on destination planning rather than individual tourism business planning, although that had started to change by the end of the 1990s (e.g. see Zhang *et al.* 2002; Evans *et al.* 2003). Since the mid-1980s, as ecotourism and sustainability have become major research areas, tourism planning has also been substantially influenced by developments in the field of environmental planning (e.g. Inskeep 1987; Dowling 1993a, 1993b, 1997; Hunter and Green 1995; Fennell and Dowling 2003; Diamantis 2004), while increasing attention is also being given to the relationship to policy (e.g. Hall and Jenkins 1995; Davidson and Maitland 1997; Hall *et al.* 1997; Andriotis 2001; *Current Issues in Tourism* 2001; Dredge and Jenkins 2007). These recent developments are extremely important for our understanding of tourism planning as no longer can it be simply seen as an exercise in land-use planning at either the regional or, more typically, the local or site level.

Undoubtedly, local or site level land-use planning is extremely important for destination regions (Gunn with Var 2002). However, such activities need to be conceived as occurring at one end of a continuum of planning-related activities that range from the local to the global and which similarly range from being land-use oriented at

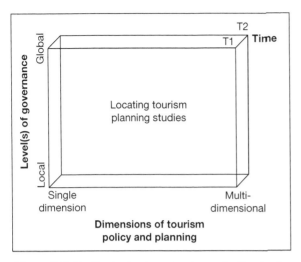

Figure 1.3 Positioning tourism planning and policy studies

the site and local level to being policy oriented at the global level (Figure 1.3). Planning for tourism therefore occurs in a number of

* forms (e.g. development, infrastructure, land and resource use, organisation, human resource, promotion and marketing);
* structures (e.g. different government, quasi-government and non-government organisations);
* scales of governance (international, transnational, national, regional, local, site, sectoral and personal);
* spatial scales (international, supranational, national, regional, local and site); and
* temporal (time) scales (for measuring change, development, implementation, evaluation and satisfactory fulfilment of planning objectives).

Furthermore, planning within public agencies is rarely exclusively devoted to tourism per se. Instead, planning for tourism tends to be an amalgam of economic, social, political and environmental considerations that reflect the diversity of the factors which influence tourism development (Heeley 1981; Hall and Page 2006).

Undoubtedly, the emergence of public and interest group concern over the perceived negative effects of tourism has led to demands for improved planning for tourism in the belief that this will help ameliorate such impacts (Hall *et al.* 1997;

Gunn with Var 2002; Dredge and Jenkins 2007). Furthermore, in recent years demand for public tourism planning has also been driven by perceived changes in the tourist marketplace and by government responses to the problems of economic restructuring in both urban and rural areas. As greater competition has begun to develop in the tourism marketplace so destinations have sought to improve various aspects of attractions, facilities and infrastructure in order that they may continue to be attractive to visitors or at least extend their product life cycle. Many areas that have recently undergone substantial economic restructuring also now want to develop tourism in order to attract investment, promote economic growth and generate employment. Some destination authorities also plain just want to attract more visitor expenditure. Such demands on tourism – and on the means by which we understand tourism-related development – are enormous, while the capacity of tourism and tourism studies as an area of academic concern to meet such challenges is mixed (Hall 2005a; Coles *et al.* 2006).

This book is concerned with the tourism planning process. Tourism policies and plans and the associate outcomes of government decisions with respect to tourism do not just 'happen'. The book therefore aims to place concerns over values, the significance of politics, and issues of scale, approach and sustainability at the centre of tourism planning in order to help reveal what happens inside the 'black box' (Easton 1953, 1957, 1990) of tourism planning and policy (Figure 1.4). It does so with reference not only to the tourism planning literature but also reference to wider work on planning in politics and policy studies, urban and regional planning, environmental planning and management, geography, business studies and regional development. The book is also primarily concerned with public tourism planning, although there is substantial discussion of private sector-related planning, particularly at the destination level. It is not a technical guide to tourism planning legislation. Being international in scope it is clearly not feasible for this book to list and discuss all relevant tourism planning legislation around the world, although various examples will be provided. Instead it is

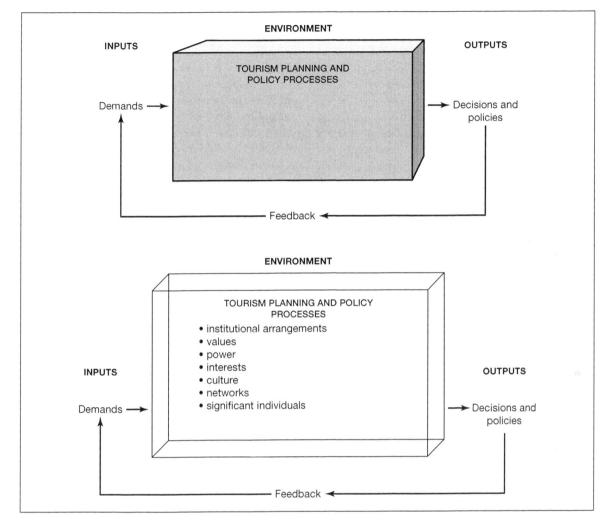

Figure 1.4 Opening the black box of tourism planning and policy systems

expected that readers will be able to follow up such legislation in their own time or as part of class exercises. Rather, the reader is being asked to see relevant legislation or land use regulations within the wider context of the tourism planning process and the tourism planning system.

Outline of the book

This book is divided into eleven chapters. This chapter sets some of the context within which tourism and tourism planning occurs including defining the fields of the key concepts of tourism, public policy and planning.

Chapter 2 identifies the sustainable tourism imperative as being one of the major driving forces behind the desire for tourism planning. It also outlines some of the key planning and policy issues with respect to understanding the relationship between tourism and change, including what are usually described as tourism impact studies.

Chapter 3 provides a brief overview of some of the major traditions or approaches to tourism planning. It discusses the traditions of booster-ism, economic approaches, the physical/spatial approach (which is increasingly becoming described under the heading of environmental planning), community-based planning and some of the emerging dimensions of sustainable tourism planning on which some of the concepts utilised in this book are based.

Chapter 4 is the most theoretical chapter of the book. It examines the nature of a systems approach to planning and how that affects our understanding of the tourism planning process. It discusses the idea of planning as theory, the nature of systems and systems thinking and how such concepts have been applied in fields such as ecology, geography, planning, management and, more recently, tourism. The chapter emphasises that process, flux and change are fundamental to a systems view of the world and need to be incorporated into our understanding of tourism. Several approaches to tourism systems are noted including the significance of the partial industrialisation of tourism. However, as part of our understanding of systems the chapter also argues that it is important to understand issues of scale, the standpoint of the participant, the role of values, the significance of relationships and the role of argument and persuasion in the planning process. The chapter concludes with a discussion of the importance of dialectical analysis to a systems view of planning and the importance of argument and persuasion in a craft approach to tourism planning.

Chapter 5 examines the development of integrated approaches towards planning in complex systems. It provides an idealised strategic model of the policy, planning and decision-making process that is then used to discuss issues in the operationalisation of planning theory, particularly with respect to identifying stakeholders, goal and objective setting, negotiation and cooperation, and our understanding of implementation. It argues for the concept of integration to be conceived of in terms of the centrality of inter-relationships, which means that problem definition becomes vital to planning as does the actual shape of planning 'solutions'.

Chapters 6–9 look at the operation of tourism policy and planning at different scales. Chapter 6 examines policy and planning at the international and transnational levels and discusses the influence of various international institutions such as the World Tourism Organization and the role of institutional arrangements through hard and soft international law on tourism development. Chapter 7 examines tourism planning and policies at the national and sub-national level. It discusses the role of government and the private sector in tourism planning and development and the key concepts of coordination, cooperation and competition in tourism. It also notes the importance of interest groups in the tourism policy and planning process and their influence on the planning process. Chapter 8 examines tourism planning at the destination level in an increasingly globalised competitive environment. It argues that the structure of destinations needs to be reconsidered in the tourism planning process with greater emphasis being placed on the need to create cooperative structures rather than simply providing greater amounts of money for destination promotion or development organisations. Chapter 9 examines the linkage between policies and operations in terms of design principles and site development. It discusses sustainable development in terms of principles of adaptivity and rates of change and their potential application to tourism.

Chapter 10 examines issues surrounding policy and planning implementation and discusses the three main approaches to implementation studies. The chapter therefore addresses the importance of understanding assumptions and frameworks with respect to the issue of how we know we have achieved what we set out to do. Chapter 11 concludes the book by reflecting on issues of cooperation, integration and relationships within complex tourism planning environments. It argues that there needs to be greater reflection on the assumptions and bases of tourism planning with the intention being that tourism planning needs to be able to reflect how the real world actually operates. In short, it argues that planning is political. This, then, has certain implications for the skill development of tourism planners. It argues that tourism planners and those involved in tourism planning need to have greater understanding of the role of communication and mediation as well as the idea of planning as argument and negotiation in addition to the more traditional technical knowledge of legislation, regulation and planning techniques.

Summary

This chapter has outlined some of the key elements of the concepts of tourism, public policy and planning, and the sub-field of tourism planning that lies at the intersection of these academic fields. Governments and destination organisations are interested in tourism because they seek to attract mobile people and manage the externalities of such mobility. Tourism planning does not just refer specifically to tourism development and promotion, although these are certainly important. Tourism must be integrated within the wider planning processes in order to promote certain goals of economic, social and environmental enhancement or maximisation that may be achieved through appropriate tourism development. Therefore tourism planning must be, as Getz (1987: 3) emphasised, 'a process, based on research and evaluation, which seeks to optimize the potential contribution of tourism to human welfare and environmental quality'.

Such a statement reflects the value basis of this book as well. The book argues that values lie at the core of tourism planning. Planning assists in determining who wins and who loses in the tourism development process. It also assists in contributing to more sustainable forms of tourism in which economic, environmental and social goals are seen to be in balance and in which there is greater equity of outcomes for stakeholders in tourism, which means not just the developers, tourism industry and the tourist but also the wider community whose destination is being consumed. Most fundamentally, tourism planning should be about the creation of sustainable places. It is hoped that this book makes at least some small contribution to such a goal.

Questions

1. To what extent can we describe the differences between planning and policy as one of degree?
2. Why is tourism described as a 'fluid' concept?
3. How do time and space affect the statistical definition of tourism?

Important websites and recommended reading

Websites

World Travel and Tourism Council: http://www.wttc.travel/

World's leading tourism industry interest group.

UN World Tourism Organization: http://www.world-tourism.org/

The World Tourism Organization (UNWTO/OMT), is a specialised agency of the United Nations, and according to their website 'is the leading international organization in the field of tourism. It serves as a global forum for tourism policy issues and practical source of tourism know-how'.

Recommended reading

1. Hall, D. and Brown, F. (2006) *Tourism and Welfare: Ethics, Responsibility and Sustained Well-Being,* CABI, Wallingford.

   Provides an excellent account of the issues of tourism development and how this relates to sustainability, ethical and quality of life concerns.

2. Hall, C.M. (2005) *Tourism: Rethinking the Social Science of Mobility,* Prentice Hall, Harlow.

   In one sense a sister companion to the present book, examines tourism mobility and associated development issues, as well as the academic dimensions of tourism.

3. Gunn, C.A. with Var, T. (2002) *Tourism Planning: Basics, Concepts, Cases,* 4th edn, Routledge, New York.

   The most recent edition of a well-cited work that primarily takes a land-use and physical planning approach to tourism planning.

4. Hall, C.M. and Jenkins, J. (1995) *Tourism and Public Policy,* Routledge, London.

   Remains one of the seminal works on tourism and policy issues. Most recent editions are published by Thomson.

5. Lew, A., Hall, C.M. and Williams, A.M. (eds) (2004) *A Companion to Tourism,* Blackwell, Oxford.

Provides a general overview of the social science of tourism with specific chapters on planning and public policy.

6. Hall, C.M. (1994) *Tourism and Politics: Policy, Power and Place,* John Wiley, Chichester.

   Remains a seminal work on the politics of tourism.

7. Church, A. and Coles, T. (eds) (2007) *Tourism, Power and Space,* Routledge, London.

   Provides a comprehensive series of chapters on issues of tourism and power.

8. Coles, T., Hall, C.M. and Duval, D. (2006) 'Tourism and post disciplinary enquiry', *Current Issues in Tourism,* 9(4–5): 293–319.

   Discussing the value of a post-disciplinary approach to tourism issues.

2 Tourism planning and policy: responding to change – the sustainable imperative

Chapter objectives

After reading this chapter you will:

- Understand the key concepts and issues of sustainable development
- Appreciate the relationship between sustainable development and sustainable tourism
- Identify the issues that affect the identification and understanding of the consequences of tourism, particularly with respect to their implications for planning
- Understand the role of change as a basis for planning intervention
- Appreciate that the effects of tourism are contextual and situational
- Be aware of tourism's contribution to change at various scales.

Tourism is intimately connected with issues of sustainable development. Indeed, since the late 1980s there has been an explosion in the number of texts and articles, plus courses and consultants, concerned with sustainable forms of development and mitigating or managing tourism's undesired effects. However, despite the plethora of discussions about sustainability in tourism we often seem no closer to finding solutions to the problems of tourism development. For every report of success it often seems that there are ten reports of failure or at least further recognition of the negative impact of tourism. Yet tourism continues to grow. Besides, it could be argued

that compared with problems of global climate change, deforestation, loss of biodiversity and cultural diversity, poverty and seemingly endless economic restructuring, tourism is not an issue. It is. Given the size of the industry and the number of people moving about the world, tourism is both a contributing factor and a response to some of these problems. Ecotourism, for example, has been posited as a means of conserving ecological diversity through offering a higher economic value for conserving plant and animal species that might otherwise be exploited in other ways. Nevertheless, tourism has also contributed to species and habitat loss through accommodation, attraction and infrastructure development, such as in many coastal areas where a golf course, a marina and a sandy beach are regarded as having greater value than mangroves and wetlands. Furthermore, one of the most pressing issues facing tourism is that even though activities by tourism at a destination may be socially, economically and environmentally friendly, their greatest environmental impact may be in actually travelling to the destination. It is these paradoxes and problems of tourism development and the hope they can be solved that creates the setting for tourism planning.

This chapter first discusses the development of the concept of sustainable development and the place of tourism within that concept. It then goes on to discuss the ways in which the consequences of tourism are identified and understood. Finally, the chapter brings issues of sustainability and impacts together within the context of the global consequences of tourism and tourism's implications for global environmental change.

Sustainable development and the sustainable tourism imperative

> Humanity stands at a defining moment in history. We are confronted with a perpetuation of disparities between and within nations, a worsening of poverty, hunger, ill health and illiteracy, and the continuing deterioration of the ecosystems on which we depend for our well-being. However, integration of environment and development concerns and greater attention to them will lead to the fulfilment of basic needs, improved living standards for all, better protected and managed ecosystems and a safer, more prosperous future. No nation can achieve this on its own; but together we can – in a global partnership for sustainable development. (Opening statement of the preamble to *Agenda 21* – United Nations 1992a: 1.1).

> We recognize that poverty eradication, changing consumption and production patterns and protecting and managing the natural resource base for economic and social development are overarching objectives of and essential requirements for sustainable development. (*Johannesburg Declaration on Sustainable Development* – United Nations 2002a: para.11)

Sustainability is primarily an outcome of the age of ecology, although the intellectual heritage of the concept dates back at least to the early nineteenth century. Although society, and key interests within society, have long been concerned with how best to utilise and conserve natural resources, it has been since the late twentieth century, and increasingly in the globalised world of the new millennium facing problems of environmental change on a global scale, that we have come to realise the way everything is tied together. Environment, economy and society are inextricably linked.

Sustainability is everyone's concern. The famous Brundtland definition, that 'sustainable development is development that meets the needs of the present without compromising the ability of future generations to meet their own needs'

(WCED 1987: 49), has come to feature in many a textbook and student essay, even though tourism was hardly mentioned in the report. Nevertheless, sustainable development and sustainability are important concepts, the interpretation and operationalisation of which have been hard fought over in policy and planning decisions throughout the world. They are not just abstract academic ideas, they are concepts that trickle down and affect the day-to-day lives of everyone on the planet, even if people never realise it. As the then Prime Minister of the United Kingdom, John Major, noted in his Foreword to *Sustainable Development: The UK Strategy*: 'Sustainable development is difficult to define. But the goal of sustainable development can guide future strategy' (HMSO 1994: 3).

The report of the World Commission on Environment and Development (WCED 1987), commonly known as the Brundtland Report, provided substantial impetus to the concept and practice of sustainable development. Five basic principles of sustainability were identified in the report:

1. the idea of holistic planning and strategy making that links economic, environmental and social concerns;
2. the importance of preserving essential ecological processes;
3. the need to protect both biodiversity and human heritage;
4. the need for development to occur in such a way that productivity can be sustained over the long term for future generations (the concept of intergenerational equity); and
5. the goal of achieving a better balance of fairness and opportunity between nations.

The focus of the Bruntland Report has come to be reinforced only by consequent international assessments of the state of the planet's environment and statements of intent with respect to sustainability in the 20 years since it was published. Key international milestones are noted in Table 2.1.

The 1992 United Nations Conference on Environment and Development held in Rio de Janeiro (often referred to as the 'Earth Summit' or 'Rio') provided an international set of principles

Table 2.1 International milestones in sustainable development

Date	Milestone
1972	United Nations Conference on the Human Environment, Stockholm
1987	Report of the World Commission on Environment and Development (Brundtland Report)
1992	United Nations Conference on Environment and Development, held in Rio de Janeiro (Earth Summit)
2000	United Nations Millennium Assessment
2002	World Summit on Sustainable Development in Johannesburg
2005	Millennium Ecosystem Assessment

and a programme of action for achieving sustainable development at a global scale. The declaration that emerged from the Rio summit and *Agenda 21,* a plan for achieving sustainable development in the twenty-first century, created a platform for government and private sector activities in sustainable development at all levels. *Agenda 21* discussed sustainable development issues and the means by which action could be taken to ensure sustainability. Significantly, it highlighted the importance of developing an inclusive approach in sustainable development stating 'Critical to the effective implementation of the objectives, policies and mechanisms agreed to by Governments in all programme areas of *Agenda 21* will be the commitment and genuine involvement of all social groups' (United Nations 1992a: 23.1). With the role of effecting planning being highlighted in focusing on participation in decision making:

> One of the fundamental prerequisites for the achievement of sustainable development is broad public participation in decision-making. Furthermore, in the more specific context of environment and development, the need for new forms of participation has emerged. This includes the need of individuals, groups and organizations to participate in environmental impact assessment procedures and to know about and participate in decisions, particularly those which potentially affect the communities in which they live and work. Individuals, groups and organizations should have access to information relevant to environment and development held by national authorities, including information on products and

activities that have or are likely to have a significant impact on the environment, and information on environmental protection measures. (United Nations 1992a: 23.2)

In 2000 the United Nations launched a series of millennium development goals as a means of bridging the north–south (developed/developing) country divide and to enhance environmental security (Table 2.2) (United Nations 2000). However, progress on achieving the goals has been slow and, as José Antonio Ocampo, Under-Secretary-General for Economic and Social Affairs stated in the foreword to the 2006 status report, 'there is still a long way to go to keep our promises to current and future generations' (United Nations 2006: 3).

The goals and implementation of the 1992 Rio Summit were revisited at the 2002 World Summit on Sustainable Development held in Johannesburg, South Africa, where the commitment of the international community to sustainable development was reaffirmed in a political declaration (United Nations 2002a) and in a new implementation plan (United Nations 2002b). Actions identified as being required at all levels in trying to achieve a move towards sustainable consumption and production to promote social and economic development are noted in Table 2.3.

However, despite a series of international agreements on sustainable development there is still considerable evidence of the extent to which humans are living beyond their natural means. For example, the Board of the Millennium Ecosystem

Table 2.2 Millennium development goals

Goals	Target
1 Eradicate extreme poverty and hunger	• Halve, between 1990 and 2015, the proportion of people whose income is less than $1 per day • Halve, between 1990 and 2015, the proportion of people who suffer from hunger
2 Achieve universal primary education	• Ensure that, by 2015, children everywhere, boys and girls alike, will be able to complete a full course of primary schooling
3 Promote gender equality and empower women	• Eliminate gender disparity in primary and secondary education, preferably by 2005, and in all levels of education no later than 2015
4 Reduce child mortality	• Reduce by two-thirds, between 1990 and 2015, the under-five mortality rate
5 Improve maternal health	• Reduce by three-quarters, between 1990 and 2015, the maternal mortality ratio
6 Combat HIV/AIDS, malaria and other diseases	• Have halted by 2015 and begun to reverse the spread of HIV/AIDS
7 Ensure environmental sustainability	• Integrate the principles of sustainable development into country policies and programmes and reverse the loss of environmental resources • Halve, by 2015, the proportion of people without sustainable access to safe drinking water and basic sanitation • By 2020, have achieved a significant improvement in the lives of at least 100 million slum-dwellers
8 Develop a global partnership for development	• Address the special needs of the least developed countries, landlocked countries and small island developing states • Deal comprehensively with developing countries' debt • Develop further an open, rule-based, predictable, non-discriminatory trading and financial system • In cooperation with developing countries, develop and implement strategies for decent and productive work for youth • In cooperation with pharmaceutical companies, provide access to affordable essential drugs in developing countries • In cooperation with the private sector, make available the benefits of new technologies, especially information and communications

Source: United Nations (2006) *The Millennium Development Goals Report 2006.* United Nations, New York. Reproduced with permission.

Table 2.3 Actions required to promote the shift towards sustainable consumption and production

- Identify specific activities, tools, policies, measures and monitoring and assessment mechanisms, including, where appropriate, life cycle analysis and national indicators for measuring progress, bearing in mind that standards applied by some countries may be inappropriate and of unwarranted economic and social cost to other countries, in particular developing countries.

- Adopt and implement policies and measures aimed at promoting sustainable patterns of production and consumption, applying, *inter alia,* the polluter pays principle described in principle 16 of the Rio Declaration on Environment and Development. (National authorities should endeavour to promote the internalisation of environmental costs and the use of economic instruments, taking into account the approach that the polluter should, in principle, bear the cost of pollution, with due regard to the public interest and without distorting international trade and investment.)

- Develop production and consumption policies to improve the products and services provided, while reducing environmental and health impacts, using, where appropriate, science-based approaches, such as life cycle analysis.

- Develop awareness-raising programmes on the importance of sustainable production and consumption patterns, particularly among youth and the relevant segments in all countries, especially in developed countries, through, *inter alia,* education, public and consumer information, advertising and other media, taking into account local, national and regional cultural values.

- Develop and adopt, where appropriate, on a voluntary basis, effective, transparent, verifiable, non-misleading and non-discriminatory consumer information tools to provide information relating to sustainable consumption and production, including human health and safety aspects. These tools should not be used as disguised trade barriers.

- Increase eco-efficiency, with financial support from all sources, where mutually agreed, for capacity building, technology transfer and exchange of technology with developing countries and countries with economies in transition, in cooperation with relevant international organisations.

Sources: United Nations (1992b) *Report of The United Nations Conference on Environment and Development* (Rio de Janeiro, 3–14 June 1992) Annex I, Rio Declaration on Environment and Development, A/CONF. 151/26 (Vol. I); and United Nations (2002b) *Johannesburg Plan of Implementation,* III, sec. 15. United Nations, New York. Reproduced with permission.

Assessment (MEA) (see Table 2.4 for a listing of the key messages of the assessment), stated that:

> At the heart of this assessment is a stark warning. Human activity is putting such strain on the natural functions of Earth that the ability of the planet's ecosystems to sustain future generations can no longer be taken for granted . . . Nearly two thirds of the services provided by nature to humankind are found to be in decline worldwide. In effect, the benefits reaped from our engineering of the planet have been achieved by running down natural capital assets.
>
> In many cases, it is literally a matter of living on borrowed time. (Board of the Millennium Ecosystem Assessment 2005: 5)

The MEA reported that over the past 50 years human action had changed the ecosystems on which we depend, 'more rapidly and extensively than in any comparable period of time in human history' (2005: 1) and noted that while some had benefited from these processes in material terms many regions and groups of people had not. (An outline of the main findings of the MEA is contained in Table 2.5.) According to the MEA (2005: 1) three major problems associated with the management of the world's ecosystems are 'already causing significant harm to some people, particularly the poor, and unless addressed will substantially diminish the

- Everyone in the world depends on nature and ecosystem services to provide the conditions for a decent, healthy, and secure life.
- Humans have made unprecedented changes to ecosystems in recent decades to meet growing demands for food, fresh water, fibre and energy.
- These changes have helped to improve the lives of billions, but at the same time they weakened nature's ability to deliver other key services such as purification of air and water, protection from disasters and the provision of medicines.
- Among the outstanding problems identified by this assessment are the dire state of many of the world's fish stocks; the intense vulnerability of the 2 billion people living in dry regions to the loss of ecosystem services, including water supply; and the growing threat to ecosystems from climate change and nutrient pollution.
- Human activities have taken the planet to the edge of a massive wave of species extinction, further threatening our own well-being.
- The loss of services derived from ecosystems is a significant barrier to the achievement of the Millennium Development Goals to reduce poverty, hunger and disease.
- The pressures on ecosystems will increase globally in coming decades unless human attitudes and actions change.
- Measures to conserve natural resources are more likely to succeed if local communities are given ownership of them, share the benefits and are involved in decisions.
- Even today's technology and knowledge can reduce considerably the human impact on ecosystems. They are unlikely to be deployed fully, however, until ecosystem services cease to be perceived as free and limitless, and their full value is taken into account.
- Better protection of natural assets will require coordinated efforts across all sections of governments, businesses and international institutions. The productivity of ecosystems depends on policy choices on investment, trade, subsidy, taxation and regulation, among others.

Source: Board of the Millennium Ecosystem Assessment (2005) *Living Beyond Our Means: Natural Assets and Human Well-being,* Statement from the Board. World Resources Institute and the UN Environmental Programme, Washington, D.C. and Nairobi, p. 3. Reproduced with permission.

long-term benefits' humankind obtain from ecosystems (MEA 2005):

1. Approximately 60 per cent (15 out of 24) of the ecosystem services examined by the MEA were being degraded or used unsustainably, including fresh water, capture fisheries, air and water purification, and the regulation of climate, natural hazards and pests.
2. There was established but incomplete evidence that changes being made in ecosystems were increasing the likelihood of non-linear ecosystem change (including accelerating, abrupt and potentially

irreversible changes) that will have important consequences for human well-being.
3. The harmful effects of the degradation of ecosystem services (the persistent decrease in the capacity of an ecosystem to deliver services) were borne disproportionately by the poor, were contributing to growing inequities and disparities, and were sometimes the principal factor causing poverty and a decline in human security.

The scope of the challenge that needs to be faced in order for economic and social activity to be environmentally sustainable is therefore immense. A response has been outlined by

Table 2.5 Main findings of the Millennium Ecosystem Assessment

- Over the past 50 years, humans have changed ecosystems more rapidly and extensively than in any comparable period of time in human history, largely to meet rapidly growing demands for food, fresh water, timber, fibre and fuel. This has resulted in a substantial and largely irreversible loss in the diversity of life on Earth.

- The changes that have been made to ecosystems have contributed to substantial net gains in human well-being and economic development, but these gains have been achieved at growing costs in the form of the degradation of many ecosystem services, increased risks of non-linear changes, and the exacerbation of poverty for some groups of people. These problems, unless addressed, will substantially diminish the benefits that future generations obtain from ecosystems.

- The degradation of ecosystem services could grow significantly worse during the first half of this century and is a barrier to achieving the Millennium Development Goals.

- The challenge of reversing the degradation of ecosystems while meeting increasing demands for their services can be partially met under some scenarios that the MEA has considered, but these involve significant changes in policies, institutions and practices that are not currently under way. Many options exist to conserve or enhance specific ecosystem services in ways that reduce negative trade-offs or that provide positive synergies with other ecosystem services.

Source: Board of the Millennium Ecosystem Assessment (2005) *Living Beyond Our Means: Natural Assets and Human Well-being,* Statement from the Board. World Resources Institute and the UN Environmental Programme, Washington, D.C. and Nairobi. Reproduced with permission.

Ekins (1993), who argued that certain conditions need to be rigorously adhered to with respect to controlling resource use, pollution and environmental impacts:

- Destabilisation of global environmental features such as climate patterns and the ozone layer must be prevented.
- Important ecosystems and ecological features must receive absolute protection in order to maintain biological diversity.
- Renewable resources must be maintained with sustainable harvesting measures rigorously enforced.
- Non-renewable resources must be used as intensively as possible.
- Depletion of non-renewable resources should proceed on the basis of maintaining minimum life expectancies of such resources, at which level consumption should be matched by new discoveries of these resources and technological innovation.
- Emissions into the biosphere should not exceed the biosphere's capacity to absorb such emissions.

- Risks of life-damaging events from human activity, i.e. nuclear power generation, must be kept at a very low level.

Clearly, meeting such conditions for sustainability is a major political, economic and environmental issue as it requires new ways of thinking about the nature and purpose of development and growth, and the role of individuals, government and the private sector in developing sustainable futures, a concern that is increasingly at the forefront of the analysis of tourism (Hall 2005a; Hall and Brown 2006).

The idea of sustainable development therefore requires a broader view of development and the natural environment than has hitherto been the case in much of western society, particularly in recent years when monetarist economics and the denial of a public interest has featured in so much government policy. 'The term "sustainable development" suggests that the lessons of ecology can, and should, be applied to economic processes' (Redclift 1987: 33). Therefore sustainable development stresses that economic development is dependent upon the continued well-being of the physical and social environment on which it is based. A purely economic approach to development does not give any appreciation of the environmental and social implications on development or an empirical measure of the quality of life and 'any development indicator based on monetary value of production is subject to both technical and conceptual shortcomings' (Smith 1977: 203). Similarly, economic data alone does not give any appreciation of the productive utilisation of resources – for example, whether or not the resources are renewable. A solely economic approach does not record the environmental and social costs that may have been associated with economic production. 'By valuing the environment predominantly in monetary terms, we may be *de*valuing its importance. We may end up, as Oscar Wilde put it, "knowing the price of everything and the value of nothing"' (Redclift and Sage 1994: 1–2). As Redclift (1987: 16) argued in one of the seminal works on sustainable development:

> From an environmental standpoint . . . GNP is a particularly inadequate guide to development since it treats sustainable and unsustainable production alike and compounds the error by including the costs of unsustainable economic activity on the credit side, while largely ignoring processes of recycling and energy conversion which do not lead to the production of goods and marketable services.

An increasingly important conception of sustainability is that of maintaining 'environmental' (Pearce and Turner 1990; Jacobs 1991) or 'natural' capital (Lovins *et al.* 1999) and, in terms of the ideas of equity which are a component of sustainability, the notion of social capital (Healey 1997). The 2005 Millennium Assessment used the concept of ecosystem services (which may be regarded as equivalent to natural capital) as a way of describing the linkages between ecosystems and human well-being. Ecosystem services are the benefits people obtain from ecosystems (Millennium Ecosystem Assessment 2005). These include:

- *provisioning services* such as food, water, timber and fibre;
- *regulating services* that affect climate, floods, disease, wastes, and the flow and quality of water;

- *cultural services* that provide recreational, aesthetic and spiritual benefits, and which serve as an important direct resource base for tourism; and
- *supporting services* such as soil formation, photosynthesis, and nutrient cycling.

The identification of the resource or capital base for development, including tourism, is important, as sustainable development requires a new way of thinking about resources that were, and to an extent still are, regarded as free and abundant. As Redclift and Sage (1994: 1) noted,

> development is about the creation of economic (often market) 'value' as natural resources are transformed into 'goods', into commodities. The process of economic development involves the substitution of resources by human-made 'capital' . . . we need to enlarge our view of capital to include nature, if we are to preserve lifeforms on the planet.

Such notions draw on economic metaphors and analysis and are based on two main principles:

1. Intergenerational equity requires passing on to the next generation a stock of 'capital', with its assumed capacity to produce at least an equivalent well-being to that enjoyed by the present generation; and
2. Biophysical capacities are not infinitely elastic. In other words, all forms of capital are not substitutable. Because some functions of the environment are vital to human well-being and are irreplaceable, 'social and economic activity should be managed at least to conserve such "critical environmental capital", which not only protects what is critical but maintains at least the present value of the environmental capital stock' (Cowell and Owens 1997: 17).

Such an interpretation is significant, because, when understood in terms of the maintenance of environmental capital, sustainability shows its relation to the older ideas of 'sustained yield', 'limits to growth' and 'capacity' (Hall 1998a). This does not mean that economic growth is necessarily limited but it does imply that, in order to be sustainable in the long term, the nature of growth must be such that it respects constraints set by the need to maintain critical environmental capital (and in some interpretations the total value of the environmental capital stock) intact. Such ideas have also been advocated by Lovins *et al.* (1999) with respect to the development of natural capitalism that is 'what capitalism might become if its largest category of capital – the "natural capital: of ecosystem services"– were properly valued' (46). The shift to natural capitalism involved four major interlinked shifts in business practice:

1. dramatically increase the productivity of natural resources;
2. shift to biologically inspired production models;
3. move to a solutions-based business model;
4. reinvest in natural capital.

As history has demonstrated, maintaining environmental capital is extremely difficult in a political–economic system within which maintaining or increasing levels of economic growth without consideration of the long-term effects of changes to or losses of ecosystem services has been a virtually unassailable policy goal. Sustainability is a qualitatively different policy goal – it is not specific, it is not easily understandable, it is not easily quantifiable, and it deals in time horizons that are not usually adopted in public or private planning and decision making. However, despite these characteristics it is still probably the most important planning and policy issue of our time. It is also the major imperative behind a thorough assessment of the manner in which tourism planning may be able to contribute to more sustainable forms of development as tourism is clearly inextricably bound up with processes of environmental, economic and social change.

Sustainable tourism

Sustainable tourism is a sub-set of both tourism and sustainable development (Figure 2.1). Sustainable tourism development is not the same as sustainable development although the principles of the latter, as outlined above, do clearly inform sustainable tourism. The key difference between

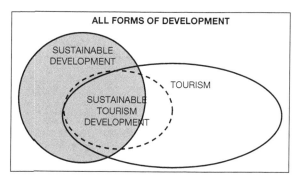

Figure 2.1 Sustainable tourism and sustainable development

the two concepts is one of scale. Sustainable tourism only refers to the application of sustainability concepts at the level of the tourism industry and consequent social, environment and economic effects, whereas sustainable development operates at a broader scale that incorporates all aspects of human interaction with the Earth's environment. The implications of such differentiation of scales of analysis are important because it can be conceived, for example, that a tourism operation may meet criteria of being sustainable although if it is placed in a community context then the function of that community as a whole may be unsustainable because of the tourism operation, as a result of other development options not being able to be pursued.

In examining sustainable development and sustainable tourism we are primarily interested in change. Change refers to the movement from one state or condition to another. Whether such a transition is positive or negative will depend on the original criteria by which change is measured. In the field of tourism studies investigations and discussion of the impacts of tourism have long been a major research theme (e.g. Mathieson and Wall 1982; Wall and Mathieson 2005) as well as a justification for planning intervention. As with the key dimensions of sustainable development the effects of tourism have typically been divided into three main categories: environmental (referring to the physical or natural environment), social and economic. These categories are not mutually exclusive and have a

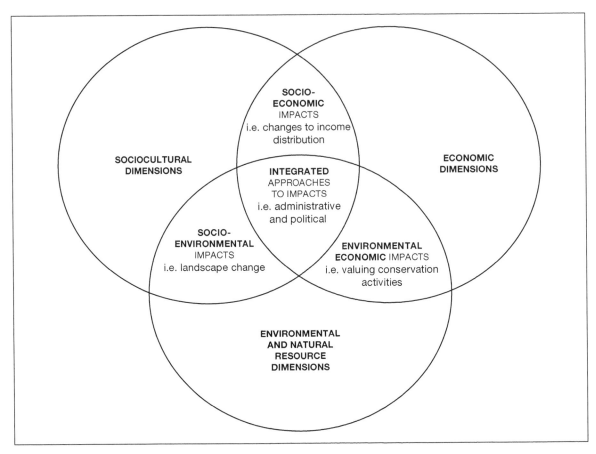

Figure 2.2 Dimensions of the impacts of tourism

significant degree of overlap but they serve as useful devices by which to discuss the impacts of tourism and their assessment (Figure 2.2).

Table 2.6 outlines some of the positive and negative effects of tourism that have been detailed in the tourism literature organised by the different types of impact. One of the immediate observations that can be made of the consequences of tourism is that the same consequence can be seen as either positive or negative – even in the same destination – depending on the perspective of the viewer and the situation in which it occurs. For example, increases in property values as a result of tourism-related development, such as the development of a sports complex or a waterfront development, are often regarded positively by property owners, real estate developers and municipalities who gain income from property taxes, but negatively by those who rent properties as they often lead to increased rents as well as making it more difficult to buy into the property market at that location (Nauright and Schimmel 2005; Hall 2005b). Such differences in the perceptions and understandings of the effects of tourism are not only different between individuals in destinations, but also between destinations, depending on the different attitudes that exist towards tourism and what it represents, other social, economic and environmental change that is occurring and the values of that society (Wheeller 1993).

The potential for different understandings of the same impact to exist has extremely important implications for our understanding of the effects of tourism that are often not fully acknowledged in tourism texts, which often represent impacts as

Table 2.6 Positive and negative dimensions of tourism

Type of impact	Positive	Negative
Economic dimension		
Economic environment	Increased expenditure	Localised inflation and price increases
	Creation of employment	Replacement of local labour by outside labour
	Increase in labour supply	Greater seasonal unemployment
	Increased value of real estate	Real estate speculation
	Increase in standard of living	Increased income gap between wealthy and poor
	Improved investment in infrastructure and services	Opportunity cost of investment in tourism means that other services and sectors do not get support
	Increased free trade	Inadequate consideration of alternative investments
	Increased foreign investment	Inadequate estimation of costs of tourism development
	Diversification of economy	Increased free trade
		Loss of local ownership
		Overdependence on tourism for employment and economic development
Industry and firm	Increased destination awareness	Acquisition of a poor reputation as a result of inadequate facilities, improper practices or inflated prices
	Increased investor knowledge concerning the potential for investment and commercial activity in the destination	Negative reactions from existing enterprises due to the possibility of new competition for human resources and state assistance
	Development of new infrastructure and facilities, including accommodation and attractions	Inappropriate destination images and brands are used
	Increase in accessibility	
	Improvements in destination image	
Environmental and natural resource dimensions	Changes in natural processes that enhance environmental values	Changes in natural environmental processes
	Maintenance of biodiversity	Loss of biodiversity
	Architectural conservation	Architectural pollution
	Preservation of natural and built heritage	Destruction of heritage
	Maintenance and re-creation of habitat and ecosystems	Destruction of habitat and ecosystems
		Exceeding physical carrying capacity

▶

Table 2.6 (continued)

Type of impact	Positive	Negative
Sociocultural dimension		
Community	Increased local participation in destination activities and events	Commercialisation and commodification of activities, events and objects that may be of a personal nature
	Community renewal	Changes in community structure
	Strengthening of community values and traditions	Weakening or loss of community values and traditions
	Exposure to new ideas through globalisation and transnationalism	Increases in criminal activity
	Creation of new community space	Loss of community space
	Greater security presence	Social dislocation
	Tourism as a force for peace	Exceeding social carrying capacity
	Revival of traditions	Loss of authenticity
Psychological/individual	Increased local pride and community spirit	Tendency towards defensive attitudes concerning host regions
	Greater cross-cultural understanding	High possibility of misunderstandings leading to varying degrees of host/visitor hostility
	Increased awareness of non-local values and perceptions	Increased alienation as a result of changes to what was familiar
Integrated		
Political/administrative	Enhanced international recognition of destination region	Economic exploitation of local population to satisfy ambitions of political elite/growth coalitions
	Greater political openness	Use of tourism to fund and legitimate unpopular decisions or regimes
	Development of new administrative institutions	Loss of local power and decision-making capacities

Sources: Mathieson and Wall (1982); Ritchie (1984); Krippendorf (1987); Hall (1992b, 2007a); Lew *et al.* (2004); Wall and Mathieson (2005); Hall and Page (2006).

being uncontestable facts (e.g. Mason 2003). Instead, interpretation of the consequences of tourism, and in some cases the effects themselves, are contextual and situational. This means that there are a number of issues which have to be clarified in seeking to identify and understand the consequences of tourism, particularly with respect to their implications for planning (Figure 2.3).

Definition

Given the problems inherent in identifying tourism phenomena and tourists and distinguishing tourism from other forms of human mobility

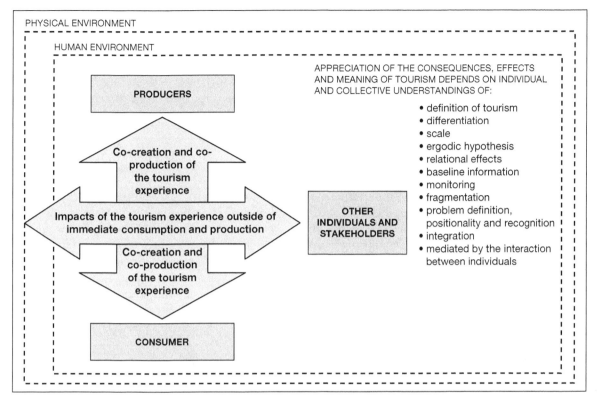

Figure 2.3 Understanding the consequences and meanings of tourism

and leisure-oriented behaviour (Coles *et al.* 2004; Hall 2005a) (see also Chapter 1) it can be difficult to isolate the impacts of tourism and tourists.

Differentiation

Human systems are extremely complex. It is only in the most simple and closed of systems that it may be possible to clearly isolate the effects of tourism from other influences on change. In the vast majority of social, economic and physical environments it is extremely difficult to identify the impacts of tourism separate from those of other industrial and cultural impacts. Yet despite this tourism has long been 'blamed' for changing places, especially when there are substantial socio-cultural and/or economic differences between tourists and members of the destination community. For example, one of the first books on tourism planning, by

Baud-Bovy and Lawson (1977: 183) commented that tourism:

> degrades irreversibly the very attractions which justified and attracted it, eroding natural resources, breaking up the unity and scale of traditional landscapes and their characteristic buildings, polluting beaches, damaging forests and rendering banal under the inundation of alien facilities of often mediocre uniform design a formerly unique country.

Perhaps this could be interpreted as a clear justification for tourism planning! Yet, simultaneously, tourism can also be seen as a means of conserving natural resources, maintaining traditional landscapes and differentiating one particular place from those around it. For example, Müller's (1999, 2002a, 2002b) research on German second home owners in Sweden demonstrated that German visitors were purchasing and maintaining building stock which may otherwise have fallen into disrepair, providing income to the local communities and contributing to the conservation of the natural and cultural landscape (also see Müller 2002c, 2004). Indeed, in some peripheral communities tourism may be one of the few development opportunities available (e.g. Hall and Boyd 2005; Jansson and Müller 2007).

Change is a normal part of human and natural systems. The reality is that *any* form of development can change the state of the physical and socio-cultural environments. Whether this is for good or for worse will depend on the perspective that is adopted by the viewer. For example, criticism of tourism has been particularly strong with respect to the effects of tourism on culture, especially in the less developed countries; yet even though tourism is clearly a part of processes of cultural globalisation its effects may be difficult to separate from those of the media and the Internet or even those of religion (Hall and Tucker 2004). The reality may be that the very visibility of tourists, as being 'different' or 'other' and the facilities which serve them may act to focus attention on tourism as a potential agent of change rather than other factors, which are less tangible or easy to criticise (Butcher 2003).

Scale

Tourism has impacts over different geographical and temporal scales. Geographical scales may range from the individual and the firm through to communities, destinations, regions, countries and the global. In addition, tourism has impacts over time. In the sciences and social sciences in general, as spatial scale increases so does the timescale of

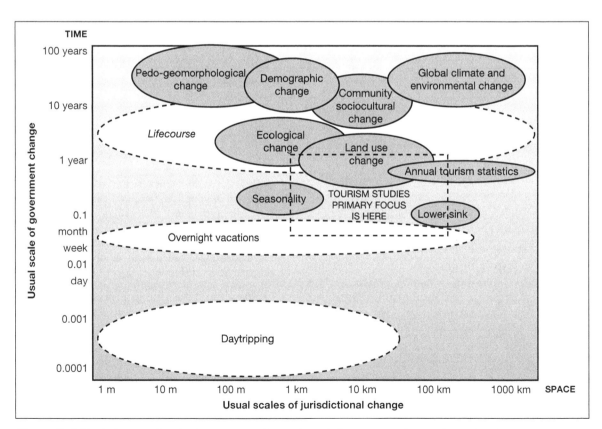

Figure 2.4 The influence of scale of temporal and spatial resolution on assessing tourism-related change
Source: Hall (2004a).

interest (Burt 2003). The corrrelation between spatial and temporal scales of analysis is not always maintained but, as Burt (2003) notes with respect to issues of scale in the physical environment, in general terms, short-term studies tend to focus on process dynamics whereas longer-term studies are more likely to involve statistical analysis of form and structure. However, in tourism the temporal and spatial scales with respect to tourism phenomena tend to be limited (Hall 2004a). In seeking to assess the impacts of tourism it is therefore extremely important to identify the spatial and temporal boundaries of analysis and the advantages and disadvantages of the boundaries used (Figures 2.4 and 2.5). For example, it has long been recognised (e.g. Clawson and Knetsch 1966), that a tourist trip consists of five stages, each with its own spatial and temporal aspects as well as psychological dimensions for the traveller (Hall 2005a):

1. decision to travel from the home environment
2. travel to destination (transit region)
3. activities at destination

4. travel from destination (transit region)
5. recollection in home environment.

Given this situation it may seem logical that in assessing the full impacts of tourism the temporal and areal boundary should include the analysis of effects from at least when the tourist leaves home to when they return. However, the majority of studies of the effects of tourism are at a site or destination level which, although obviously still important from the destination's perspective, may mean that some of the broader effects of tourism may be missed (Gössling and Hall 2006). Figure 2.6 provides a matrix that presents the relative consequences of tourism in relation to the stages of tourism as well as the different dimensions in which effects occur. A good example of the importance of understanding scale in relation to the environmental dimensions of travel is a study of the impacts of tourism in the Seychelles. Gössling et al. (2002) found that more than 97 per cent of the energy used by tourists was a result of air travel to and from the destination, leading Gössling et al. (2002) to comment 'Existing

Sociocultural/economic/political systems	Biodiversity	Climate
International	Global	Macroclimate
Supranational	Continental	
National	Biome	
Regional	Bioregion	
	Landscape	
Local firm	Ecosystem	
Family	Stand/field/communities	Mesoclimate
Individual	Individual species	Microclimate

Figure 2.5 Scale in tourism analysis: primary foci in socio-economic systems, biodiversity and climate research in terms of research outputs

Note: Shading indicates the extent to which certain scales of analysis have been studied.

Sources: Hall (2004a) and Gössling and Hall (2006).

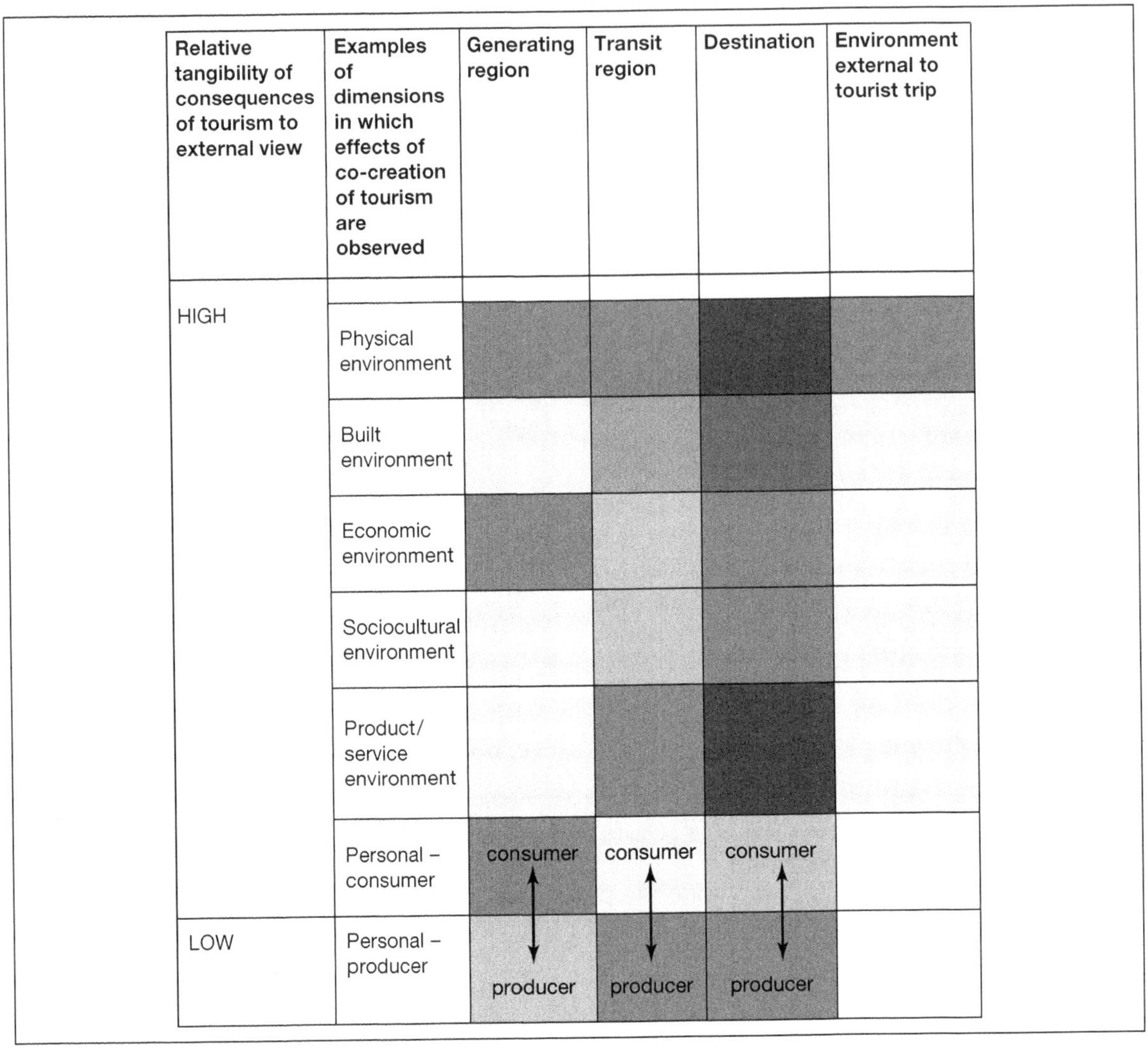

Relative tangibility of consequences of tourism to external view	Examples of dimensions in which effects of co-creation of tourism are observed	Generating region	Transit region	Destination	Environment external to tourist trip
HIGH	Physical environment				
	Built environment				
	Economic environment				
	Sociocultural environment				
	Product/ service environment				
	Personal – consumer	consumer	consumer	consumer	
LOW	Personal – producer	producer	producer	producer	

Figure 2.6 A matrix of the consequences of tourism by dimension and environment

Note: Shading indicates relative change as a consequence of the consumption and production of tourism. The darker the shading, the more substantial the change.

Source: Hall (2004a).

concepts [of tourism and the local environment] are thus insufficient to make clear statements about the sustainability of particular forms of travel or the sustainability of certain destinations'. Just as significantly, many tourism studies are one-offs rather than being a part of a longitudinal or time series study, a situation that potentially affects our understanding of how tourism affects a location over time – particularly in the absence of a clear and workable ergodic hypothesis for tourism development.

Ergodic hypothesis

A system is ergodic if the long-term observation of a single motion leads to the same frequency of measured values as the observation of many motions with different starting points. In ecology an ergodic hypothesis is an expedient research strategy which links space and time so that different areas in space are taken to represent different ecological stages in time (Bennett and Chorley 1978). In ecology the concept of succession is used to refer to the colonisation of a new physical environment by a series of vegetation communities until a final equilibrium state, the climax, is achieved. The presence of the colonisers, the pioneer plants, modifies the environment so that new spiecies can join or replace the initial colonisers. Changes are rapid at first but slow to a more or less imperceptible rate of change at the climax stage (Allaby 1985).

In tourism possibly the nearest that exists to an ergodic hypothesis is the concept of a tourist area cycle of evolution (Butler 1980, 2006) which is often described as a tourism, destination or resort cycle of evolution (Papatheodorou 2004). Unfortunately, despite numerous studies, its capacity to explain the pattern of tourist area development on the basis of single location, short-term studies is extremely limited although it does provide a useful heuristic device. However, more recent spatially oriented reinterpretations of the model may provide the basis for a more quantitative approach with greater predictive capacities grounded in the importance of accessibility (e.g. Hall 2005a, 2006b; Coles 2006).

Relational effects

The consequences of tourism are often discussed as if tourism had a one-way impact, i.e. tourism only affects a destination, without it being highlighted that in reality the impacts and effects of tourism are two-way in that tourism affects a destination and vice versa, the destination affects tourism. This is also an important issue as it stresses that there is an exchange process occurring at all levels with respect to tourism, i.e. from personal exchange between visitors and members of the destination community through to economic and environmental flows. This perspective of the relational aspects of tourism in part emerged from our understanding of services. Because tourism is an experiential service product – 'the application of specialised competencies (skills and knowledge), through deeds,

processes, and performances for the benefit of another entity or the entity itself (self-service)' (Vargo and Lusch 2004) – it means that in order to be able to understand tourism phenomenon we need to be able to understand its consumption and production through the relational processes of co-creation and co-production in which the value of the tourism experience is determined by both the consumer and the producer of the experiential product. The importance of relational effects in tourism planning is discussed further in Chapter 5.

Baseline information

In order to understand the consequences of tourism it is desirable to understand what a location was like before tourism began or at least large numbers of visitors arrived relative to the local population. Unfortunately, in all but a very few circumstances such pre-tourism baseline information does not exist. Therefore, in some cases an approximate estimate may be made by examining conditions in a comparable location that can be used as a control while change is monitored in the primary tourism location. Although this is most easily done with physical environmental information, such as biodiversity and geomorphology, it may also be undertaken with sociocultural or economic environments. The difficulties and dangers implicit in this approach relate to the lack of an appropriate ergodic hypothesis as outlined above.

Monitoring

There is often little specific and ongoing monitoring of the effects of tourism. Typical of this situation on a national basis is a review of the environmental impacts of tourism developments in Australia, with Warnken and Buckley (2000) noting that only 7.5 per cent of tourism developments were subject to a formal monitoring process. When monitoring did occur there was a greater use of BACIP environmental impact assessment designs (before, after, control, impact, paired sampling). However, Warnken and Buckley observed that there was often a lack of baseline data, control sites, and the implementation of monitoring programmes were often subject to constraints in finance and time (2000: 459–60):

> One common deficiency is the absence or inadequacy of predevelopment baseline monitoring; the before, after (BA) comparison in the BACIP design. Some human disturbances are unforeseen, and monitoring can take place only after the event. More commonly, however, entrepreneurs are simply reluctant to invest in monitoring until development approvals have been granted, and then want to commence construction immediately after having received approval, without time for predevelopment baseline monitoring.

Issues of monitoring and evaluation are dealt with at depth in Chapter 10.

Fragmentation

Our knowledge of the consequences of visitation are extremely fragmented. This is partially because of some of the problems outlined above but also because tourism research is often concentrated on some locations, environments and issues and not on others. For example, there is arguably a disproportionate amount of research at some locations, such as national parks; environments, such as rainforest; or on some types of tourism, such as ecotourism, when compared to mass tourism destinations (which is what the bulk of leisure tourists engage in) or in fragile environments such as deserts in which tourists may have an impact out of proportion to their numbers.

Problem definition, positionality and recognition

The issue of what constitutes a problem in terms of the consequences of tourism is a significant concern for planners and those concerned with managing tourism's impacts effects. Tourism resources are recognised as such because of a utility value. In exactly the same way many of the problems arising from tourism development are also perceptual in nature; the exception being something that is understood as being life threatening in an immediate sense. However, even serious pollution may be ignored if it means that employment may be maintained (e.g. see Lukes 2005).

To rework the seminal observations of Zimmermann (1951) with respect to the perceptual nature of resources in the case of the consequences of tourism: problems are not, they become; they are not static but expand and contract in response to human actions, perceptions and wants. Many of the consequences of tourism are recognised by some people and not others. This is because of such factors as knowledge, interests, values, and the tangibility of the impact. Environmental change may be much easier to see than social change, although how it is interpreted, i.e. whether it is derived from tourism or not, may remain problematic. In addition, evidence suggests that your position in the tourism system may also affect how you perceive the consequences of tourism, with those working in the industry often having very different understandings of its effects from those who work outside it (Singh *et al.* 2003); a situation that clearly creates major issues for assessing the consequences of tourism in conjunction with stakeholders who may benefit from tourism development.

Integrated assessment

Despite the fact that the imperative of sustainable development is that tourism-related change should be addressed in an integrated manner which brings together the sociocultural, economic and environmental dimensions of problem definition and solution, the reality is that the majority of change issues are addressed in a disciplinary or one-dimensional fashion (Coles *et al.* 2006). This will often mean that problems are only partly defined, meaning that solutions can only be partial in scope. However, the complexity of the consequences of tourism and tourism development suggests that more than one disciplinary viewpoint or set of values and interests are required to help solve problems associated with change.

In order to address these issues two related approaches are increasingly being utilised. First, the development of new institutional approaches and methods to encourage integrated problem solving, including more collaborative approaches, which serve as a major theme throughout the remainder of the book. Second, the utilisation of post-disciplinary approaches to tourism issues (Coles *et al.* 2006), which provide a philosophical underpinning to integrated institutional arrangements as well as problem-based research. They argued that the unprecedented levels of tourism-related mobility and its consequences were such that the complexity of tourism relationships to change at all scales, but particularly the global, exceeded the capabilities of an individual disciplinary approach. As Visnovsky and Bianchi (2005: no pages), the editors of *Human Affairs: A Postdisciplinary Journal for Humanities and Social Sciences*, commented:

> Postdisciplinarity in our understanding does not mean that the traditional disciplines have disappeared or indeed should disappear, but rather that they are changing and should change in order to solve complex issues of human affairs. It is not sufficient to approach such complex issues from any single discipline.

From the local to the global

This chapter has highlighted that the identification and understanding of the impacts of tourism are as problematic as they are complex, contextual and situational. However, this does not make them any less real or significant. Indeed, the concept of sustainability would not have developed unless it was emerging in response to a series of global concerns over the state of the world. Many of the development challenges are expressed at a local level, which is the scale at which most tourism planning problems are usually perceived and managed. Yet there is a growing recognition that there is a global set of problems to which tourism contributes and that also affect destinations and their level of well-being (Gössling and Hall 2006).

Figure 2.7 illustrates the relationship of tourism to changes in ecosystem services (natural capital) and human well-being. These changes occur over space (as indicated by scale relationships) and time (from the short to the longer term). The physical, sociocultural and economic environments are always changing although change is never uniform across time and space.

Nevertheless, 'all changes are ultimately connected with one another through physical and social processes alike' (Meyer and Turner 1995: 304). The scale and rates of change have increased dramatically since the Industrial Revolution of the nineteenth century because of human actions within which tourism is deeply embedded, for example the growth of mass mobility and its consequent effects. Concern over the consequences of tourism has grown hand in hand with the realisation of the changed scale within which these impacts occur. When the effects of tourism were regard as highly localised, if not unique, then concern was often only expressed at a local level. However, as impacts have become more commonplace and widespread so it is that concern has also grown. Tourism is not alone in this phenomenon. In fact, it characterises the growth of environmental and social awareness overall. Yet in recent years it has come to be recognised that although tourism is often characterised as a 'smokeless' industry it is certainly not harmless, with the capacity to have undesirable impacts increasingly causing concern where it is a significant development option. Tourism has therefore become recognised as a contributor to global environmental change (GEC).

Human impacts on the environment can be described as global in two ways. First, 'global refers to the spatial scale or functioning of a system' (Turner *et al.* 1990: 15). For example, the climate and the oceans have the characteristic of a global system and both influence and are influenced by tourism production and consumption. A second kind of GEC occurs if a change 'occurs on a worldwide scale, or represents a significant fraction of the total environmental phenomenon or global resource' (Turner *et al.* 1990: 15–16), in this sense GEC is the sum of a host of changes at the local scale. Tourism is significant for both types of change (Gössling and Hall 2006).

At the global level Gössling (2002) sought to identify the extent of tourism-related environmental change. With respect to land use Gössling (2002) estimated that, worldwide, leisure-related land use might account for 515,000 km², representing 0.34 per cent of the terrestrial surface of the Earth or 0.5 per cent of its biologically

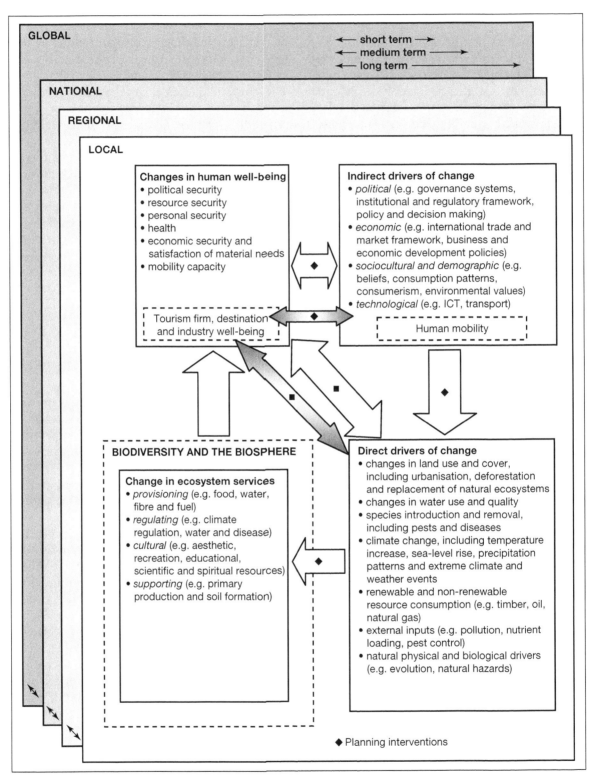

Figure 2.7 Tourism and changes to ecosystem services and human well-being

Sources: Hall (2000, 2005a); Millennium Ecosystem Assessment (2005) and Gössling and Hall (2006).

Ecological footprint analysis

A number of methods have been developed to evaluate the environmental impacts of tourism, including:

- environmental impact assessments (EIAs) – which evaluate the environmental consequences of tourism;
- limits of acceptable change (LAC) and tourism optimisation management model (TOMM) – which attempt to set standards for the toleration of change.

However such methods, although valuable, focus only on the destination or local environment rather than on the full consequences of tourism over all stages of the travel process. In the case of tourism this will mean that the consequences of travel to and from the destination are therefore ignored in any assessment exercise of sustainability. In response to these types of issues a new generation of integrated assessment (IA) modelling frameworks has been developed in order to assess the dynamics and consequences of GEC. One family of approaches has used traditional economic money-based measures of societal welfare in a bid to determine costs and benefits. However, the relevance of money as a metric of societal and environmental well-being and the ecological implications of human consumption is debatable (Senbel *et al.* 2003).

In response to such issues a new potential approach to IA has been developed that serves as an ecologically based measure of consumption as well as an indirect indicator of long-term ecological risk as a result of future consumption choices. This metric is referred to as the ecological footprint (EF) and is a measure of the intrinsic sustainability of a given area. EF analysis applies the ideas of carrying capacity to humans, but turns it on its head by asking how large an area is required to support a community, firm or region, given certain assumptions about biological productivity and consumption patterns, rather than asking how many individuals a given area can support. Therefore the ecological footprint of a specified

population is the area of land and water ecosystems required on a continuous basis to produce the resources that the population consumes and to assimilate the wastes which the population produces, wherever on Earth the relevant ecosystems are located (Rees 1991, 1995, 2000, 2001; Senbel *et al.* 2003: 84), with measures using space equivalents such as hectares of land or water surface. In simple terms, EF produces a net ecological budget, expressed in areal terms, by dividing human consumption (demand) by ecosystem productivity (supply) (Figure 2.8).

Gössling *et al.* (2002) undertook an ecological footprint analysis of the approximately 117,690 international leisure tourists who visited the Seychelles in 2000 with an average length of stay of 10.4 days. According to Gössling *et al.*'s research the land used directly for tourism infrastructure was on average 105 m^2 per tourist. The average footprint for food and fibre consumption was 1086 m^2, excluding the energy requirements for their transport to the Seychelles. In comparison the ecological footprint of fossil energy land was substantial, amounting to 1.73 ha., with about 97.5 per cent of this footprint as a result of air travel. Overall, the average tourist's holiday required more than 1.8 ha. of world average space to maintain the necessary resource flows and offset greenhouse gas emissions. The combined ecological footprint of all leisure travel to the islands was over 212,000 ha. or 2120 km^2. This can be compared to the total land area of the Seychelles of 455 km^2. However, perhaps more significantly, the Seychelles study indicated the environmental consumption of long-distance travel in real terms. An average ten-day holiday in the Seychelles corresponds to 17–37 per cent of the annual EF of a citizen of a country in the developed world: 'the biologically productive area available on a global per capita level is only 2 ha . . . A single journey to the Seychelles thus required almost the same area as available per human being on a global scale' (Gössling *et al.* 2002: 206). The authors concluded, 'environmental conservation based

▶

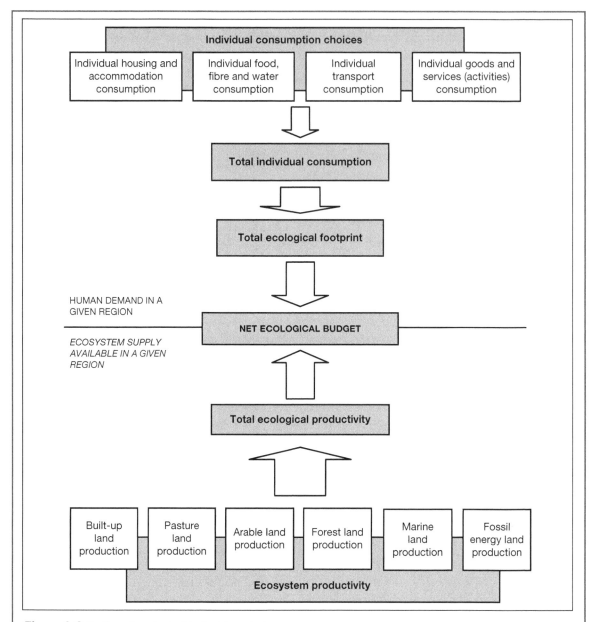

Figure 2.8 Outline of ecological footprint analysis

on funds derived from long-distance tourism remains problematic and can at best be seen as a short-term solution to safeguard threatened ecosystems' (2002: 209). One solution of course may be to attract tourists from nearer markets, thereby reducing the EF of tourism. Unfortunately, the Seychelles, like many other peripheral and island destinations, often has limited market options available to it.

productive area. Of this less than 1 per cent is due to accommodation, with the vast majority (97 per cent) being accounted for by transportation requirements. However, it should be recognised that tourism is often highly concentrated in its land use impacts, leading to what has been described as tourism urbanisation. In Italy over 43 per cent of the coastline is completely urbanised, 28 per cent is partly urbanised and less than 29 per cent is still free of construction. There are only 6 stretches of coast over 20 km long that are free of construction and only 33 stretches between 10 and 20 km long without any construction (Hall 2006b).

Tourism-related energy use is also substantial. According to the results of Gössling's (2002) review, in 2001 tourism may have been responsible for the consumption of 14,080 PJ of energy (approximately 3.2 per cent of global energy use), resulting in emissions of 1400 million tonnes of CO_2 equivalent emissions (5.3 per cent of global emissions). Transport, accommodation and activities are responsible for 94 per cent, 4 per cent, and 2 per cent of the total, respectively. However, this estimate is regarded as conservative, because energy used for the construction and maintenance of infrastructure, etc. has not been considered. This estimate may seem to be a minor share, but Gössling's (2002) analysis also revealed that the industrialised countries, which constitute only 15 per cent of the world's population, accounted for 82 per cent of global leisure-related transport (distances). Gössling's work also reinforces Hall's (2005a) perspective that tourism is the realm of the rich in terms of money and time, as Gössling (2002: 298) concluded 'that a minor proportion of the world's population (the better educated and wealthy, possibly less than 5 per cent of the world's population) accounts for a major share of the leisure-related energy use (assumingly more than 40 per cent)'. Importantly, with respect to tourism and climate change concerns per unit of energy used,

air travel has the greatest impact on global warming. Even though it accounts for only 15 per cent of the leisure-related distances traveled globally, it is responsible for about 18 per cent of the energy use

and 37 per cent of the contribution of leisure-travel to global warming. (Gössling 2002: 298)

Biological exchanges are also a significant part of tourism's contribution to environmental change but are difficult to quantify. However, tourism has been a significant factor in hastening species and disease movement around the world. They, too, are difficult to measure on a global scale. Tourism may also increase overall demand for water as well as affecting water quality. For example, in the Balearic Islands (Spain), water consumption during the peak tourism month in 1999 (July) was equivalent to 20 per cent of that by the entire local population in the entire year (De Stefano 2004). The impact of the large numbers of visitors to the Mediterranean on water quality is exacerbated by the overall infrastructure quality of tourism destinations. Scoullos (2003) reports that only 80 per cent of the effluent of residents and tourists in the Mediterranean is collected in sewage systems, with the remainder being discharged directly or indirectly into the sea or to septic tanks. However, only half of the sewage networks are actually connected to wastewater treatment facilities, with the rest being discharged into the sea. The United Nations Environment Programme Mediterranean Action Plan Priority Actions Programme (UNEP/MAP/PAP) (2001) estimated that 48 per cent of the largest coastal cities (over 100,000 inhabitants) have no sewage treatment systems, 10 per cent possess a primary treatment system, 38 per cent a secondary system and only 4 per cent a tertiary treatment system.

The potential contribution of tourism to environmental change is substantial and is the most quantified at a global scale. However, tourism also contributes substantially to sociocultural and economic change. The consequences of tourism act as a major driver for demands for tourism planning so that destinations can be developed in a more sustainable fashion. However, before examining some of the issues and practices of planning intervention at a number of different scales we will next discuss some approaches to tourism planning so that the context of intervention is better understood.

Summary

This chapter has discussed the development context within which tourism occurs and the significance of the consequences of tourism. The first part of the chapter outlined some of the key components of sustainability, which is a major justification for planning intervention. The chapter then went on to examine some of the key issues that have to be clarified in order to identify and understand the consequences of tourism, particularly with respect to their implications for planning. The importance of the issues discussed with respect to context, situation and relationality cannot be overestimated as they help explain why planning is often such a problematic and frustrating exercise for those who believe that rational decision making should work otherwise. Unfortunately, for those who prefer such an outcome the reality of planning is that neither the process nor the outcomes may end up being regarded as rational. Instead, planning, like democracy, is 'messy', though no less important for being so. The final section of the chapter outlined some of the characteristics of global environmental change to which tourism both contributes and is affected by. This last section also provided further empirical justification as to why sustainable development, discussed in the first section, is so important. In a very real sense tourism planning is the link between the goals of sustainable development and tourism-related change. As the remainder of the book emphasises, it is therefore the overarching task of tourism planning to promote human welfare, derived in part from the stock of economic, human and social capital, and to maintain and enhance ecosystem services (the stock of natural capital).

Questions

1. Why does the idea of 'sustainability' challenge conventional ways of thinking about development?
2. Is there a difference between sustainable tourism and sustainable development?
3. What are the nine issues identified in relation to the identification and understanding of the consequences of tourism?
4. What is an ergodic hypothesis and why is this significant for understanding tourism development?
5. What are the two ways by which environmental change can be described as global and how do these relate to tourism?

Important websites and recommended reading

Websites

Millennium Ecosystem Assessment:
http://www.millenniumassessment.org/

UN Millennium Development Goals:
http://www.un.org/millenniumgoals/index.html

United Nations (1992) *Agenda 21: Earth Summit – The United Nations Plan of Action from Rio*:
http://www.un.org/esa/sustdev/documents/agenda21/

The report of the World Commission on Environment and Development (WCED 1987) is available in its original form from the United Nations:
http://daccessdds.un.org/doc/UNDOC/GEN/N87/184/67/IMG/N8718467.pdf?OpenElement

Johannesburg Plan of Implementation:
http://www.un.org/esa/sustdev/documents/WSSD_POI_PD/English/POIToc.htm

The UN World Tourism Organization has a sustainable development programme:
http://www.world-tourism.org

Recommended reading

1. Hall, D. and Brown, F. (2006) *Tourism and Welfare: Ethics, Responsibility and Sustained Well-Being*, CABI, Wallingford.

   Provides an excellent account of the issues of participation in tourism and how this relates to sustainability, ethical and quality of life concerns.

2. Gössling, S. and Hall, C.M. (eds) (2006) *Tourism and Global Environmental Change,* Routledge, London.

    Provides an account of the consequences of tourism at a global level and how GEC also affects tourism.

3. Wall, G. and Mathieson, A. (2005) *Tourism: Change, Impacts, Opportunities,* Pearson, Harlow.

    An updated account of one of the seminal works on the impacts of tourism.

4. Hall, C.M. (2005) *Tourism: Rethinking the Social Science of Mobility,* Prentice Hall, Harlow.

    Provides an account of the significance of mobility as a means of understanding tourism and its consequences.

5. Hall, C.M. and Page, S. (2006) *The Geography of Tourism and Recreation: Space, Place and Environment,* 3rd edn, Routledge, London.

    Has a number of chapters devoted to outlining the effects of tourism and tourism development.

6. Coles, T., Hall, C.M. and Duval, D. (2006) 'Tourism and post disciplinary enquiry', *Current Issues in Tourism,* 9(4–5): 293–319.

    Details the implications of post-disciplinary approaches for problem definition in tourism.

7. Bramwell, B. and Lane, B. (1993) 'Sustainable tourism: an evolving global approach', *Journal of Sustainable Tourism,* 1(1): 6–16.

    A frequently cited paper in the first issue of the influential *Journal of Sustainable Tourism.*

8. Hall, C.M. and Lew, A. (eds) (1998) *Sustainable Tourism: A Geographical Perspective,* Addison Wesley Longman, Harlow.

    An edited book that includes a number of highly cited chapters on various aspects of sustainable tourism.

9. Mowforth, M. and Munt, I. (2003) *Tourism and Sustainability: Development and New Tourism in the Third World,* 2nd edn, Routledge, London.

    An excellent account of some of the issues of sustainable tourism examined in the context of developing countries.

10. Sharpley, R. and Telfer, D. (eds) (2002) *Tourism and Development: Concepts and Issues,* Channel View Publications, Clevedon.

    An edited book that provides a good general overview of issues associated with tourism development processes.

3 The changing dimensions of tourism planning

Chapter objectives

After reading this chapter you will:

- Understand the reasons why tourism planning and policy problems change
- Appreciate the way in which the tourism policy agenda changes over time
- Identify the stages of the issue attention cycle
- Understand the focus of the five broad approaches or traditions that have been identified with respect to public tourism planning
- Appreciate the difficulties in undertaking community-based tourism
- Be aware of the key elements of a sustainable approach to tourism planning.

The focus and methods of tourism planning have not remained constant but have evolved to meet the new demands that have been placed on the tourism industry. International tourism policies among the developed nations can be divided into five distinct phases (Table 3.1). Of particular importance has been the increased direct involvement of government in regional development, environmental regulation and the marketing of tourism, although more recently there has been reduced direct government involvement in the supply of tourism infrastructure and greater emphasis on the development of public–private partnerships, support for destination branding and marketing strategies and industry self-regulation (Hall 1994). In particular, the attention of government

to the potential benefits of economic and regional development has provided the main driving force for tourism planning, but the result has often been top-down planning and promotion. Sustainability has also been an area of increased concern, though the concept has been interpreted in many different ways. However, since 2000 new issues have made it on to the tourism policy agenda – such as global environmental change (see Chapter 2), security and renewed focus on the reduction of tourism trade barriers.

The fact that the focus of tourism planning has changed over the past 50 years suggests that there must be reasons why planning 'problems' also change. Several reasons can be given for this:

- New problems arise in the physical environment that must be responded to, such as natural disasters.
- Changes in the economic, social, technological, political and physical environment need to be responded to. As noted in Chapter 2 the more rapid the change the more likely it will be perceived as a problem.
- There are changes in thinking about how government should act, i.e. not only changes in who holds power in government but also changes in political philosophy.
- There are changes in planning and social theory. This makes us see the world differently and, particularly, changes our rankings of what the problems are.
- New knowledge gives us new problem-solving powers and therefore allows us to focus on new issues.

Table 3.1 International tourism policies from 1945 to the present

Phase	Characteristics
1945–1955	The dismantling and streamlining of the police, Customs, currency and health regulations that had been put into place following the Second World War.
1955–1970	Greater government involvement in tourism marketing in order to increase tourism earning potential.
1970–1985	Government involvement in the supply of tourism infrastructure and in the use of tourism as a tool of regional development.
1985–2000	Continued use of tourism as a tool for regional development, increased focus on environmental issues, reduced direct government involvement in the supply of tourism infrastructure, greater emphasis on the development of public–private partnerships and industry self-regulation.
2000–present	Continued use of tourism as a tool for regional development; greater focus on network development, collaboration and clustering. Security and crisis management new dimensions of tourism policy. Environmental issues such as climate change are prominent along with broader issues of global environmental change. In developing countries pro-poor tourism initiatives are identified by Non-government Organisations (NGOs) as a significant policy issue. Reduction of trade barriers also significant.

Sources: After OECD (1974); Hall (1994, 2005a); Hall and Jenkins (1995); Gössling and Hall (2006).

Plate 3.1 Bristol City Treasury, England. This picture of a road sign outside of the Bristol City Treasury sums up the changed priorities for government with respect to tourism very nicely and the continuing challenges which local government face.

The issue attention cycle

One of the most significant concepts in understanding the relationships between the media and how important certain issues are to consumers is the concept of the 'issue attention cycle' (Downs 1972). According to Downs, modern publics attend to many issues in a cyclical fashion. A problem 'leaps into prominence, remains there for a short time, and then, though still largely unresolved, gradually fades from the center of public attention' (1972: 38). Originally applied to an understanding of social issues of the 1960s, and environmental issues in particular, the notion of an issue attention cycle has also been found to be extremely important in explaining the relationship between domestic and foreign policy decisions, the media and the level of public interest in certain issues. One of the main reasons for this is the 'ecology of news' in that there is competition between news stories for the finite amount of media space and new stories will usually have greater impact than old ones. For example, it can be noted that the objective danger of something to tourists will not usually correlate to the amount of news coverage an issue will get and therefore the policy or planning response. For example, there is a far greater likelihood of being killed in a car crash or catching a tropical disease as a tourist than being killed by terrorists or hijacked (Hall 2005a). Nevertheless, it is the exceptional event that often seems to grab the headlines, influence public opinion and therefore influence policy and planning decisions.

The issue attention cycle is divided into six stages (Figure 3.1) which may vary in duration depending upon the particular issue involved, but which almost always occur in the following sequence:

1. The pre-problem stage

At this stage an issue only exists for experts and those directly involved. Few members of the public are aware of the issue.

2. Alarmed discovery and euphoric enthusiasm

Immediate measures are taken with respect to the problem.

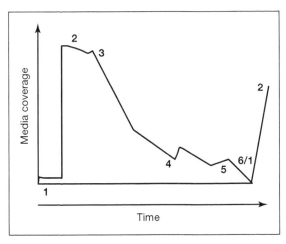

Figure 3.1 The issue attention cycle

Note: The issue attention cycle is divided into six stages, which may vary in duration depending upon the particular issue involved, but that almost always occur in the following sequence:

1. The pre-problem stage.
2. Alarmed discovery and euphoric enthusiasm.
3. Realising the cost of significant progress.
4. Gradual decline of intense public interest. Sporadic recapture of issue may occur on the anniversary of an event or when a similar event occurs that is related to the overall policy area.
5. The post-problem stage.
6. Issue re-emergence/alarmed discovery and euphoric enthusiasm.

Source: From Hall, C.M. (2005a) Tourism: *Rethinking the Social Science of Mobility,* Prentice Hall, Harlow. Reproduced with permission.

3. Realising the cost of significant progress

In this stage winners and losers in the policy process are identified.

4. Gradual decline of intense public interest

This phase develops as the original problem loses its novelty to both media and public. The public also begin to understand how difficult a solution will be, and how

▶

costly it has become. Indeed, it may also be acknowl-edged that some problems, such as those associated with security, are never 100 per cent solvable. Four re-actions may result: discouragement, a sense of threat, boredom, or a combination of these feelings (Downs 1972). So long as the initial problem does not make the media or is seen to be occurring 'elsewhere' then public interest and hence policy concern will dimin-ish. Public attention no longer focuses on the issue but is transferred instead to another problem that is entering stage two, diverting policy attention and gov-ernment funding with it. The carrying capacity of the media means that the ecological competition between issues leads to a situation in which new issues arise replacing the original issue in terms of extent and quality of coverage. Indeed, the amount of attention an issue gets is clearly not always related to its 'seri-ousness' as an issue. Media coverage is therefore di-minished and routinised with only sporadic recapture,

Sources: See Hall (2002, 2005a).

review or anniversary stories that mark the effects of the original event on policy, planning and administra-tive processes.

5. The post-problem stage

In this final stage the problem is managed in an orderly way by agencies through routine programmes and policies. The situation becomes one of incre-mental change or no change at all until another crisis affects the administrative system.

6. Issue re-emergence/alarmed discovery and euphoric enthusiasm

Arguably these stages well describe not only changes since 2001 with respect to travel safety measures and policies (Hall 2002), but are also indicative of government response towards public opinions with respect to other tourism-related issues, such as envi-ronmental protection or the cost of fuel for transport.

- The public's perception of what the planning issues are changes and government and planners respond to this.

Within western society considerable debate has emerged in the past two decades over the appro-priate role of the state in society. Such a debate has considerable impact on both the form of, and the organisations that undertake tourism planning. Throughout most of the 1980s and the early 1990s, 'Thatcherism' (named after Conservative Prime Minister Margaret Thatcher) in the United Kingdom and 'Reaganism' (named after Republi-can President Ronald Reagan) in the United States saw a period of supposed retreat by central gov-ernment from active intervention. At the national level, policies of deregulation, corporatisation, privatisation, free trade, the elimination of tax incentives, and a move away from discretionary forms of macro-economic intervention, have been the hallmarks of a push towards 'smaller' govern-ment and lower levels of central government inter-vention in various countries around the world.

Tourism is clearly not immune from changes in political philosophy in its wider policy

environment. The dominant ideological trend in western societies in the 1980s and for much of the 1990s to deregulate the market and reduce the extent of government involvement has led to government often becoming entrepreneurial in its involvement with tourism in order to increase the financial contribution of tourism to government income. Therefore, government has increasingly been involved in the promotion and marketing of destinations, and the joint development of tourist attractions or facilities, with the private sector (see Burns 1999 for an excellent discussion on the changing role of tourism planning in develop-ing countries).

Tourism is subject to direct and indirect gov-ernment intervention often because of its em-ployment and income-producing possibilities and therefore its potential to diversify and contribute to national and regional economies. Given calls from some interests for reduced government in western society in recent years, there have been increasing demands from conservative national governments and economic rationalists in the public and private sectors for less regulation of the industry and also for a stronger business interest in government with respect to tourism promotion and planning, often through the privatisation or corporatisation of tourism agencies or boards. However, in many cases this has not meant that tourism businesses have had to shoulder a greater share of the cost of national and regional tourism promotion. The implications of such a deregulated or 'neoliberal' approach for the tourism industry are substantial.

For example, the World Travel and Tourism Council (WTTC) policies with respect to government's role in tourism states: 'The most effective policy responses are those that focus on key government tasks, such as coordinating infrastructure development and fostering competitiveness, rather than focusing on short-term protectionism or micro-intervention in market mechanisms' (2003: 6). Measures that 'will help deliver on the promise' include:

- Long-term tourism planning at national and regional/local levels.
- Creating a competitive business environment that avoids inflationary taxation, guarantees transparency, and offers more attractive corporate ownership rules.
- Ensuring that quality statistics and information feed into policy and decision-making processes.
- Bringing new professionalism, funding and coordination into promotion and marketing, employment and training needs, infrastructure and regional/local policy.
- Developing the human capital required for Travel & Tourism growth. Governments should lead investment in human resources – through education and by bridging the gap between authorities and the industry – to help plan ahead for future needs. An online and easily accessible market-monitoring network could link reliable tourism market information with data on employment.
- Liberalizing trade, transport and communications and easing barriers to travel and to investment.
- Confidence building for customers and investors on safety and security.
- Promoting product diversification that spreads demand.
- Planning sustainable tourism expansion in keeping with cultures and character.

- Investing in technological advances to facilitate safe and efficient Travel & Tourism development, such as satellite navigation systems (WTTC 2003: 7).

Such sentiments are very distant from ideas of the role of the state in tourism espoused by the International Union of Travel Organizations (IUOTO), the forerunner to the UN World Tourism Organization (UNWTO), which, in the 1970s, argued that tourism was such an important sector that in order to foster and develop tourism

on a scale proportionate to its national importance and to mobilize all resources to that end, it is necessary to centralize the policy-making powers in the hands of the state so that it can take appropriate measures for creating a suitable framework for the promotion and development of tourism by the various sectors concerned (IUOTO 1974: 71).

Over 30 years later, the comments of IUOTO are far removed from contemporary debates concerning the role of the state and government in tourism or even the role of the UNWTO (see Chapter 6 for a more recent perspective on UNWTO's approach to tourism development). For example, The UNWTO now has a Business Council as part of

a partnership approach to tourism as a method to promote public and private integration and as a model of understanding between the two sectors. To achieve their objectives, UNWTOBC aids Members in expanding their tourism businesses through industry networking, forming contacts with the necessary government officials strengthening industry–education relationship, and conducting specialized research projects of the private sector (World Tourism Organization 2007a).

Indeed, the UNWTO 'recognizes that the private sector is the driving force behind tourism growth and advocates a partnership approach to development on the local and international level' (2007d).

Much intervention in tourism and other public policy arenas (e.g. education, health and welfare) is related to market failure, market imperfection and social need. The market method of deciding who gets what and how is not always adequate, and therefore government often changes the distribution of income and wealth by measures that work within the price system. Across the globe almost every industry has been supported at various times by subsidies, the imposition of tariff regulations, taxation concessions, direct grants and other forms of government intervention, all of which serve to affect the price of goods and services and therefore influence the distribution of income, production and wealth. The size or economic importance of the tourism industry, so commonly emphasised by the public and private sector sectors (e.g. WTTC 2003; World Tourism Organization 1997, 2001, 2006b, 2007b), is no justification in itself for government intervention; within market-driven economies justification must lie in some aspect of: (1) market failure; (2) market imperfection, or (3) public/social concerns about market outcomes. In other words, 'implicit in each justification for political action is the view that government offers a corrective alternative to the market' (Hula 1988: 6).

Market failure takes many forms. For instance, the market often fails to protect adequately the environment on which much of the tourist industry depends for its survival. One would expect that a business or industry which receives income from environmental quality would largely maintain that quality. However, there is a real risk that, where several businesses rely on the same environmental space or where others are competing for resources, the 'tragedy of the commons' (Hardin 1968) – the inability of individuals or the private sector on many occasions to come together to coordinate a strategy to protect (or enhance) the environment because they regard it as a 'free' resource to which their own individual activities do little harm – will emerge. This arises for such reasons as the inclination of businesses to freeload on the activities of others, and the difficulty in getting private interests to pool their resources. In addition, business is rarely interested in long-term social and environmental need as opposed to short-term revenue and profits, and yet tourism development may impact adversely on some sections of the community to the extent that government has to step in to rectify the problem (Hall and Jenkins 1998).

Infrastructure supply is another avenue for market failure, market imperfection or social need. This is illustrated in the manner in which governments in many parts of the world usually find themselves as the main providers and managers of roads, airports, railways, power supply, sewage and water supply, although increasingly infrastructure is being provided by way of public–private sector partnerships or statutory or corporate authorities in which government is a major shareholder or partner.

Market imperfections can be found in areas where the market does not cater to the needs of individual citizens. In many countries government, in consultation with industry, unions and other interests, has established equal employment opportunity legislation, anti-discrimination legislation, occupational health and safety practices, minimum wage structures, the provision of facilities for disabled people, and other workplace and social/cultural arrangements. Public consensus may also deem that a particular market outcome is unacceptable. A prime example is social welfare policy because there is usually a political consensus that aid ought to be targeted to those who are unable to compete in the market (Hall and Jenkins 1998; Dredge and Jenkins 2007).

Tourism, as does any other industry, has problems that stem from market failures and imperfections and from subsequent government responses. However, as an industry, tourism is poorly understood, as are its various impacts. Hard to define because of its particular service and structural characteristics, tourism is consequently beset by problems of analysis, monitoring, coordination and policy making. Moreover, until recently, tourism research, and notably analysis of tourism public policy and planning (Hall and Jenkins 1995), has been a low priority, with the tourism industry and governments at all levels more often concerned with promotion and short-term returns than strategic investment and sustainability. The major proportion of tourism industry and even government tourism agency research has therefore been focused on understanding the market and the means by which potential consumers can be persuaded to buy tourism products. According to Hall and Jenkins (1998) understanding of

- the dynamics of the tourism destination system in terms of the most appropriate set of supply-side linkages to maximise the returns from visitor expenditure;
- the long-term effects of tourism on the socio-cultural and physical environment; and
- the relationship of tourism to other industries, is minimal.

To this we can perhaps add our understanding of the dynamic nature of tourism planning as a whole. While the desirability for tourism planning is generally accepted, the most effective form and method of planning remains an essentially contested concept. The consequences of tourism development are wide ranging and often unpredictable. As a result, planning can often only articulate concerns or uncertainties, society must guide planners in assessing their acceptability. Furthermore, as the discussion below illustrates, planning occurs at different levels and within a number of planning traditions, each with its own set of values, methods, problems and solutions. Although we have substantial numbers of local case studies of tourism planning and development on the one hand, and a desire for more sustainable tourism on the other (often being driven by international agreements regarding sustainability and the environment), the development of more appropriate forms of tourism on anything in the space in between has not been terribly successful.

Planning for tourism has traditionally been associated with land-use zoning or development planning at the local or regional government level. Concerns have typically been focused on site development, accommodation and building regulations, the density of tourist development, the presentation of cultural, historical and natural tourist features, and the provision of infrastructure including roads and sewage. However,

as noted above, tourism planning at all levels of government has increasingly had to adapt its tourism planning programme in recent years to include concerns over the environmental and social impacts of tourism, the competitiveness of destinations and, given the changing context within which government occurs, demands for 'smaller government', particularly from some business interests which argue that self-regulation is more economically efficient than government regulation. As the following pages will indicate, economic motivations have been foremost in tourism planning. However, attention is gradually becoming focused on the social and environmental aspects of tourism development, and the creation of more sustainable forms of tourism overall.

Approaches to tourism planning

Five broad approaches or traditions of public tourism planning can be identified:

1. 'boosterism';
2. an economic, industry-oriented approach;
3. a physical/spatial approach;
4. a community-oriented approach that emphasises the role the host plays in the tourism experience;
5. a sustainable tourism approach.

As Getz (1987: 5) noted, such tourism planning 'traditions are not mutually exclusive, nor are they necessarily sequential'. Nevertheless, this categorisation is a convenient way to examine the different and sometimes overlapping ways in which problems of tourism planning are perceived, and the research and planning assumptions, methods and models associated with each approach. The following sections will review each of these traditions and conclude with a discussion of the development of a sustainable model of tourism planning. The various approaches to tourism planning are outlined in terms of timelines and key events or perspectives in Table 3.2 and by several dimensions of tourism planning in Table 3.3.

Table 3.2 Timelines for traditions of tourism planning

Dates	Boosterism	Economic	Physical/spatial	Community	Sustainable tourism
1850s	Established by the 1850s with the advent of industrialised mass tourism				
1890s		Established by the late 1890s with respect to discussions of development alternatives of natural area destinations	Antecedents emerge with respect to the conservation of natural areas although secondary to economic approaches		Debates over 'sustained yield' forestry antecedent for sustainable development
1930s		State's role in managing the economy becomes extremely important	Land-use zoning becomes established practice in urban and regional planning	Idea of planner as expert well established in urban and regional planning	
1960s		Economic analysis of development decisions becomes more commonplace	Emergence of modern conservation movement with environmental agencies established for the first time	Idea of planner as expert comes to be challenged in the late 1960s and early 1970s	UN Habitat and Man and Biosphere programmes begin to be developed in the late 1960s
1980s	Neoconservative political approaches with respect to role of the state give boosters a stronger role in destination growth coalitions	Economic analysis dominant in public planning and decision making	Spatial approaches are weakened as public–private approaches become a popular planning strategy	Increased application of community approaches to tourism through public participation exercises	Sustainable development key concept in World Conservation Strategy and the Brundtland Report; ecotourism as a response to sustainability issues
2000	Continued role of growth coalitions reinforced by rise of concept of 'place wars' and destination competition	Economic analysis remains dominant. Tourism satellite accounts become important evaluation tool while idea of competitiveness influences destination planning	Spatial planning tools remain important especially as a result of new geographic information technologies; spatial planning approached at multiple scales; interest in physical dimensions of climate and global environmental change, including natural areas as refugia	Public participation standard in much destination planning although extent to which it affects planning outcomes problematic; increased association of participation with stakeholder relations	Sustainable tourism a significant planning concept although application is contested; increased concern over climate change and global environmental change; increased awareness of tourism and human welfare/quality of life issues, including in relation to 'pro-poor tourism'

Table 3.3 Tourism planning approaches: assumptions, problem definition, methods, models and literature

Planning tradition	Underlying assumptions and related attitudes	Definition of the tourism planning problem	Some examples of related methods	Some examples of related models	Some examples of related literature
Boosterism	• tourism is inherently good • tourism should be developed • cultural and natural resources should be exploited • industry as expert • development defined in business/corporate terms	• how many tourists can be attracted and accommodated? • how can obstacles be overcome? • convincing hosts to be good to tourists	• promotion • public relations • advertising • growth targets	• demand forecasting models	Usually associated with tourism policy statements from government and industry
Economic	• tourism equal to other industries • use tourism to: create employment, earn foreign revenue and improve terms of trade, encourage regional development, overcome regional economic disparities • planner as expert • development defined in economic terms	• can tourism be used as a growth pole? • maximisation of income and employment multipliers • influencing consumer choice • providing economic values for externalities • providing economic values for conservation purposes	• supply–demand analysis • benefit–cost analysis • product-market matching • development incentives • market segmentation	• management processes • tourism master plans • motivation • economic impact • economic multipliers • hedonistic pricing	Economic impact statements and feasibility studies. Examples would be analyses of the potential benefits of hosting an Olympics; Jackson *et al.* 2005

Table 3.3 (continued)

▲

Planning tradition	Underlying assumptions and related attitudes	Definition of the tourism planning problem	Some examples of related methods	Some examples of related models	Some examples of related literature
Physical/spatial	• tourism as a resource user • ecological basis to development • tourism as a spatial and regional phenomenon • environmental conservation • development defined in environmental terms • preservation of genetic diversity	• physical carrying capacity • manipulating travel patterns and visitor flows • visitor management • concentration or dispersal of visitors • perceptions of natural environment • wilderness and national park management • designation of environmentally sensitive areas	• ecological studies • environmental impact assessment • regional planning • perceptual studies	• spatial patterns and processes • physical impacts • resort morphology • LAC (limits of acceptable change) • ROS (recreational) opportunity spectrum • TOS (tourism opportunity spectrum) • destination lifecycles	Gunn 1994; Inskeep 1991; Dowling 1997; Gunn with Var 2002; Newsome *et al.* 2001; Newsome *et al.* 2005; Gössling *et al.* 2002
Community	• need for local control • search for balanced development • search for alternatives to 'mass' tourism development • planner as facilitator rather than expert • development defined in sociocultural terms	• how to foster community control? • understanding community attitudes towards tourism • understanding the impacts of tourism on a community • social impact	• community development • awareness and education • attitudinal surveys • social impact assessment	• ecological view of community • social/perceptual carrying capacity • attitudinal change • social multiplier	Murphy 1985; Blank 1989; Macbeth 1997; Jain and Triraganon 2003; Singh *et al.* 2003

Table 3.3 (continued)

Planning tradition	Underlying assumptions and related attitudes	Definition of the tourism planning problem	Some examples of related methods	Some examples of related models	Some examples of related literature
Sustainable	• integration of economic, environmental and sociocultural values • tourism planning integrated with other planning processes • holistic planning • preservation of essential ecological processes • protection of human heritage and biodiversity • inter- and intra-generational equity • achievement of a better balance of fairness and opportunity between nations • planning and policy as argument • planning as process • planning and implementation as two sides of the same coin • recognition of political dimension of tourism	• understanding the tourism system • setting goals, objectives and priorities • achieving policy and administrative coordination in and between the public and private sectors • cooperative and integrated control systems • understanding the political dimensions of tourism • planning for tourism that meets local needs and trades successfully in a competitive marketplace • change as multi-scalar	• strategic planning to supersede conventional approaches • raising producer awareness • raising consumer awareness • raising community awareness • stakeholder input • policy analysis • evaluative research • political economy • aspirations analysis • stakeholder audit • environmental analysis and audit • interpretation	• systems models • integrated models focused on places and links and relationships between such places • resources as culturally constituted • environmental perception • business ecology • learning organisations • governance	Krippendorf 1987; Hall and McArthur 1998; Mathieson and Wall 1982; McKercher 1997; Lindberg and McKercher 1997; Gössling 2002; Gössling and Hall 2006; Hall and Härkonen 2006; Hall and Brown 2006

Sources: After Getz (1987); Hall (1998b); Hall *et al.* (1997).

Boosterism

Boosterism has been the dominant tradition towards tourism development and planning since mass tourism began. Indeed in many ways it is debatable whether one can describe boosterism as form of planning at all. Boosterism is a simplistic attitude that tourism development is inherently good and of automatic benefit to the hosts. Under this approach little consideration is given to the potential negative economic, social and environmental impacts of tourism and instead cultural and natural resources are regarded as objects to be exploited for the sake of tourism development. Therefore, in many ways boosterism may be more aptly described as a form of non-planning. However, boosterism has had a marked impression on the economic and physical landscape.

Elements of the idea of boosterism have their origins not only in nineteenth-century European laissez-faire economic utilitarianism and North American frontier capitalism but also in the relatively small size of organised tourism for much of the past 150 years. When tourist numbers were so small and natural resources so overwhelming in some areas, such as the frontier United States where the first national parks were created, then the effects of tourism were relatively small. However, although tourism grew, the perception of tourism as a benign, 'smokeless' industry did not change until relatively recently.

Under the boosterism tradition, residents of tourist destinations are not involved in the decision-making and planning processes surrounding tourism development and those who oppose such development may be regarded as unpatriotic or excessively negative. In recent years boosterism is probably best noted in the hosting of mega-events, such as the Olympic Games, in which such large events are held to be automatically good for the host city and region (Olds 1998; Nauright and Schimmel 2005). Research in this tradition focuses on the forecasting of tourism demand primarily for the purposes of promotion and development rather than to ensure that levels of demand are appropriate to the resources and social carrying capacity of a region. According to Getz (1987: 10):

> Boosterism is still practiced, and always will be, by two groups of people: politicians who philosophically or pragmatically believe that economic growth is always to be promoted, and by others who will gain financially by tourism. They will go on promoting it until the evidence mounts that they have run out of resources to exploit, that the real or opportunity costs are too high, or that political opposition to growth can no longer be countered. By then the real damage has usually been done.

The economic tradition: tourism as an industry

Under the economic tradition, tourism is seen as an industry that can be used as a tool by governments to achieve certain goals of economic growth and restructuring, employment generation, and regional development through the provision of financial incentives, research, marketing and promotional assistance. Although the economic model does not claim tourism to be the panacea for all economic ills, the approach does emphasise the potential value of tourism as an export industry, sometimes nebulously defined, which can positively contribute to national and regional imbalances in such things as terms of trade, balance of payments or levels of foreign exchange. For example, in promoting tourism as a response to the substantial economic restructuring of agriculture in rural Australia, the Department of Tourism (1993: 24) noted

> Diversification of traditional rural enterprises into tourism would provide considerable benefits to local rural economies including:
>
> - wider employment opportunities;
> - diversifying the income base of farmers and rural towns;
> - additional justification for the development of infrastructure;
> - a broader base for the establishment, maintenance and/or expansion of local services;
> - scope for the integration of regional development strategies; and
> - an enhanced quality of life through extended leisure and cultural opportunities[.]

without also acknowledging some of the down-sides of rural tourism or the difficulties for some marginal farming operations to get into the tourism business.

Within the economic tradition, government utilises tourism as a means to promote growth and development in specific areas. Therefore the planning emphasis is on the economic impacts of tourism and its most efficient use to create income and employment benefits for regions or communities. Attention is given to the means by which tourism can be defined as an industry in order that its economic contribution and production can be measured, and so the role of government regulation and support can be adequately appraised (see Lew *et al.* 2004). Under the influence of the WTTC and UNWTO this has meant the development of a series of tourism satellite accounts at national and regional levels (Lennon 2003). In addition, there has been a focus on the competitiveness of destinations and the development of approaches that support competitiveness such as clustering and networks (Michael 2007). However, the role that tourism actually plays in regional development is regarded as somewhat problematic as it is possible that a focus on tourism development may not be the most appropriate strategy in terms of regional competitiveness (Malecki 2004).

One of the main characteristics of the economic approach is the use of marketing and promotion to attract the type of visitor who will provide the greatest economic benefit to the destination given the destination's specific tourist resources. Both government and industry emphasise market segmentation studies and matching product and markets. Economic goals are given priority over social and ecological questions; however, issues of opportunity costs, the assessment of visitor satisfaction and the economic necessity of generating a positive attitude towards tourists in host communities does mean that limited attention is paid to the negative impacts of tourism. Significantly, social and environmental questions when they are examined are examined with an economic framework, i.e. treated as externalities, rather than treated within frameworks such as 'rights' or 'welfare' (Hall and Brown 2006). Under the economic approach the issue of who benefits and who loses from tourism development does not usually arise.

The land-use/physical/spatial approach

The physical/spatial approach has its origins in the work of geographers, urban and regional land-use planners and conservationists who advocate a rational approach to the planning of natural resources. Land-use planning is one of the oldest forms of environmental protection. For many readers the land use/spatial approach is the dominant form of public tourism planning through its close relationship with regional and destination planning, for example the early work of Gunn (1979, 1988) before he incorporated the concept of sustainability in his later work (Gunn 1994).

Physical or spatial planning refers to 'planning with a spatial, or geographical, component, in which the general objective is to provide for a spatial structure of activities (or of land uses) which in some way is better than the pattern existing without planning' (P. Hall 1992: 4). Typically, spatial planning is multi-dimensional and multi-objective. Within this approach, tourism is often regarded as having an ecological base with a resultant need for development to be based upon certain spatial patterns that would minimise the negative impacts of tourism on the physical environment. Comprising one of the main focuses within this framework are the related issues of physical and social carrying capacity (e.g. Mathieson and Wall 1982), environmental thresholds (e.g. Hill and Rosier 1989), and limits to or acceptable/desirable rates of change (e.g. McCool 1994; Wight 1998).

In order to minimise the impact of tourists on the physical environment many visitor managers seek to manipulate travel patterns by concentrating or dispersing tourists in sensitive areas. For example, many national parks and marine parks have management plans that zone sections of the park in relation to certain levels of visitation, the provision of certain desired experiences and the nature of the resource itself (Newsome *et al.* 2001). However, visitor management strategies

Plate 3.2 Canterbury, Kent, England. The large number of visitors to the city has created substantial congestion problems which various tourism planning strategies have sought to overcome.

at heritage attractions are increasingly being revised as past strategies appear not to be able to cope with either the increased numbers or the increased demands for positive experiences being placed on such sites (Hall and McArthur 1998; Newsome *et al.* 2005). As Lindberg and McKercher (1997: 72) noted:

> As soon as an area starts to show signs of damage through overuse, the walking paths, roads, boating and other activities can be shifted to a different location . . . the common strategy of dispersion may be misguided . . . From the perspective of minimizing overall environmental change due to ecotourism, shifting locations may be the wrong strategy, because the new location may be damaged before the old location recovers.

Within the spatial tradition, geographers have emphasised the tendency for destinations to evolve and decline in relation to the market (an economic approach) and the resources of a region (the physical approach) (e.g. Butler 1980; Hall and Page 2006). It is therefore not surprising that the spatial tradition emphasises the production of tourism development plans that are based on the natural resources of a region and on the

capacity or limitations of sites to withstand tourism infrastructure (e.g. Priskin 2001). However, while such plans provide valuable insights into the potential natural resource capacities and travel patterns that occur within a region, they often fail to give attention to the social and cultural attributes of a destination. Therefore another significant strand within the land-use and physical planning aspects of the spatial tradition is the attention given to environmental impact and social impact assessments and statements (Warnken and Buckley 2000; Diamantis 2004; see also Chapter 2). Such statements have increasingly become required under planning law for the development of major infrastructure projects (e.g. airports and roads), resort developments and facilities (e.g. visitor centres in wilderness areas). Although often thought of as primarily being related to developments in nonurban areas, the impacts of tourism-related development in urban areas, particularly large waterfront developments, are also often subject to an environmental impact statement, which will often include a number of social factors. For example, some of the urban impacts considered

Plate 3.3 Canterbury Cathedral, Kent, England. Large numbers of tourists have placed enormous stress on the physical and spiritual fabric of the Cathedral. A Visitor Centre had to be built to help manage crowds as has the development of a visitor management strategy for the cathedral and its grounds.

appropriate for inclusion in an EIS by Haughton and Hunter (1994: 256) are:

- employment
- accessibility
- safety
- air and water quality, pollution
- urban sprawl
- displacement
- community facilities and services
- tax base.

As the land use/spatial approach has evolved it has increasingly taken on aspects of wider developments in the land-use and physical planning field. Indeed, land-use planning has increasingly sought to integrate social and cultural planning concerns within an ecological approach as environmental problems have come to be defined in terms of human–environment relationships, particularly as land-use planners have sought to respond to the challenge of sustainable development (Gunn with Var 2002). This new development in the physical planning field is often broadly described under the heading of environmental planning. According to Evans (1997: 5), contemporary environmental planning 'is conceived as an integrated and holistic approach to the environment that transcends traditional departmental and professional boundaries, and is directed towards securing the long-term goal of environmental sustainability'.

According to Cowell and Owens (1997), an environment-led system of planning will have certain implications, including:

- the construction of defensible arguments for protecting any particular function of the environment as 'environmental capital';
- defining what is sustainable in the first place will create conflict as it pre-empts future decisions;
- issues will be intensely political because of the constraints they will place on economic activity;
- there will be debate over the various technical discourses of impact management and compensation;
- issues of linkages will arise – with other policy instruments and between localities and scales.

The issues noted by Cowell and Owens bear great similarity to a number of the issues identified in the first chapter and, as we shall see, are points that the following chapters will frequently return to. Nevertheless, as Cowell and Owens (1997: 21) emphasise, 'These issues must be confronted if we are to make sense of sustainability in real policy contexts.' Similarly, as Evans (1997: 8) argues, 'if environmental planning for sustainability . . . is to be anywhere near effective, the political processes of public debate and controversy, both formal and informal, will need to play a much more significant role than has hitherto been the case'.

Community-oriented tourism planning

Since the late 1970s increasing attention has come to be given to the negative environmental, cultural and personal impacts of tourism and the social context within which they occur. Although the negative effects of tourism were initially associated with the less developed nations (e.g. de Kadt 1979; Smith 1989a, 1989b; Harrison 1992) it was gradually recognised that as tourism grew undesirable impacts were also occurring in the developed nations and in parts of Europe and North America in particular. Indeed Craik (1988: 26) argued that despite difficulties in quantifying the social impacts of tourism 'in the same way as carrying capacities, bed requirements and even environmental impacts . . . it is perhaps the most important aspect of tourism development'. Therefore an examination of the social impacts of tourism came to be regarded as essential not only from an ethical perspective of the need for community involvement in decision-making processes but also because without it, tourism growth and development may become increasingly difficult. As Ross (1991: 157) observed in the light of rapid international tourism growth to some Australian destinations:

> If pleasant and satisfying experiences involving local residents are important in the destination images of tourists, and in their decision-making processes, then a consideration of the well-being of local residents in the context of tourist development would seem critical. Should residents of tourist communities come to believe that continual tourist development is destroying their physical and social environment, and that tourists are the symbols of this process, then a degree of unpleasantness may eventually characterize many resident–visitor interactions, which would ultimately damage the image of friendliness in the locals, so prized by overseas tourists at present.

In response to the perceived negative effects of tourism development, alternative strategies of tourism development were espoused in the 1980s and 1990s, including what we now describe as ecotourism, which highlighted the social and physical context within which tourism occurred (e.g. Smith and Eadington 1992; Fennell and Dowling 2003; Diamantis 2004). Similarly, McIntosh and Goeldner (1986: 308, 310) highlighted the need for wider community involvement in tourism in their five goals of tourism development, in which they argued that tourism development should aim to:

1. provide a framework for raising the living standard of local people through the economic benefits of tourism;
2. develop an infrastructure and provide recreation facilities for both residents and visitors;
3. ensure that the types of development within visitor centres and resorts are appropriate to the purposes of these areas;
4. establish a development programme that is consistent with the cultural, social and economic philosophy of the government and the people of the host area; and
5. optimise visitor satisfaction.

One of the earliest and most influential statements of the community approach to tourism development is to be found in Murphy's book *Tourism: A Community Approach* (1985). Murphy advocated the use of an ecological approach to tourism planning that emphasised the need for local control over the development process. One of the key components of the approach is the notion that in satisfying local needs it may also be possible to satisfy the needs of the tourist, a 'win–win' philosophy that is immensely attractive. Nevertheless, despite the undoubted conceptual attraction to many destinations of the establishment of a community approach to tourism planning, substantial problems remain in the way such a process may operate and how it may be implemented (Haywood 1988; Murphy 1988; Singh *et al.* 2003). Indeed, even in the case of Murphy's work local control was often expressed through the role of interest groups, particularly business groups, rather than a broader degree of community control.

Community tourism planning is a response to the need to develop more socially acceptable guidelines for tourism expansion. For example, Cooke's (1982) seminal work on social sensitivity to tourism in British Columbia provides some important insights into the manner in which the social impacts of tourism on a community can be ameliorated through appropriate planning measures. Cooke (1982) identified several sets of conditions that are appropriate to local tourism development:

- tourists respect local cultural and ethnic traditions and values;
- opportunities for extensive local involvement in the tourism industry through decisions made by local government; community-wide support for volunteer tourism programmes; and active participation in the direction of tourist development;
- tourism is an economic mainstay, compatible with other economic sectors, or is viewed as a desirable alternative to other industries;
- themes and events that attract tourists are supported and developed by the local community.

Conditions associated with locally inappropriate tourism development include:

- tourists do not respect local or ethnic traditions and values;
- uncertainties about the future direction of tourism development with local people feeling that they have little control;
- residents feel that visitors are catered to ahead of locals, and that infrastructure and facilities have been designed for the benefit of tourists rather than the local community;
- growth in the host community is proceeding faster than what the residents feel appropriate;
- perceived or actual conflicts over natural resource use.

Cooke's study recommended that all tourism planning be based on the goals and priorities of residents. Indeed she even went further and recommended that local attractions be promoted only when endorsed by residents. While many readers may have sympathy with this approach and while this idea underlies much of the community development literature (Singh *et al.* 2003), its practical exercise will have substantial implications for tourism development that could even mean stopping certain types of development which may be favoured by certain stakeholders in the planning process. For example, opposition has often emerged towards the development of casinos by various interests in a destination because of the perceived impact of casinos on host communities, particularly in relation to a perceived increase in crime and prostitution and the effectiveness of governments at regulating casino gambling (Nichols *et al.* 2002).

A community approach to tourism planning is therefore a 'bottom-up' form of planning, which emphasises development *in* the community rather than development *of* the community. As Blank (1989: 4) recognised, '*Communities* are the destination of most travellers. Therefore *it is in communities that tourism happens*. Because of this, *tourism industry development and management must be brought effectively to bear in communities*'. Under this approach, residents, not tourists, are regarded as the focal point of the tourism planning exercise, and the community, which is often equated with a region of local government, is regarded as the basic planning unit. Nevertheless substantial difficulties will arise in attempting to implement the concept of community planning in tourist destinations. As Dowling (1993a: 53) noted, 'research into community attitudes towards tourism is reasonably well developed, although incorporation of such views into the planning process is far less common'.

One of the major difficulties in implementing a community approach to tourism planning is the political nature of the planning process (Singh *et al.* 2003). Community planning implies a high degree of public participation in the planning process (Haywood 1988). As has been long recognised, public participation implies that the local community will have a degree of control over the outputs of the planning and decision-making process and possibly even the process itself (Arnstein 1969). Therefore, a community approach to tourism planning implies that there will be a need for partnership in, or community control of, the tourism development process (Timothy and Tosun 2003). However, such a community approach has generally not been adopted by government authorities, often because of complaints from business interests of the economic impact of decision-making delays that arise out of any statutory requirement for participation. Moreover, for many government officials, whether elected or otherwise, community control can also be interpreted as a loss of their power and their control over the planning process. Indeed, the level of public involvement in tourism planning throughout most of the world can be more accurately described as a form of tokenism in which decisions or, just as importantly, the direction of decisions has already been prescribed by government. Communities rarely have the opportunity to say no.

Substantial problems also exist in implementing public participation programmes at the community level (Sewell and Phillips 1979; Timothy 1999). For example, formal legalistic processes of consultation usually require the hosting of public meetings. However, public meetings can be exploited by those individuals and organisations who best know how to utilise meeting procedures and dynamics in their favour. Indeed, the more formal the participation process the more legalistic it tends to become, thereby disadvantaging poorer resourced stakeholders. Several impediments to public participation in tourism planning have been identified (Jenkins 1993; Singh *et al.* 2003; Murphy and Murphy 2004):

- some members of the public generally have difficulty in comprehending complex and technical planning issues;
- some members of the public are not always aware of or understand the decision-making process;
- the difficulty in attaining and maintaining representativeness in the decision-making process;
- the apathy of many citizens unless they feel their interests are being directly affected;
- the increased costs to planning authorities in terms of staff and money;

- the prolonging of the decision-making process;
- adverse effects on the efficiency of decision making.

An additional complication of public participation processes in a number of situations is the growing cultural diversity of many locations. Such diversity requires not only meeting the challenge of soliciting the voices of multiple publics but also communicating across language barriers and culture-based epistemologies. Five specific challenges can be identified in such situations (Unemoto 2001):

1. traversing interpretative frames embedded in culture, history and collective memory;
2. confronting otherness in the articulation of cultural values and social identities;
3. understanding the multiple meanings of language;
4. respecting and navigating cultural protocols and social relationships; and
5. understanding the role of power in cultural translation.

A further problem in utilising a community approach to tourism planning is the structure of government. The nature of systems of governance leads to difficulties in ensuring that tourism policies at different levels of government are adequately coordinated and that decisions and policies at one level are not at odds with decisions at another. For example, a locally based community decision not to allow tourism development at a particular site may well be at odds with a regional or national tourism plan that has been drawn up by a superior level of government. Alternatively, a local government decision to proceed with a tourism-related development may be opposed at another level if it impinges on legislative requirements or policy settings. However, if tourism resource conflicts are to be resolved at the community level then the institutional arrangements for decision-making processes related to management also need to be based at the local level (Millar and Aiken 1995). One major concern with such measures is the role that local elites may have in skewing decisions towards their own interests rather than wider community needs. However, the holding of reserve powers at higher levels of government can often act as a restraint on the roles of local elites (Ostrom 1990).

Despite the difficulties in implementing a community approach to tourism development, elements of the approach have proven to be attractive in the tourism planning literature, particularly since the early 1990s (e.g. Getz 1994; Ryan and Montgomery 1994; Simmons 1994). Many readers would likely agree with Murphy that, 'If tourism is to become the successful and self-perpetuating industry many have advocated, it needs to be planned and managed as a renewable resource industry, based on local capacities and community decision making' (Murphy 1985: 153). However, on reflection, one could argue that Murphy's statement was made over two decades ago and in aggregate tourism has kept on growing in that time despite its many environmental and social deficiencies, so perhaps local capacity does not really matter. Or perhaps, as Chapter 2 noted, in observing the negative affects of change it might just be a matter of time?

As noted above, tourism planning is not static. Planning approaches evolve in relation to the demands made upon them by various stakeholders and interests, the changing values of a community and a society, and the broader socio-economic–environmental context within which planning occurs. Nevertheless, elements of a community approach to planning would appear to provide a basis for the formulation of tourism policies that would assist both residents and visitors in the longer term, satisfying local desires to control the rate of change, if any, and meeting visitor interest in the maintenance of unique attributes of a destination. However, a community approach is only a starting point. Tourism planning must also be able to accommodate the physical and economic dimensions of tourism, not only in order to ensure the long-term viability of the tourism industry but also to assist in the creation of sustainable places. The next section will examine some of the aspects of the emerging sustainable approach to tourism planning.

A sustainable approach to tourism planning: towards integrated tourism planning and development?

As noted in Chapter 2, sustainable development has a primary objective of providing lasting and secure livelihoods that minimise resource depletion, environmental degradation, cultural disruption and social instability. The WCED (Bruntland Commission) (1987) report extended this basic objective to include concerns of equity; the needs of economically marginal populations; and the idea of technological and social limitations on the ability of the environment to meet present and future needs.

While tourism ostensibly seeks to meet the primary objective of sustainable development (i.e. 'not to shit in its own nest' and in so doing to continue over time to return benefits to society), there are many contradictions within both the concept of sustainable development and the nature of tourism that will mean that complete satisfaction of the concept will be extremely difficult (e.g. Bramwell and Lane 1993; Hall and Butler 1995; Hall and Lew 1998; Diamantis 2004). For example, Pearce *et al.* (1988) noted that sustainability implies an infinite time horizon, whereas practical decision making requires the adoption of finite horizons. Although these factors complicate the attainment of sustainable development planning objectives, they are not 'hard barriers'. Rather, they serve to emphasise the pre-conditions for tourism to become a sustainable land use. Paramount among these is an effective coordination and control mechanism – a system that is able to give practical and ongoing effect to the policy and planning intent of sustainable development.

The complex nature of the tourism industry and the often poorly defined linkages between its components are major barriers to the integrative strategic planning that is a prerequisite for sustainable development. Tourism development is often fragmented and poorly coordinated (Hall and Jenkins 1995). The poor record of synchronisation of policy and practice therefore appears to be one of the major impediments to attainment of sustainable development objectives. The existence of tourist infrastructure and 'ready-made' attractions alone are not sufficient by themselves to ensure the long-term future of a tourist destination, although they may be successful in the short run. Furthermore, an imbalance between the supply and demand components of tourism, together with inadequate attention to factors determining economic, social and environmental sustainability, have the potential to lead to undesirable and unforeseen consequences (Butler 1990, 1991; Singh *et al.* 2003).

As tourism developed around the world in the immediate post-Second World War era, there was little evidence to suggest that the nature and scale of tourism activities was not sustainable. The number of people travelling was minimal by today's standards. It is only since the rapid growth of international tourism in the early 1970s with the advent of the jumbo jet that questions about factors affecting sustainability, such as environmental and social constraints to development, have become prominent (Hall 2005a). Therefore it should not be surprising that the need for incorporation of sustainable development principles into tourism development has only recently emerged as one of the key management issues in tourism.

Community planning provides a basis for the development of a longer-term approach to tourism, but the tenets of community-based planning need to be extended to incorporate the coordinative, iterative, integrative and strategic aspects of planning before a sustainable approach can be realised. One of the means to developing more sustainable forms of tourism lies in convincing government and the tourism industry of the importance of incorporating sustainable development principles into planning and operations. Dutton and Hall (1989) identified five mechanisms by which this goal can be achieved:

1. cooperative and integrated control systems;
2. development of industry coordination mechanisms;
3. raising consumer awareness;
4. raising producer awareness;
5. strategic planning to supersede conventional approaches.

Cooperative and integrated control systems

Unfortunately, in a typical public planning process, stakeholders are often consulted minimally, near the end of the process, and often via formal public meetings. In contrast, an interactive and cooperative style may result in better decisions in terms of stakeholder acceptance (Wight 1998). An integrative planning approach to tourism planning and management at all levels (from the regional plan to individual resort projects) would assist in the distribution of the benefits and costs of tourism development more equitably, while focusing on improving relationships and understanding between stakeholders may also assist in agreement on planning directions and goals. However, cooperation alone will not foster commitment to sustainable development without the incentive of increased mutual benefits. In addition, a cooperative planning process will still need to be 'steered' in order to ensure that planning outputs are generated.

Development of industry coordination mechanisms

The development of improved coordination mechanisms is regarded as a mechanism to improve firm and destination collaboration towards common goals as well as being a means by which the concerns of industry stakeholders can be better articulated to decision makers. The support by industry groups of voluntary development codes, environmental codes or codes of conduct is perhaps indicative of possible directions if common needs can be agreed upon. However, for such guidelines to be effective, it must be ensured that they do not constitute a 'lowest common denominator' approach to development and implementation. Therefore, it becomes imperative that government, at all levels, uses its influence to encourage greater industry coordination on planning issues by creating structures and processes that enable stakeholders to talk to each other and create effective relationships and partnerships.

Raising consumer awareness

In many cases the difference between a sustainable and non-sustainable tourism operation can be difficult for consumers to detect, particularly in the short term. Even in the long term the various market segments will react differently to different levels of impact. For example, some users of national parks continue to use areas even when they become crowded, while others divert elsewhere. Nevertheless, if consumers are to enjoy the benefits of better quality experiences, while minimising the costs of that experience to their own or external communities, then they will be more likely to make informed judgements about the types of tourism products and services. For example, the shift in some markets from consumptive to experiential services (i.e. from hunting to wildlife photography) is illustrative of the capacity of markets to readjust and make value judgements compatible with the values inherent in the philosophy of sustainable development.

In recent years there has been a growth in 'conscious consumption' in which consumers have thought about their purchases with respect to such factors as organic foods, environment conservation and human rights. Such conscious consumerism has influenced tourism with respect to the growth of ethical tourism considerations, codes of tourism conduct, types of tourism such as volunteer tourism as well as destination boycotts. However, while alterations to the demand side of the tourism equation may well be possible through the modification of tourist behaviour, it may be argued that the tourists who read and take note of such material as codes of behaviour are those who represent the least worry in terms of negative impacts on the physical and social environment (Mason and Mowforth 1996). Therefore, if sustainable forms of tourism are to be developed, then it clearly becomes essential to develop more sustainable forms of tourist product that are supplied to the consumer.

Raising producer awareness

Making tourism production more sustainable can be undertaken through a combination of regulatory and voluntary approaches. Educating producers to make their products more sustainable is one way of seeking to ensure that destinations benefit, however in some cases having more sustainable product may also increase the product appeal in certain markets. Many producer groups have developed codes of conduct and good practice in an effort to make their businesses more environmentally friendly. However, the more cynical commentator may note that such developments have only occurred in order to reduce the likelihood of greater government regulation of the tourism industry.

Strategic tourism planning to supersede conventional approaches

Strategic tourism planning at the destination level is facilitated by greater involvement of host communities in the decision-making process (Gunn with Var 2002; Singh *et al.* 2003). Such an approach requires a willingness on the part of decision-making agencies to actively solicit and take account of host community attitudes if genuine public involvement in planning is to be achieved. Moreover, strategic tourism planning at the destination level needs to be conceived of in terms of strategic planning for the destination rather than strategic planning for destination organisations, which are related but significantly different things. Strategic tourism planning in its fullest sense is proactive, responsive to community needs, perceiving planning and implementation as part of a single process, and ongoing.

Strategy is a means of achieving a desired end, e.g. the objectives identified for the management of tourism resources. In the case of sustainable tourism planning and development, 'the strategy' is the use of appropriate visitor management, marketing, management and planning practices to achieve three basic strategic objectives:

1. ensuring the conservation of tourism resource values;
2. enhancing the experiences of the visitors who interact with tourism resources;
3. maximising the economic, social and environmental returns to stakeholders in the host community (Hall and McArthur 1998).

The five mechanisms identified by Dutton and Hall (1989) for sustainable tourism practice still appear to be applicable planning strategies at a destination or operational level but do not deal with the contextual issues that emerge in attempting to implement such tourism strategies. A decade later Lew and Hall (1998), in a review of research on sustainable tourism development identified a number of 'lessons' regarding sustainable tourism that do provide more of the context which planners need to understand in order to be able to make principles of sustainability work:

- Sustainable tourism represents a value orientation in which the management of tourism impacts takes precedence over market economics – although tensions between the two are ever present.
- Implementing sustainable tourism development requires measures that are both scale and context specific.
- Sustainable tourism issues are shaped by global economic restructuring and are fundamentally different in developing and developed economies.
- At the community scale, sustainable tourism requires local control of resources.
- Sustainable tourism development requires patience, diligence and a long-term commitment.

Yet some ten years on sustainable tourism still appears to be something of a pipedream. Indeed, the challenges of global environmental change and the fact that tourism is a significant contributor to climate change (see Chapter 2) suggests that the mechanisms of sustainable tourism planning have not been adopted to the extent that is required. Therefore, a sixth dimension of sustainable tourism would seem to be required – industry and visitor regulation.

Increased regulation

Where voluntary procedures to promote sustainability have failed then increased regulation may be the only option available to gain the required outcomes. A range of potential regulatory measures exist, with some of the more popular approaches including increased charging for resource use or undesirable impacts, such as pollution; new taxation regimes; licences and permits. However, while the need for such measures to change behaviour may be recognised (e.g. Gössling and Hall 2006), governments are often fearful of industry and consumer backlash with respect to increased regulation, particularly if it also increases the cost of travel or products.

It is the implications of these lessons for the successful application of sustainable tourism strategies that the following chapters will address.

Summary

As with all forms of resource development, tourism requires appropriate management regimes. The free market is not an adequate mechanism by itself to protect the interests of all parties and stakeholders in the tourism development process. Management regimes evolve as a solution to the challenge of collective action (Ostrom 1990). In the case of tourism planning we are looking at a way in which such collective action can be understood and furthered within the context of tourism development. As this chapter has highlighted, a number of approaches to tourism planning have developed, ranging from unrestrained boosterism through to economic emphasis and, more recently, there have been approaches that emphasise the environmental and community dimensions of tourism. Since the mid-1980s several strands of these approaches have become integrated to various degrees in an attempt to formulate more sustainable approaches towards tourism development. An examination of the most cited publications in the tourism planning and policy literature (Table 3.4) indicates the significance of community-based and sustainable approaches in academic literature along with significant attention being given to issues of public participation, collaboration, land-use planning and sustainability. Yet, given the effects of tourism development, there also appears to be a significant disjoint between the focus of academic attention on tourism planning and the actual sustainability of tourism.

The increasing recognition by government and industry of the nexus between tourism and

Table 3.4 Key readings/influences in tourism planning and policy as assessed by number of citations

Author	Date	Title	Journal name or book edition	Number of citations	Average citations/year since published
Inskeep	1991	*Tourism Planning*	1st edn	253	15.8
Gunn	1988	*Tourism Planning*	3rd edn	230	12.1
Hall	1994	*Tourism and Politics: Policy, Power and Place*	1st edn	155	11.9
Gunn with Var	2002	*Tourism Planning: Basics, Concepts, Cases*	4th edn	152	30.4
Jamal and Getz	1995	Collaboration theory and community tourism planning	*Annals of Tourism Research*	113	9.4
Hall and Jenkins	1995	*Tourism and Public Policy*	1st edn	100	8.3
Hall	2000	*Tourism Planning: Policies, Processes and Relationships*	1st edn	103	8.3
Richter	1989	*The Politics of Tourism in Asia*	1st edn	62	3.4
Reed	1997	Power relations and community-based tourism planning	*Annals of Tourism Research*	59	5.9
Simmons	1994	Community participation in tourism planning	*Tourism Management*	57	4.3
Getz	1986	Models in tourism planning: towards integration of theory and practice	*Tourism Management*	56	2.7
Elliott	1997	*Tourism: Politics and Public Sector Management*	1st edn	51	5.1
Edgell	1990	*International Tourism Policy*	1st edn	51	3
Sautter and Leisen	1999	Managing stakeholders: a tourism planning model	*Annals of Tourism Research*	47	5.9
Getz	1992	Tourism planning and destination life cycle	*Annals of Tourism Research*	47	3.1
Bramwell and Lane	2000	*Tourism Collaboration and Partnership: Politics, Practice and Sustainability*	1st edn	43	6.1
Keogh	1990	Public participation in community tourism planning	*Annals of Tourism Research*	41	2.4

▶

Table 3.4 (continued)

Author	Date	Title	Journal name or book edition	Number of citations	Average citations/year since published
Inskeep	1994	*National and Regional Tourism Planning*	1st edn	40	3.1
Getz and Jamal	1994	The environment-community symbiosis: a case for collaborative tourism planning	*Journal of Sustainable Tourism*	37	2.8
Haywood	1988	Responsible and responsive tourism planning in the community	*Tourism Management*	36	1.9
Ryan	2002	Equity, management, power sharing and sustainability: issues of the 'new tourism'	*Tourism Management*	33	6.6
Dredge	1999	Destination place planning and design	*Annals of Tourism Research*	31	3.9
Pigram	1990	Sustainable tourism-policy considerations	*Journal of Tourism Studies*	28	1.6
Getz	1987	Tourism planning and research	Conference paper	26	2.0
Hall	1999	Rethinking collaboration and partnership: a public policy perspective	*Journal of Sustainable Tourism*	25	3.1
Yuksel *et al.*	1999	Stakeholder interviews and tourism planning at Pamukkale, Turkey	*Tourism Management*	23	2.9
Murphy	1988	Community driven tourism planning	*Tourism Management*	22	1.2
Selin	1999	Developing a typology of sustainable tourism partnerships	*Journal of Sustainable Tourism*	21	2.6

Note: Number of citations derived from Google Scholar survey undertaken 25 April 2007. Where there were two citation records for the same publication they were combined. Only tourism journals or book publications with over 20 citations were included.

sustainable development does augur well for a more socially responsive and environmentally sensitive tourism industry. However, the design, planning and management of tourism environments requires more than the simplistic adoption of codes and guidelines or industry self-regulation, valid though these strategies may be. Instead, a sustainable tourism industry requires a commitment by all parties involved in the planning process to sustainable development principles. Only through such widespread commitment can the long-term integration of social, environmental and economic goals be attained, issues that we will return to as we progress through the various dimensions and scales of tourism planning and policy.

Questions

1. How does market failure provide a justification for government intervention in tourism?
2. Why are community-based approaches to tourism planning difficult to implement?
3. To what extent are Dutton and Hall's (1989) five mechanisms to achieve sustainable tourism development still relevant in the twenty-first century?

Important websites and recommended reading

Websites

World Travel & Tourism Council: http://www.wttc.travel/

World's leading tourism industry interest group.

UN World Tourism Organization: http://www.world-tourism.org/

The World Tourism Organization (UNWTO/ OMT), is a specialised agency of the United Nations, and is the leading international organisation in the field of tourism.

Recommended reading

1. Hall, D. and Brown, F. (2006) *Tourism and Welfare: Ethics, Responsibility and Sustained Well-Being*, CABI, Wallingford.

   Provides an excellent account of the issues of tourism development and how this relates to sustainability, ethical and quality of life concerns.

2. Hall, C.M. (2005) *Tourism: Rethinking the Social Science of Mobility*, Prentice Hall, Harlow.

   In one sense a sister companion to the present book, examines tourism mobility and associated development issues, as well as the academic dimensions of tourism.

3. Gunn, C.A. with Var, T. (2002) *Tourism Planning: Basics, Concepts, Cases*, 4th edn, Routledge, New York.

The most recent edition of a well-cited work that primarily takes a land-use and physical planning approach to tourism planning. An examination of the different editions of the book produces a good insight into the trends and changes in approaches to tourism planning, particularly within the spatial/physical tradition.

4. Inskeep, E. (1991) *Tourism Planning: An Integrated and Sustainable Development Approach*, Van Nostrand Reinhold, New York.

   Prescriptive land-use and site-based approach to tourism planning that has been well cited.

5. Michael, E.J. (2007) *Micro-clusters and Networks: The Growth of Tourism*, Oxford: Elsevier.

   One of the best accounts of the role of state with respect to the development of tourism clusters and networks.

6. Hall, C.M. (2002) 'Travel safety, terrorism and the media: the significance of the issue attention cycle', *Current Issues in Tourism*, 5(5): 458–66.

   Applies the issue attention cycle to travel security issues post-9/11.

7. Murphy, P.E. and Murphy, A.E. (2004) *Strategic Management for Tourism Communities*, Channelview, Clevedon.

   Updates some of Murphy's earlier work on community tourism within a more contemporary strategic planning perspective.

8. Sharpley, R. and Telfer, D.J. (eds) (2002) *Tourism and Development, Concepts and Issues*, Channelview, Clevedon.

9. Campbell, S. and Fainstein, S. (eds) (2003) *Readings in Planning Theory*, Blackwell, Oxford.

   Provides a useful comparison of theory and approach in general public planning with tourism planning.

10. Singh, S., Timothy, D. and Dowling, R.K. (eds) (2003) *Tourism in Destination Communities*, CABI, Wallingford.

    Provides a good overview of community-based tourism.

4 Tourism planning systems: theory, thinking and exorcism

Chapter objectives

After reading this chapter you will:

- Understand the differences between prescriptive and descriptive approaches to tourism planning and policy
- Appreciate the way planning and policy acts as theory
- Identify the elements of a systems approach to tourism planning
- Understand the importance of scale in public tourism planning
- Appreciate the significance of standpoint in tourism planning process
- Be aware of the key elements of a dialectical approach to tourism planning
- Appreciate appreciative inquiry as a potential planning tool.

Theory allows for both professional and intellectual self-reflection. It tries to make sense of the seemingly unrelated, contradictory aspects of urban development and create a rational system with which to compare and evaluate the merits of different planning ideas and strategies. It seeks the underlying conceptual elements that tie together the disparate planning areas, from housing and community development to transportation planning and urban design (Campbell and Fainstein 2003a: 3).

The concept of a system is a very powerful analytical tool. At its simplest level a system is an integrated whole whose essential properties arise from the relationships between its constituent parts. Systems thinking is therefore the understanding of a phenomenon within the context of a larger whole (Capra 1997). Systems and systems thinking has greatly influenced fields of study such as biology, ecology and physics, from which some of the first ideas regarding systems were developed early in the twentieth century, through to engineering, building construction, sociology, geography, planning and, of course, tourism studies.

This chapter aims to provide an overview of the nature of systems and systems thinking. It examines how some of the ideas of systems have been applied to tourism, and aims to understand the complex environment within which tourism occurs and that it influences. Finally, the chapter outlines the shape of the tourism planning system adopted in this book and some of the various elements within such a system. Key issues to be addressed include such concepts as scale, standpoint and relationships.

Planning and policy as theory

Planning and public policy are troublesome as a research focus because of their inherent complexity, 'specifically because of the temporal nature of the process, the multiplicity of participants and of policy provisions, and the contingent nature of theoretical effects' (Greenberg *et al.* 1977: 1532). As Lyden *et al.* (1969: 156–157) wrote:

> Altogether the realistic working assumption is that a public decision is an amalgam of a variety of contributions – public attitudes amongst them – fed into a

network of social interactions. The interaction path rarely shows a constant, unchanging structure; instead it develops, evolves, and changes shape and form over time. One of the primary reasons why the public policy process has always appeared to be such a mystery to many people is this fluidity, this refusal to remain within the confines of institutional structures designed to deal with public issues.

This highly complex and volatile situation has given rise to a wide and diverse body of theoretical approaches to the study of planning and policy although many of these approaches have not been fully articulated within the context of tourism (Hall and Jenkins 1995). The study of policy and planning has become an interdisciplinary field; however, 'popularisation of the field has not led to a great deal of theoretical cohesion . . . interpretations . . . may differ sharply depending on the pedigree of the analyst' (Jenkins 1978: ix). Similarly, Campbell and Fainstein (2003a: 2) note that 'the amorphous quality of planning theory means that practitioners largely disregard it'. Nevertheless, as they went on to observe, 'theory can inform practice. Planning theory is not just some idle chattering at the margins of the field. If done poorly, it discourages and stifles; but if done well, it defines the field and drives it forward' (Campbell and Fainstein 2003a: 3).

Different models exist to interpret the same events, leading in many cases to different conclusions (e.g. Rakoff and Schaefer 1970; Allison 1971; Fagence 1979; Allison and Zelikow 1999). Yet this situation, while frustrating to many students of planning and tourism who wish to see 'solutions' in black and white, reflects the importance of understanding the various standpoints from which planning problems may be perceived. Different values and interests of individuals involved in the planning process will give rise to different interpretations of the planning problem and, therefore, of planning solutions. Moreover, such a situation reflects the interrelationship between planning and policy and theory.

One of the basic tenets of this book is that plans and policies imply theories. Planning and policy making reflect assumptions about the manner in which people, organisations and, in some cases, the environment, will act given an authoritative decision or set of decisions. As Pressman and Wildavsky (1979: xv) stated:

> Whether stated explicitly or not, policies point to a chain of causation between initial conditions and future consequences. If X, then Y. Policies become programs when, by authoritative action, the initial conditions are created, X now exists. Programs make the theories operational by forging the first link in the causal chain connecting actions to objectives. Given X, we act to obtain Y.

Similarly, Majone (1980a: 178) has argued that 'policies may be viewed as theories from two different but related perspectives'. First, 'they can be seen as an analyst's rational reconstruction of a complex sequence of events'. Second, 'they can be seen from the point of view of actions, giving them stability and internal coherence' (Majone 1980a: 178). More recently, Campbell and Fainstein (2003a: 2) observed, 'In their day-to-day work planners may rely more on intuition than explicit theory; yet this intuition may in fact be assimilated theory.' Theory and planning therefore go hand in hand. However, planning theory, and tourism planning theory in particular, is often regarded as having a soft theoretical base – if it is regarded as having a theoretical foundation at all. Nevertheless, planning theory has the capacity to inform practice and make explicit previous assumptions about the nature of tourism planning, thereby offering the opportunity for reflection and improvement of the planning process toward certain goals and objectives.

As Chapter 3 indicated, tourism planning has been characterised by a number of different approaches, each of which reflects a certain range of assumptions and values, utilises a limited range of methodologies, and defines problems in particular ways. Each of these we can argue is characterised by a particular theoretical orientation. There is not sufficient space to fully elucidate the way in which each of the planning approaches frames the world in a particular way. That would require a book in itself. Instead, this chapter examines one of the main theoretical constructs which underlies the developing sustainable approach towards tourism planning, that of systems and systems thinking.

Prescriptive and descriptive approaches to tourism planning and policy

Tourism planning and policy research and, indeed, much research throughout the social sciences, can be built up on two main types of theory: that which adopts prescriptive models and that which adopts descriptive models (Mitchell 1989; Hall and Jenkins 1995). 'Prescriptive or normative models seek to demonstrate how [planning and] policy making should occur relative to pre-established standards,' whereas 'descriptive models document the way in which the policy process actually occurs' (Mitchell 1989: 264). Prescriptive (normative) models serve as a guide to an ideal situation. Several tourism planning texts have adopted prescriptive models of the planning process (e.g. Inskeep 1991; Gunn 1994; Gunn with Var 2002). However, while these may be useful rational models against which to compare reality, they do not provide detailed insights into the real world of planning and policy and its associated set of values, power and interests. Instead, approaches, methods and techniques need to be evaluated within the context of the goals, objectives and outcomes of tourism planning and development (Hall and McArthur 1998; Dredge and Jenkins 2007).

Descriptive approaches give rise to explanations about what happened during the decision-making, planning and policy-making processes. Indeed, one of the great problems with prescriptive tourism planning approaches is that their value has often failed to be evaluated in terms of their economic, cultural, environmental and political context. Many tourism plans are never or only partially implemented. Perhaps one of the main reasons for this is that they represent 'rational' planning approaches that fail to consider the world in which the plans will operate. In other words, although prescriptive tourism planning models are deductive, one cannot deduce in the absence of prior knowledge. This book uses a combination of both descriptive and prescriptive approaches. While several of the chapters outline what is happening with respect to tourism planning and policy they also outline ways in which it might be improved. Although the model of the policy and planning process used in this book is essentially descriptive in that it focuses on power, institutional arrangements and values as elements of planning and decision-making processes, the articulation of values of sustainability, the proposed establishment of certain forms of institutional arrangements, and arguments for certain approaches towards sustainable tourism are prescriptive. It is hoped that by placing arguments and values at the forefront of tourism planning that the planning and policy process will be seen in terms of the contested, political, terrain that it really is (see Chapter 10 for a further extension of these issues). However, rather than be regarded as a weakness, a public sphere of debate should be seen as a strength, as it is only through open debate, communication and exchange of ideas that the public interest which tourism planning arguably seeks to represent can actually be gained.

Systems and systems thinking

A system is an object of study. A system comprises:

1. a set of elements (sometimes also called entities);
2. the set of relationships between the elements;
3. the set of relationships between those elements and the environment.

Systems analysis is valuable because simple linear relationships and casual chains, while being the realm of classical science that most of us learnt in secondary school and 'learn by numbers' management texts, cannot adequately describe or explain many of the complex situations encountered in either the physical or social sciences. Instead we are often faced with the problem of trying to explain the multiple and complex interactions that take place in everyday life. A system is therefore a means of abstracting from reality in a manner that makes it more understandable.

The structure of a system is composed of elements and the relationships between elements. Elements are the basic unit of a system. However, part of the art of systems analysis and definition will be the construction of a set of entities that form a relatively coherent object of study which has a well-defined relationship with its environment. Systems analysis cannot proceed without such abstraction. As Ashby (1966: 16) observed, any real system will be characterised by 'an infinity of variables from which different observers (with different aims) may reasonably make an infinity of different selections'. Similarly, Wilson (1986: 476) noted,

> while the definition of any particular system of interest obviously reflects the object of study, it is constructed by the analyst, and so different system definitions of the same object of study will be created by different people for different purposes.

For example, as Hall (1998b: 4) notes,

> one of the most frustrating things for a student starting a tourism course is that almost every text provides a different definition of tourism. This is not necessarily because authors are trying to be difficult and confuse the student, although some may have suspicions that this is indeed the case! Rather the author is trying to be specific about exactly where the text fits into the broad spectrum of tourism studies and is trying to delimit the boundaries of the book.

In other words, the definition is a convenient abstraction that can contribute to analysis. The above approach is fundamental to any subject. Each discipline and area of scholarship and research has as one of its first tasks the identification of the things that comprise the foci for study. By defining terms we give meaning to and provide a basis for the understanding of what we are doing. Moreover, we are able to give terms a specific, technical basis that can be used to help communicate more effectively and improve the quality of our research and management.

One of the most substantial problems in understanding the elements within a system is that of scale. Systems are embedded within systems. What we regard as an element of a system at one level of analysis may itself constitute a system at a lower level of analysis. For example, we often examine the flows of tourists within an international tourism system by analysing the flows of tourists between different countries, which are the elements of such a system. However, if we change our resolution we may then examine the flows of tourists within a country, by looking at the intraregional flows of tourists. In the latter example it is the country that is the system and the regions the elements. How we define an element therefore depends on the scale at which we conceive the system, otherwise referred to as the resolution level.

> Every element is characterised by forming, from the point of view of the corresponding resolution level (at which the system . . . is defined), an indivisible unit whose structure we either cannot or do not want to resolve. However, if we increase the resolution level in a suitable manner . . . the structure of the element can be distinguished. In consequence, the original element loses its meaning and becomes the source of new elements of a relatively different system, i.e. of a system defined at a higher resolution level (Klir and Valach 1967: 35 in Harvey 1969: 454).

The other component in the structure of a system is the relationship or links between the elements that make up a system. Three basic forms of relationship can be identified: (1) a series relation (in which A leads to B), which is the characteristic cause-and-effect type relation of classical science; (2) a parallel relation in which two elements are affected by another element; (3) a feedback relation, which describes a situation in which an element influences itself. Both the elements and the relationships between them are part of the environment, which is most simply thought of as everything there is. However, when trying to model a system it is important to recognise the relevant elements in the environment that affect the operation of the system. Therefore, these are abstracted out from the environment and tied into a specific systems model for the purposes of analysis.

Another important element in systems analysis is defining the boundaries of a system. In mathematical terms this is extremely easy. However, in operational terms it can be extremely difficult. Sometimes the boundary of a system may be set by defining it in terms of something that is self-evident in terms of the questions being asked. For example, if one were examining a political systems problem then an appropriate boundary might be a government boundary. Similarly, a problem of water resource management may be dealt with in ecological terms through selecting a watershed as a boundary. Indeed, planning problems typically emerge when the different boundaries of different systems overlap, making management extremely difficult, a point we will return to later. Many boundaries are not so easy to identify. Therefore boundaries may be imposed through the application of judgement as to where a system begins and ends and in relation to the problem we are trying to solve. This does not mean that such boundaries are arbitrary, rather they should be related to the goals of the study and experience of such systems, as clearly the selection of a boundary can have a major impact on research results. Nowhere has this been more clearly demonstrated in tourism than with respect to economic analysis.

A multiplier may be regarded as 'a coefficient which expresses the amount of income generated in an area by an additional unit of tourist spending' (Archer 1982: 236). It is the ratio of direct and secondary changes within an economic region to the direct initial change itself. The size of the tourist multiplier is a significant measure of the economic benefit of tourism because it will be a reflection of the circulation of the tourist dollar through an economic system. In general, the larger the size of the tourist multiplier the greater the self-sufficiency of that economy in the provision of tourist facilities and services. Therefore, a tourist multiplier will generally be larger at a national level than at a regional level (e.g. state, province, county), because at a regional level leakage will occur in the form of taxes to the national government and importation of goods and services from other regions. Similarly, at the local level, multipliers will reflect the high importation level of small communities and tax payments to regional and national governments. As a measure of economic benefit from tourism, the multiplier

technique has been increasingly subject to question, particularly as its use has often produced exaggerated results (Bull 1994), one reason being that the selection of the boundary of the economy being studied is so critical. The smaller the area to be analysed, the greater will be the number of 'visitors' and hence the greater will be the estimate of economic impact, while the selection of the boundary will also affect the extent to which there is leakage out of the system, for example through the importation of goods and services for tourism. Boundary selection is therefore a key determinant in influencing the result of any analysis of an economic system (Burns and Mules 1986).

One area in which systems thinking has been especially influential and that will be familiar to most readers is in the biological and ecological sciences. For example, the concept of the 'web of life' conveys the idea that all life is interrelated in a network of relationships. The central organising idea of ecology is that of the ecosystem, a term developed by Arthur Tansley in 1935 to replace the more anthropomorphic term 'community': 'All the parts of such an ecosystem – organic and inorganic, biome and habitat – may be regarded as interacting factors which, in a mature ecosystem, are in approximate equilibrium: it is through their interactions that the whole system is maintained' (Tansley 1935: 207).

An ecosystem is therefore a model of interrelatedness in nature that includes a hierarchy of systems at different levels of complexity and extent. The ecosystem concept presents both the biological and non-biological aspects of the environment in one entity, with strong emphasis on the cycling of nutrients and the flow of energy in the system – whether it be a lake, a forest or the earth as a whole (Worster 1977). Fosberg (1963 in Stoddart 1972: 157) defined an ecosystem as:

> a functioning interacting system composed of one or more living organisms and their effective environment, both physical and biological . . . The description of an ecosystem may include its spatial relations; inventories of its physical features, its habitats and ecological niches, its organisms, and its basic reserves of matter and energy; the nature of its income (or input) of matter and energy; and the behaviour or trend of its entropy level.

The ecosystem idea has been influential not just in ecology. Stoddart (1965, 1967), for example, argued that the ecosystem concept has four main properties that makes it suitable as a tool in geographic research, First, it is monistic, in that it brings together the environment, humans, plants and animals into a single framework, within which the interaction between components can be examined. Second, ecosystems are structured in an orderly, comprehensible manner. Third, ecosystems function, in that they involve the continuous throughput of matter and energy.

> In geographic terms, the system involves not only the framework of the communication net, but also the goods and people flowing through it. Once the framework has been defined, it may be possible to quantify the interactions and interchanges between component parts. . . . (Stoddart 1972: 158)

Fourth, the ecosystem is a general system thereby providing for application to a range of different situations where systems analysis may prove fruitful. However, while Stoddart's hope of systems analysis providing a methodological foundation for geography proved unfulfilled (see Johnston 1991), ecosystem and systems thinking did have substantial influence in related areas such as planning, management and, more recently, tourism (see below).

Within the planning tradition, systems models of planning have been particularly influential since the mid-1960s. For example, Chadwick (1971) in *A Systems View of Planning,* which sought to integrate engineering, ecological and societal systems in a comprehensive theory of the urban and regional planning process, argued

> that planning is a process, a process of human thought and action based upon that thought – in point of fact, forethought, thought for the future – nothing more or less than this is planning, which is a very general human activity. (1971: 24)

Hall's explanation of what planning should do supports Chadwick's case:

> it [planning] should aim to provide a resource for democratic and informed decision-making. This is all planning can legitimately do, and all it can pretend to do. Properly understood, this is the real message of the systems revolution in planning and its aftermath. (P. Hall 1982: 303)

More recently, Peter Hall noted that fundamental to the idea of systems planning 'was the idea of interaction between two parallel systems: the planning or controlling system itself, and the system (or systems) which it seeks to control' (P. Hall 1992: 230).

The systems influence has been equally significant in corporate planning and management thinking. In the late 1950s and early 1960s writers, such as Burns and Stalker (1961), began to stress more 'organic' modes of business organisation and management that highlighted the manner in which successful organisations are able to adapt to and change their environments. Organisations are therefore regarded as sets of interacting subsystems (e.g. strategic, technological, structural, human-cultural and managerial) operating within the business environment, receiving inputs in the form of human, financial, informational and material resources and producing organisational outputs in the form of goods and services, ideally at an effective and efficient level of production that allows the organisational system to be maintained (Kast and Rosenzweig 1973). This 'contingency' approach to organisation is now the dominant perspective in contemporary organisational analysis (Morgan 1986). Indeed it is now such a part of our everyday thinking and analysis about business and organisation that it is hard for us to appreciate how revolutionary the idea was and, perhaps, to reflect on the tremendous implications that such a systems analogy may have for understanding issues such as sustainability. As Morgan (1986: 71) observed,

> By exploring the parallels between organisms and organizations in terms of organic functioning, relations with the environment, relations between species, and the wider ecology, it has been possible to produce different theories and explanations that have very practical implications for organization and management.

The organism metaphor therefore offers a number of strengths in terms of the insights it offers on organisations (Morgan 1986):

- It emphasises the importance of understanding relations between organisations and their environments.

Organisations are best thought of as open systems continually adapting and changing, they are therefore an ongoing process rather than just a collection of parts.

- It draws attention to the importance of understanding the 'needs' that must be satisfied if an organisation is to survive. Therefore the various demands of the strategic, technological, structural, human-cultural and managerial subsystems all need to be met.
- There are many different 'species' or types of organisation each with characteristics that may allow it to adapt or fit better into different environmental circumstances.
- Organic ideas of organisation that stress adaptation and innovation may provide a better mind-set, organisational culture and/or vision to actually provide for such innovation.
- The focus on ecology and interorganisational relations in terms of cooperation and competition may provide a far better foundation for creating organisational frameworks that provide for the development of cooperative structures in complex environments.

More recently the systems metaphor and systems thinking has been influencing the realms of business and organisation research through interest in ideas of organisations as self-reproducing systems and organisational evolution and change (Morgan 1986).

Process, flux and change are fundamental to a systems view of the world. One of the most influential writers in advancing this perspective has been David Bohm (1980), who argued that the world we see at any given moment needs to be understood as but a moment within more fundamental processes of change and reality. Bohm describes this fundamental reality as being implicate (or enfolded) order, in contrast to the explicate (or unfolded) order that we see in our everyday view of the world. Explicate reality (or forms) can be likened to the eddies, waves and whirlpools that we see in fast-flowing rivers as the water rushes through rapids. Think of these

eddies – while seemingly having a relatively stable form, they have no existence other than in terms of the movement of the flowing water in which they exist (the implicate order). Bohm therefore suggests that underlying explicate reality there are hidden processes and relations, termed by Morgan (1986: 234) as 'logics of change', that help explain 'reality' at any given point of time. 'To discover these, we have to understand the movement, flux, and change that produce the world we experience and study' (Morgan 1986: 234).

The idea of process and change has also become associated with systems thinking at the level of the individual. For example, writers such as Gergen (1991: 170) emphasise the significance of relational psychology which recognises that:

> We realize increasingly who and what we are is not so much the result of our 'personal essences' (real feelings, deep beliefs, and the like) but of how we are constructed in social groups . . . Relationships make possible the concept of self. Previous possessions of the individual self – autobiography, emotions, and morality – become possessions of relationships. We appear to stand alone, but we are manifestations of relations.

The identity of an individual involved in the planning process is therefore constituted by membership of particular sets of relational networks. Such an observation may have significant implications for the stewardship of resources, because resources are also part of network relationships as they are shaped and extracted from the environment through human perception and patterns of behaviour. Deep ecologists, for example, would argue that the relationship of individuals to resources may also be conceived as implying a moral relationship which would require the adoption of more sustainable ways of behaviour. While such a notion may be absurd to some readers, the ideas of relatedness to both others and the natural world is of increasing influence in the conservation movement around the world and underlies many of the policy developments that surround sustainability.

Systems analysis relates to the abstraction rather than the reality (Harvey 1969). However, this does not make systems thinking 'unreal'. We all have our ideas, models or theories about how the world or people operate. These are our abstractions that we use to understand the world, explain what is happening, and act accordingly in various situations. In the physical sciences or in engineering some of the systems models may be isomorphic, that is the abstracted model and the original system will be symmetrically related in terms of the elements within them and the relationships between such elements. The vast majority of abstractions though, particularly in the social sciences, are homomorphic, that is the relationship to the original system is asymmetrical. For example, imagine yourself on a walk in the countryside reading a map. Think of the relationship between the map (which is an abstraction) and the countryside (reality/the original system). Every element in the map can be assigned to an element in the countryside, yet the countryside contains many elements (or entities to use the terms above) that are not recorded on the map. The geometric relationships (physical distances) represented on the map also hold in the countryside, but there are also many geometric relationships around you in the countryside that cannot be portrayed on the map. 'We may treat the map as a model of the countryside, but we cannot treat the countryside as a model of the map' (Harvey 1969: 471). Nevertheless, we may get easily lost without a map. So it is therefore that other abstractions based on systems modelling may be most useful for helping us find our way through the complexity of tourism and tourism planning.

Tourism systems

The idea of a tourism system has been widely used in the international tourism literature since the early 1970s (e.g., Preobrazhensky *et al.* 1976; Leiper 1989; Farrell and Twining-Ward 2004; Hall and Page 2006), with the term being popularised in a number of tourism texts. For example, according to Mill and Morrison (1985) the system consists of four parts: market, travel, destination and marketing. As noted above, a system is an assemblage or combination of things or parts forming a complex or

unitary role. Tourism is often termed as a system in order to describe the interrelationships between the various sectors that enable leisure travel to and from a destination. Several different types of systems models have been utilised in tourism studies. For example, at a geographical level, four basic elements may be identified (Figure 4.1):

- *Generating region:* this is the source region of the tourist and the place where the journey begins and ends.
- *Transit region or route:* this is the region the tourist must travel through to reach their destination.
- *Destination region:* this is the region the tourist chooses to visit and where the most obvious consequences of the system occur.
- *The environment:* within which the travel flows are located and with which the tourist interacts.

The basic geographical tourism system model is useful for identifying the flows of tourists from the generating region to the destination region. Of course there may be more than one destination and therefore a whole pattern of destination regions and transit route regions may be built up. In addition, the different stages of the travel experience that describe the individual traveller's encounter with the tourism system has psychological and industrial dimensions as well (Figure 4.1).

Other system models have emphasised the supply and demand dimensions of tourism. For example, texts by Murphy (1985), and Hall (1998b, 2005a) (Figure 4.2) all developed models which focus on the importance of the tourist experience that occurs at the point where consumption and production coincide. As Murphy (1985: 10) noted, 'the travel experience is this industry's product, but unlike other industries it is the consumer who travels and not the product'. Nevertheless, from a production perspective, which is that usually taken in tourism policy terms by destinations, a number of distinct elements can be identified in different locations (Figure 4.3). Significantly, such a framework reinforces the fact that destination institutions

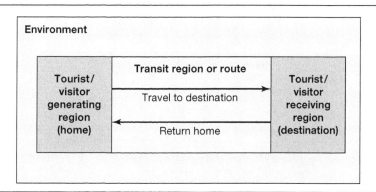

Geographical elements	Psychological elements	Industrial elements
Generating region	Decision to travel	Travel agencies/wholesalers
	Decision to purchase	Destination marketing, promotion and imaging
		Transport infrastructure such as airports
Transit route	Travel to destination	Transport and transit route infrastructure such as motels, highway cafés and restaurants, service stations, information services
Destination region	Behaviour and activities at destination	Tourist accommodation, restaurants, tourism information services, attractions, retailing, events, conventions and meetings, tourism business districts, vacation and second homes, souvenir shops, vacation and second homes
	Social interaction with hosts	
	Demonstration effects	
Transit route	Travel from destination	Transport and transit route infrastructure such as motels, highway cafés and restaurants, service stations
Generating region	Recollection stage	Ongoing efforts by travel agencies, destination and businesses within destination to encourage return visits
	Activities and behaviours on return home	
	Reverse demonstration effects	

Relationship of geographical elements to other dimensions of tourism system

Figure 4.1 Geographical elements of a tourist system and associated psychological and industrial elements
Source: From Hall, C.M. (2005a) *Tourism: Rethinking the Social Science of Mobility,* Prentice Hall, Harlow. Reproduced with permission.

usually operate in both generating areas and in transit regions in order to attract visitors.

Another approach to tourism systems at the level of the tourist destination has been developed by Le Pelley and Laws (1998) in a study of visitor management in Canterbury, England. According to the authors, 'the method focuses attention on the outcomes of the system's functioning for

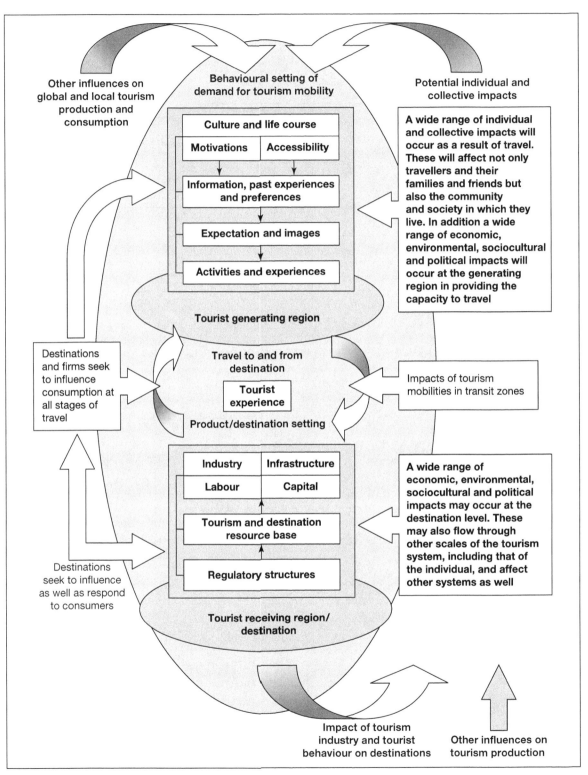

Other influences on global and local tourism production and consumption

Behavioural setting of demand for tourism mobility

Potential individual and collective impacts

Culture and life course

| **Motivations** | **Accessibility** |

Information, past experiences and preferences

Expectation and images

Activities and experiences

Tourist generating region

A wide range of individual and collective impacts will occur as a result of travel. These will affect not only travellers and their families and friends but also the community and society in which they live. In addition a wide range of economic, environmental, sociocultural and political impacts will occur at the generating region in providing the capacity to travel

Destinations and firms seek to influence consumption at all stages of travel

Travel to and from destination

Tourist experience

Product/destination setting

Impacts of tourism mobilities in transit zones

| **Industry** | **Infrastructure** |
| **Labour** | **Capital** |

Tourism and destination resource base

Regulatory structures

Tourist receiving region/ destination

A wide range of economic, environmental, sociocultural and political impacts may occur at the destination level. These may also flow through other scales of the tourism system, including that of the individual, and affect other systems as well

Destinations seek to influence as well as respond to consumers

Impact of tourism industry and tourist behaviour on destinations

Other influences on tourism production

Figure 4.2 The tourism system

Source: From Hall, C.M. (2005a) *Tourism: Rethinking the Social Science of Mobility,* Prentice Hall, Harlow. Reproduced with permission.

Tourist/visitor generating region (home)	Transit region or route	Tourist/visitor receiving region (destination)
Environment		

Tourist/visitor generating region (home)	Transit region or route	Tourist/visitor receiving region (destination)
		Facilities and attractions • accommodation (hotels and motels) • exhibition and conference centres • theme parks • national and state parks • retail stores • events and festivals • casinos • interpretation and visitor centres informal/semi-formal: communities, culture, landscapes
Linking transport infrastructure in generating region		**Destination transport infrastructure** • airports • sea ports • railway stations • bus stations
	Commercial transport link(s) between home and destination • airlines • bus and coach services • railway services • car hire services • ferry services	Commercial transport at destination
Distribution channels for destination in generating region • retail travel agents • wholesale travel agents • tour operators • online retailers and distributors	Communication links between generating region and destination that enable the distribution and promotional channels as well as enabling financial transactions. Also relates to communication links within destination	**Distribution channels at destination** • tourist firms accessed directly • destination intermediaries, e.g. visitor centres • tour operators
Promotional channel for destination in generating region		Promotional channel for destination
Destination related labour force in generating region	Transit labour force	Destination labour force

Figure 4.3 Formal destination production elements of a tourism system

particular stakeholder groups during a given period of time' (Le Pelley and Laws 1998: 89). The Le Pelley and Laws model divided the tourism system into:

- a series of inputs (tourists' expectations, entrepreneurial activity, employee skills, investors' capital, local authority planning, residents' expectations and attitudes);
- components of what was described as the 'Canterbury Destination System', which included a series of primary (cathedral and historic city centre) and secondary elements (hotels, catering, retailing, attractions, information services, parking and infrastructure), along with external influences (transport developments, competition, tastes, legislation and currency exchange rates);
- outcomes in terms of impacts (economic, community, environment and ecology) and stakeholder outcomes.

As the reader will hopefully now realise, the idea of a tourism system can be conceptualised in a number of ways. Yet each of these may be regarded as appropriate in terms of the various emphases they give to the study of tourism. Such a situation is not uncommon in the analysis of a social phenomenon in which it is virtually impossible to model all of the elements that may be regarded as forming a part of the social system in question. In the case of tourism this situation is all the more complex because of the nature of tourism itself:

- It is hard to define, and is defined by different stakeholders in different ways.
- It is 'diffuse' in the way it filters through economies and communities.
- It is usually regarded as a service industry, with the corresponding difficulties in dealing with the study of the intangible and perishable nature of services.

The concept of partial industrialisation is one attempt to describe the complex nature of tourism and the consequent problems of coordination, management and strategic development that are typically associated with it. According to Leiper (1989: 25) partial industrialisation refers to the condition

> in which only certain organisations providing goods and services directly to tourists are in the tourism industry. The proportion of (a) goods and services stemming from that industry to (b) total goods and services used by tourists can be termed the index of industrialisation, theoretically ranging from 100% (wholly industrialised) to zero (tourists present and spending money, but no tourism industry).

One of the major consequences of the partial industrialisation of tourism is its significance for tourism development, marketing, coordination and network development. Although we can recognise that many segments of the economy benefit from tourism, it is only those organisations which perceive a direct relationship to tourists and tourism producers that become actively involved in fostering tourism development or in marketing. However, there are many other organisations such as food suppliers, petrol stations and retailers (sometimes described as 'allied industries') which also benefit from tourists but that are not readily identified as part of the tourism industry (Hall 2005a). Therefore, in most circumstances, businesses that regard themselves as non-tourism businesses will often not create linkages with tourism businesses for regional promotion unless there is a clear financial reward. It will often require an external inducement, such as promotion schemes established by government at minimal or no cost to individual businesses, or regulatory action such as compulsory business rating tax for promotion purposes, before linkages can be established (Michael 2007).

Although under-appreciated in the tourism literature, the concept of partial industrialisation is a powerful explanatory tool when trying to understand the nature of tourism, particularly when attempting to explain why coordination is so difficult with respect to the various components of tourism at the community, destination or even at the national level. Nevertheless, partial industrialisation provides only a partial insight into the complexities of tourism. Other aspects of trying to create a better foundation for understanding tourism, and tourism planning, also need to be considered. First, the issue of scale in tourism analysis. Second, the standpoint of the viewer or participant in the tourism planning process.

The issue of scale

Issues of scale of analysis have been given very little coverage in the tourism literature (see also Chapter 2). Yet scale is a critical element in environmental and social science research. Scale refers to the level at which we are representing reality in our research and our thinking. It can also be thought of as the level of resolution at which we are trying to understand things. For example, Figure 2.5 noted that within research on tourism and global environmental change with respect to sociocultural and economic systems, biodiversity and climate change some scales of analysis had been studied while others were virtually complete unknowns. Three basic questions have arisen with respect to scale (Haggett 1965; Harvey 1969):

1. *Scale coverage* – do we have regular and comprehensive monitoring of the world at all relevant scales? This issue is obviously clearly important with the collection of tourism statistics and the understanding of tourist flows.
2. *Scale standardisation* – do we have comparable data from equivalent sampling frames? This issue often arises when comparing the tourism statistics from one country or region to another. Not only do we need to know that the methodologies of collecting tourism statistics are the same but also the areas being investigated must be equivalent. Similarly, the collection of case study data from a number of different studies and then the aggregation of the information also create difficulties of equivalency between the various cases.
3. *Scale linkage* – three different connections between the various scale levels can be identified (Harvey 1969):
   (i) same level – which refers to a comparative relationship;

(ii) high to low level – which is a contextual relationship; e.g. tourism policy at the national level forms the context within which changes in tourist numbers at the local level can be analysed;
(iii) low to high level – which is an aggregative relationship, e.g. tourist flows at the national level are the result of the activities of individual firms.

Substantial inferential problems arise in the last two cases because generalisations we make at one level may not hold for another. Indeed, the idea of emergence, i.e. that the whole is greater than the sum of the parts, makes this virtually a certainty. Such a situation creates substantial difficulties for explanation in tourism studies that the field has not addressed, especially as most tourism analysis often does not acknowledge the scale at which work is being undertaken, or the contexts of that scale, and the capacity to generalise from one scale to another. Issues of scale, if they are noted at all, tend to be dealt with in terms of the possibilities for comparison. The capacity to perceive or illustrate the linkages and relationships between scales is rarely acknowledged. Table 4.1 outlines three general scales of analysis in tourism from the macro to the micro and the key concepts that can be identified within these scales.

The issue of relationships between scales is especially important for tourism planning. We have acknowledged in the previous chapters that tourism planning and planning issues occur at different scales – national, state/provincial, regional, local – yet how are those levels of analysis and levels of action linked? Moreover, how do we incorporate the supranational level, e.g. organisations such as the European Union, or the role of the individual into the tourism planning equation? Arguably the issue of scale becomes even more problematic when we seek to mesh policy and planning scales (and boundaries) with scales that are utilised with respect to environmental issues (Gössling and Hall 2006). We recognise that tourism, like the environment, is a global issue that tends to be acted out at a local or place level by individuals and organisations

Table 4.1 Scales of analysis in tourism

Scale of analysis and description of tourism	Focus	Key concepts with respect to travel behaviour	Planning and policy focus	Key concepts with respect to tourism policy and planning behaviour
Macro	Aggregate	• Distribution, patterns, flow • Activity	• Nation state • Structure • Ideology	• National interest • State interest • Political culture • Institutional arrangements
Meso	Combines aggregate and individual analysis	• Mobility, trip stage, lifecourse, travel career	• Organisation • Decision making	• Individual organisations as policy actors • Political parties • Policy networks
Micro	Individual	• Personality, psychographics/lifestyle • Motivation, expectation, satisfaction	• Individual • Agency	• Political psychology • Personality • Motivations • Individual political values • Individual actors

who are aiming to satisfy their values and interests or, to use a well-worn environmental activist phrase which illustrates the connectivity between the individual and the local to the global – 'Think Globally, Act Locally'. Therefore, any conception of the tourism planning process needs to be able to accommodate the different scales or levels at which tourism planning occurs and the context of such planning in terms of the linkages and relationships between the various levels. Or, as Mill and Morrison (1985: xix) observed with respect to the concept of a tourism system: 'The system is like a spider's web – touch one part of it and reverberations will be felt throughout.'

Standpoint

Another issue that has received only passing consideration in tourism is the standpoint of the viewer or participant in the tourism planning process. Where do we stand as students of tourism in terms of what we regard as appropriate in tourism? How do our work, interests and

values influence such perspectives of tourism? How do we act on our values in our day-to-day lives through our involvement in tourism planning and tourism policy? There is no absolute standpoint in tourism planning. Our perspectives and actions will shift over time in relation to our changing experiences, knowledge base, values and ideologies, contact with different stakeholders, changed legislative and institutional frameworks, and changes in our desired environment, to name just a few factors. Our perspectives and actions will also change according to our position in the planning process. Are we working for a government agency, a private developer, or as a facility manager? Are we a member of an environmental interest group trying to preserve a building or save a species, or are we just wanting better facilities in our community, or simply trying to stop yet another tower block being built that will block our view or change our streetscape? We may even occupy some of these roles simultaneously. However, these questions are not just academic. How we perceive tourism planning and policy and how we utilise the

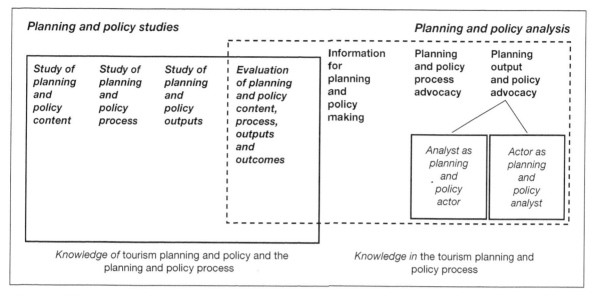

Figure 4.4 Types of tourism planning and policy analysis

analysis that is conducted will depend on a particular intersection of factors at any given time, where we sit in the wider tourism planning system and the type of tourism planning and policy analysis we are conducting (Figure 4.4) (Hogwood and Gunn 1984; Hall and Jenkins 1995; Hall 2005a). Our place in, and ability to influence the planning system is therefore relational.

Such a perspective is not as radical as it seems. As Healey (1997: 65) observed, 'it is now widely understood in the planning field that planning is an interactive process, undertaken in a social context, rather than a purely technical process of design, analysis and management'. This is a crucial point. Many textbooks relate planning as a technical process in which the writer is out of screen somewhere and the book seems to be written as a series of facts or statements which suggests that this is the way it must be. It isn't. As Chapter 3 illustrated, there are different traditions of tourism planning, each having its own focus. Each tradition is not inherently wrong or right. We judge it as being wrong or right upon a particular set of criteria that in turn reflect what we believe tourism planning is and should be trying to achieve in terms of outcomes. This shifting base is a reflection of wider perceptions of the tourism 'expert' and the 'planner' in society.

As Peter Hall (1992: 248) noted, 'Whatever the planner's ideology, it appears that people are no longer willing, as once apparently they were, to accept his or her claim to omniscience and omnipotence.' Such a perspective does not mean that planning is obsolete or redundant as,

> almost by definition, . . . planners will never be completely ineffective, or completely omnipotent. They will exist in a state of continuous interaction with the system they are planning, a system which changes partly, but not entirely, owing to processes beyond their mechanisms of control. (P. Hall 1992: 230)

We therefore need to recognise that our position in tourism planning is relational to where we lie in the tourism system and the various stakeholders, interests and factors with which we interact. As Hall argued, we are constantly interacting with the people, institutions and environment around us that are themselves in a constant state of change and flux:

> Planning in practice, however well managed, is therefore a long way from the tidy sequences of the theorists. It involves the basic difficulty, even impossibility, of predicting future events; the interaction of decisions made in different policy spheres; conflicts of values which cannot be fully resolved by rational discussion and by calculation; the clash of

organized pressure groups and the defence of vested interests; and the inevitable confusions that arise from the complex interrelationships between decisions at different levels and at different scales, at different points of time. The cybernetic or systems view of planning is a condition towards which planners aim; it will never become complete reality. (P. Hall 1992: 246)

This relational perspective of planning is inherent in a systems view of society and of tourism planning, in that we acknowledge that we are part of, rather than separate from, the tourism planning process. When we espouse a particular course of planning action or interpretation of a planning situation we are not merely offering impartial, objective, technical advice but our advice is value and interest laden and has the power to have substantial social, economic, environmental and political impacts, some of which may be unintended. It is likely that our decisions as well as our perspectives will favour some stakeholders and not others. This applies as much to this author while in the act of writing this book which, as you read it and hopefully reflect on it, may influence your own notion of what tourism planning is, and what it can be, and how you might act, just as it does the person who is laying out the land-use plans for a new resort.

As I write this section at about 1 a.m. on an April morning in a relatively small city in the South Island of New Zealand, I am surrounded by several piles of books, photocopies and field notes (and listening to Nick Cave and KCRW's *Rare on Air 3*). I am conscious that I am arguing for a particular set of values and positions to be an appropriate structure for understanding tourism planning and perhaps achieving certain goals relating to sustainability that I regard as important. I am making such comments because I wish to encourage the reader to think about how they perceive tourism and how we both understand it and seek to achieve certain goals and objectives through tourism planning. You, me, people, actively construct their worlds. What world do we want to or are we able to construct through tourism? (see Hall 2004c for a further discussion of issues of reflexivity and a rare opportunity to use the word 'fuck' in the tourism literature).

Knowledge is related to action. Knowledge and values are actively constituted through social, interactive processes. As Healey (1997: 29) observed, public policy and planning are 'social processes through which ways of thinking, ways of valuing and ways of acting are actively constructed by participants'. Such an approach variously described as argumentative (Majone 1980a, 1989; Wildavsky 1987; Fischer and Forester 1993; Hall 1994, 2005a; Hall and Jenkins 1995), communicative (Healey 1992a, b, 1993, 1996; Sager 1994) or interpretative planning theory (Innes 1995; Campbell and Fainstein 2003b) recognises:

- that all forms of knowledge, including policy and planning knowledge, are socially constructed;
- that the development and communication of knowledge and reasoning takes many legitimate forms;
- the significance of the social context and the interactions within that context which provide for the development of an individual's interests and knowledge;
- the role of power relations in influencing the social context and interactions of planning both at the level of decision making and non-decision making and at deeper levels of social relations and ideology;
- that public policies and the development of the knowledge and reasoning which determine such policies need to be owned by all the stakeholders who are affected by the policy-making process, particularly when it is spatially organised around place needs and goals;
- that the above observation means that greater emphasis needs be provided on collaborative consensus-building rather than competitive interest bargaining. In several polities this may require the formation of more participatory political cultures than exist at present;
- that therefore planning, as part of the context of social relations within which decision making and policy development occur, has the capacity to improve the context of social relations in order to develop more participatory and equitable practices (Healey 1997).

Appreciative inquiry

Appreciative inquiry (AI) can be approached as a theory, a process, a field of knowledge, a philosophy or a worldview (Mellish 2000; van der Haar 2002; van der Haar and Hosking 2004; Grant and Humphries 2006). While it originated in the organisational development field (Cooperrider 1986; Cooperrider and Srivastva 1987), and is most commonly used as a methodology for change in organisational management (e.g. Peelle III 2006), it has also been adapted as an approach to community planning (e.g. Jain and Triraganon, 2003), evaluation (Preskill and Catsambas 2006; Reed *et al.* 2005), a means of framing research questions (Carter 2006) and an interview tool for field research (Michael 2005).

Due to its adaptability, numerous definitions of AI have developed. However, Cooperrider and Whitney's (2005: 8) description of AI provides a basic practice-oriented definition:

> Appreciative Inquiry is the cooperative, coevolutionary search for the best in people, their organisations, and the world around them. It involves systematic discovery of what gives life to an organisation or a community when it is most effective and most capable in economic, ecological, and human terms.

This planning insight begins by looking at the origins of AI, exploring why and how it developed as a complementary form of action-research. Some practical guidelines for conducting an AI are then given. Subsequently, examples are provided to illustrate the variety of applications of AI. Finally, an example is given to highlight the potential for adapting this approach as a methodology for conducting tourism research.

The development of appreciative inquiry

The intellectual and spiritual roots of action-research are perhaps most frequently associated with Kurt Lewin who coined the term in 1944 (see Cooperrider and Srivastva 1987; Egan and Lancaster

2005). Lewin (1948: 211) argued that 'we should consider action, research, and training as a triangle that should be kept together'. The aim of action-research was to close the gap between science and practical affairs, so that new social theory could be developed, as well as practical results (Bushe 1999).

Although there is some debate regarding an exact definition of action-research, it is generally understood to refer to a 'participatory, democratic process concerned with developing practical knowing in the pursuit of worthwhile human purposes, grounded in a participatory worldview which we believe is emerging at this historical moment' (Reason and Bradbury 2006: 1). The purpose of action-research therefore continues to focus on bringing together theory and practice so that problems can be identified, understood and addressed. However, despite the continued use of conventional action-research, it has also received much criticism. It has been argued that it has lost much of the spirit with which it was originally developed and that it has been unable to meet its potential as a vehicle of social innovation (Cooperrider and Srivastva, 1987). As a result, a number of complementary forms of action-research have been developed, such as AI.

The concept of AI originated with Cooperrider's (1986) doctoral dissertation 'Appreciative inquiry: toward a methodology for enhancing organisational innovation' and the subsequent article by Cooperrider and Srivastva (1987). Following these publications, AI has gained much recognition and is now perceived as 'one of the more significant innovations in action-research in the past decade' (Bushe 1999: 61). AI therefore represents a complementary, but also essentially new and distinct approach to action-research. It differentiates itself from action-research based on three key factors that are summarised in Table 4.2.

▶

Table 4.2 Comparison of action-research and appreciative inquiry

Key criticisms of action-research	Justification of criticism	Alternative offered by appreciative inquiry	Justification of alternative
Underestimates the power of theory.	Focusing too much on 'action' is a major barrier to advancing social knowledge.	• Leaves behind the common dualistic view of theory and practice by trying to achieve both practical action and the generation of new theory. • Shifts the focus of theory from its predictive capacity to its generative capacity.	Through closing the gap between theory and practice and focusing on the generative capacity of theory, AI challenges assumptions and generates new alternatives for social action.
Concentrates excessively on problem solving.	Concentrating on problems creates a discourse of 'deficit'. It also limits the potential to generate altogether new ideas, visions and theory.	• Focuses on the positive and productive aspects of a situation. • Assumes that all social systems 'work' to some extent and therefore organisational practices can be developed by doing more of what works (rather than less of what does not).	By moving away from negative images, AI is able to create new beliefs rather than reinforce existing ones, create whole system change, and give an organisation or community a sense of identity and strength.
Uses logical positivistic assumptions that consider reality as stable and enduring.	Such assumptions result in the use of standardised rules for solving problems and limit the potential to generate imaginative and creative theory.	• Turns towards sociorationalism, assuming that social order is constructed, fluid, impermanent and open to multiple interpretations. Under such assumptions, the researcher is also understood to be an active participant of the research process.	Through the adoption of the sociorationalist approach, this improves our capacity to create generative theory and encourages creative thought.

Sources: Derived from Cooperrider and Srivastva (1987); Hammond (1998); van der Haar (2002); Jain and Triraganon (2003); Bushe and Kassam (2004); Reed *et al.* (2005); Ludema *et al.* (2006); Reason and Bradbury (2006); Appreciative Inquiry Commons (2007).

Conducting an appreciative inquiry

Conducting an AI typically involves a three-stage process.

1. The *change agenda* is considered: 'What are you trying to accomplish? What is your purpose?' (Whitney and Trosten-Bloom 2003: 24). This step thus focuses on establishing a positive topic and developing clear objectives for the AI.
2. The *form of engagement* is considered: 'What is the most appropriate form of engagement, given your change agenda, your organisation culture,

time frame, and resources?' (Whitney and Trosten-Bloom 2003: 24). The form of engagement that is developed can range from a 'mass-mobilised inquiry' (thousands to millions of interviews are conducted throughout a city, community or the world) to a 'core group inquiry' (a small group of people select topics, craft questions and conduct interviews).
3. An *inquiry strategy* is developed: 'Having identified the purpose and form of engagement, what decisions and steps must you take along the way to ensure the project's success?' (Whitney and

▶

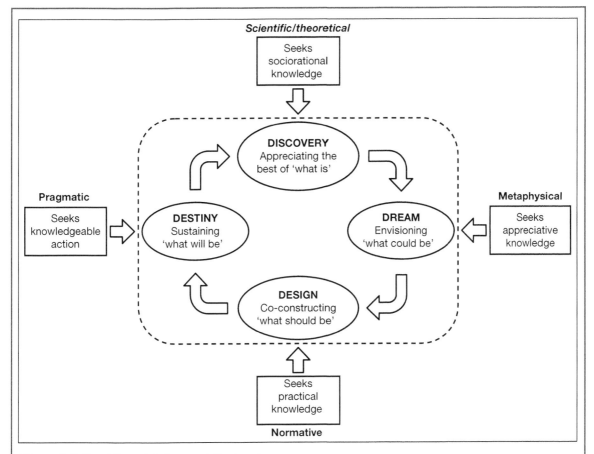

Figure 4.5 The 4-D model of appreciative inquiry
Sources: Derived from Cooperrider and Srivastva (1987) and Ludema *et al.* (2006).

Trosten-Bloom 2003: 24). This stage generally involves micro-level choices regarding how the objectives of the AI are to be met. Existing AIs have tended to adapt the '4-D model' (Ludema *et al.* 2006) in order to develop an appropriate inquiry strategy. This model is based on the scientific, metaphysical, normative and pragmatic approach of AI and is summarised in Figure 4.5.

While the 4-D model can be adapted and applied to suit a variety of different agendas, it is important to consider the eight principles of AI throughout the process (Whitney and Trosten-Bloom 2003). These principles are based on sociorationalism, combined with social constructionism (Gergen 1985), image theory, grounded research and Vickers' (1980) notion

of 'appreciative systems' (Whitney and Trosten-Bloom 2003; van der Haar and Hosking 2004):

1. the constructionist principle (words create worlds)
2. the simultaneity principle (inquiry creates change)
3. the poetic principle (we can choose what we study)
4. the anticipatory principle (image inspires action)
5. the positive principle (positive questions lead to positive change)
6. the wholeness principle (wholeness brings out the best)
7. the enactment principle (acting 'as if' is self-fulfilling)
8. the free choice principle (free choice liberates power).

▶

Applications of appreciative inquiry

Since its conception in 1986 there has been much experimentation with AI and it has been adapted for use in a variety of settings (see Bushe and Kassam 2004). The following four examples have been selected to highlight the range of scales and applications of AI, as well as the way in which it can be combined with other approaches. They illustrate the potential for applying AI as a means to facilitate positive organisational change, as a community planning approach, as an evaluation technique, and as an interview tool.

Organisation change. The Global Relief and Development Organisation (GRDO) (Ludema *et al.* 2006) is a non-governmental organisation based in the United States and Canada with 120 partner organisations around the world. The organisations were involved in a three-year AI in order to identify 'best practices of organisational capacity-building from around the world'. This AI incorporated all four stages of the 4-D process. Initially, large-group conferences were held with GRDO staff and partner organisations to introduce AI, craft unconditional positive questions and plan a 'listening tour' in which hundreds of organisations and community groups were involved in discovering the core factors that support organisational capacity (discover). Following this 'listening tour' a second round of conferences was held in which best practices were shared and possible futures were envisioned (dream). Subsequently a global summit meeting was held and new initiatives for interorganisational capacity-building were launched (design). Once GRDO staff and partner organisations had returned to their respective countries these initiatives were then implemented (destiny). Finally, a third round of conferences was held to discuss experiences with the new approach and develop follow-up initiatives.

A community planning approach. AI can be adapted to plan for, and develop, community-based tourism. Jain and Triraganon (2003) developed a training manual based on an Appreciative Participatory Planning and Action (APPA) approach developed by the Mountain Institute in the 1990s. This approach to planning and management combines AI with Participatory Learning and Action (PLA). APPA thus incorporates the 4-D model and focuses on strengths and successes as a means to empower communities, groups and organisations. However, through the adoption of PLA it also places a strong emphasis on the active involvement of local people, so that local communities have the ultimate control over the development process. The three key principles of APPA are thus to focus on success, participatory learning and sustainability. Since its development in the 1990s APPA has gained much popularity and is now used in over ten countries by communities, NGOs, governments and the private sector.

An evaluation technique. Reed *et al.* (2005) adapted AI as a means to evaluate small voluntary organisations in the United Kingdom. Ten small-scale, not-for-profit schemes for older people were selected as examples of effective, creative and innovatory community action. These schemes were each visited for two days so that AI interviews (with users, volunteers, staff and stakeholders) could be carried out and the projects could be observed. The first three stages of the 4-D process were adapted to form appreciative interview questions and data was subsequently analysed using the AI questions as an analytic framework to illustrate the specific characteristics and achievements of each project. AI data was then combined with the 'impact grid' (see Reed *et al.* 2005).

An interview tool. AI has been used specifically as an interview tool for field research. As with Reed *et al.*'s (2005) adaptation of the 4-Ds, Michael's (2005) study also suggests that it is possible to select and adapt these four stages in order to meet the specific objectives of a study. In this example indigenous NGOs in Africa were researched over 12 months through conducting interviews that represented 'mini-versions' of the discovery phase. Michael (2005) was particularly concerned with understanding what made local NGOs 'tick' and therefore chose to focus only on appreciating the 'best of what is'. She concludes that AI 'can be as valuable as a research tool for interviewing in the field as it has proved as a methodology for organisational change' (Michael 2005: 229).

Appreciative inquiry as a tourism inquiry strategy

An AI was conducted to assess the development of good practice within volunteer tourism sending organisations. The form of engagement involved a

▶

Table 4.3 Inquiry strategy

Stage	Steps	Purpose
DISCOVERY (appreciating and valuing the best of 'what is') AND DREAM (envisioning 'what could be')	a) Contact sending organisations and invite their participation. b) Observe the positive aspects of volunteer tourism programmes by focusing on what they are visibly achieving and how they are doing this (discovery). c) Conduct interviews with representatives of sending organisations and host organisations. Explore what is effective and successful in current practices (discovery) and discuss ideals and aspirations for the future (dream). d) Conduct focus groups with volunteer tourists. Explore what is effective and successful in current practices (discovery) and discuss ideals and aspirations for the future (dream)	• Reinforce existing positive imagery and develop positive visions by focusing on the benefits and successful management strategies of each organisation. • Bring together characteristics of successful management from each organisation so that a preliminary framework of good practice for sending organisations can be developed.
DESIGN (co-constructing 'what should be')	e) Encourage comment and discussion between participants from the discovery and dream stages by placing the preliminary framework of good practice in an online forum (blog) f) Revise and adapt framework of good practice based on comments made in the forum.	• Encourage dialogue between different sending organisations with similar goals. Allow them to find common ground by sharing ideals and empower them to adopt positive ideas from each other. • Develop revised framework of good practice that represents shared ideas.
DESTINY (sustaining 'what will be')	g) Essentially beyond the scope of this study although final results were sent to each sending organisation.	• Communicate stories and good practices to encourage organisations to adopt some of these ideas.

multiple case study inquiry, in which ten different sending organisations were selected to represent the variety of different organisations and volunteer tourism programmes that exist. The inquiry strategy essentially followed the 4-D process and is summarised in Table 4.3.

The study used relatively conventional data collection techniques, but approached the whole research process as an AI (Table 4.4). It was therefore important to maintain the eight principles of AI throughout the study. Initially, the focus of the study was carefully selected so that it would generate enthusiasm and appreciation within the researched sending organisations (the *poetic principle*). Subsequently, interview

and focus group questions were carefully developed so that they were successful in stimulating ideas, innovation and invention, based on the *simultaneity principle* that inquiry creates change. This was particularly apparent in the dream phase of interviews and focus groups in which questions were developed that would encourage visions and ideals to be enacted in the present (the *enactment principle*).

In addition, unconditionally positive questions were used throughout fieldwork to shift participants' attention towards potentials, dreams and visions (the *positive principle*). This encouraged participants to focus on the positive core of the sending organisation so that positive images could be generated (the

▶

Table 4.4 The appreciative inquiry interview process

Step*	Purpose	Sample questions (from interviews with representatives of sending organisations)
1. Stage-setting questions	Build rapport with interviewee and allow them to relax.	What exactly does your job involve? Why did you choose to work for . . . (name of sending organisation)? / Why did you choose to set up . . . (name of sending organisation)? What do you value most about working for . . . (name of sending organisation)?
2. Discovery questions	Discover and appreciate the strengths and successes of the sending organisation in general and the Volunteer travel program (VTP) in particular. Build an understanding of how these successes are achieved.	Can you tell me a bit more about your organisation? E.g. What is the aim of your organisation? What is your philosophy? What makes your organisation special/unique? In what ways do you think that the programmes run through your organisation are benefiting: • the host organisations? • the volunteers? In what ways are your volunteer programmes having broader or long-term benefits? What are the main strengths about the way your programmes are organised? Of all the programmes you are involved with, which one do you think is the most successful? Why?
3. Dream questions	Encourage interviewee to think creatively about how their organisation could be improved.	How do see your organisation in a few years time? Are there any changes that you would make? How? Why? Imagine that in five years your organisation wins an international award for its volunteer programmes. What would the award be for? Why would you deserve such an award?
4. Concluding questions	Conclude the interview and allow interviewee to summarise their main opinions and ideas.	What defines a successful volunteer tourism experience? What are the key factors that ensure your organisation's success?

*Before the interview began, participants were given a verbal and written explanation of the purpose of the research, the appreciative inquiry approach, the interview process and how the interview data would be used. If they agreed to participate, written consent was collected.

anticipatory principle). Developing an online forum helped transform these images into a collective one, encouraging communication and collaboration (the *constructionist principle*). In order to incorporate the *wholesome principle*, the opinions of as many people as possible who were involved with the organisation were accessed (volunteer tourists, host organisations and sending organisations). However, each individual was given the option of whether or not they wished to participate (the *free choice principle*). While interviews and focus groups were semi-structured, Table 4.4 provides an example of the steps followed in

▶

a typical interview, as well as some sample questions from the interviews conducted with representatives of the sending organisation.

The study highlights a number of potential advantages of using an appreciative approach in tourism planning research. In particular, by maintaining the positive principle throughout interviews and focus groups, it was possible to collect imaginative data. While it has been claimed that focusing only on the positive can lead to distorted results (see Grant and Humphries 2006), it is argued that taking this approach was valuable for this research because it provided opportunities to access new possibilities and capture constructive organisational stories.

In addition, the study parallels previous research that has pointed to the enjoyment and excitement associated with the AI process (e.g. Bushe 1999; Arcoleo 2001; Michael 2005). Several participants involved in this study stated that they had valued the positive reflection that the AI-oriented interview/focus group had encouraged. Importantly, however, while the researcher attempted to maintain an appreciative approach throughout interviews and focus groups, issues and challenges still arose. In particular, during the dream phase of the interview questions participants often compared their 'dreams' for the future with current problems they were experiencing. This suggests that although previous researchers have argued that AI limits the potential for discussing feelings of frustration (McLean 1996; Egan and Lancaster 2005; Grant and Humphries 2006) this is not always the case. Conducting an AI can enable participants to approach difficulties in a more positive manner by focusing on how the situation could be improved, rather than on the problem itself (see also Elliott 1999; Whitney and Trosten-Bloom 2003; Reed *et al.* 2005). In some cases this may also have encouraged participants to speak more openly about the problems they had experienced because they were able to approach these problems in a constructive manner.

The potential of AI for tourism planning

AI has the potential to provide a new approach in tourism planning by focusing on the positive, creating generative theory and shifting towards sociorationalism. AI thus represents an attempt to address several of the shortcomings of action-research. AI is commonly associated with the 4-D process, but these steps of discovery, dream, design and destiny should not be interpreted as a fixed structure. Instead, they provide a number of stages that can be selected and adapted as appropriate to meet the agenda of a particular AI. While AI is firmly based on a number of key ideas and principles, it is an adaptable process. As Whitney and Trosten-Bloom (2003: 23) state, 'no two Appreciative Inquiry processes are ever exactly the same'. AI is still developing and new approaches are continuously evolving. Each AI should therefore be 'home-grown' (Cooperrider and Whitney 2005: 15) so that it meets the unique change agenda and challenges with which it is involved. Taking such an approach can be valuable not only in facilitating positive organisational or community development, but also as an evaluation technique, as an interview tool and as a research method. It is therefore argued that AI has significant potential to advance our knowledge in a range of areas within the study of tourism planning.

Source: Eliza Raymond.

'Introducing' planning, then, means the introduction of ways and means to bring about changes that would otherwise not occur. 'The ongoing stream of life does not wait for planners to give it direction' (Friedmann 1973: 347). Planners act upon social, physical and economic processes in order to guide society towards desired objectives. Tourism planning in this sense reflects the position of Friedmann (1973: 346–347) that planning is the *guidance of change within a social system.* Specifically, this means a process of self-guidance that may involve *promoting differential growth* of subsystem components (sectors), *activating the transformation of system structures* (political, economic, social), and *maintaining system boundaries* during the course of change.

Friedmann's comments also reflect the essentially political nature of planning and policy and the difference between planning and policy studies and policy analysis – knowledge of versus knowledge in – the planning and policy process (see Figure 4.4). Cullingsworth's (1997: 5) comment that

> Rational planning is a theoretical idea. Actual planning is practical exercise of political choice that involves beliefs and values. It is a laborious process in which many public and private agencies are concerned. These comprise a wide range of conflicting interests. Planning is a means by which attempts are made to resolve these conflicts.

reinforces Peter Hall's (1992) observations on the political nature of planning. Similarly, the significance of politics, who gets what, when, where, how and why is reflected by Wildavsky (1987: 25), with respect to policy, when he argues, 'we must first exorcise the ghost of rationality, which haunts the house of public policy'. A statement that applies equally well to the field of tourism planning and policy.

Sustainability, politics and planning: exorcising the ghost of technical rationality

Sustainability is an 'essentially contested concept' (Gallie 1955–56); that is, a concept the use and application of which is inherently a matter of dispute. The reason for this is the degree to which the concept is used to refer to a 'balance' or 'wise use' in the way in which natural resources are exploited. The appropriateness of such an approach and the very way in which 'wise use' is defined will depend on the values and ideologies of various stakeholders. However, the history of natural resource management over the last century would suggest that sustainable development is another term which has emerged in an attempt to reconcile conflicting value positions with regard to natural resources and the environment and the perception that there is a crisis which requires solution (Gössling and Hall 2006). In a review of the historical antecedents of the concept of the sustainable development of natural resources, Hall (1998b: 22) made three observations regarding present-day issues that surround sustainability:

1. Debate over the sustainable development of natural resources in industrialised countries dates from the middle of the nineteenth century and cannot be seen as a new policy issue, at least at the local or national level.
2. Tourism has long been a key factor in the justification for environmental conservation.
3. There has been no easy middle path in attempting to find a balanced use of natural resources. Political reality, rather than ecological reality, has been the order of the day.

Therefore sustainability, and tourism planning as a mechanism of achieving more sustainable and appropriate forms of tourism, need to be seen both within a political context in order to be able to understand the structure of planning issues and as a political goal in terms of their achievement. As Evans (1997: 8) observed,

> sustainability is, at its very heart, a political rather than a technical or scientific construct, and the variety of interpretations of the notion reflect this. For this reason, there is unlikely to be a 'universal theory' of sustainability to inform or guide practice, and sustainability cannot be technicised or reduced to a series of indicators or standards, useful and necessary as these aids undoubtedly are.

One of the key issues in operationalising the concept of sustainability is the extent to which governments intervene in the market in order to achieve policy goals and initiatives that meet the sustainable vision. Public planning, of which tourism planning is usually a component, is by its nature interventionist. Planning seeks to reconcile individual interests in terms of arriving at decisions and actions that meet some notion of the public good. As Friedmann (1959: 329) noted, 'Planning is nothing more than a certain manner of arriving at decisions and action, the intention of which is to promote the social good of a society undergoing rapid changes.' Planning, and tourism planning, is therefore something we do in order to meet or satisfy the ideal of the public interest. However, unfortunately in my opinion, in recent years private preferences and economic measures, backed by the supposed legitimacy of 'the market', 'efficiency' and 'rational behaviour', have supplanted in many cases debate on political ideals and the idea of a common good (Saul 1995). According to de-Shalit (1997: 96), 'this philosophy holds that society is an instrument for the benefit of individuals; all the more, therefore, should nature be subjugated by humans, who through its progressive transformation fulfil their individualistic desires'. In this idea of politics and governance private interests, which are mediated in the market, hold sway of the public interest. Such a situation does not bode well for the environment or for notions of equity, which is one of the cornerstones of sustainability. As Porritt (1984: 116) recognised:

> There may well have been a time, at the start of the Industrial Revolution, when Adam Smith's assertion that the sum of individual decisions in pursuit of self-interest added up to a pretty fair approximation of public welfare, with the 'invisible hand' of the market ensuring that individualism and the general interest of society were one and the same thing. But in today's crowded, interdependent world, these same individualistic tendencies are beginning to destroy our general interest and thereby harm us all.

Planning and markets are not necessarily in conflict or incompatible; indeed, appropriate public planning may provide a degree of certainty regarding government policy and the regulatory environment that can be welcomed in the marketplace. As Jacobs (1991: 125) observed, planning 'stands in contrast to the operation of market forces, but it does not preclude the existence of markets'. As noted in Chapter 3, one of the central reasons for government intervention and public planning is the experience of market failure. In an ideal world the marketplace provides a mechanism for the continued readjustment of production in relation to consumer preferences and ability to pay. However, we do not live in an ideal world. Some markets may take the form of producer oligopolies and monopolies that may exclude new entrants into the marketplace (Healey 1997).

'The belief in market solutions has led to the vigorous search for economic instruments as a means of valuing environmental assets, giving signals to consumers and producers that will lead to resource conservation and lower pollution' (Blowers 1997:35). Nevertheless, business has long been resistant to environmental regulations, even in areas such as tourism in which supposedly businesses have a direct financial incentive to maintain the quality of the environment. Indeed Schrecker (1991) characterised many businesses as being 'bitter' in their opposition to regulation of their activities, with the courts often being used to oppose the actions of public interest groups and government agencies. This is not to deny that individual businesses can act in an appropriate manner. However, if the marketplace alone sets the extent to which businesses utilise the physical and social environment, then history clearly suggests that the loss of environmental and social capital is inevitable.

Purely economic and self-interested individual preferences can easily lead to the continuing degradation and depletion of resources. One of the best examples of this idea, and one of the theoretical underpinnings of contemporary understanding of the problems of sustainability, is Garret Hardin's (1968) well-known 'Tragedy of the commons'. According to Hardin, the state of the environment resembles an open pasture that is open to all. Each herder tries to keep as many cattle on the common land as possible. Each herder sees the utility of adding one more animal to his herd, with an advantage of +1. In contrast, the personal disadvantage to the herder of such a move is only a fraction of −1 as any effects of overgrazing will be shared by all the herders. The tragedy is that all herders who are seeking to economically maximise their position will arrive at the same conclusion and the herders as a collective then proceed to exceed the carrying capacity of the land.

Many issues regarding the sustainability of tourism resources, e.g. impacts of tourists in wilderness areas, accommodation or second home development without consideration of sewage disposal, air pollution in national parks or destruction of the ozone layer by jet aircraft, all illustrate that issues of sustainability are related to such concepts as 'collective action', the 'public good' and the 'public interest'. Therefore, as Ophuls (1977: 186) recognised, 'environmental imperatives are basically matters of principle that cannot be bargained away in an economic fashion'. Clearly, 'not all of us think of ourselves primarily as consumers; many of us regard ourselves as citizens as well' (Sagoff 1988: 27). Notions of public good or public interest are therefore central to ideas of sustainability and tourism planning (see also Dredge and Jenkins 2007). Issues surrounding sustainability call for a politics of the common and consequently for interventionism, such a measure

> must make some assumptions about the idea of the good, since the argument rests on a theory of value, that is, on the idea of an intrinsic, noninstrumental value. And such a theory value is simply a theory of the good. (de-Shalit 1997: 98)

Intervention, often through public planning, is the mechanism that provides for the implementation of the public ideal. As Blowers (1997: 35) stated, 'Intervention is needed that gives priority to the public or common interest and to the needs of future generations. There needs to be a shift from private to public interest.' However, notions of public good and the public interest shift over time according to processes of argument and debate within a civil society. The concept of sustainability and its applications are not a given, they have to be argued and fought for. Within academic circles there has clearly been some argument over the nature of sustainable tourism and how it can be operationalised (e.g. see any volume of the *Journal of Sustainable Tourism*). Yet such arguments, and recognition of the value and interest position of the author, have clearly not permeated into much of the writing on tourism planning, where tourism planning and its outcomes are still presented as being primarily a technical issue and not a political problem.

Yet, perhaps just as importantly in terms of public debate on the public interest with respect to tourism planning, the debate in the academic institutions and academic associations has tended not to reach the wider public sphere. In part this is because universities 'are in crisis and are attempting to ride out the storm by aligning themselves with various corporatist interests. That is short-sighted and self-destructive. From the point of view of their obligation to society, it is simply irresponsible' (Saul 1995: 177).

One of the difficulties of so-called postmodern approaches to the analysis of society, and tourism as a part of the wider social system, is that ideas of a public good on which action can be based has been severely undermined. All action is related to interest. The corporatist mentality, which dominates many institutions as well as ideas of governance at the various international, national, regional and local scales, and which gives sway to private interest in the ascendancy of 'the market' over the public interest of 'the public good' in government action or inaction, lies at the heart of the lack of debate.

> The citizen's great difficulty in making public debate work begins . . . with the crisis in our language. I have talked about the division between the powerless public language and the rhetoric, propaganda and dialects of corporatism. The resulting blockage in public debate is enormous . . .
>
> The difficulty with many of the arguments used today to examine reigning fallacies is that they have fallen into the general assumptions of deconstructionism. They do not seek meaning or knowledge or truth. They seek to demonstrate that all language is tied to interest. The deconstructionists have argued against language as communication in order to get at the evils of rhetoric and propaganda. But if language is always self-interest, then there is no possibility of disinterest and therefore no possibility of the public good. The net effect has been to reinforce the corporatist point of view that we all exist as functions within our corporations.
>
> . . . the best hope for a regeneration of language lies not in academic analysis but in citizen participation (Saul 1995: 174, 177).

As was noted in Chapter 3, participation is a significant issue in tourism planning (e.g. Murphy 1985; Dredge and Jenkins 2007). However, participation and the shaping of the way communities manage tourism is a product of the institutional arrangements, individuals, power structures, interests and values that affect the decision-making process on different scales. The capacity of individuals and groups to participate in the tourism planning system is not just the result of cultural or democratic values, it is also a product of the structures of public governance and the extent to which such structures are genuinely open to participation and debate. Moreover, it is a product of the set of relationships that develop between those involved in the tourism planning and policy process. Participation is therefore a relationship within the tourism system. Indeed the choice of techniques used in tourism planning – identification of indicators, selection of objectives and the production of outputs (what is conventionally recognised as a plan in the form of a document) – are all determined by the set of relationships that exist between the various stakeholders and how exclusive or inclusive they are. The nature of those relationships will determine who wins and who loses in the political system that is tourism planning.

In any system, there are large areas of indifference where political behaviour is possible without planned intervention. Nevertheless, the relative influence of the planning function in guiding the social and economic change that sustainability calls for will depend chiefly on five variables:

1. the clarity of the system objectives;
2. the extent of consensus about them;
3. the relative importance that politicians attach to them;
4. the degree of variance relative to objectives expected in the performance of the system;
5. the extent to which a technical (as opposed to a purely political) approach is believed capable of making system performance conform to these objectives (Friedmann 1973: 353).

Understanding interdependence: the importance of dialectical analysis

One of the most critical problems facing the analysis of tourism phenomenon from a systems perspective, and the construction of the tourism landscape in particular, is the relationship between process and form. Unfortunately, much analysis of tourism merely accounts for form with there being little attention to the processes by which such forms have been created. In addition, where processes are considered they are often examined from a positivist ontological perspective. However, positivism is only one of several possible ways of understanding the human condition and the spaces within which human life unfolds. One alternative to positivism is that of dialectical thinking.

Dialectical analysis has been noted by a number of authors (e.g. Hollinshead 1992; Roche 1992; Hall 1994; Hall and Jenkins 1995) as a valuable tool in examining tourism, particularly in the area of tourism policy. Hall (1994: 200) argued that 'The process of dialectical inquiry would appear to be essential to the study of the political dimensions of tourism,' given that 'the vast majority of tourism research is one-dimensional and fails to adequately account for *both* tourism as a complex social phenomenon and the theoretical frameworks that are being utilised' (1994: 199). Similarly, Roche (1992: 591) argued that dialectical forms of conceptualisation are needed.

> to appreciate the difference and interdependence between social facts and social values, between theory and description, and between theory and policy. But further it requires [students of tourism] to appreciate the unity-in-difference in social reality of such complex phenomena as action and structure, continuity and change, consciousness and material conditions, micro and macro levels and so on.

However, despite the potential significance of dialectical analysis for broadening the scope of tourism knowledge there has been little detailed discussion of the nature and relevance of dialectical thinking. Therefore the remainder of this section outlines the key elements of dialectical thinking along the lines of principles identified by Ollman (1993) and Harvey (1995), and their application to tourism.

Relations and flows

Dialectical analysis emphasises the understanding of processes, relations and flows over the analysis of elements, things, structures and organised systems. The self-evident world of things identified within a positivistic framework is transformed through dialectical inquiry into a more confusing world of relations and flows manifested as things. Ontologically, dialecticians hold that 'elements, things, structures and systems do not exist outside of, or prior to, the processes and relations, that create, sustain, or undermine them' (Harvey 1995: 4). Such a step may be too bold for many readers; as Ollman (1993: 34) observed, it is extremely difficult for social scientists to abandon the 'common sense view' that 'there are things and there are relations, and that neither can be subsumed in the other'. Nevertheless, it should be emphasised that such a way of viewing the world is increasingly gaining support in other areas of academic endeavour including physics (e.g. Bohm 1980), biology (e.g. Capra 1997), psychology (e.g. Gergen 1991) and Christian theology (e.g. Cupitt 1987).

Dialectical analysis, which emphasises the role of process, of continually becoming, is therefore explicitly denying the validity of Cartesian, positivistic modes of enquiry. In a manner that recalls the analyses of Hewison (1987, 1991) and Hollinshead (1992) in heritage tourism, Harvey (1995: 5) observed that 'The more we treat the world as being made up of finished products separate from the continuous flow of experience out of which such products are created, so we reduce everything to the past.' Conventional tourism analysis therefore explores relations between things rather than the continuous processes of formation, maintenance and dissolution of things, which therefore has substantial implications for the manner in which culture tends to be represented in tourism research. Students of tourism should take heed of Williams' (1997: 128) excellent commentary:

> In most description and analysis, culture and society are expressed in an habitual past tense. The strongest barrier to the recognition of human cultural activity is this immediate and regular conversion of experience into finished products. What is defensible as a procedure in conscious history, where on certain assumptions many actions can be

definitively taken as having ended, is habitually projected, not only into the always moving substance of the past, but into contemporary life, in which relationships, institutions and formations in which we are still actively involved are converted, by this procedural mode, into formed wholes rather than forming and formative processes. Analysis is then centred on relations between these produced institutions, formations, and experiences, so that now, as in that produced past, only the fixed explicit forms exist, and living presence is always, by definition, receding.

Wheels within wheels

Things (elements) are constituted out of flows, processes and relations operating within bounded fields that constitute structured systems, yet from a dialectical approach both individual things and the system itself 'rests entirely on an understanding of the processes and relations by which they are constituted' (Harvey 1995: 5–6). Dialectical analysis therefore sees systems within systems, patterns within patterns, in a sort of Mandelbrot set of the social sciences. 'Things' are 'internally heterogeneous [contradictory] at every level' (Levins and Lewontin 1985: 272). 'Any "thing" can be decomposed into a collection of other "things" which are in some relation to each other' (Harvey 1995: 6) (also refer to the discussion of systems in Chapter 3). While analysis may be focused on the destination, for example dialectical analysis emphasises the problematic nature of reduction by noting the significance of relationships to processes occurring at further meta and micro scales and relationships to things outside of the destination. Destinations and their analysis are therefore perceived to be embedded within a complex web of sociocultural, economic, political and environmental relationships within which the social scientist also crafts their understanding of such relationships. These, in turn, can be decomposed into the various things that make up a destination: businesses, communities, infrastructure and environments. This is not to say that destinations or individuals are merely a passive product of external processes. As Mellor (1991: 114) noted with respect to analyses of heritage by melancholic postmodernists who have assumed:

> that people are not in active negotiation with their symbolic environment, but are passively shaped by it. The problem with this wretched scenario is that it has been devised by people who are compulsive readers of texts. They pay close attention to their semiotic surroundings and believe that others do too . . . The alternative is to treat people as active agents interacting with real structures. People make their own cultures, albeit not in circumstances of their own choosing. Amongst those circumstances – within and towards which their activity is directed – are structures of representation; but so too, are structures of class, ethnicity, and gender, along with deliberate economic and political strategies that bear upon these. These things are real. They do not merely exist in discourse. Their reality and their consequences exceed their representation. But people are not merely passively constructed by them. Even in leisure, people act intentionally; although in doing so they may slice the world along a different grain to that expected by the melancholic intellectual.

As Harvey (1995) noted, there are several implications that arise from the heterogeneity of things. First, every thing is decomposable – there is no basic unit. It is therefore legitimate to investigate 'each level of organization without having to search for fundamental units' (Levins and Lewontin 1985: 278). Nevertheless, as Harvey (1995: 7) also observed, 'critical practice in the humanities is very much guided these days, perhaps overly so, by concerns to dissolve fixed categories within conflicting fields and fluxes of socio-linguistic and representational practices'. Second, given that all things are heterogeneous the only way we can understand the attributes of things is to understand the processes and relations they internalise. Third, and following on from the second, there is no fixed or a priori boundary to the system within which a thing is located. This therefore raises the important problem of where one sets boundaries in analysis. Changes in boundaries will change not only the nature of theories but also answers. This problem has already been well recognised with respect to economic analysis in tourism in terms

of where one sets the boundary of the economic region but also with respect to issues of pollution and sustainability, e.g. what is sustainable at one level may not be sustainable at another (Hall and Butler 1995). This does not mean that one should stop setting boundaries. Such a venture would make analysis impossible. Rather it means that the arbitrary nature of boundary setting needs to be made more overt in the process of research and evaluation (see Majone 1980b for a further exposition of this problem from within a dialectical framework). Similarly Morgan (1986: 337), in his excellent discussion on the nature of organisational analysis, observed:

> People who learn to read situations from different (theoretical) points of view have an advantage over those committed to a fixed position. For they are better able to recognize the limitations of a given perspective. They can see how situations and problems can be framed and reframed in different ways, allowing new kinds of solutions to emerge.

Significantly, in an implicit reference to dialectical modes of thinking, Morgan then went on to note:

> the trick is to learn how to engage in a kind of conversation with the situation one is trying to understand. Rather than impose a viewpoint on a situation, one should allow the situation to reveal how it can be understood from other vantage points . . . as one develops the art of reading situations, critical analysis and evaluation becomes a way of thinking. (1986: 337)

What does this mean for some of the key concepts that we face in examining tourism planning?

Space and time

Space and time are not absolute. Instead, they are actively constructed by various processes. Dialectical thinking emphasises that there are multiple spaces and times that are contingent and contained within different biological, physical and social processes. Space and time are therefore relative properties, awareness of which has already partially infiltrated into tourism studies from research into the different space–time conceptions of many indigenous peoples.

Parts and wholes

'Parts and wholes are mutually constitutive of each other' (Harvey 1995: 8) – an observation that anticipates the work of Giddens (1984) on structuration theory, in which agency makes structure and structure makes agency. This holistic approach to the analysis of social systems has been particularly influential in human geography and cultural studies. However, it has had barely little substantive impact on mainstream tourism studies, although it was clearly influential in the work of Britton (1989, 1991) in his efforts to get capital recognised as a key concept in the geography of tourism (also see Hall and Page 1999a).

Cause and effect

Given the nature of the relationship between parts and the whole in dialectical analysis, it also follows that cause and effect, subject and object are also interchangeable. This therefore means that dialectical thinking makes only very limited reference to cause and effect type argument.

Contradiction and creativity

The heterogeneity that exists in things and systems gives rise to contradictions (a well-known characteristic of dialectical analysis) out of which creative tensions or, as Harvey (1995: 9) described them, 'transformative behaviours'. Such dialectical relationships between opposing forces and concepts is therefore held to be the basis of the tensions that give rise to the evolving social (Levins and Lewontin 1985) and personal world. Through dialectical analysis one learns about others through oneself, and oneself through others.

Change

In dialectical analysis change is a constant. Change and instability are the norm, not the exception. Nevertheless, in research we tend to focus on the 'moments' and 'forms' that are embedded within processes. The critical issue, though, is to be aware of the mechanisms and transformations that may give rise to those forms rather than just the form itself. In tourism studies the emphasis has generally been on the latter.

Argument

Dialectic analysis does not lie outside of its own form of argumentation but remains subject to it. It is a process that produces things in the form of concepts and theories which in themselves will be supported or undermined in terms of the ongoing process of critique and enquiry. The observer is not outside of the process he or she is examining. As soon as a researcher begins to examine a process, she or he has entered into a relationship with that process and has become part of the process itself. Observation is intervention. Similarly, the success or otherwise will be judged by other constituents of processes and systems of which the researcher is a part. The success of any argument therefore does not rely on any objective criteria. Instead, it is founded on the shifting criteria of particular groups and individuals that change over time. Several authors have focused on the role of argument, particularly with respect to tourism planning and policy that are themselves very process driven (see Hall 1994; Hall and Jenkins 1995).

Education – the search for possibilities

Finally, let us deal with eduction, which is 'the exploration of potentialities for change, for self-realization, for the construction of new totalities (for example, social ecosystems) and the like, rather than deduction or induction – the central motif of dialectical praxis' (Harvey 1995: 10). Praxis is totalisation, totalisation is praxis. Dialectical analysis highlights the role of values in social processes, e.g. tourism policy and planning, and sees the constructed knowledge that results as discourses situated in a realm of power and interests. Values are not universal truths or abstractions but this does not mean that value choice is unimportant. Far from it. Dialectical reflection forces the researcher to confront the implicit and explicit nature of values in the development and reporting of academic research. Unfortunately, a wander through the increasing number of tourism journals and books that weigh down the library shelves would suggest that such reflection, if it does exist, remains well hidden in the confines and strictures of academic writing which has tended to reinforce the fact–value dichotomy of Cartesian views of the world within which the researcher appears to lie outside of the world he or she studies. The relevance of much academic research in tourism could well be questioned – relevant to what and to whom? Results tend to be produced and reproduced for the greater benefit of narrow industry and personal interests (e.g. promotion, greater status within the walls of academia) rather than actually seeking to improve the lot of the individuals who are most affected by the vagaries of tourism.

The act of tourism planning and research, as with the subject matter of such research, needs to be located within the continuous flows of processes, relationships and systems from which it is constituted and which it informs. Dialectical thinking, for this author at least, is a crucial component of tourism analysis which needs to be put at the forefront of tourism knowledge, rather than cast to the rear. The unfolding and becoming of one's life is the search for possibilities. To paraphrase Harvey (1995): the search for such possibilities is embedded within, rather than articulated after, the research process, and it is to the discussion of some of these possibilities that this book now turns.

Summary

This chapter has outlined some of the key issues and concepts underlying the development of some of the argumentative and collaborative approaches that are part of the emerging framework of non-technocratic sustainable tourism planning. This chapter is also rich in metaphor: concepts such as a system, ideas of scale, standpoint and relationships are powerful metaphors that can be used to help describe the complexity of tourism planning. As Morgan (1986: 331) noted, 'The images or metaphors through which we read organizational situations help us describe the way organizations are, and offer clear ideas over the way they could be.' However, it should also be noted that the concept of a tourism system can be analysed in more that a metaphorical fashion and can also actually be studied empirically in a rigorous mathematical fashion, particularly with respect to spatial analysis (see Hall 2006a). The chapter has also argued that it is the notion of the public good or interest which lies at the core of sustainable tourism planning. The next chapter will attempt to describe how the tourism planning system looks and prescribe how it might be improved in terms of the overriding vision of sustainability. Chapters 6 to 9 then look at the tourism planning system at various scales of operation and the interrelationships between those scales. Throughout all of these chapters the idea of relationship and the relational way in which we all 'see' tourism planning problems will serve as an important thread in the search for more sustainable forms of tourism.

Questions

1. What is the significance of the concept of partial industrialisation for tourism planning?
2. How do issues of scale affect tourism plannng?
3. Why is argument such an important component of tourism planning and policy?
4. How might appreciative inquiry differ in its focus from other analytical methods?

Important websites and recommended reading

Websites

Journal of Planning Literature:
  http://jpl.sagepub.com/

Journal of Planning Education and Research:
  http://intl-jpe.sagepub.com/

Planning Theory (journal):
  http://plt.sagepub.com/

Current Issues in Tourism:
  http://www.multilingual-matters.net/cit/

Journal of Sustainable Tourism:
  www.multilingual-matters.net/jost/

Tourism Geographies:
  http://www.tandf.co.uk/journals/titles/
  14616688.asp

Recommended reading

1. Majone, G. (1989) *Evidence, Argument and Persuasion in the Policy Process*, Yale University Press, New Haven.

   A seminal work with respect to the realities of planning and policy analysis (also see his earlier Majone, G. (1980) 'The uses of policy analysis', in B.H. Raven (ed.), *Policy Studies Annual Review*, vol. 4, Sage, Beverley Hills, 161–80.

2. Fischer, F. and Forester, J. (1993) *The Argumentative Turn in Policy Analysis and Planning*, UCL Press, London.

   A significant text with respect to the role of argument in planning

3. Hall, C.M. (2005) *Tourism: Rethinking the Social Science of Mobility*, Prentice Hall, Harlow.

   First and last chapters in particular comment on issues of tourism theory and their formulation.

4. Hall, C.M. (2004) 'Reflexivity and tourism research: situating myself and/with others', in J. Phillimore and L. Goodson (eds) *Qualitative Research in Tourism: Ontologies, Epistemologies and Methodologies*, Routledge, London, 137–55.

   Personal comments on reflexivity and its implications in a tourism context.

5. Allmendinger, P. and Tewdwr-Jones, M. (eds) (2002) *Planning Futures: New Directions in Planning Theory*, Taylor & Francis, London.

Useful text with respect to providing an overview of planning theory.

6. Allison, G. and Zelikow, P. (1999) *The Essence of Decision*, 2nd edn, Longman, Boston.

   The second edition of one of the most influential books in policy analysis. The books studies the Cuban missile crisis from various perspectives and highlights how different frameworks can provide different 'readings' of events.

7. Farrell, B.H. and Twining-Ward, L. (2004) 'Reconceptualizing tourism', *Annals of Tourism Research*, 31(2): 274–95.

   Useful overview of systems thinking in tourism, particularly with respect to the implications for adaptive management strategies.

8. Healey, P. (1997) *Collaborative Planning: Shaping Places in Fragmented Societies*, Macmillan Press, Basingstoke.

   Influential book with respect to the 'communicative turn' in planning.

9. Hall, D. and Brown, F. (2006) *Tourism and Welfare: Ethics, Responsibility and Sustained Well-Being*, CABI, Wallingford.

   Discusses some of the ethical and value issues in tourism.

10. Rydin, Y. (2007) 'Re-examining the role of knowledge within planning theory', *Planning Theory*, 6(1): 52–68.

    Discusses the implications of different knowledge claims for planning processes.

5 The integrated and strategic tourism planning process: dealing with interdependence

Chapter objectives

After reading this chapter you will:

- Have developed working definitions of vision, mission, goal, objective and target
- Appreciate some of the key issues with respect to connecting the different parts of strategic planning
- Understand the significance of identifying and involving stakeholders in the strategic planning process
- Understand the role of evaluation and monitoring in tourism planning.

Tourism planning is often highly complex, reflecting Peter Hall's observation that planning 'is merely an acute instance of the central problem of society' (1992: 249). By this Hall meant that problems in contemporary society have a habit of becoming 'interconnected', in that what was initially seen as a problem in one sphere, say unemployment, may then become connected to other policy and planning concerns such as the environment. Such planning and policy 'messes' (Ackoff 1974) may also be well described as metaproblems.

Tourism planning often poses metaproblems. Several reasons account for this. Most significant is the nature of tourism itself, difficult to define, diffuse through economy and society and, typically, with no clear control agency. Instead, tourism tends to cut across agency boundaries. Nevertheless, planning for tourism is still regarded as important because its effects are so substantial

and potentially long-standing. Indeed concern with making tourism, along with all development, sustainable has provided an even greater imperative for improved tourism planning.

As the previous chapter argued, systems approaches to tourism may provide valuable opportunities for the understanding of tourism and how it may be steered in one direction or another. Such a systems approach to planning, particularly one that consciously sets out to identify and articulate different sets of value choices, bears strong parallels to developments that are occurring in public planning. According to Peter Hall,

> The old planning was concerned to set out the desired future end state in detail, in terms of land-use patterns on the ground; the new approach . . . concentrated instead on the objectives of the plan and on alternative ways of reaching them, all set out in writing rather than in detailed maps. (P. Hall 1992: 229)

In the new planning

> the emphasis was on tracing the possible consequences of alternative policies, only then evaluating them against the objectives in order to choose a preferred course of action; and, it should be emphasized, this process would continually be repeated as the monitoring process threw up divergences between the planner's intentions and the actual state of the system. (P. Hall 1992: 229)

The current planning paradigm, which is heavily influenced by cybernetics and systems analysis, emphasises the pattern of goals, continuous information, projection and simulation of alternative futures, evaluation, choice and continuous monitoring. For example, many readers will be familiar with the following steps in the planning process identified by Anderson (1995):

1. identify issues and options;
2. state goals, objectives, priorities;
3. collect and interpret data;
4. prepare plans;
5. draft programmes for implementing the plan;
6. evaluate potential impacts of plans and implementing programmes;
7. review and adopt plans;
8. review and adopt plan-implementing programmes;
9. administer implementing programmes, monitor their impacts.

Similar models have been applied in terms of planning for tourism. For example, the state government tourism agency in South Australia, Tourism South Australia, developed the most integrated planning model for a government authority for tourism in Australia in the 1990s. Tourism South Australia (1991: 28) noted that traditional approaches to tourism planning, as outlined in Chapter 3, were 'limited because they ignore research and evaluation of tourism demand (market needs and expectations) and tourism supply (resource utilisation consistent with demand preferences and environmental sustainability)'. Therefore, in order to provide the unique, satisfying tourism experiences that differentiate products and destinations in the marketplace, create long-term appeal and sustain the resource base on which tourism products and destinations are based, they argued that tourism planning must integrate market- and resource-driven processes. The elements of such a 'synergistic' tourism planning process that is vision and goal oriented, integrative, market driven, resource driven, consultative and systematic is detailed in Table 5.1.

A planning process for regional and local tourism that utilises a synergistic and integrated approach to tourism planning, and is based on the South Australian and other regional tourism planning experiences, is illustrated in Figure 5.1 and Table 5.2. Such a process may not be applicable in all situations; instead the succession of stages indicate 'the investigative logic that is required for proper tourism planning' (Tourism South Australia 1990: 28). The key elements identified in Figure 5.1 should be utilised in such a way as to ensure that the planning process is systematic, pinpoints the needs, values and interests of the various stakeholders in the tourism planning and

---

Table 5.1 Elements of a synergistic tourism planning approach

Vision oriented	Clear recognition of tourism's role in achieving broad community goals
Objective oriented	Clear recognition of the need for measurable objectives that allow monitoring and evaluation
Integrative	Including tourism planning issues in the mainstream of planning for the economy, society, conservation, parks, heritage, land use and infrastructure
Market driven	Planning for development that meets the needs of visitors and so will trade successfully in a competitive marketplace
Resource driven	Developing assets that build on the destination's inherent strengths while protecting and enhancing the attributes and experiences provided by tourism resources
Consultative	With meaningful community and stakeholder input to determine what is acceptable to the local population
Systematic	Drawing on, or undertaking research to provide conceptual or predictive support for tourism planning. In particular, drawing on the experience of other tourism destinations by appropriate benchmarking

Sources: Tourism South Australia (1991); Hall *et al.* (1997); Hall (2005a); Dredge and Jenkins (2007).

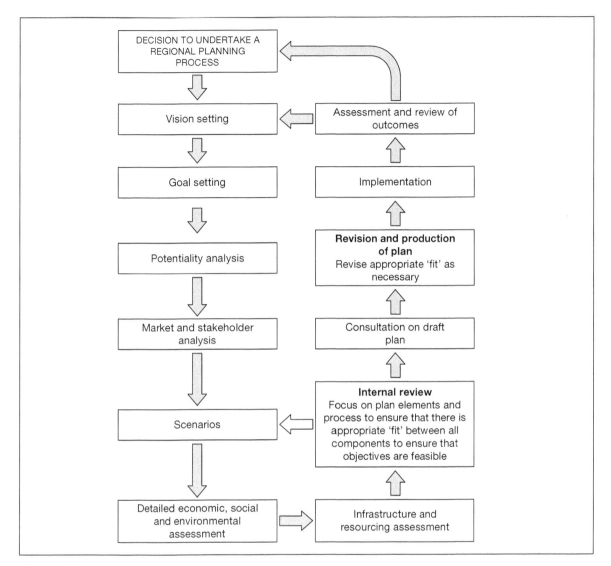

Figure 5.1 A regional planning process for tourism

development process, and incorporates an understanding of the market and the tourism resource base.

Nevertheless it should be pointed out that a good process and series of outcomes from one perspective may not be regarded as such from another. For example, in the case of South Australia, while the model was well respected by environmental and community interests, particularly for the manner in which it sought to integrate sustainability issues into the planning process, its effectiveness was limited by developments at other levels of governance. A change of government in South Australia meant that the goals of Tourism South Australia shifted to concentrate on tourism promotion so as to encourage greater visitor numbers. In this new policy setting long-term sustainable planning goals became secondary to short-term increases in the number of tourists (Hall 2007a).

Such a situation is not unusual with respect to tourism planning (Dredge and Jenkins 2007).

Table 5.2 Steps and outcomes in a regional planning process for tourism

Step	Outcomes
1 Decision to undertake a regional planning process	
Usually undertaken as an answer to negative community responses to rapid tourism development or some other crisis or, more rarely, a proactive decision as the result of an awareness of changes in the tourism business environment	Clear statement with respect to planning process and its intended outcomes
Identification of legislative, regulatory and institutional basis for regional planning process	
2 Vision Setting	
Provides a broad vision of what the region wants to be with respect to tourism and its role in the region. This will usually be revised through the consultation process	Draft statement of vision
3 Goal Setting	
Within the tourism, economic, social and environmental philosophies and policies of government, establish what is to be achieved by the process	Clear statement of purpose
Develop draft objectives	
4 Potentiality analysis	
Examine broad tourism market trends	Statement of tourism's potential and priority in the region and in community development
Analyse area's tourism assets, strengths and weaknesses	
Undertake competitor analysis and benchmarking	
Determine community and regional goals	
Determine the existing and potential role of tourism in the area's economy, especially with respect to accessibility issues and travel times to destination	
5 Market and stakeholder analysis	
Analyse the tourism market – trends, market segments, characteristics and needs, growth potential with respect to demographic, economic and accessibility change	Target markets identified
	Statement of market positioning
Identify fit between market forces and the area's assets, resources and stakeholders	Major product strengths, gaps and opportunities identified
Determine market position	

▲

Table 5.2 (continued)

Step	Outcomes
Identify stakeholder interest and commitment	
Identify major product strengths and gaps	
6 Scenarios	
Identify preliminary 'primary values'	Draft statement of desired future role and character of tourism in the area
Identify alternative future tourism scenarios and their economic, social and environmental implications for the region	Draft statement of objectives and strategies and revised statement of vision and goals
Select preferred scenario(s)	
Identify constraints to achieving preferred scenario(s)	
Establish tourism objectives and strategies	
At this stage preliminary consultation can be done if resources allow to identify at an early stage preferences for desired futures	
7 Detailed assessment of economic, social and environmental sustainability	
Identify and evaluate natural and built tourism resources	Revise objectives and strategies
Specify potential development opportunities consistent with positioning	High visitor level tourism areas or precincts identified specifying appropriate types and scales of development
Analyse environmental and landscape values	Revisit development principles and planning specifications
Identify conflicts and constraints to tourism development	Major development opportunities and performance criteria specified
Identify linkages and relationships to other regional industries and tourism's effect on these	Where tourism may have a negative effect on other sectors and businesses the total effect on the region must be assessed in case tourism development results in a net loss
8 Detailed assessment of infrastructure and resource support	
Identify and detail infrastructure required to support investment and provide for visitor and local needs, including transport infrastructure	Prioritised programme of infrastructure works and identification of funding mechanisms and sources
Identify and detail infrastructure required to manage visitors' impact	Where funding is taken from existing budgets the opportunity costs of resource reallocation must be assessed
Identify and describe opportunities for the interpretation of features of visitor interest	
Identify funding and resources required for plan	

Table 5.2 (continued)

Step	Outcomes
9 Internal review	
Focus on plan elements and process to ensure that there is appropriate 'fit' between all components so to ensure that objectives are feasible	Decision to proceed to public release of draft plan for consultation or revise process or elements if plan is not regarded as feasible
10 Consultation on draft plan	
Consult with key organisations, stakeholders and the community	Concise document outlining stages 1 to 9
Consult with other levels of government to ensure acceptability of plan	Outline monitoring and evaluation process on plan
Consult with other agencies to ensure tourism plan is integrated with other policies and planning statements	Amendment to existing policies, plans and regulations outlined as appropriate
11 Revision and production of plan	Revised, final version of plan is produced and made available via a variety of mechanisms
12 Implementation	
Devise implementation mechanisms – programmes of work, organisational responsibilities and timelines, funding as well as further information meetings on plan where required. In some cases the development of an implementation network may be appropriate	Implementation strategy
Undertake/identify required changes to existing legislation, regulation and policies	Periodic reports on implementation and recommendations for plan amendments
Ensure that monitoring, evaluation and appropriate benchmarking is undertaken and that stakeholders agree on both what is being measured and how results will be interpreted	
13 Assessment and review of outcomes	
A review and assessment is undertaken of the results of monitoring, evaluation and benchmarking against the objectives that were set and other objectives and benchmarks as appropriate	A formal progress report is provided to stakeholders and decision makers
Review implementation procedures	Decisions are made with respect to the need to further revise plan or other elements associated with its successful implementation, i.e. resourcing, indicator selection

Sources: Tourism South Australia (1991); Hall *et al.* (1997); Hall (2005a, 2007); Dredge and Jenkins (2007).

Indeed, within the public sphere it may even be the norm as governments, policies and institutional arrangements for tourism are constantly changing. Yet such a situation also provides a valuable lesson for understanding tourism planning, as it illustrates:

- the multiscale nature of planning, in other words what occurs at one level may not be compatible with another. Furthermore, changes in policy will filter through the various levels of the planning system;
- the implications of different sets of values affecting policy settings and planning processes;
- that planning models and tools do not operate in isolation from the people who develop and implement them. You can have the best planning model in the world. However, unless you have the capacity to operate it, which may involve arguing your case to politicians and those to whom you are responsible, it is of little practical value, although it may still provide a stimulus for change elsewhere. Winning policy arguments, like sustainability itself, may take time.

As Cullingsworth (1997: 25) observed, 'Planning is a process of formulating goals and agreeing the manner in which these are to be met. It is a process by which agreement is reached on the ways in which problems are to be debated and resolved.' This chapter will examine various aspects of the planning process and key issues that arise in trying to make planning and plans happen. The

> focus upon the processes of planning and land-use policy, rather than a concern with policy outcomes, might be viewed as irrelevant or even obsessional. However, it *is* important since the outcomes of policy are, in large part, a consequence of how that policy is framed, organised and implemented. (Evans 1997: 5–6)

The policy, planning and decision-making process: the setting

As previous chapters have discussed, public policy making and planning are first and foremost political activities. Public policy is influenced by the economic, social and cultural characteristics of society, as well as by the formal structures of government and other features of the political system. Policy making therefore involves the economic, physical, social and political environments in a process of action and reaction over time (Barrett and Fudge 1981). Policy and planning are therefore consequences of the political environment, values and ideologies, the distribution of power, institutional frameworks and decision-making processes (Simeon 1976; Hall and Jenkins 1995; Church and Coles 2007).

Policy analysis is a vital tool for understanding how tourism planning and policy operates. As Davis *et al.* (1993: 16) observed,

> 'Policy is not a self-evident, independent behaviour fact. Policy acquires meaning because an observer perceives and interprets a course of actions amid the confusions of a complex world' [Heclo 1974: 4]. If public policy is the choices (intended and unintended) acted upon within a society, then public policy analysis becomes a method for disentangling those decisions, for exploring why issues arise on the agenda, and how they are resolved. Public policy analysis therefore requires us to 'puzzle out' (to use another apt phrase from Heclo) this interaction of values, interests and resources, specify how they are shaped by prevailing organisational arrangements and explore the way politics can intervene to confirm or upset the expected result.

Policy analysis is multi-dimensional in examining the range of factors that affect the policy making and planning process. There are both different stages and different levels of analysis. Ham and Hill (1984: 17–18) noted that:

> Precisely how many levels are investigated is likely to vary according to the nature of the enquiry being undertaken, but it can be suggested that three levels will often be appropriate. These levels are: first, the micro level of decision-making within organisations; second, the middle range analysis of policy formulation [and implementation]; and third, macroanalysis of political systems including examination of the role of the state. It is the interaction between levels which is particularly significant and problematic.

What is often regarded in tourism as 'planning' refers to the first two levels, with questions of 'policy' often being consigned to the macro level. However, as noted earlier, planning and policy may best be conceived as a continuum along the three levels. Nevertheless, the level of understanding of the three levels and the interactions between them is not particularly great. At the macro level there is widespread ignorance of institutional arrangements and, particularly, the role of the state in tourism public policy. At the meso level there is little understanding of how and why decisions are made and actions are taken, while at the micro level understanding of the relationship between individuals, their values and interests, and organisations and the state is lacking. The elements of each level and the relationships between them is illustrated in Figure 5.2. While substantial progress has been made in understanding the various operations of these levels in different

parts of the world, in overall terms our level of understanding is still relatively low (Church and Coles 2007; Dredge and Jenkins 2007) compared with other planning and policy fields.

However, while the model may assist in conveying the manner in which interaction exists between the different levels of analysis of policy and planning, it still does not adequately express the multi-dimensional set of tourism policy and planning relationships that occur at different scales of governance. Figure 5.3 seeks to illustrate the different dimensions of tourism planning that occur at different scales – from the local to the international, using the example of ecotourism (Hall 2003a, 2004b, 2006d). Although ecotourism is a significant area of tourism planning it has very few specific policies and institutions. Instead,

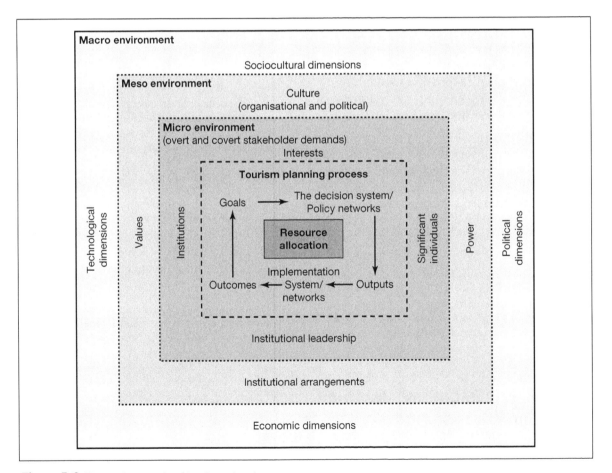

Figure 5.2 The environments of tourism planning

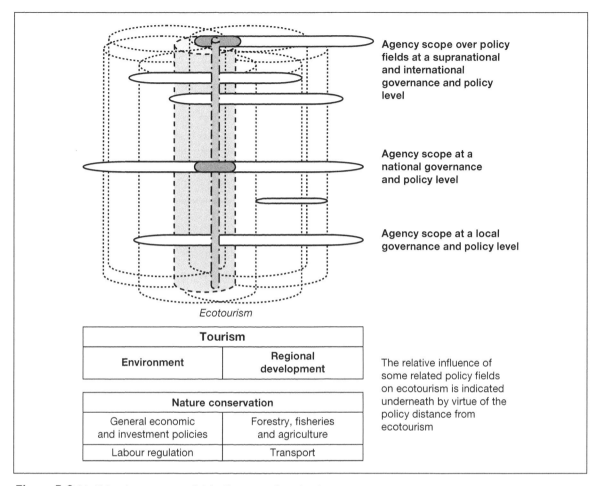

Agency scope over policy
fields at a supranational
and international
governance and policy
level

Agency scope at a
national governance
and policy level

Agency scope at a local
governance and policy level

Ecotourism

Tourism	
Environment	**Regional development**

Nature conservation	
General economic and investment policies	Forestry, fisheries and agriculture
Labour regulation	Transport

The relative influence of
some related policy fields
on ecotourism is indicated
underneath by virtue of the
policy distance from
ecotourism

Figure 5.3 Multi-level governance fields: the case of ecotourism

ecotourism policies are usually found within tourism policies (Fennell and Dowling 2003; Diamantis 2004). Therefore the ecotourism policy field is represented as being embedded within the broader tourism policy field. However, in turn ecotourism (as well as tourism) is affected by a much wider array of policies than just what is contained in tourism policy. The broken lines surrounding the particular fields are representative of the permeability and fluidity of policy arenas (horizontal fields) in contrast to the more fixed boundaries of policy action and concern of specific public agencies (vertical fields). What is important to note is that the relationships between the various components of the governance framework for tourism planning and policy exist both vertically (over different levels of governance) and horizontally (within specific regulatory space). The tourism planning system therefore comprises the set of constant interactions between the various components of the system from the individual to the global. As will be discussed later, what happens at one level of tourism governance or in a policy arena will be affected by other levels and arenas. The more complex a planning problem is to solve, invariably the more levels and regulatory spaces it will occupy. It is the analyst who draws the boundaries within the tourism planning system in terms of trying to define and manage the planning problem.

One of the ways in which the implications of different scales for tourism planning can be seen is by examining the different levels of institutional arrangements that have been created to manage and plan tourism. For example, tourism organisations have been established at the international (global) level, e.g. the UN World Tourism Organization; the supranational level, e.g. European Union tourism organisations; and through to national, regional and local tourism organisations (Table 5.3).

The internationalisation of environmental issues also reveals the multiscale aspects of institutional arrangements that can be seen in the plethora of environmental legislation and regulation from the international (e.g. *Agenda 21*) through to the local scale (e.g. local government site regulations and planning schemes). There are very few legal agreements that deal specifically with tourism and the environment. Instead, the relationship between tourism and the environment tends to be managed within general environmental and planning law. Table 5.4 identifies the various levels at which such legal frameworks operate from the international through to the national and the sub-national level, using the Nordic countries of Finland, Norway and Sweden as an example (Gössling and Hultman 2006; Hall 2006d).

A number of international conventions operate in the region. These conventions range from international agreements on the Law of the Seas (which is clearly of major importance to the cruise ship industry and marine tourism) to the World Heritage Convention, which serves to establish World Heritage listing for cultural and natural heritage sites of universal significance that are typically of great significance as visitor attractions; and to provisions for the conservation of fauna and flora (e.g. the Ramsar Convention, which governs habitat for migratory birds) that may also serve as important ecotourism attractions.

At the supranational level there are European, Baltic and Nordic agreements on the environment and on tourism. One of the most important institutions in the Nordic context is the European Union: Denmark, Finland and Sweden are members, while Iceland and Norway have well-developed economic and political relationships with the EU. The EU does not have a specific directorate for tourism, although tourism is used as a tool in a number of policy areas, particularly with respect to regional development and peripheral regions (see Clement *et al.* 2004 for a review of the environment and sustainable development integration in Nordic structural funds). In terms of nature conservation that provides sites for ecotourism visitation, the EU has a range of policy mechanisms which, in turn, may be integrated with international policies and institutions. For example, EU nature conservation policy is founded upon a combination of international agreements, the most important of which is the Convention of Biodiversity, which was adopted in 1992, and European policy measures such as the Birds Directive (1979) and the Habitats Directive (1992). These agreements provide the institutional basis for European biodiversity programmes such as Natura 2000 and wider EU conservation policy (Hall 2006d).

Under Natura 2000 all EU states are required to take steps to ensure that natural habitats and species in the network receive 'favourable conservation status':

> Natural habitats must be large enough, important structures and functions must exist, and there must be viable populations of species typical of the habitat. With respect to species there must be a sufficient number of individuals within the area, reproduction must take place and the species habitat must be large enough. (Swedish Environmental Protection Agency 2003: 6)

There are approximately 4,000 Natura 2000 sites in Sweden, covering a combined area of more than 6 million hectares. The procedures by which sites have been recognised illustrates the interrelationship between different levels of governance and policy making with the sites having been selected by administrative boards in each county following consultation with landowners and other authorities. Selection decisions were then reviewed by the Swedish Environmental Protection Agency prior to a decision by the Swedish government, with the sites then being proposed in turn to the EU Commission (Swedish Environmental Protection Agency 2003: 8). Each site must have a conservation plan that states permissible and non-permissible

Table 5.3 Tourism and related organisations from the international to the local scale

	Government and intra-government organisations	Producer organisations	Non-producer organisations	Single interest organisations
International	United Nations World Tourism Organization; World Heritage Committee (UNESCO); Committee for the Development of Sport; OECD (Organization for Economic Cooperation and Development)	World Travel and Tourism Council; International Air Transport Association; International Olympic Commitee	Tourism Concern; World Wildlife Fund (WWF); Association for Tourism and Leisure Education (ATLAS); Greenpeace; Friends of the Earth	World Congress Against the Commercial Sexual Exploitation of Children
Supranational	Asia Pacific Economic Cooperation (APEC) tourism working group; Tourism Council of the South Pacific; Association of South East Nations (ASEAN) Promotion Centre on Trade and Investment; European Commission	Pacific Asia Travel Association (PATA); Baltic Sea Tourism Commission; Play Fair Europe; European Surfing Federation; National Olympic Committees	Sierra Club; International Downtown Association; Travel and Tourism Research Association	End Child Prostitution in Asian Tourism (ECPAT)
National	Indonesian Directorate General of Tourism; English Sports Council; Countryside Commission; Australian Tourist Commission; Irish Tourist Board (Bord Fáilte)	British Sports and Allied Industries Federation; Tourism Council Australia; Institute of Leisure and Amenity Management (ILAM); Irish Tourist Industry Confederation	National Trust; Australian Conservation Foundation; Australian Consumers Association	The Wilderness Society; Hispanic Association for Corporate Responsibility; ECPAT (Australia)
Regional (including provincial and state)	Tourism Alberta; Natal Parks Board; Western Australian Tourism Commission (WATC); Scottish Tourist Board; Tourism British Columbia	Tourism Council Australia (WA Division); Scottish Confederation of Tourism; Shannon Development; Coalition of Minnesota Business	Western Australian Conservation Council	Tasmanian Wilderness Society
Local	Local government involvement in leisure and tourism provision, e.g. Tourism Canterbury; Calgary Economic and Development Authority; Tourism Vancouver	Local chambers of commerce and industry associations; local sporting clubs and private sport and leisure centres	Ratepayers and resident associations, e.g. Waikiki Improvement Association	Single issue organisations such as a 'friends of a park' or a group that has been formed in order to prevent particular developments such as a hotel or airport

Table 5.4 Multiple scales of institutional arrangements for ecotourism policy and planning in the Nordic countries: the case of Finland, Norway, and Sweden

Scale	Examples
International	1972 Convention concerning the Protection of the World Cultural and Natural Heritage (Paris) [World Heritage Committee, UNESCO]; 1992 Framework Convention for Climate Change (New York); 1992 Convention on Biodiversity (Rio de Janiero); 1971 Convention on Wetlands of International Importance especially as Waterfowl Habitat (Ramsar); 1979 Convention on the Conservation of Migratory Species of Wild Animals (Bonn); 1981 Law of the Seas; UNESCO Biosphere Reserves programme.
Supranational	European Union; Nordic Council of Ministers; Nordic Council; Nordic Environmental Cooperation; Baltic Council; Northern Forum
National	Metsähallitus (Finland); Miljøverndepaertementet (Norway); Naturvårdsverket (Sweden)
Subnational	Provinces; counties; communes; municipalities

activities, with visitor access usually being encouraged where this does not endanger high-value species or habitats. The value of such a programme for ecotourism is that it helps secure the resource base on which ecotourism depends through regulatory protection, management plans and nature conservation agreements. In addition, such programmes may assist with the transfer of management and planning knowledge between locations as well as being of assistance in gaining financial support for projects (Hall 2006d).

At the national level, a number of legislative and regulatory instruments may affect the relationship between tourism and the environment, while within most countries decisions taken at the local level in the form of development permissions and local plans will also have a major effect on the environmental impacts of tourism development and tourist activities (Hall and Page 2006). For example, Metsähallitus, the Finnish Forest and Park Service, states that 'the economic utilisation of protected areas for ecotourism, for example, is permissible where it does not endanger the achievement of conservation aims' (Metsähallitus 2000: 7). Indeed the growth of ecotourism and an increase in the number of visitors to protected areas is used by Metsähallitus as an indication of a more favourable opinion towards nature conservation. Yet tourism is regarded as only one out of ten different uses of the

Finnish protected area system that require a policy statement (the others being everyman's right, fishing and hunting, photography, local residents, traffic, forestry, mineral prospecting and mining and leasing land). Ecotourism is not explicitly defined within management guidelines although its economic dimension is noted, which therefore suggests that ecotourism is regarded as commercial tourism use of protected areas by firms as opposed to access by independent visitors and recreationists. Interestingly, the agency's management guidelines outline the policy boundaries with respect to tourism planning. According to Metsähallitus (2000: 42) the agency does not intend to develop its own activities in the field but instead will

> aim to provide a framework and opportunities for independent enterprises in the field of ecotourism. The aims of sustainable ecotourism must be agreed upon with all interested parties (local residents, the tourism sector, other local organisations) by drawing up a strategy for tourism following the principles of participatory planning.

The multi-scale institutional arrangements that surround tourism and the environment are only one aspect of the difficulties of planning for tourism. The same pattern of multi-level governance and policy relationships exists in many other areas that affect tourism, e.g. employment, investment, trade, taxation, visa and regional development incentives, adding to the complexity of the environment in which tourism planning occurs.

This section has discussed some aspects of the setting within which planning occurs. The environment for tourism planning and policy making is seen to be highly complex, with multiple sets of vertical and horizontal relationships. Within this tourism planners develop planning procedures and plans, which are the output of such procedures. Having noted the setting within which planning occurs we will now return to the difficulties of establishing planning strategies within such an environment.

Strategic planning for tourism

As Chapter 3 noted, strategic planning is regarded as an essential component of sustainable tourism planning. A 'strategy' is a means to achieve a desired end. As Evans *et al.* (2003: 9) observed, 'A plan is probably the way in which most people use the word strategy. It tends to imply something that is intentionally put in train and its progress monitored from the start to a predetermined finish'. Porter (1980: xvi), who focused on the idea of thinking competitively, stated that 'essentially, developing a competitive strategy is developing a broad formula for how a business is going to compete, what its goals should be, and what policies will be needed to carry out those goals'. Strategic planning is the process by which organisations effectively adapt to their environment over time by integrating planning and management in a single process and seeks to deal with the following questions:

- Where are we now? – Check (monitor and evaluate).
- Where do we want to get to? – Plan.
- How do we get there? – Do (action).

The strategic plan is therefore the document that is the output of a strategic planning process and which serves to guide future directions, activities, programmes and actions. The outcome of the strategic planning process is the impact that the process has on the organisation, its activities and its environment, including the various stakeholders. Such impacts are then monitored and evaluated through the selection of appropriate indicators as part of the ongoing revision and readjustment of the organisation to its environment. Strategic planning therefore emphasises the process of continuous improvement as a cornerstone of organisational activity in which strategic planning is linked to management and operational decision making (Hall and McArthur 1998), with the three key mechanisms required to achieve this being:

1. a planning framework that extends beyond organisational boundaries and focuses on strategic decisions concerning stakeholders and resources;
2. a planning process that stimulates innovative thinking and provides a capacity to adapt to environments;
3. an organisational values system that reinforces commitment to the organisational strategy.

A key point that readers will observe with the above is the use of the word 'organisation'. This is because tourism planning, even when it is for a region or a destination, is undertaken within an organisational context. Although the best plans are often highly inclusive of the stakeholders within a region or location for which tourism activities are being planned, the planning process is still being done by individuals within an organisation, while organisations such as local councils or municipalities, tourism departments or even elected bodies are the ones then held responsible for the planning process and outcomes.

Strategic planning has been a part of business literature since the late 1950s and early 1960s (see Evans *et al.* 2003 for a good basic introduction within a travel and tourism context), and the fact that it is 'oriented towards process rather than towards the production of one-shot (or end-state) plans' (P. Hall 1992: 11) is a reflection of the wider influences of systems theory in the planning field. Strategic planning and the business ecology metaphor of the organisation and a destination responding and adapting to its environment in a state of constant interaction is a classic representation of the ideas of systems thinking presented in the previous chapter. Strategic planning is therefore both a process, which leads to specific planning outputs, and a way of thinking about the world. As Ohmae (1983: 79) stated:

> The drafting of a strategy is simply the logical extension of one's usual thinking processes. It is a matter of long-term philosophy, not short-term expedient thinking. In a very real sense, it represents the expression of an attitude to life. But like every creative activity, the art of strategic thinking is practiced most successfully when certain operating principles are kept in mind and certain pitfalls are consciously avoided.

Similarly, according to Primozic *et al.* (1991: 15):

> Strategic thinking must be a continuous cycle. The cycle begins with formulating a strategic vision for the organization, proceeds through creating strategies that determine how the vision can be used to guide the organization's efforts, continues with developing appropriate tactics to implement the strategic plans, and leads to the implementation and operational steps that all members of the organization must carry out in the day-to-day running of the enterprise.

However, while perhaps being more conducive to sustainable thinking, strategic planning by itself will not necessarily lead to more sustainable forms of tourism or even intrinsically better outcomes. Instead, strategic planning may well be an important conceptual and practical tool that, given a set of sustainable objectives, may well be more suitable for actually achieving the objectives of sustainable tourism than non-strategic planning methods. According to Hall and McArthur (1998), there are a number of advantages in adopting a strategic approach in visitor planning, as it:

- provides a sense of purpose and the foundation of criteria for the formulation of new projects;
- stresses the need for both short- and long-term objectives that can accommodate changing circumstances, e.g. a change in the level of government funding for tourism;
- gives stakeholders a clear indication of the current and long-term level of support required for tourism management programmes;
- provides for potential integration of stakeholder objectives into an organisational or programme strategy, thereby increasing the likelihood of success;
- encourages strategic and increased receptiveness to opportunities in the external environment;
- can create a sense of ownership and involvement in planning processes and outputs with a consequent likely increase in performance and level of support;
- can make organisations more effective and efficient in attaining programme and/or organisational goals.

Yet, as noted above strategic planning always has an organisational focus (Swart 2005). Even in the case of destination planning, for example, an organisation will still be responsible for the development, evaluation and implementation of the plan. The difficulty of course is for any destination's tourism organisation to be able to distinguish between a strategic plan for the organisation and a strategic plan for a destination for which it has responsibility. These are two different things. Unfortunately, the destination plan is often equated with the former.

Figure 5.4 outlines a model of a strategic tourism planning process that identifies key components of the process, some of which, in turn, will correspond to some of the components of a formal planning document. The process is encompassed by the environment within which tourism planning and management operates. This includes, therefore, such factors as institutional arrangements, institutional culture and stakeholder values and attitudes as well as broader economic, social, political and economic trends. Such factors are extremely important. For example, public sector tourism strategic plans will be developed and written in line with the legislative and regulatory powers and organisational structures of the implementing organisation(s),

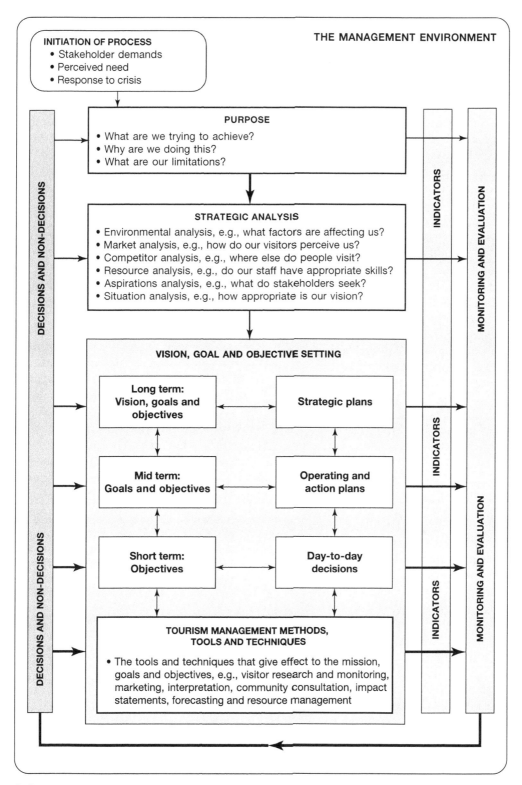

Figure 5.4 Strategic tourism planning process
Source: Hall (1995).

broader policy settings and, in some cases, ministerial directive. However, as Hall and McArthur (1998) observed, it may also be the case that once the strategic planning process is under way, goals and objectives formulated and the process evaluated, the institutional arrangements, including legislation and organisational structures, may be recognised as inadequate for the successful achievement of certain goals and objectives. Indeed, strategic planning for tourism at the destination level often seems to give rise to new organisational structures and/or responsibilities in order to try and achieve more effective implementation of planning strategies. In order to be effective the strategic planning process also needs to be integrated with the development of appropriate organisational structures and values, yet, at the destination level, such measures may give the impression that stakeholders are not adequately included in the planning process. In such situations the strategic planning process is as important as its output, i.e. a plan. By having an inclusive planning process by which those responsible for implementing the plan are also those who helped formulate it, the likelihood of 'ownership' of the plan and, hence, effective implementation will be dramatically increased.

A strategic planning process is usually initiated for a number of reasons, including:

- *Stakeholder demands* – demand for the undertaking of a strategic plan may come from the pressure of stakeholders, e.g. the tourism industry, conservation groups or government.
- *Perceived need* – the lack of appropriate information by which to make decisions or an appropriate framework with which to implement legislative requirements may give rise to a perception that new management and planning approaches are required. This factor has become extremely important with respect to the need to develop new arrangements, structures and strategies with which to develop sustainable tourism.
- *Response to crisis* – the undertaking of strategic planning exercises is often the result of a crisis in the sense that the management

and planning system has failed to adapt to aspects of the management environment, e.g. failure to conserve a heritage site or a rapid decline in the number of visitor arrivals.
- *Best practice* – heritage managers can be proactive with respect to the adoption of new ideas and techniques. Therefore a strategic planning process can become a way of doing things better including benchmarking destinations or developments with competitors.
- *Adaptation, innovation and the diffusion of ideas* – individuals within an organisation can encourage strategic planning processes as part of the diffusion of ideas within and between tourism planning and management agencies.

As Figure 5.4 indicates, the strategic planning process is hierarchically structured, from a vision or mission statement through to goals, objectives and action statements. Each level expands on the other in terms of detail, direction and ability to be achieved. The hierarchical structure also reflects the various layers or scales of the planning system within which planning problems are 'solved'. For example, as McLoughlin (1969: 105) stated with respect to physical planning in the urban environment:

> It follows from the hierarchical or tree-like nature of choices and alternatives that lower-level decisions tend to require higher-order choices to be clarified. For example, it is often found that a particular proposal such as the rebuilding of a row of older shops and houses cannot be resolved without consideration of the question of the future width and alignment of the street, which itself cannot be decided until the circulation and access system for that part of the city (and thus perhaps the whole city) is decided upon; this in turn forces attention onto the land use patterns which the transport system is to be designed to serve.

Once under way, strategic planning is also designed to be iterative. That is, planning systems should be able to adapt and change to the internal and external forces with which they interact, that is, they *learn* how to be effective in terms of the most appropriate set of goals, objectives, actions, indicators, institutional arrangements and practices. As the environment changes so the planning system, and the components within it, also change.

Figure 5.4 illustrates the process dimensions of current planning paradigms that we noted at the start of the chapter. However, while we typically talk of 'stages' of the planning process, and we write them up as such in books such as these, one should always remember that the process is never purely linear (i.e. A leads to B leads to C leads to D and returns to A). There is constant feedback, adjustment and change between all the components of the process; sometimes this is formal, e.g. when new legislative arrangements are established in order to meet the goals and objectives of a plan, but often such accommodation occurs informally during the process, e.g. objectives emerge over a period of behind-the-scenes negotiation between stakeholders as to what is acceptable and required. Indeed, one of the biggest frustrations in reading about planning is that one often comes across the phrase 'establish objectives' or something similar, as if it is a perfectly rational and self-evident process. Yet in reality there tends to be a whole series of, often heated, interaction between various stakeholders and interests over objective setting, because such a process sets the direction of planning in motion, determines what the planning problems are, how they might be solved and who is responsible (see Sautter and Leisen 1999). Most significantly, by clearly stating the purposes of planning it becomes possible to state:

- what an organisation is trying to achieve;
- why an organisation is undertaking the planning process;
- what the limitations of the process are.

Where do we want to go?

The first step in the strategic planning processes is to identify the purposes the planner seeks to achieve, to order them in terms of their importance, and to consider how far they are reconcilable each with the other. As Peter Hall stated, 'unless objectives are made explicit, no one can be sure that they are shared by the people they are being planned for; nor is it possible rationally to prefer one plan to another' (1992: 233).

Mission, goal and objective formulation is therefore a critical component of strategic tourism planning. An organisation's mission or vision, goals, objectives and targets are highly interdependent. The formulation of mission statements and the development of goals and objectives needs to be conducted hand in hand with the strategic analysis and vision setting, i.e. a statement as to what an organisation is trying to achieve. As Heath and Wall (1992: 63) noted with respect to strategic tourism marketing, management strategies 'grow out of and reflect the environmental analysis, resource analysis and goal formulation steps. Unless . . . goals have been set to be accomplished, there is no purpose in strategy formulation'. The key outputs of a strategic planning process are: there is a mission statement, a vision, a series of goals, a series of objectives and a set of targets, which are also usually accompanied by a statement with respect to the resources that will be required to fulfil them.

- The *vision* is a statement with respect to what the organisation would like to fulfil. In tourism this is usually done in terms of its stakeholders, i.e. it will be a statement about what the destination should be.
- The *mission statement* describes what the organisation is trying to accomplish in the longer term.
- *Goals* generally emphasise long-range intentions of the organisation and are not usually quantified; they are abstract and tend to express areas of organisational concern.
- *Objectives* are measurable goals that are capable of being carried into action and which have been made more specific with respect to magnitude, time and responsibility and that are judged to be attainable within a specific time. Objectives therefore also imply an element of competition for scarce resources.
- *Targets* represent specific programmes in which *criteria of performance* (i.e. benchmarks, indicators, standards) are set against target dates by which they will be accomplished.

The selection of goals, objectives and targets is extremely important in terms of tourism planning because they lead to the selection of indicators by which success in meeting objectives, and therefore the overall goal of sustainability, can be evaluated. In addition the selection will influence the allocation of resources, and/or the identification of new resources, including partners, in order to be able to achieve the strategic plan.

Nevertheless, the selection of goals, objectives, targets and indicators is not easy. The problem emerges of seeking to integrate individual programmes into a coherent plan. This operates not only at the level of what is contained within the planning document but also with respect to organisational structures and values held by those who are responsible for both the formulation and implementation of planning strategies. Indeed, as noted earlier, the process itself, by which different interested parties, groups and individuals come together to communicate different options and possibilities, is as important as what the plan eventually looks like. Indeed it can sometimes be argued that this is the most important part of strategic tourism planning as it should ideally bring a sense of realism as to what can be achieved – and what cannot.

Communication and involvement in planning processes can lead to ownership of any plan, thereby leading to increased possibilities of successful implementation. In tourism planning this becomes extremely important because at the destination level it is the sum of all the components that make up the destination product (which therefore includes the local community) rather than just members of the destination promotion organisation or even the members of the tourism industry. Such a situation means that one of the key tasks of any tourism planner is seeking the involvement and collaboration of the various stakeholders in the tourism planning process from outside of the organisational context within which they work.

'The task of reconciliation is the essence of the job of the . . . planner' (P. Hall 1992: 10). However, such a task helps explain why tourism planning is so difficult in terms of the amount of information and expertise that is required and

'the need to frame and then weigh up different objectives' (P. Hall 1992: 10) which may be sought by different interests and stakeholders in the planning process – although it should be noted that there is no necessary relationship between the scale and expense of a planning programme and the complexity of the objectives behind it (P. Hall 1992).

Integrated approaches towards tourism planning are therefore neither *top down*, 'where goals at each level in the organisation [or spatial area] are determined based on the goals at the next higher level' (Heath and Wall 1992: 69), or *bottom up*, where the goals of individual units are aggregated to become the strategic plan. Instead, integrated tourism planning is an *interactive* or *collaborative* approach that requires participation and interaction between the various levels of an organisation or unit of governance and between the responsible organisation and the stakeholders in the planning process.

How do we get there? The problem of coordination

> Finding creative solutions in a world of growing inter-dependence requires envisioning problems from perspectives outside our own. We need to re-design our problem-solving processes to include the different parties that have a stake in the issue. Achieving creative and viable solutions to these problems requires new strategies for managing interdependence (Gray 1989: xviii).

The lack of single authorities responsible for tourism development has meant that local authorities and private industry have often been confused by the tourism development and planning process. Furthermore, the diverse structure of the industry has meant that coordination of the various elements of the planning process has been extremely difficult. However, perhaps paradoxically, it is the very nature of the industry that makes planning so important. As Gunn (1977: 85) observed, because of the fragmented growth of the tourism industry 'the overall planning of the total tourism system is long overdue . . . there is no overall policy, philosophy or coordinating force that brings the many pieces of tourism into harmony and assures their continued harmonious function'.

The need for coordination has become one of the great truisms of tourism planning and policy (Hall 1994; Testoni 2001). For example, Lickorish *et al.* (1991: vi) argued that

> There is a serious weakness in the machinery of government dealing with tourism in its co-ordination, and co-operation with operators either state or privately owned. Government policies or lack of them suggest an obsolescence in public administration devoted to tourism . . . Political will is often lacking.

One therefore has to ask why?

'"Co-ordination" usually refers to the problem of relating units or decisions so that they fit in with one another, are not at cross-purposes, and operate in ways that are reasonably consistent and coherent' (Spann 1979: 411). Coordination for tourism occurs both horizontally, e.g. between different government agencies that may have responsibilities for various tourism-related activities at the same level of governance (i.e. national parks, tourism promotion, transport), and vertically, e.g. between different levels of government (local, regional, provincial, national) within an administrative and policy system. Two different types of coordination are covered under Spann's definition: administrative coordination and policy coordination. The need for administrative coordination can be said to occur when there has been agreement on aims, objectives and policies between the parties that have to be coordinated but the mechanism for coordination is undecided or there are inconsistencies in implementation. The necessity of policy coordination arises when there is conflict over the objectives of the policy to be coordinated and implemented. The two types of coordination may sometimes be hard to distinguish as coordination will nearly always mean that one policy or decision will be dominant over others. Furthermore, perhaps the need for coordination only becomes paramount when it is not occurring. Most coordination occurs in a very loose fashion that does not require formal arrangement. In addition, some conflict can also be productive in the formulation of new ideas or strategies for dealing with problems

(Hall 1998b). Nevertheless, coordination is a political activity and it is because of this that coordination can prove extremely difficult, especially when, as in the tourism industry, there are a large number of parties involved in the decision-making process. As Edgell (1990: 7) observed, 'there is no other industry in the economy that is linked to so many diverse and different kinds of products and services as is the tourism industry'.

In a collaborative or interactive approach towards tourism planning the emphasis is on planning *with* rather than planning *for* stakeholders. The approach reinforces the complex nature of tourism destination products, by recognising that the opinions, perspectives and recommendations of external stakeholders are just as legitimate as those of the planner, or the 'expert', or of industry. Such an approach may well be more time consuming than a top-down approach but the results of such a process will have a far greater likelihood of being implemented because stakeholders will have a degree of ownership of the plan and of the process. Furthermore, such a process may well establish greater cooperation or collaboration between various stakeholders in supporting the goals and objectives of tourism organisations, and also create a basis for responding more effectively to and for change (Hall and McArthur 1998).

Coordination refers to formal institutionalised relationships among existing networks of organisations, interests and/or individuals, while cooperation is 'characterized by informal trade-offs and by attempts to establish reciprocity in the absence of rules' (Mulford and Rogers 1982: 13). Often the problem of developing common approaches towards tourism planning and policy problems, such as the metaproblem of sustainability, is identified in organisational terms, e.g. the creation of new ones or the allocation of new responsibilities to old ones. However, such a response does not by itself solve the problem of bringing various stakeholders and interests together. Instead, by recognising the level of interdependence that exists within the tourism system, it may be possible for 'separate, partisan interests to discover a common or public interest' (Friedmann 1973: 350).

Table 5.5 The collaborative process

Phase 1: Problem setting
- common definition of problem
- commitment to collaborate
- identification of stakeholders
- legitimacy of stakeholders in terms of both internal and external acceptance
- convenor characteristics
- resource identification and availability for participation and collaboration.

Phase 2: Direction setting
- establishing ground rules
- agenda setting
- organising subgroups, e.g. task forces
- joint information search
- exploring options
- reaching agreement and closing the deal.

Phase 3: Implementation
- dealing with constituencies
- building external support
- structuring
- monitoring the agreement and ensuring compliance.

Source: After Gray, B. (1989) *Collaborating: Finding Common Ground for Multiparty Problems*, Jossey-Bass, San Francisco. Reproduced with permission.

Collaboration is one important means to advance the collective good of stakeholders in tourism. Collaboration is essentially an emergent process rather than a prescribed state of organisation (see Table 5.5) (Gray 1989; Wood and Gray 1991). According to Gray (1989: 15), 'Typically, collaborations progress from "underorganized systems" in which individual stakeholders act independently, if at all, with respect to the problem . . . to more tightly organized relationships characterized by concerted decision making among the stakeholders', with stakeholders being defined as 'all individuals, groups or organizations that are directly influenced by actions others take to solve the problem' (Gray 1989: 5). Under conditions of interdependence the range of interests associated with any particular problem

is wide and therefore differences between interests can often become controversial. Depending on the scale of analysis and the issue being examined, the number of stakeholders that an organisation has to contend with may be extremely large. For example, in terms of agreements with stakeholders, the United States Forest Service has developed more than 12,000 agreements with other agencies at all levels of government, universities and colleges, rural communities and organisations, and other outside interests (Ungar 1994). In the state of Vermont alone, the Forest Service has working agreements with the Abenaki Nation, the Catamount Trail Association, the Nature Conservancy, Lyndon State College, the University of Vermont, the Vermont Association of Snow Travelers, the Ecotourism Society, the Green Mountain Club, Tree Talk, Inc., the Vermont Department of Forests, Parks and Recreation, the Vermont Department of Fish and Wildlife, Division of Water Quality, County Sheriffs, and the Youth Conservation Corps, and numerous other stakeholders (Ungar 1994). Large numbers of stakeholders can clearly make satisfactory outcomes difficult to achieve, but if legitimate stakeholders are excluded or ignored the quality and degree of acceptance of any recommendations will be highly suspect. As Healey (1997: 70) noted, 'unless all stakeholders are acknowledged in the [planning] process, policies and practices will be challenged, undermined and ignored'. Indeed there are a number of interrelated judgements that stakeholders weigh up when deciding whether or not to collaborate:

- Does the present situation fail to serve my interests?
- Will collaboration produce positive outcomes?
- Is it possible to reach a fair agreement?
- Is there parity among the stakeholders?
- Will the other side agree to collaborate? (Gray 1989: 59).

A legitimate stake means the perceived right and capacity to participate in the negotiations. Those actors with a right to participate are those impacted by the actions of other stakeholders. They become involved in order to moderate those impacts. However, to be perceived as legitimate, stakeholders must also have the capacity to participate. (Gray 1985: 922)

Stakeholder audit

The concept of 'stakeholders' is becoming increasingly important in tourism planning. Stakeholders are the individuals, groups and organisations with an interest in a planning problem, issue or outcome that are directly influenced or affected by the actions or non-actions taken by others to resolve the problem or issue. Traditionally focused on the resource and on expert opinion with respect to determining definition and management of planning issues, tourism planning is now far more externally oriented. Several reasons can be put forward for this significant shift:

- The claims of 'expert' perspectives, such as those held by planners, have come to be challenged by other groups in society.
- There has been a recognition that some 'voices' have previously been ignored in the planning process because of lack of recognition by dominant elements of society, lack of resources to articulate their concerns, different traditional consultation mechanisms to those adopted by planning authorities, or a combination of all three.
- Changes in government funding, philosophies and arrangements has meant that many tourism

planners have had to engage in developing partnerships and collaborative relationships with external groups.
- And, related to the above, some planners and agencies may now actively seek support from a range of interests in order to improve the likelihood that their policies and recommendations will be adopted.

Stakeholder audits are one mechanism which can assist planners in identifying the interests, groups and individuals that are stakeholders in the tourism planning process as well as help in understanding and confronting the complex web of relationships that surround tourism planning and management (Roberts and King 1989). Hall and McArthur (1996) identified seven steps in the undertaking of a stakeholder audit (Table 5.6). The audit is a useful tool for managers as it provides a framework for the identification of the various interests and values that impinge on the successful undertaking of organisational objectives. Managers and staff of tourism planning organisations often have a mental map of the individuals and groups that affect their work and act accordingly

---

Table 5.6 Steps in the stakeholder audit

1 Identification of stakeholders.

2 Determination of stakeholder interests, goals, priorities and values.

3 Review of past stakeholder behaviour in order to assess their strategies relating to issues and the likelihood of their forming coalitions with other stakeholders.

4 Estimation of the relative power (legal authority, political authority, financial, human and physical resources, access to media) of each stakeholder and stakeholder coalitions.

5 Assessment of how well your organisation is currently meeting the needs and interests of stakeholders.

6 Formulation of new strategies, if necessary, to manage relations with stakeholders and stakeholder coalitions.

7 Evaluation of effectiveness of stakeholder management strategies, with revisions and readjustment of priorities in order to meet stakeholder interests.

Sources: After Roberts and King (1989); Hall and McArthur (1996).

▶

in relations with them. Stakeholder analysis is therefore a systematic way of identifying the range of interests in a particular tourism planning issue and their ability to affect planning processes and actions.

Many stakeholders can be categorised as being 'interest groups'. The term 'interest group' tends to be used interchangeably with the terms 'pressure group', 'lobby group', 'special interest group' or 'organised interests'. An interest group can best be defined as any association or organisation that makes a claim, either directly or indirectly, on government so as to influence policy without itself being willing to exercise the formal powers of government. Several features of interest groups can be observed:

- While attempting to influence governments, interest groups do not seek government. Even if an interest group runs a single issue candidate in an election this is usually an attempt to gain further publicity for the group's cause.
- Not all activities of an interest group need be political.
- Interest groups will often seek to influence government policy indirectly by attempting to shape the demands that other groups and the general public make on government, e.g. through the conduct of public relations campaigns.

Interest groups operate at multiple scales of governance, e.g. international, national, regional and local. However, interest groups can also be classified along a continuum, according to their degree of institutionalisation, as producer groups, non-producer groups and single interest groups. Producer groups, such as business organisations (e.g. tourism industry associations, chambers of commerce), labour organisations (e.g. unions and employee associations) and professional associations (e.g. planning associations), tend to have a high level of organisational resources, a stable membership maintained by the ability of the group to provide benefits to members, ability to gain access to government, and a high level of credibility in bargaining and negotiations with government, tourism organisations and other interest groups. In non-producer groups, institutionalisation has occurred on the basis of a common interest of continuing relevance to members, such as heritage

and environmental conservation (e.g. the World Wildlife Fund, the National Trust in the United Kingdom, the Historic Places Trust in New Zealand, and the Sierra Club in North America) or social issues (Tourism Concern). Single interest groups are at the other end of the continuum from producer groups and are characterised by their limited degree of organisational permanence, as they will likely disappear altogether once their interests have been achieved or have been rendered unattainable. This typically refers to locally based organisations that were established specifically to conserve a particular environmental resource, for example local campaigns to stop motorway development in rural areas in the United Kingdom or logging of a forest.

The categorisation of interest groups can be extremely useful in understanding their resources, methods and effectiveness in the policy-making process. The continuing relevance of group objectives to their members and the corresponding degree of organisational permanence will clearly influence the resource base of groups and their continued visibility. For example, the Sierra Club in the United States grew from a small, local, hiking and nature appreciation society in the late nineteenth century and a regionally based nature preservation group in the early twentieth society to what is presently one of the most influential conservation organisations in the nation, with concerns covering the full range of environmental issues. Similarly, the Wilderness Society in Australia developed from the Tasmanian Wilderness Society that was originally formed to stop the construction of the Franklin Dam in the early 1980s.

In addition to identifying stakeholders it is also useful to note their positions on issues, their relationships with each other, and their relative strength in affecting the heritage management process. Such material can then serve as the basis for discussion among staff on how best to communicate with stakeholders and the ability to meet their interests. Another way of describing the relationship of various interests in tourism planning is with respect to their attitudes and behaviour or involvement in the planning process. Figure 5.5 illustrates such a classification method with respect to attitudes towards a tourism planning issue. A useful exercise is for readers to

▶

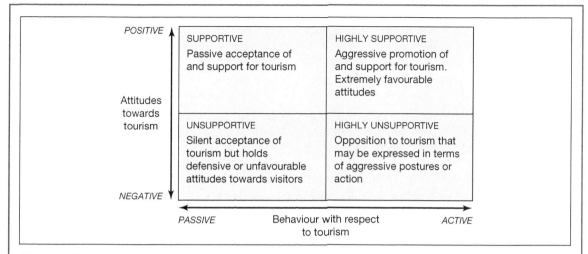

Figure 5.5 Categorisation of stakeholder attitudes towards tourism

examine a particular planning issue and then slot organisations and individuals into each category upon examination of the figure. However, it should be realised that much of tourism planners' time is spent in dealing with those who are most for or against a particular policy, outcome or decision. Yet, in the majority of cases, these stakeholders will only represent a relatively small number of people in comparison to the wider pool of stakeholders. The challenge for the tourism planner is therefore to try and accommodate into the planning process not only the more extreme perspectives but also much of the middle range of interests and values. Therefore, stakeholder input into the planning process is an important aspect of connecting aspirations analysis with the development of planning strategies over the short and long term.

Collaboration therefore operates on a model of shared power that is in keeping with the idea of the existence of a shared or public interest (Wood and Gray 1991). Nevertheless, for the planner, 'successfully advancing a shared vision, whether in the public or the private sector, requires identification and coordination of a diverse set of stakeholders, each of whom holds some but not all of the necessary resources' (Gray 1989: 9). Collaboration is a highly dynamic process consisting of a number of elements:

- Stakeholders are interdependent.
- Solutions emerge by dealing constructively with differences.
- Joint ownership of decisions is involved.
- Stakeholders need to assume collective responsibility for the future direction of the domain.
- Collaboration is an emergent process.

Collaborative planning approaches have been extensively used with respect to multi-party environmental disputes, e.g. land and water use, natural resource management and public land-use issues (Bingham 1986) and are becoming increasingly recognised as significant for tourism (Selin and Beason 1991; Selin 1993; Selin and Chavez 1994, 1995; Jamal and Getz 1995; Selin and Myers 1995, 1998; Bramwell and Sharman 1999; Bramwell and Lane 2000). Gray (1989) identified a number of benefits of collaboration:

- Broad comprehensive analysis of the domain improves the quality of solutions.
- Response capacity is more diversified.
- It is useful for reopening deadlocked negotiations.
- The risk of impasse is minimised.
- The process ensures that each stakeholder's interests are considered in any agreement.

- Parties retain ownership of the solution.
- Parties most familiar with the problem, not their agents, invent the solutions.
- Participation enhances acceptance of solution and willingness to implement it.
- The potential to discover novel, innovative solutions is enhanced.
- Relations between the stakeholders improve.
- Costs associated with other methods are avoided.
- Mechanisms for coordinating future actions among the stakeholders can be established.

The emphasis on sharing power and participation means that collaborative approaches fulfil one of the social pillars of sustainability, namely the requirement for equity. As Blowers (1997: 42) noted, 'Inequality is about power relationships.' Collaboration therefore becomes a means of involving all affected parties to search for common interests and outcomes (see Table 5.5).

> Instead of trying to restrict participation, a common tactic, the professional manager gains more control over the situation by ensuring that all the necessary parties are there at the table, recognizing that parties in a dispute often engage in adversarial behaviour because no other approach is available to protect their interests. (Carpenter and Kennedy 1988: 26)

Furthermore, 'joint ownership means that the participants in a collaboration are directly responsible for reaching agreement on a solution' (Gray 1989: 13). Waddock and Bannister (1991; see also Selin and Myers 1998) found the following factors to be significant predictors of partnership effectiveness:

- Partners need to trust other partners.
- Partner representatives need to have adequate power to make decisions for their organisations.
- Appropriate partner organisations need to be identified and included in the partnership.
- Partners need to sense that there will be benefits to all members of the partnership from their efforts.
- Partners need to recognise that they are interdependent.

- Issues being dealt with need to be salient to partners.
- Partners need to feel that they add value to the partnership.
- Power needs to be balanced among partners.
- Objectives for the partnership should be clear and well defined.
- Competent staff are required for successful implementation of the partnership.
- Feedback to partners is important.
- A strong vision of the partnership must be articulated by leaders.
- Strong leadership is required to maintain the partnership.

Waddock and Bannister's (1991) observations were borne out in further research by Selin and Beason (1991) and Selin and Chavez (1994) on tourism partnerships, with the latter study also noting the significance of several organisational and operational characteristics for successful partnerships. Organisational characteristics included:

- administrative support
- flexible protocols
- staff continuity
- mediator roles

and operational characteristics such as

- a written plan
- meeting environment
- cooperative agreement
- the setting of new goals.

Selin and Chavez (1994: 59) observed that 'partnerships form a complex system of interrelationships between agencies and interests that is constantly changing'. For example, in research on ecotourism policy in the United States Edwards et al. (1998) identified a wide variety of government tourism agencies that collaborated in respect of ecotourism policy, with one of the conclusions being that even though some agencies may not have policies or activities that are ecotourism related, such as commerce or labour, they may work closely with other government agencies which do. Nevertheless, significant barriers to collaborative planning also exist.

Selin *et al.* (1997) in a study of collaborative planning in the US Forest Service noted that the four greatest perceived barriers to collaboration were

1. initiatives constrained by personal agenda;
2. the Federal Advisory Committee Act;
3. the lack of full support of line offices;
4. initiatives becoming too politicised.

In the case of the Forest Service

> many managers were skeptical of collaborative forums characterized by shared decisionmaking, joint ownership, and collective responsibility; their concept of collaborative planning contradicts Gray's (1989). Most preferred to see collaborative planning as an advisory function, with the Forest Service retaining primary control over final decisions. (Selin *et al.* 1997: 27)

Furthermore, in a wider setting, protracted conflict between stakeholders that has led to substantial mistrust, the vesting of power in elite organisations and a lack of incentives to participate may all constrain the effectiveness of collaborative strategies (Selin 1998).

In a more positive vein we can also note that collaborative planning approaches also encourage planners, and others, to reflect on the manner in which planning and implementation represent two sides of the same coin. As Friedmann (1973: 359) observed,

> *the kind of implementing mechanism adopted will itself influence the character of the plan and the way it is formulated*. The formulation and implementation of plans are closely interdependent processes, so that the choice of one will in large measure also determine the second.

The inclusiveness of collaborative approaches may therefore help assist in dealing with some of the key problems of problems of implementation:

- Many policies represent compromises between conflicting values.
- Many policies involve compromises with key interests within the implementation structure.
- Many policies involve compromises with key interests upon whom implementation will have an impact.

- Many policies are framed without attention being given to the way in which underlying forces (particularly economic ones) will undermine them (Barrett and Hill 1993 in Ham and Hill 1994).

The importance of having those stakeholders who will be responsible for implementing the solution that emerges from the planning process cannot be emphasised enough. Acceptance of and support for a solution is enhanced when those who must abide by it are included in designing the solution (Delbecq 1974); such a situation may be extremely important in such areas as codes of environmental practice by tour operators or developers, for example. Furthermore, insufficient consideration of implementation of outputs within the planning process 'may result in settlements that create devastating precedents that may result in reluctance to negotiate in the future; damage interpersonal relationships; and financial, time or resource loss' (Moore 1986: 248).

How do we know we've got there? The role of evaluation and indicators

Through evaluation and performance monitoring governments and agencies seek to establish whether public sector activities are achieving their goals or objectives, or are achieving them to an increased extent over time, and to determine whether objectives are being pursued as efficiently as possible. Evaluation can also seek to establish why public planning activities do or do not achieve their objectives, allowing lessons from successes to be applied elsewhere and failures to be dealt with (O'Faircheallaigh and Ryan 1992).

Evaluation is increasingly becoming a significant component of tourism planning and policy as they are undertaken on a more strategic basis (Miller and Twining-Ward 2005). Nevertheless, 'The word "evaluation" needs careful definition. To most lay observers, it conveys a connotation of economic criteria . . . But essentially, *evaluation consists of any process which seeks to order preferences*' (Hall 1982: 288). Peter Hall's definition of evaluation is insightful for two principal reasons. First, many other definitions of evaluation confine evaluation to the 'what happened after the policy was implemented' phase (e.g. Dye 1992). Although evaluation tends to be more focused on determining performance for outcomes such as impact assessment, justification, accountability, planning and resource allocation, improvement, and continued support (Cauley 1993), there is no reason why evaluation cannot be undertaken before a policy is put into effect. Indeed it makes good sense to include an objective whereby responses to policy proposals are evaluated, 'Because errors are to be expected projects should be planned to facilitate early detection and correction' (Hollick 1993: 125). Similarly, Hall and Jenkins (1995) argued that constant monitoring of the tourism policy process can alert decision makers and policy makers to situations in which public officials carry out different activities from those envisaged, or perhaps when policies fail to reach intended clients. In other words, to simply 'evaluate the programme in terms of its original objectives might lead to a conclusion that the policy was a failure, yet this might be misleading since the policy as originally envisaged might not actually have been put into effect' (Hogwood and Gunn 1984: 220). Policy failure or success could be the result of various aspects of policy design (e.g. ambiguous statements of objectives and intent), policy implementation (e.g. bureaucratic discretion or uncontrollable global forces), or from unforeseen forces (e.g. economic, political and social) creating changes in public need (Hall and Jenkins 1995).

Second, Hall's (1982) definition acknowledges that 'evaluation is not simply concerned with carrying out technically correct evaluations; it has to be concerned with how evaluation results are consumed and utilized' (Hogwood and Gunn 1984: 220). Tourism planning and policy evaluation should therefore be concerned with who requested the evaluation, why the evaluation was requested, the estimation, assessment or appraisal of policy, including its development, content, implementation and effects, and the manner in which that evaluation will be consumed and utilised. Evaluations of policy must consider who got what, where, and why and the outcomes and impacts of policy. That said, goals and objectives may be ambiguous or covert and therefore difficult to detect. This in itself means policy evaluation must go beyond simply measuring outcomes and impacts with respect to goals and objectives (Hall and Jenkins 1995).

Evaluation involves making judgements about the results of some sort of measurement against specific objectives. This is typically done by collecting and analysing information, judging the worth of something and making informed decisions for the future. Table 5.7 outlines some of the reasons for which evaluation and monitoring is undertaken in tourism planning and policy. However, evaluation rarely occurs for a single reason and the roles that evaluation undertakes are multiple and interrelated. According to Hall and McArthur (1998), some of the principles that should be kept in mind when undertaking evaluation are:

- What needs to be measured is determined before the measurement technique.
- The only aspects assessed are those that will provide the necessary critical information.
- Stakeholders clearly understand the rationale and nature of the evaluation programme.
- What is to be evaluated already has some form of measurable objectives or performance criteria.
- Relevant information can be collected.
- Results are balanced and reliable, and recommendations are relevant, feasible and timely.
- Information is presented in a way that increases the possibility of acceptance.
- The right information reaches the right people.
- The programme is delivered to stakeholders in a way that reflects their interests and abilities (e.g. comprehension and cognitive).

Evaluation is both an ongoing task of strategic planning and a key element of strategic thinking (Phillips and Moutinho 2000). If we accept Lindblom's (1980: 64) notion that 'Most, perhaps all, administrative acts make or change policy in the process of trying to implement it', then this observation in itself justifies the need for

Table 5.7 Roles of evaluation and monitoring in the tourism planning and policy-making process

- Assessing the degree of need for government/agency/stakeholder intervention and policy.
- Continuous function of the policy-making process to enlighten, clarify and improve policy. Evaluation allows for the testing of assumptions regarding the way in which the process operates, the nature of outcomes and the effectiveness of programmes.
- Conceptual and operational assistance to decision makers, planners and policy makers, particularly as shifts in implementation and target needs and expectations occur. Evaluation allows access and integration of relevant information that improves the quality of decision making in areas such as resource allocation and other policy and programme directions.
- Specification of policy outcomes and impacts.
- Review of performance indicators through consideration of whether the original objectives or desired outcomes remain realistic and appropriate.
- Review of planning strategies and processes.
- Help gain acceptance of outcomes and agreement on strategies.
- Assessing or measuring the efficiency and cost effectiveness of tourism policies and plans in terms of the financial, human and capital resources.
- Accountability reporting for resource allocation, distribution and redistribution, through assessment and demonstration of the degree to which a policy or programme is meeting its objectives.
- Symbolic reasons (to demonstrate that something is being done).
- Political reasons (to use the results of evaluation for political ends in order to win policy and planning arguments).

Sources: Hall and Jenkins (1995); Hall and McArthur (1998); Miller and Twining-Ward (2005).

monitoring and evaluation. By incorporating monitoring and evaluation at the very beginning and throughout the tourism planning and policy-making process, the type of information required from monitoring and evaluation can be specified during the formation of the plan/policy and in advance of the plan's/policy's implementation (Pechlaner and Sauerwein 2002). Moreover, the policy analysis approach to evaluation, which acknowledges the politics of tourism planning and public policy, is not simply concerned with carrying out technically correct evaluations; it has to be concerned with how evaluation results are ordered, consumed and utilised (Hogwood and Gunn 1984). In other words, the planner needs to be aware of the power of argument and the communication of ideas to the various stakeholders who receive them. 'The process of critical evaluation . . . requires that we explore competing explanations and arrive at judgments regarding the way that they fit together' (Morgan 1986: 331).

Interpretations need to be played off against each other and, when necessary, choices need to be made between them.

Although monitoring, auditing and evaluation are closely related concepts there are significant differences between them. Monitoring is a process of repetitive observation of one or more elements or indicators according to prearranged schedules in time and/or space. Auditing is the comparison of predicted outcomes with those outcomes that have already occurred. Evaluation research is at the other end of a spectrum of evaluative activity from auditing with evaluation referring to the systematic assessment of the effectiveness, efficiency (or) appropriateness of a policy, programme or part of a programme (Hall and McArthur 1998) (see Table 5.8). Auditing and monitoring are therefore a component of the wider field of evaluation.

Environmental auditing has become a well-recognised technique within environmental

Table 5.8 Characteristics and purposes of audit and evaluation

Audit	Evaluation
• Typically the agent of an external third part (e.g. Parliament); focused on accountability, with a consequent strong emphasis on independence of the area under review.	• Pursued in collaborative relationship with programme managers; scope includes accountability, but main areas of concern are the appropriateness and effectiveness of programme activities.
• Generally attempts to assess performance against established (i.e. well-documented if not statutory) standards; focus is on internal processes.	• Aims to assess the impact of programmes in terms of policy objectives/programme goals; focus is on stakeholders.
• Takes policy settings and strategies as given.	• Critically examines existing policy settings and strategies within programmes and may recommend change.
• Confined to an examination of what is already done or has been completed.	• Can be used to form a judgement about the appropriate design of policy for future implementation as well as to review work in progress or completed.
• Strong focus on accountability and control.	• Focus on programme improvement with accountability being a secondary consideration.
• A well-defined profession based in accountancy.	• An emerging profession drawn from a wide range of academic fields and that is substantially interdisciplinary in nature.

Sources: After Douglas (1992); Hall and McArthur (1998).

planning and, increasingly, within tourism planning as well (e.g. World Travel and Tourism Council 1990). Nevertheless, with respect to the conduct of auditing of environmental impact statements, Selman (1992: 140) notes:

> often it is impossible to conduct an adequate audit because of the vague wording of predictions. Auditing of many impacts can only be undertaken when monitored data allow statistically valid interpretations of cause–effect relationships to be derived for projects with a long operational life . . . monitoring may be required for long periods before trends can be identified.

One of the great difficulties, therefore, with assessment of tourism's impacts, along with other forms of evaluation of tourism, is the creation of appropriate baseline data along with reliable monitoring practices (see Chapter 2). Nevertheless, environmental auditing for tourism is becoming increasingly important as businesses and organisations seek to ensure that they are complying with regulations and legislation (e.g. with respect to

pollution) and evaluate their performance in relation to membership of voluntary environmental programmes (e.g. Green Globe) and more broadly assumed environmental responsibility. Relevant types of environmental audits that may be undertaken include:

- *compliance audits,* which ensure that regulations are not being breached;
- *site audits,* comprising spot checks of known problem areas;
- *corporate audits,* which examine the performance of an entire business or agency, and more positively, ensuring that technical and advisory support on environmental matters is available throughout the organisation;
- *issues audits,* which are a response to specific environmental issues (such as energy use, recycling or use of rainforest timber);
- *associate audits,* in which vetting of environmental action is extended to an organisation's contractors, agents and

suppliers in order to ensure that they are operative in appropriate ways;

- *activity audits,* which evaluates policies in activities that cut across business boundaries, such as distribution and transport networks (after Selman 1992).

Whether it be auditing or part of a broader evaluation process, indicators play a major role in measuring success in meeting goals and objectives. Sustainable development indicators measure sustainability or sustainable development performance.

> Sustainability indicators need to take account of economic linkages, quality of life and perhaps future welfare aspects, as well as environmental quality… The challenge is to strike a balance between having a small number so that the main messages are clear, while not oversimplifying the issues or omitting significant areas, or suppressing significant geographical variations. (HMSO 1994: 220)

Development of sustainable indicators provides a theoretical and practical framework for defining the meaning of sustainability at various scales, from global to the community, and for measuring progress towards that goal. Sustainability indicators serve as a 'reality check' to ensure that strategic, planning and management processes are moving in desired directions and that agencies and individuals are held accountable for their decisions and actions. Sustainable indicators also enable comparison between different regions, but are most valuable when measuring a nation, region, community or place against itself over time.

The role of an indicator is to make complex systems understandable or perceptible, 'those things which a decision-maker needs to know to reduce the risk of unknowingly taking poor decisions' (World Tourism Organization 1993: 8). As Jacobs (1991: 237) noted, 'without accurate and systematic information about the state of and changes in the environment (which many countries surprisingly lack) it is impossible to set sustainability targets and to direct policy to meet them'. An effective indicator or set of indicators helps nations, regions, communities and organisations determine where they are, where they are going, and how far they are from chosen goals. Indicators of sustainability also provide information on long-term viability based on the degree to which economic, environmental and social systems are efficient and integrated. To measure the degree of efficiency and integration, a set of numerous indicators is often required. At the community level, for example, these indicators may incorporate several broad categories such as economy, environment, society/culture, government, resource consumption, education, health, housing, transportation and quality of life. The usefulness and accuracy of indicators of sustainability depends on their ability to create a 'snapshot' of economic, environmental and social systems at a given scale. This 'snapshot' must be appropriate to the scale at which the evaluation is occurring and for which goals and objectives have been developed. In addition, the indicators used at one scale should be related to the indicators used at other scales in order to ensure integration of objectives for and evaluation of sustainability. Choosing the appropriate indicators and developing a programme is a complex process requiring collaboration between many sectors including government agencies, the public, research institutions, civic and environmental groups and business. Indicators should be developed in accordance with the following criteria:

- recognition of scale and relationship between various scales;
- relevant to the main objective of assessing progress towards sustainable development;
- understandable in that they are clear, simple and unambiguous;
- realisable within the capacities of governments, organisations and communities, given their logistic, time, technical and other constraints;
- conceptually well founded;
- limited in number, remaining open-ended and adaptable to future developments;
- broad in coverage of all aspects of sustainable development;
- representative of an international consensus, to the extent possible;

- where possible, dependent on data that are readily available or available at a reasonable cost/benefit ratio, of known quality and updated at regular intervals; where this is not the case new data will be required.

Indicators for sustainable tourism are most often used to provide information for tourism planners and managers at various scales of operation ranging from individual businesses through to national agencies and even international businesses in some cases (Miller and Twining-Ward 2005). According to the World Tourism Organization (1993) the type of indicators that tourism sector managers need to know include:

- *warning indicators* which sensitise decision makers to potential areas of concern and the need to act to anticipate and prevent problems, e.g. visitor numbers;
- *measures of pressures or stresses* that measure key external factors of concern or trends which must be considered in any management response, e.g. changing community expectations or changing levels of visitor satisfaction;
- *measures of the state of the natural resource base (product) and measures of level of its use,* e.g. changing use levels, measures of biodiversity, or pollution levels for a given site;
- *measures of impacts,* usually related to measures of physical, social and economic impact, which examine the cause and effect relationships between the decisions and actions and the external environment, e.g. changing attitudes to tourism due to changes in visitor numbers or days of beach closures due to unacceptable pollution levels;
- *measures of management effort/action* that examine the question of 'is enough being done?', e.g. extent of area declared as national park or conservation reserve or amount of funds spent on visitor management strategies;
- *measures of management impact* that evaluate the effectiveness of management decisions and actions, e.g. levels of visitor-related

degradation in areas set aside as national parks or conservation reserves.

Undoubtedly the selection of indicators is fraught with difficulties. They must meet the criteria noted above, must be appropriate to measuring the efficiency and effectiveness of goals and objectives and must also provide a clear indication of cause and effect relationships. However, the use of indicators has also been criticised at a deeper level for its 'managerial' approach towards sustainability (Bayliss and Walker 1996), in which indicators are used to measure environmental assets to ensure that the total stock of assets is not diminished between generations (the principle of intragenerational equity). In this setting

the environment is likened to a stock of natural capital yielding a flow of services to the economic system (i.e. its essential economic functions), then sustainable development of that system involves maximising the net benefits of economic development, subject to maintaining the services and quality of the stock of natural resources' (Pearce *et al.* 1989: 42).

Bayliss and Walker (1996) criticise this approach as they note that not only have there been inconsistencies in gathering data, difficulties in selecting criteria and high levels of variability and uncertainty throughout the process of monitoring sustainability, but that there are inherent problems in such a positivistic/scientific approach to sustainability in the first place. Indeed McConnell (1981) criticised such positivistic comprehensiveness in planning by noting that theory, without being spatially, temporally and stakeholder group specific, cannot be falsified, leaving a lack of any basis to establish the reliability of the claims it makes to producing reliable knowledge (Bayliss and Walker 1996). Such a powerful critique reflects wider concerns as to the way in which the concept of sustainability and its implementation cannot be separated from the political arena (e.g. see Sachs 1993). However, as this book has consistently pointed out, policy and planning outputs, such as the selection of indicators and monitoring results, should not be taken as a given. They should be part of a contested public domain in which their selection, suitability, operation and outputs are subject to debate and discussion in order to ensure that they meet the widest possible notion of the public interest at that level. Indicators and the evaluation process need to be as much a part of the process of argument and debate as any other component of planning. This does not mean that indicators are without value, far from it; appropriate indicators can be invaluable in determining the value of policy settings and the efficiency and effectiveness of planning processes. If well done they provide a basis for policy renewal and targeting that is even more appropriate to the task in hand. However, as with any planning tool, their use needs to be seen within the wider political context of interests, values and power.

Strategic planning is a powerful conceptual tool and approach. It puts in operational terms the dynamic nature of tourism systems and the wider set of interrelationships and interdependencies that operate in the human and physical environment. It is also ongoing and seeks to both respond to and stimulate appropriate change. However, as noted earlier, it does not by itself automatically lead to sustainable outcomes in the environment external to the organisation that is undertaking such activities. Indeed, again as previously observed, there is a common tendency in tourism to assume that strategic planning processes undertaken by destination organisations are automatically the same as a strategic plan for a destination. They are not; the objectives, stakeholders, interests, values and outcomes that are related to such a process will be different. There is a difference between determining the long-term survival of a tourism organisation and the long-term sustainability of a destination.

The idea of interdependence in planning has run very strongly through this chapter. Before moving on to examine the policy and planning process at various scales we shall discuss the role of dialectical analysis that underpins much of the thinking about the importance of relational and communicative planning theories and strategies.

Summary

This chapter has emphasised the importance of systems thinking in tourism planning and the corresponding role of strategic planning in tourism. Strategic tourism planning is designed to be holistic, integrated and comprehensive. Integration in tourism planning and management refers to an awareness that tourism is a system of interrelated social, economic, physical and political variables and the corresponding establishing of a series of institutional arrangements and planning processes that reflect such a system. At an organisational level, to be comprehensive, three conditions must be met:

1. Functional programmes and activities must be in keeping with the wider values, mission, principles, goals and objectives of the management organisation.
2. Any programme or activity must be monitored and evaluated in terms relevant to the wider values, vision, mission, goals and objectives.
3. All relevant variables must be considered in the design of individual programmes and activities.

This chapter has also outlined a process of strategic tourism planning. It has emphasised the significance of the reasons for the initiation of strategic planning and the construction of an integrated set of goals, objectives and actions that can then be implemented and evaluated over time horizons ranging from the day to day to the long term. The chapter has also provided a strategic planning process that is geared towards stakeholders. As Colenutt (1997: 109) observed, 'The participation of local residents makes a difference to how the local authority conducts itself and can also affect how the developers and landowners act'. However, such a philosophy applies throughout the planning process. As Colenutt went on to argue in the context of town planning:

> The purpose of planning, its values and vision should, therefore, be redefined. Communities and their needs should be at the centre not simply responding to the demand (or lack of it) of the property market. If we

move down this path, it then becomes possible within the framework of planning consultation to debate explicitly how to create and protect jobs, house the homeless, create a decent healthy environment, ensure adequate public transport and reduce crime. These issues are real, and, if they are not brought into the planning system, town planning will die as an instrument of social policy, leaving it to be manipulated by rich and powerful corporate elites (Colenutt 1997: 115).

Such sentiments apply equally to tourism planning. If the creation of sustainable places is a goal of tourism planning, then tourism planning must be a process that is geared not only to government, industry and tourist satisfaction but to a broad notion of stakeholders which is inclusive of the local community and the public interest.

Questions

1. How might a concern with the policy and planning process improve outcomes?

2. What are the key elements of a strategic approach to tourism planning?

3. Why is a strategic planning process usually initiated?

4. Explain the similarities and differences between the concepts of coordination and collaboration.

5. What are the differences between conducting an audit and undertaking an evaluation?

6. How are goals and objectives different? And why does this matter?

Important websites and recommended reading

Websites

Tourism Victoria (Australia), site contains example of strategic plan and reviews: http://www.tourismvictoria.com.au/strategicplan/

East Gippsland (Victoria, Australia) Strategic Tourism Plan (This plan is interesting as you can judge the interrelationships between state planning strategies (above) and local level strategies): http://www.egipps.vic.gov.au/Page/Page.asp?Page_Id=52&h=1&p=1

Michigan (USA) Tourism Strategic Plan: http://www.tourismplan.msu.edu/

Maine (USA) Nature Tourism Initiative: http://www.fermatainc.com/maine/

Gold Coast City Council (Queensland, Australia). The 'strategic tourism focus' of one of Australia's major destinations: http://www.goldcoast.qld.gov.au/t_standard2.aspx?pid=2450

Kangaroo Island (South Australia) Strategic Tourism Plan/Tourism Optimisation Model: http://www.tomm.info/home.aspx

Hawaii Tourism Authority, strategic planning: http://www.hawaiitourismauthority.org/

New Zealand Tourism Ministry planning toolkit: http://www.tourism.govt.nz/tourism-toolkit/tkt-strategic-planning/tkt-latplanning.html

Recommended reading

1. Hall, D. and Brown, F. (2006) *Tourism and Welfare: Ethics, Responsibility and Sustained Well-Being*, CABI, Wallingford.

   Provides an excellent account of the issues of participation in tourism and how this relates to sustainability, ethical and quality of life concerns.

2. Heath, E. and Wall, G. (1992) *Marketing Tourism Destinations: A Strategic Planning Approach*, John Wiley, New York.

   Remains one of the best books written on strategic planning in tourism.

3. Simpson, K. (2001) 'Strategic planning and community involvement as contributors to sustainable tourism development', *Current Issues in Tourism*, 4(1): 3–41.

   Examines stakeholder driven strategic planning as a contributor to sustainable tourism development.

4. Ruhanen, L. (2004) 'Strategic planning for local tourism destinations: an analysis of tourism plans', *Tourism and Hospitality Planning and Development*, 1(3): 239–53.

    Reviews plans of tourism destinations in Australia and identifies that destinations were not incorporating principles of sustainability into their planning processes.

5. Dredge, D. and Jenkins, J. (eds) (2007) *Tourism Planning and Policy*. John Wiley, Brisbane.

    Australian- and New Zealand-oriented textbook on tourism planning and policy.

6. Soterlou, E.C. and Roberts, C. (1998) 'The strategic planning process in national tourism organizations', *Journal of Travel Research*, 37(1): 21–9.

    Reported that the comprehensiveness of the strategic planning process in National Tourism Organisations (NTOs) is determined by the internal capacity for undertaking strategic planning and factors in the external environment.

7. Benckendorff, P.J. and Pearce, P.L. (2003) 'Australian tourist attractions: the links between organizational characteristics and planning', *Journal of Travel Research*, 42(1): 24–35.

    Indicated that attraction organisations which had greater levels of planning also had higher levels of perceived performance and faced the future with better growth prospects and business confidence (also see Benckendorff 2006).

8. Gray, B. (1989) *Collaborating: Finding Common Ground for Multiparty Problems*, Jossey-Bass, San Francisco.

    Remains the seminal work on collaboration.

9. Evans, N., Campbell, D. and Stonehouse, G. (2003) *Strategic Management for Travel and Tourism*, Butterworth-Heinemann, Oxford.

    Although primarily examining strategy within a corporate context the book nevertheless provides a useful introduction to some of the issues of strategic management for tourism.

10. Treuren, G. and Lane, D. (2003) 'The tourism planning process in the context of organized interests, industry structure, state capacity, accumulation and sustainability', *Current Issues in Tourism*, 6(1): 1–22.

    Provides a framework for the analysis of the tourism planning process that holds tourism planning to be primarily a complex and contingent process occurring within and between three locations: the individual organisation, the industry and the state.

6 Tourism planning and policy at the international and supranational level

The concept of the absolute sovereignty of states will have to make concessions as never before in face of today's emerging environmental crisis. There will have to be a high degree of willing subordination of national sovereignty in favour of the common good of all nations.

This new common interest lies in the preservation, for the peoples of the globe and for their future generations, of a world no less habitable than it is today, while at the same time rehabilitating those parts of it that man is making, or has already made, relatively uninhabitable. (Stephen 1991: 185)

Chapter objectives

After reading this chapter you will:

- Have developed working definitions of governance in relation to tourism
- Appreciate some of the key issues with respect to tourism policy planning at the supranational level and their potential influence at the local level
- Understand the relationship between the concepts of hard and soft international law
- Understand the influence of other policy fields, such as international trade and the environment, on tourism policy.

As a result of political and economic globalisation there have been significant shifts in the role of the state in recent years that have affected the way in which tourism is governed and how policy and planning processes are undertaken. Issues that were at one time a local concern, such as the environmental impacts of tourism, are now of international interest and subject to new sets of institutional arrangements which, although being developed at an international or global scale, have an effect on what happens at the local scale. Therefore this chapter will discuss some of the issues associated with the changing nature of governance before examining the international scale of governance with respect to tourism planning and policy.

The changing nature of governance

Arguably one of the most significant dimensions of globalisation has been the transformation of political and regulatory practices. State authority, power and legitimacy have ceased to be bounded on a strict territorial basis, which has been the basis for sovereign governance for most of the past 150 years. Instead, in the condition of postsovereign governance, the governance of key cultural, economic and financial issues is being increasingly handled by the transfer, whether temporary or permanent, of goal-specific authority from nation states to regional or multilateral supranational and international organisations and to the local or subnational state. Under this set of conditions the governance of a number of policy and planning areas is being maintained not just by territorial state-bounded authorities, as in much of the past, 'but rather by a network of flows of information, power and resources from the local to the regional and multilateral levels and the other way around' (Morales-Moreno 2004: 108).

In this context there is therefore the need to examine not only the role of the nation state in tourism but, perhaps more critically, the roles and interactions of international and supranational bodies, private actors such as transnational corporations and non-governmental organisations, and the important role of the local state in both domestic and international policies and issues relating to tourism. These new policy actors along with the regulatory mechanisms of the nation state are contributing to the development of a new multi-layered governance architecture (e.g. Scholte 2000; Hall 2005a) for numerous policy and issue areas including tourism (e.g. see the multi-scaled nature of governance with respect to ecotourism in Figure 5.3).

The term 'governance' has a number of meanings (Rhodes 1996, 1997; Kooiman 2003), and in particular has often come to imply changes in the public sector that minimise the role of formal governmental actors and give a greater role to the private sector and to non-government organisations (Pike *et al.* 2006). For example, Rhodes (1997) adopts a definition of governance which assumes that government has lost its capacity to govern, and that governance is now the product of self-organising, inter-organisational networks. Similarly, Kooiman (1993a: 6) argues that governance has become an interorganisational phenomenon, and that it is best understood through terms such as 'co-managing, co-steering and co-guidance', all implying more cooperative methods for identifying and achieving policy goals. Kooiman (1993b: 258) defines governance as: 'The pattern or structure that emerges in a socio-political system as a "common" result or outcome of the interacting intervention efforts of all involved actors. This pattern cannot be reduced to one actor or group of actors in particular.' Although not denying the importance of decentralisation Peters (1996, 1998) nevertheless emphasises that governance implies 'steering', or the employment of some mechanism(s) of providing coherent direction to society by nation-state governments.

This theme is also picked up by Morales-Moreno (2004: 108–9) who argues that,

> we could define governance as the capacity for steering, shaping, and managing, yet leading the impact of transnational flows and relations in a given issue area, through the inter-connectedness of different polities and their institutions in which power, authority, and legitimacy are shared.

The identification of transnational relations here is significant as there are many issues that are not transnational and are clearly the domain of territorial-based state sovereignty. However, tourism is one area that is marked by substantial transnational flows and relations, although their political and policy significance has often not been fully appreciated (Hall 1994, 2005a).

Governance does not mean the end of state sovereignty. Sovereignty still lies in the hands of nation states who clearly remain the main actors in the international sphere, especially when some states do not fully ascribe to the notion of a multi-levelled polity. States may join supranational and international agreements but they can also leave. In the case of the European Union, which is often used as an example of supranationalism, it may even be argued that the power of the state has been increased rather than eroded as a result of integration since the tendency does appear to be for the supranational European Union to take over from the state those functions the state performs less well under contemporary conditions of globalisation, e.g. regulation of financial markets and international trade (Majone 1996). The notion that the state is finished or is a 'hollow' vessel may therefore be substantially premature (Pike *et al.* 2006). Of course, as Peters (1998) observes, the capacity of states to behave as a unitary actor is sometimes greatly overstated or misinterpreted in the 'state' literature as well, 'but it still appears easier to begin with that more centralised conception and find the exceptions than to begin with a null hypothesis of no order and find any pattern'. However, there is no disputing the tremendous transformation of sovereignty that has occurred and which points to the formation of a multi-levelled polity (Peters and

Pierre 2001) that have a number of implications for tourism which will be examined below and in the following chapters. However, this chapter will look at the significance of new actors and structures in supranational and international relations within the overall development of multi-layered governance architecture.

Tourism and international relations

For a field as international in scope as tourism there are surprisingly few international agreements and regulations that are directly concerned with managing tourism activity. Tourism is a significant component of international relations and diplomatic activity, with the ease of access between countries often being an indirect measure of the degree of positive relations between them. As Derek Hall (1991: 53) observed:

> The numbers, and to a lesser extent nature, of tourist flows can be comprehensively influenced by administrative and bureaucratic controls and impositions. These can cover such areas as visa regulations, currency exchange controls and proscriptions, on tourist movements and activities. In other words, constraints may be imposed before, at and subsequent to the tourist's point of entry.

Despite the existence of international tourist organisations, such as the UN World Tourist Organization, there is little in the way of specific international regulation of tourism services, except for the area of air transport where there are a number of conventions covering landing rights and safety. Arguably such a position reinforces the position of authors who argue that rather than privileging tourism as an industrial category we should be considering tourism as a means of describing all forms of voluntary human mobility (e.g. Coles *et al.* 2004), especially given that governments regulate the movement of 'people' rather than the movement of 'tourists'.

Perhaps more surprisingly given the enthusiasm of such organisations as the UNWTO and the WTTC for the industry and economic benefits of travel and tourism, tourism has also received little attention in international trade agreements and conventions. However, the overall liberalisation of the services area agreed to in the 1993 conclusion to the Uruguay Round of the General Agreement on Tariffs and Trade (GATT) and the subsequent efforts to liberalise trade in services and overseas investment within the General Agreement on Trade in Services have focused more policy attention specifically on tourism and its development. Despite the relative paucity of international agreements related directly to tourism there is a significant institutional framework for tourism policy and planning at the international level consisting of international organisations with direct and indirect interests in tourism, and a range of international laws and agreements related to cognate areas, including such areas as the environment, heritage, trade, labour relations, migration and transport. In addition there has been substantial development of supranational institutional arrangements for tourism that, though not global in scope, create a series of formal sectoral relationships between a number of countries, usually within a regional context.

Yet tourism policy and planning is clearly impacted by a far wider range of policy areas than just tourism, especially within the context of multi-layered governance when decisions at an international level with respect to an area, such as 'heritage' or 'environment', affect 'tourism' at the local or firm level (Figure 6.1). In fact it could be argued that policies for other areas, such as trade or the environment, have a much greater impact on tourism than tourism-specific policies. For example the UNWTO has only a minor advisory role with respect to regulation of tourists and tourism investment and trade while the World Trade Organization clearly has pre-eminence in that policy field. However, at the same time that changes in governance are occurring at the international level so are they also occurring at the regional and local level, what is usually referred to as subnational government or the local state.

Whereas for most of the modern period of international relations the local state had no substantial international role to play, subnational actors are becoming increasingly important in two main ways. First, where the subnational government is a primary actor when they engage directly in international relations, e.g. through

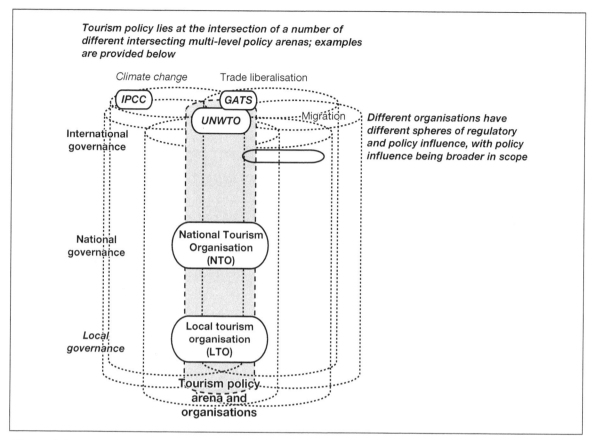

Figure 6.1 Multi-layered tourism governance

Source: Hall, C.M. (2005a) *Tourism: Rethinking the Social Science of Mobility*, Prentice Hall, Harlow. Reproduced with permission.

direct international promotion. Second, where the subnational government is a mediating actor and seeks to affect international relations by attempting to influence the central government in its policy deliberations and actions for the purpose of promoting policies that will be beneficial to local conditions, e.g. trade policy and targeted international tourism promotion. It should be noted that increasingly it is not just provincial/state governments that are playing such an international role, but also cities. For example, in the case of tourism and place competition (Hall 2005a), cities are increasingly lobbying to host international events, such as the Olympics and international expositions, and also competing to be able to attract international investment for tourism infrastructure, such as conference and exhibition centres and sports stadia. The changes in the international relations and the development of multi-level governance are illustrated in Figures 6.2 to 6.6. This chapter will now examine the international level in more depth, while the following chapters discuss the national and local state levels.

Governance architecture and regulation: 'hard' and 'soft' international law

One of the most important components of institutional arrangements for tourism at the international level is that of international law. International law helps proscribe the extent to

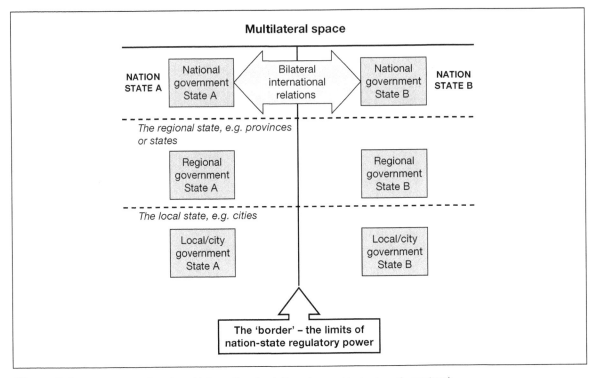

Figure 6.2 The 'traditional' realm of international relations (pre-mid-nineteenth century)

Note: Development of sets of bilateral international relations. Limited formal international relations at the regional and local level.

Source: Hall, C.M. (2005a) *Tourism: Rethinking the Social Science of Mobility,* Prentice Hall, Harlow. Reproduced with permission.

which agreements undertaken between nations at the international level affect domestic arrangements. International law may be described as either 'hard' or 'soft'. Hard international law refers to firm and binding rules of law such as the content of treaties and the provisions of customary international law to which relevant nations are bound as a matter of obligation. Soft law refers to regulatory conduct that, because it is not provided for in a treaty, is not as binding as hard law. Soft law is also often a precursor to hard law. Examples of soft law include recommendations or declarations that are made by international conferences or organisations (Lyster 1985). For example, the Convention on Biological Diversity adopted at the United Nations Conference on Environment and Development (UNCED) in June 1992 in Rio de Janeiro may be regarded as hard international law (see Chapter 2). However, the recommendations of the same conference with

respect to such matters as poverty alleviation were an example of soft international law.

Soft law is particularly important in the area of international conservation and environmental law because treaties and conventions often require parties to attend regular meetings that make recommendations for implementation. For example, the World Heritage Convention has annual meetings of its members to discuss the progress of the implementation of the treaty. Agreed procedures under the Antarctic Treaty, the Man and the Biosphere Programme and the World Conservation Strategy are all examples of soft environmental law that arose out of United Nations conferences and which have affected tourism development, planning and policy in various countries throughout the world.

One of the central issues in the enactment of treaties and conventions is the obligation that the international agreement places on the signatory.

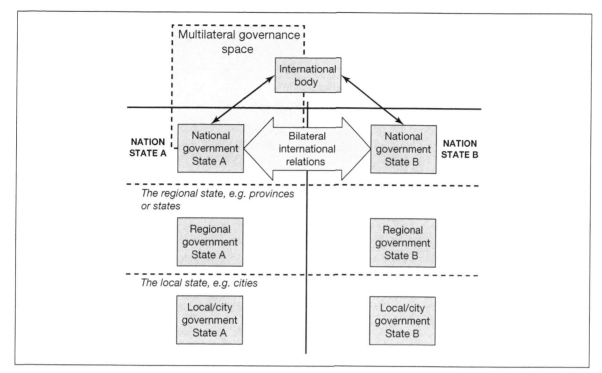

Figure 6.3 Growth in the international scale of governance (late nineteenth century)

Note: Limited growth in multilateral relations, e.g. International Postal Union. Limited formal international relations at the regional and local level.

Source: Hall, C.M. (2005a) *Tourism: Rethinking the Social Science of Mobility,* Prentice Hall, Harlow. Reproduced with permission.

International law cannot be enforced in the same manner as domestic law, because nations can only rarely be compelled to perform their legal obligations, i.e. through the use of force. However, the moral obligations that accrue to members of the international diplomatic community and the norms of international relations are usually sufficient to gain compliance from nations. Soft law fixes norms of behaviour that nations should observe, but which cannot usually be enforced. Nation states usually make every effort to enforce a treaty once they have become party to it, although in some political systems, particularly federal systems, ratification may be subject to domestic political interests that can slow down or even renege on agreements signed by the national government. Nevertheless, it is in the interests of almost every state that order, and not chaos, should be the governing principle of civil society, and if treaties were made and

freely ignored chaos would soon result. Matters of international concern, for example, those covered by soft international law, do not necessarily have to be the subject of international treaties. However, the existence of a treaty, a convention or an agreed declaration may serve to provide evidence for such concern in domestic political life. For example, the World Heritage Convention (discussed below), obliges signatories to protect World Heritage property on their territory (Wall 2004; Fyall and Leask 2006).

In contrast, implementation of the World Conservation Strategy (WCS), a forerunner to UNCED and the foundation for much contemporary thinking on sustainability and global environmental change (see Chapters 2 and 4), was promoted by the IUCN, which issued progress reports on the various requirements and actions. Implementation was not marked by the same set of legal obligations that characterise the

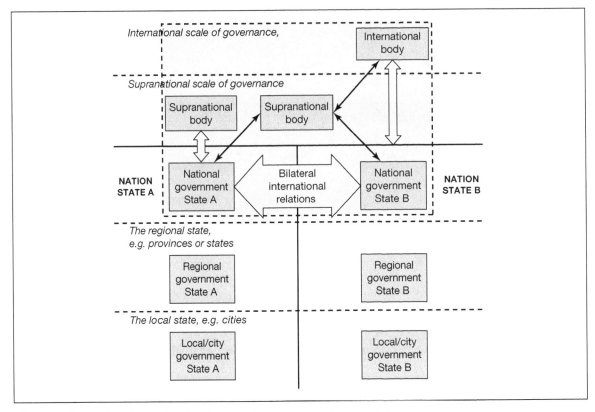

Figure 6.4 Growth in international and supranational bodies (1945–1960s)

Note: Growth in international and supranational bodies, e.g. European Common Market, United Nations, and multilateralism. Increasing but ad hoc development of formal international relations at the regional and local level.

Source: Hall, C.M. (2005a) *Tourism: Rethinking the Social Science of Mobility,* Prentice Hall, Harlow. Reproduced with permission.

World Heritage Convention. Instead, it rested upon the moral urgency that surrounds environmental problems and the priorities created by the strategy within the international community of nations. Hence some nations were far more active with respect to WCS than others. However, the WCS (IUCN 1980: Sec. 15.3) noted that 'perhaps the most important form of international action is the development of international conservation law and of the means to implement it' and specifically noted the 'four main global conservation conventions' (Sec. 15.4):

1. the Convention on Wetlands of International Importance, Especially as Waterfowl Habitat (Wetlands Convention);

2. Convention Concerning the Protection of the World Cultural and Natural Heritage (World Heritage Convention);

3. Convention on International Trade in Endangered Species of Wild Fauna and Flora (CITES); and

4. the Convention on Conservation of Migratory Species of Wild Animals (Migratory Species Convention).

These have since been complemented by the Convention on Biological Diversity and to an extent action with respect to climate change. In this way soft international law may act as a forerunner to the establishment of hard international law.

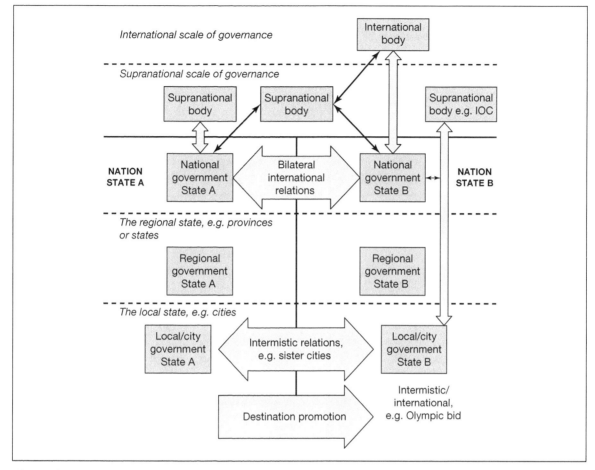

Figure 6.5 Growth in transnational relations at all levels (1970s)

Note: Continued growth in multilateralism and international and supranational bodies, e.g. economic unions. Substantial growth in intermistic relations at the city level with sister city relations, as well as international destination promotion campaigns at the regional and local level

Source: Hall, C.M. (2005a) *Tourism: Rethinking the Social Science of Mobility,* Prentice Hall, Harlow. Reproduced with permission.

Trade

Probably the most significant series of international agreements for tourism policy at the macro level of policy making are those concerned with trade. International tourism trade issues are usually dealt with on either a bilateral or multilateral basis, although unilateral action may be taken by governments when they feel that their interests are being impeded. Many bilateral trade agreements relating to tourism are usually in the area of transport (e.g. air transport agreements) or investment (e.g. protection for foreign investment under most-favoured-nation status),

although increasingly agreements with respect to security and migration, including visa requirements, are also significant. Multilateral negotiations are often conducted under the auspices of international organisations. Three international trade organisations with an interest in tourism are the International Monetary Fund (IMF), the Organization for Economic Cooperation and Development, and the World Trade Organization (WTO). Organisations with a more specific interest in tourism activities include the World Tourism Organization, the International Civil Aviation Organization (ICAO), the International Maritime Organization (IMO), the Customs

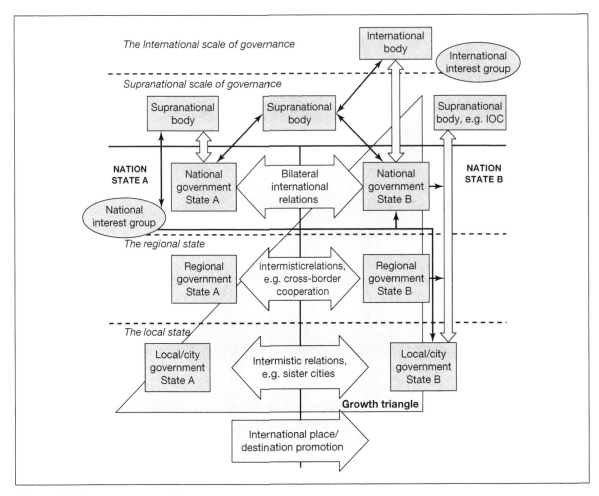

Figure 6.6 Contemporary multi-level governance

Note: Extensive international- and transnational-related networks as a result of continued multilateral growth in policy actors, e.g. environment human rights, and growth in intermistic relations including sister cities and international associations. Development of multi-level regional governance structures to manage economic performance, e.g. growth triangles. Broadening of international destination promotion concept to include place promotion and the 'world city' concept.

Source: Hall, C.M. (2005a) *Tourism: Rethinking the Social Science of Mobility,* Prentice Hall, Harlow. Reproduced with permission.

Cooperation Council (CCC), and regional bodies such as the Tourism Council of the South Pacific (TCSP) and the Tourism Program of the Organization of American States.

At the global level the United Nations Conference on International Travel and Tourism in Rome in 1963 was perhaps the first to highlight the role of tourism in economic development and in improving international relations, with the conference considering 'that it is incumbent on governments to stimulate and coordinate national tourist activities' (1963: 17). Despite the economic significance of tourism to many countries and to the global economy as a whole, the establishment of trade regimes for tourism has not had the high profile of the agricultural or manufacturing sectors. This is most likely because of tourism's position as a service industry and as an 'invisible' export or import in many countries' trade balances. Such a situation has meant that, for many years, tourism was not taken seriously as a priority area for international policy development, particularly in developed countries (Kearney 1992; Hall 1994; Davidson and Maitland 1997; Dredge and Jenkins 2007). However, economic restructuring of traditional industries and the recognition of service industries, including telecommunications and finance, as potential growth poles for economic development and employment purposes in western economies has increased interest in tourism. Indeed, the Uruguay Round of GATT, concluded in December 1993, gave substantial attention to mechanisms to encourage freer trade in the area of services that has since been taken up in the General Agreement on Trade in Services (GATS).

GATS defines four ways (or "modes") to trade services:

1. services supplied from one country to another, such as international telephone calls; officially known as "crossborder supply" (mode 1);
2. consumers or firms making use of a service in another country, such as tourism; officially termed "consumption abroad" (mode 2);
3. a foreign company setting up subsidiaries or branches to provide services in another country, such as foreign banks; officially named "commercial presence" (mode 3);
4. individuals travelling from their own country to supply services in another, such as consultants; officially referred to as "presence of natural persons" (mode 4).

Liberalising trade in these types of services is designed to allow easier movement of companies, capital and people across boundaries and borders. Nevertheless, the place of tourism in GATS' negotiations is at times almost as problematic as the pace at which agreements are reached within the WTO. For example, with respect to the UN World Tourism Organization's proposed annexe of tourism to GATS, the European Community (EC) was the only WTO member to formally submit a reaction to the proposed annexe. Although the EC stated its support for 'the main intentions' of the proposal, it did not explicitly endorse the establishment of a new tourism annexe to GATS. Instead, the EC proposed that the list of sectors intended to be included in the annexe were too

broad, as well as also noting that air transport services were currently excluded from GATS' negotiations, and that some of the issues raised by the sponsors could be better addressed in the WTO's Working Party on Domestic Regulation (WPDR) (Dunlop 2003). Interestingly, Dunlop (2003: 10) also noted that the EC, along with the United States, suggested that sustainable development needed to be considered within the annexe, with the EC stressing 'the importance of access to high-quality environmental services – a key offensive negotiating interest for the EC (and US) in the GATS negotiations', which would have significant impact in a wide range of countries with respect to tourism trade with the EU. In addition, the EC sought to use any annexe to eliminate restrictions on foreign direct investment in tourism.

The organisation that has historically probably focused most on trade liberalisation in the area of tourism services is the Organization for Economic Co-operation and Development based in Paris. Created in 1961, the OECD groups 30 member countries in an organisation that,

> provides governments a setting in which to discuss, develop and perfect economic and social policy. They compare experiences, seek answers to common problems and work to coordinate domestic and international policies that increasingly in today's globalised world must form a web of even practice across nations. (OECD 1999)

OECD countries produce two-thirds of the world's goods and services and account for about 70 per cent of the world's international tourism trade. However, the OECD does not perceive itself as an exclusive club, instead regarding membership as limited only by a country's commitment to a market economy and a pluralistic democracy.

Although the OECD provides economic statistics and forecasts, the latter of which may be particularly influential in affecting investment flows and currency exchange rates, it is as a policy forum that the OECD has had the most significant long-term effect on tourism policy, particularly with respect to international tourist trade liberalisation (Davidson and Maitland 1997) and the enhancement of international tourism trade. Although more recently it has taken an overt interest in tourism and climate change (Agrawala 2007).

As the OECD's website stated at the beginning of 2007, 'The OECD produces internationally agreed instruments, decisions and recommendations to promote rules of the game in areas where multilateral agreement is necessary for individual countries to make progress in a globalised economy' (OECD 2007). At an informal level the policy debate within the OECD leads to 'policy learning' between countries, by which we mean that elements of policies and institutional arrangements in one country are modelled on another country's experiences. This has been particularly important with respect to the organisation of tourism at the national, and even state/provincial level in Australia, Canada and New Zealand, for example. In formal terms policy discussion can lead to the development of formal agreements, e.g. by establishing legally binding codes for free flow of capital and services.

In examining obstacles to trade in international travel and tourism, a number of issues that affect tourist trade can be identified:

- Government attention to tourism is usually focused more on promotion of inbound tourism rather than on a more general approach that deals with reduction or removal of restrictions to human mobility on a multilateral basis.
- Governments have not usually assessed the impact of laws and regulations specifically on tourism, as there are very few tourist or tourism-specific laws.
- Government international trade and diplomatic policies often conflict with, and override, tourism policies. This is particularly the case with respect to security policies in a post-9/11 environment.
- International organisations that focus on trade issues have historically addressed tourism primarily in piecemeal fashion and not with tourism as an integral unit. This is changing with respect to the OECD and GATS, although because of the diffuse nature of tourism in many policy fields substantial

gaps still remain, particularly as new issues arise.
- There is only limited coordination among international organisations on tourism matters.

Obstacles to tourism can also be classified as to whether they constitute tariff or non-tariff barriers. Non-tariff barriers include travel allowance restrictions, restrictions on credit card use, limitations on duty-free allowances, and advance import deposit-like measures (e.g. compulsory deposits prior to travel). Tariff barriers include import-duty measures, airport departures or airport taxes, and subsidies, for example a consumer-subsidy measure such as an official preferential exchange rate for foreign tourists or price concessions. Although tourism tariff barriers may be lowered by specific tourism agreements, tariffs are usually dealt with under broader multilateral negotiations on tariff reductions on trade in goods and services, e.g. the World Trade Organization, or negotiations within a specific trading bloc such as the European Community, the Association of South East Asian Nations (ASEAN) or the North American Free Trade Agreement (NAFTA) between Canada, Mexico and the United States; or through bilateral agreements, e.g. the Closer Economic Relations agreement between Australia and New Zealand (Hall 1994). In addition, attempts to liberalise international trade in tourism services are also encouraged through the action of international organisations such as the UNWTO and the WTTC.

The World Tourism Organization

The UNWTO is the leading international policy organisation in the tourism field, being particularly influential in less developed nations and in the United Nations' system of organisations of which it is a member. In 1998 its membership included 138 countries and territories and over 350 Affiliate Members representing local government, tourism associations, private sector companies and educational institutions. In 2006, the UNWTO's membership comprised 150 countries, seven territories and more than 300 Affiliate Members.

According to the Statutes of the World Tourism Organization:

1. The fundamental aim of the Organization shall be the promotion and development of tourism with a view to contributing to economic development, international understanding, peace, prosperity, and universal respect for, and observance of, human rights and fundamental freedoms for all without distinction as to race, sex, language or religion. The Organization shall take all appropriate action to attain this objective.

2. In pursuing this aim, the Organization shall pay particular attention to the interests of the developing countries in the field of tourism. (UNWTO, 1970, Article 3. The Statutes came into force on 2 January 1975 in accordance with Article 36)

Although a member of the United Nations system its origins predate the establishment of the UN. The World Tourism Organization was originally formed in 1925 as the International Union of Official Travel Publicity Organizations based at The Hague in the Netherlands. After the Second World War it was renamed the International Union of Official Travel Organizations (IUOTO) and moved to Geneva. As international tourism and the corresponding complexity of intergovernmental relations with respect to tourism grew in the 1960s, IOUTO sought to have a stronger role in international tourism and the United Nations system in a similar fashion to the World Health Organization (WHO), the United Nations Educational, Scientific and Cultural Organization (UNESCO) and the International Civil Aviation Organization. In December 1969 the UN General Assembly passed a resolution that recognised such a role, with the resolution being ratified in 1974 by 51 of the nations whose official tourism organisations were members of IUOTO.

In 1975 IUOTO was renamed the World Tourism Organization, with its first General Assembly being held in Madrid, where the Secretariat was also installed in the following year at the invitation of the Spanish government, which provided a building and other financial assistance for the organisation. In 1976 the organisation became an executing agency of the United Nations Development Programme (UNDP) and in 1977 a formal cooperation agreement was signed with the United Nations itself. Although full (national) and affiliate memberships have grown over the years, it is noticeable that a number of OECD member countries, such as Australia, Canada, New Zealand and the United States, were not members of the organisation for many years. In part this is because officials from these countries, while cooperating with the organization, rightly or wrongly do not perceive the organisation as 'providing value for money' and, perhaps, do not have the influence on the direction of the organisation's policies and undertakings they might wish. However, this position has shifted substantially given that in 2003 the UNWTO became a specialised agency of the United Nations.

One of the greatest challenges facing the UNWTO is the generation of funding to finance its activities, which is leading to an increasing focus on partnerships with industry and, possibly, changes in the focus of UNWTO's organisational philosophies. UNWTO is primarily financed by members' contributions. Full Members, open to all sovereign states, pay an annual quota calculated according to the level of economic development and the importance of tourism in each country. Associate Membership is open to territories not responsible for their external relations. Membership requires the prior approval of the government that assumes responsibility for their external relations. Affiliate Members consist of organisations and firms that work in the tourism and travel sectors and which pay an annual fee (€2,000 in early 2007). Affiliate membership requires endorsement by the government of the state in which the headquarters of the applicant is located.

Such is the importance of public–private partnerships that in 1998 the UNWTO announced the composition of a Strategic Group to advise the UNWTO Secretary-General on implementation of an active public–private partnership within UNWTO. The members of the Strategic Group were announced as being, representing the government sector: Brazilian Tourism Board President Caio Luiz de Carvalho; Egyptian

Tourism Minister Mamdouh El Beltagui; Maldives Tourism Minister Ibrahim Hussain Zaki; Honorary UNWTO Secretary-General Antonio Enriquez Savignac; Swiss Tourism Chief Peter Keller; and the Tunisian Tourism Minister Slaheddine Maâoui. Representing the private sector were: Martin Brackenbury, chairman of the UNWTO Business Council and President of the International Federation of Tour Operators; Geoffrey Lipman, President of the World Travel and Tourism Council; Isao Matsuhashi, Chairman of the Japan Travel Bureau and the Japan Association of Travel Agents; Bill Norman, President and CEO of the Travel Industry Association of America; and Stefano Torda, Deputy Secretary-General of confederazione generale del commercio (CONFCOMMERCIO) and formerly tourism director of Italy (WTO 1998e). The composition of the group is interesting as it conveys an appreciation of the networks that exist both within and between the UNWTO and other organisations. These networks now have a formal structure within the UNWTO through the Affiliate Member category.

Affiliate members have the opportunity to participate in UNWTO policy fora and may also be in a better position to enter into partnership arrangements with the UNWTO in development projects. According to the UNWTO (WTO 2007c):

> Affiliate membership in the World Tourism Organization offers a chance to participate in the give and take of the international tourism business at its very highest levels. Members not only benefit from increased exposure and visibility, they gain access to all UNWTO meetings and seminars. They find out about new business opportunities and they have a chance to influence policy makers on issues vital to the positive growth of the tourism industry – issues such as travel advisories, taxation, the Global Code of Ethics, the Tourism Satellite Account and short-term market forecasts.

At the policy level the activities of the UNWTO have been substantial. Although its outputs may be regarded as soft international law their influence is still significant. For example, former UNWTO Secretary-General Antonio Enrìquez Savignac attended the Rio Earth Summit in 1992 and was instrumental in getting tourism included in *Agenda 21* as one of the only industries capable of providing an economic incentive for preservation of the environment (WTO 1999). Although sustainable development has been one focus of WTO policy activity, other areas such as trade liberalisation (WTO 1998a, 1998b), public–private partnerships (WTO 1998c, 1998d) and health and safety have also been important. Examples of such policy measures include the development of:

- Tourism Bill of Rights and Tourist Code (1985, resolution of Sofia conference)
- Recommended Measures for Safety
- Creating Tourism Opportunities for Handicapped People
- Health Information and Formalities in International Travel
- WTO Statement on the Prevention of Organized Sex Tourism
- The Manila Declaration on World Tourism (1980)
- The Hague Declaration on Tourism (declaration of the Inter-Parliamentary Conference on Tourism, jointly organised with the Inter-Parliamentary Union) (1989)
- The Bali Declaration on Tourism (1996)
- Global Code of Ethics for Tourism (1999)
- International Year of Ecotourism (2002)
- Tourism 2020 Vision.

Soft law initiatives such as the Manila Declaration on World Tourism in 1980 had a considerable impact on the tourism policy process in some countries as it helped redefine the concept of tourism impacts to include the sociocultural dimension (Davidson and Maitland 1997). Similarly, the Hague Declaration on Tourism, which built on the Brundtland Commission's call for 'sustainable development', helped establish sustainable tourism as a national and regional policy concern in some member countries (Davidson and Maitland 1997).

In addition to its policy function, the WTO also has substantial influence on national and regional tourism development and plays an important role as a land-use and tourist resource planner. This function is significant not only for its direct impact on tourism development, particularly in developing countries, but also because it illustrates the manner in which the activities of international bodies operate at lower scales of the tourism policy and planning process all the way through to the regional and local level, affecting various stakeholders at all these levels. The UNWTO acts as an executing agency of the United Nations Development Programme (UNDP), while other planning and development activities are secured through consultancies and financing from other national and international agencies. According to the WTO (1999), US$4.4 million worth of development activities was undertaken in 42 countries in the operating period 1996–97. In 2001–02 the figure was 70 countries with a value of US$2.5 million (World Tourism Organization 2007a). Examples of UNWTO planning and development projects include:

- strategy for environmentally sustainable development of India's Andaman Islands (1996);
- tourism master plan in Ghana (1996);
- reconstruction and development plan in Lebanon (1997);
- action plan for sustainable tourism development in Uzbekistan (1997);
- Tourism Master Plan for Pakistan (2001);
- Tourism Master Plans for eight Chinese provinces (2000–2002);
- development of national parks in Rwanda (1999);
- tourism development strategy for Moldova (1999);
- integrated development programme for Palestinian Authority (2000).

Although the UNWTO has a significant role to play in tourism at the international level, the growth in international tourism has also led to the development of international organisations with interests in tourism, particularly at the supranational level. Private sector organisations such as the WTTC, the OECD and supranational organisations such as the EC and the Organization of American States are all competing for policy ascendancy in influencing international tourism policy debate and the subsequent development of

international agreements on tourism matters. Substantial policy shifts have occurred in recent years, including within the UNWTO, where greater emphasis has been given to liberalisation of trade and encouragement of further development. The observations of Burns in 1994 still apply to the present day:

> it is clear . . . that WTO is actively promoting the expansion of tourism at a global level. WTO survives not so much through its membership fees (governments and affiliates) but through spin-off activities such as consulting and project management. It therefore actually needs more tourism! (in Davidson and Maitland 1997: 119)

A sustainable UNWTO therefore requires tourism to continue to exist and grow. That the UNWTO perceives itself as assuming the leadership role in world tourism is beyond doubt. As the UNWTO Secretary-General, Francesco Frangialli, stated, 'In the absence of the European Union's capacity to make itself felt in the tourism sphere, the World Tourism Organization remains today the principal body concerned with tourism cooperation between European countries' (WTO 1998f). With the Secretary-General adding that it was unfortunate that the world's two most important tourist areas, Europe and the United States, lack overall strategies and vision for tourism development (WTO 1998f). Nevertheless, both Europe and the Americas have significant supranational bodies developing strategies for tourism development.

The development of international conservation and environmental law

The institutional arrangements surrounding conservation and the environment clearly have substantial impact on tourism planning and development. It is not as easy to define the precise boundaries of environmental law as it is to define a traditional area such as criminal law. Since the Second World War environmental law has expanded as concerns over environmental quality have arisen not only on a domestic level

6.1 TOURISM PLANNING INSIGHT

The transboundary air pollution calendar of East Asia

May–October (Singapore and Malaysia): south-west monsoon winds blow sulphur dioxide, nitrogen dioxide and particulate-laden smoke from Indonesia over downwind neighbours Singapore and Malaysia.

March–May (North and South Korea, Japan): spring sandstorms from the Gobi and its desertified fringes carry yellow dust through northern China (including Beijing) across North and South Korea to Japan. In 2006 Beijing was hit by 17 spring sandstorms.

November–March (North Asia): surge in air pollution particulates as a result of increased burning at coal-fired power plants to provide winter heating.

Transboundary environmental problems can be a significant source of international dispute and can affect tourism. Within national jurisdictions the cost of solving a pollution problem is usually borne by the polluter under the 'polluter pays' principle or government will step in to regulate offending polluters. However, transboundary pollution can be much more difficult to manage as it can be perceived as one country interfering in the affairs of another and as a means of imposing costs on production. The transfer of blame is also commonplace. For example, China blames Hong Kong companies for polluting the Hong Kong Special Autonomous Region and Guandong province because they own some of the polluting factories in the province. Similarly, Indonesia argues that Singaporean and Malaysian companies own the oil palm and timber plantations where the fires used as part of the land clearance are causng the smoke.

Relevant international agreements may exist. For example, Malaysia and Singapore are parties to the 2002 ASEAN haze pact, but even though Indonesia is a member of ASEAN it has not signed the pact, thus limiting Malaysia's and Singapore's legal capacities to encourage the Indonesian government to act. Furthermore, even though such forest fires, along with emissions from China's coal-fired power stations, are substantial contributors of greenhouse gas emissions under the Kyoto Protocol, developing countries such as Indonesia and China were excluded from the first (2008–2012) round of emissions cuts. The situation in East Asia is therefore potentially only going to get worse for some tourism destinations, as well as the people who live there, before it gets better.

See: Singapore Institute of International Affairs Haze Watch: http://www.siiaonline.org/hazewatch. A web-archive feature to provide public access and awareness building for the Institute's advocacy/research activities and resources related to ongoing transboundary haze prevention efforts in the region.

---

but also in the international sphere. Ecological processes do not recognise legal boundaries. Acid rain, the ozone layer, the greenhouse effect, sea level rise and the Chernobyl disaster are all testimony to the transnational basis of environmental problems. Issues of pollution, wildlife protection, conservation of biodiversity and the preservation of cultural and natural heritage have become international in scope. In East Asia for example there are a number of transboundary air pollution issues that affect tourism as well as the day-to-day quality of life of citizens (see Tourism planning insight above).

Environmental law may be defined as:

any regulation which affects the natural environment *per se;* or which declares the right of any person to take action to develop or protect it; or which might affect the scenic, historical, artistic or cultural beauty or appreciation of man's efforts to harmonize the built and natural environments. (Bates 1983: 2)

Environmental law may be broadly categorised as having two components: 'protective' and 'exploitative'. 'Protective' rules protect the natural environment from human activity and conserve the built and cultural environments, while 'exploitative' rules control the disposition of natural resources and facilitate development. Legislation may combine both components, but conceptually it may be useful to separate them.

Although the setting aside of areas (such as national parks, wilderness areas and reserves) that are also significant tourist attractions for the protection of species and biodiversity is an important part of international strategies for sustainable development, such a protective component is not new at the international level. For example, the Convention for the Preservation of Wild Animals, Birds and Fish in Africa was signed in London in May 1900. The first convention to refer to the preservation of wilderness areas was the 1940 Convention on Nature Protection and Wildlife Preservation in the Western Hemisphere, which was restricted to members of the Organization of American States (formerly the Pan American Union). This Convention defines in Article 1(4) the expression 'Strict Wilderness Reserve': 'A region under public control characterized by primitive conditions of flora, fauna, transportation and habitation wherein there is no provision for the passage of motorized transportation and all commercial developments are excluded.' This definition is complemented by Article 4, which states: 'The contracting governments agree to maintain the strict wilderness reserves inviolate as far as practicable except for duly authorized scientific investigations or government inspection or such uses as are consistent with the purposes for which the area was established.'

As Lyster (1985: 96) commented, the Convention 'was a visionary instrument, well ahead of its time in terms of the concepts it espouses'. It preceded the United States Wilderness Act by some 24 years. Its great weakness was that it did not establish an administrative structure to implement its terms. This may be compared with the World Heritage Convention, which we shall examine below, which has a World Heritage Bureau and a mechanism with which to implement its terms. Nevertheless, the objectives of the Western Hemisphere Convention set an important precedent in the field of international conservation and environment agreements. The Convention's preamble states that it is the desire of the parties to:

> protect and preserve in their natural habitat representatives of all species and genera of native flora and fauna, including migratory birds, in sufficient numbers and over areas extensive enough to assure them from becoming extinct through any agency within man's control.
> . . . protect and preserve scenery of extraordinary beauty, unusual and striking geologic formations, regions and natural objects of aesthetic, historic or scientific value, and areas characterized by primitive conditions in those cases covered by this Convention. (World Heritage Convention 1981)

These goals were to be achieved through the establishment of national parks, reserves, nature monuments and strict wilderness reserves. Although the Convention has become something of a 'sleeping treaty' (Lyster 1985: 111), in terms of its implementation throughout much of the Americas, it still remains a significant agreement in international conservation. The precedent established by the Convention has also had implications in domestic disputes surrounding the preservation of wilderness areas. For example, Guilbert (1973, in Coggins and Wilkinson 1981: 785) argued that the convention places an obligation on the United States to keep wilderness areas inviolate. However, 'no court has yet accepted or even seriously considered Mr Guilbert's unique thesis' (Coggins and Wilkinson 1981: 787). In Australia, the Convention was referred to in the Franklin Dam case (Coper 1983) in the High Court in establishing the degree of international concern surrounding the preservation of the world's heritage. Therefore international institutional arrangements, such as those of conservation law and regulation, can substantially influence domestic conservation policies from the national through to the local level, an issue discussed with respect to the implementation of the World Heritage Convention.

The World Heritage Convention

The philosophy behind the Convention is straightforward: there are some parts of the world's natural and cultural heritage which are so unique and scientifically important to the world as a whole that their conservation and protection for present and future generations is not only a matter of concern for individual nations but for the international community as a whole (Slatyer 1983: 138).

World Heritage Sites are contemporary tourism magnets and national icons that continue to influence present values. They are treasures in the fullest and deepest sense. They must be managed in such a way that they are preserved for future generations and at the same time presently made accessible to the public for its education and enjoyment. Finding the proper balance between these two demands is the difficult and important task of World Heritage Site managers (ICOMOS 1993: 1).

The Convention for the Protection of the World's Cultural and Natural Heritage (WHC), to give it its full name, was adopted by a UNESCO Conference on 16 November 1972. The Convention came into force in December 1975, when 20 nations ratified it. The Convention is 'an innovative legal instrument' (Slatyer 1984: 734), designed to enable nations to cooperate in the protection of cultural and natural sites of outstanding value to humanity. 'The Convention provides a permanent legal, administrative and financial framework for international co-operation for the safe guarding of the cultural and natural heritage of mankind' (Australian Heritage Commission 1983: 5.1) and may be regarded as one of the pinnacles of world conservation (Fyall and Leask 2006).

The signatories commit themselves to assist in the identification, protection, conservation and preservation of World Heritage properties. They undertake to refrain from 'any deliberate measure which might damage directly or indirectly' cultural or natural heritage (Art. 6(3)), and to 'take appropriate legal, scientific, technical, administrative and financial measures necessary for [its] identification, protection, conservation, presentation and rehabilitation' (Art. 5d).

The Convention is administered by the Intergovernmental Committee for the Protection of

Plate 6.1 Franklin Dam site, Tasmania, Australia. Australia's accession to the World Heritage Convention provided the necessary legal basis to stop the dam from being built in 1983 and reducing the high wilderness qualities of the region. The case was an important precedent with respect to the interpretation of obligations under international heritage law.

the World Cultural and Natural Heritage, commonly referred to as the World Heritage Committee, which is composed of 21 states elected at a general assembly of State Parties to the Convention every two years. The committee is the key policy and decision-making body. It is responsible for all decisions pertaining to nominations to the World Heritage List and the World Heritage in Danger List, and to requests for assistance under the World Heritage Fund. As the operational guidelines for the implementation of the Convention noted, the committee has three essential functions:

(i) to identify, on the basis of nominations submitted by State Parties, cultural and natural properties of outstanding universal value which are to be protected under the Convention and to list those properties on the 'World Heritage List';

(ii) to decide which properties included in the World Heritage List are to be inscribed on the 'List of World Heritage in Danger';

(iii) to determine in what way and under what conditions the resources in the World Heritage Fund can most advantageously be used to assist State Parties, as far as possible, in the protection of their properties of outstanding universal value (World Heritage Committee 1984: 3).

The committee elects a bureau that is responsible for detailed examination of new nominations and requests for funding. The bureau consists of a chairperson, a rapporteur and five vice-chairpersons elected from World Heritage Committee membership. The committee and the bureau receive technical advice for 'cultural' sites from the International Council for Monuments and Sites (ICOMOS) and the International Center for Conservation in Rome (ICCROM), while for 'natural' properties the advisory body is the International Union for Conservation of Nature and Natural Resources (IUCN). UNESCO provides a secretariat to help implement the decisions of the committee. A World Heritage Fund has also been established to provide financial and technical assistance to those nations that otherwise would not be in a position to fulfil their obligations under the Convention.

All signatories to the Convention are invited to identify and submit nominations of outstanding universal value to the World Cultural and Natural Heritage List. This is a 'select list of the most outstanding' cultural and natural properties 'from an international viewpoint' (World Heritage Committee 1984: 4). Cultural property nominated to the World Heritage List (WHL) should:

(i) represent a masterpiece of human creative genius; or

(ii) exhibit an important interchange of human values, over a span of time or within a cultural area of the world, on developments in architecture or technology, monumental arts, town-planning or landscape design; or

(iii) bear a unique or at least exceptional testimony to a cultural tradition or to a civilization which is living or which has disappeared; or

(iv) be an outstanding example of a type of building or architectural or technological ensemble or landscape which illustrates (a) significant stage(s) in human history; or

(v) be an outstanding example of a traditional human settlement or land-use which is representative of a culture (or cultures), especially when it has become vulnerable under the impact of irreversible change; or

(vi) be directly or tangibly associated with events or living traditions, with ideas, or with beliefs, with artistic and literary works of outstanding universal significance (the Committee considers that this criterion should justify inclusion in the List only in exceptional circumstances and in conjunction with other criteria cultural or natural). (UNESCO 1999: Sec. 24)

In addition cultural sites have to meet the test of authenticity in design, material, workmanship or setting and in the case of cultural landscapes their distinctive character and components and have adequate legal and/or contractual and/or traditional protection and management mechanisms to ensure the conservation of the nominated cultural properties or cultural landscapes. Natural property nominated to the WHL should:

(i) be outstanding examples representing major stages of earth's history, including the record of life, significant on-going geological processes in the development of land forms, or significant geomorphic or physiographic features; or

(ii) be outstanding examples representing significant on-going ecological and biological processes in the evolution and development of terrestrial, fresh water, coastal and marine ecosystems and communities of plants and animals; or

(iii) contain superlative natural phenomena or areas of exceptional natural beauty and aesthetic importance; or

(iv) contain the most important and significant natural habitats for in-situ conservation of biological diversity, including those containing threatened species of outstanding universal value from the point of view of science or conservation. (UNESCO 1999: Sec. 44)

Nominations need to provide a detailed account of the characteristics of each site (World Heritage Committee 1984). Each nomination must be endorsed by the national government, and be signed by the government authority responsible for the implementation of the convention. Following endorsement, the nomination is sent to the UNESCO Secretariat via the UNESCO National Commission of the nominating signatory. The Secretariat passes nominations for cultural properties to ICOMOS or ICCROM and for natural properties to IUCN. These bodies rigorously analyse the nomination to determine whether the property concerned meets the World Heritage criteria and is of outstanding universal value. The World Heritage Bureau, acting upon the advice of ICOMOS, ICCROM or the IUCN, can make three types of recommendations to the World Heritage Committee. Nominations may be accepted, rejected or deferred until further information is available.

The commitment of the World Heritage Committee to ensure that the WHL retains the criterion of universal significance in the assessment of nominations is indicated in its willingness to reject or defer unsuitable nominations. The acceptance of nominations to the list which are clearly not of World Heritage standard is regarded as devaluing the purpose of the Convention and the protection that it provides for the world's cultural and natural heritage. Through the international and national attention focused on the nomination process, 'the inclusion of a property on the World Heritage List should give added protection to the site' (Slatyer 1983: 142). In addition to the prestige attached to a World Heritage site, a degree of protection under international law, and a possible increase in the attraction of the site as a tourism destination may be expected. Yet, the WHL is not necessarily unchanging.

Properties that have been degraded through either human or natural causes may be deleted from the WHL and placed on the World Heritage in Danger List. It is hoped that the prospect of a site being placed on the latter list will focus enough attention to save it before the 'symbolic fate' of deregistration occurs. Furthermore, the World Heritage Committee is constantly seeking

Table 6.1 World Heritage List sites by status, 1998–2006

Category	Number of sites		Percentage of sites (%)	
	1998	2006	1998	2006
Cultural	445	644	76.5	77.6
Natural	117	162	20.1	19.5
Mixed	20	24	3.4	2.9
Total	582	830	100	100

Source: UNESCO.

to update the procedures by which nominations are reviewed in order to ensure that nominated properties fit the criteria for World Heritage listing.

The sites of the WHL can be classified into cultural, natural or mixed sites depending on which criteria they meet. Table 6.1 reports the numbers and percentages of cultural, natural and mixed heritage sites on the WHL as of December 1998 and 2006. Cultural listings far outnumber natural sites, in spite of the fact that the Operational Guidelines recommend a balance between the two categories. However, according to von Droste (1995), Director of the World Heritage Centre and editor of the *World Heritage Newsletter,* despite the continuous expansion of properties on the WHL each year it does still not fully reflect the world's cultural and natural diversity. Pocock (1997) is also critical of the greater attention given in the Operational Guidelines to the inscription criteria for cultural properties compared to natural properties. The Committee has recommended that measures be taken to improve the balance between cultural and natural heritage. One way they hope to achieve this is by offering assistance in the preparation of nominations of types of properties under-represented in the WHL. There have been a number of suggestions as to why the existing imbalance has occurred, including the fact that there are few parts of the natural world untouched or influenced by humankind in some

Plate 6.2 Mount Cook National Park, New Zealand. The park is part of the South Westland World Heritage Area and is a major attraction for visitors interested in natural history and the environment.

way, and nominations for often larger natural areas can be associated with controversy and opposed at a local level for commercial and economic reasons. For example, the nomination of Australia's Wet Tropics World Heritage area resulted in conflict between environmentalists and professional scientists with logging companies and the Queensland government (Hall 1992a, 2006d).

It has been argued that the nomination process and the additional prestige gained by receiving World Heritage status serves to increase the attraction of a site as a potential tourist destination for both domestic and international tourists (Fyall and Leask 2006). Given the qualities possessed by World Heritage sites it is not surprising that they are popular tourist attractions and destinations. For example, Shackley observes that, 'such sites are magnets for visitors and the enrolment of a new property on the World Heritage List, with the concomitant publicity, is virtually a guarantee that visitor numbers will increase' (Shackley 1998, Preface). Similarly, Cook (1990 in Drost 1996: 481) observes, 'It appears that designation does increase

visibility through public information generated by the World Heritage Committee, the host State and the private sector.' However, Ashworth and Tunbridge (1990) take a more jaundiced view, noting, 'The coveted UNESCO designation of World Heritage Site is used for national aggrandizement and commercial advantage within the international competition for tourists, more often than it is a celebration of an international identity.' Indeed, empirical research suggests that the causal link between World Heritage listing and increased visitation over and above existing tourism trends is tenuous (Hall and Piggin 2001; Buckley 2002).

Despite a lack of empirical evidence of a causal relationship between World Heritage listing and tourism growth, tourism is still perceived as a means to justify listing to some stakeholders who might otherwise be opposed and also as a way to help ensure the conservation of World Heritage sites through revenue generation, awareness raising and, possibly, improved management and planning practices (Harrison and Hitchcock 2005; Fyall and Leask 2006). The philosophy underlying the Convention also has implications

Plate 6.3 Cliff Palace World Heritage Site, Mesa Verde National Park, Colorado, USA.

unique, while also reinforcing ideas of authenticity. In addition, the reservation process clearly identifies the boundaries of any listing which can then correspond to the space that tourists may seek to occupy.

The WHC therefore clearly has implications for tourism. To reiterate the theme picked up earlier in the chapter – decisions and actions taken at the international level clearly have the capacity to reverberate through the national, regional and local levels in a manner that has substantial implications for tourism planning and policy. Hales (1984) in discussing the status and direction of the WHC noted that 'Conventions, like babies, must crawl before they can walk, and walk before they can run. This Convention is both precocious and far from recognizing its potential.' McMichael and Gare (1984: 262) noted that international conventions, such as World Heritage, 'will be used to give status, and therefore additional protection, to important protected areas'. While increased protection is a possibility created, the relationship between World Heritage listing and tourism may also create substantial tension between local and global policy goals and institutions:

> Many World Heritage Sites are in countries that simply do not have the money or the expertise to meet international conservation standards. Even when there is a national awareness, financial support for even minimal conservation is 15 or 20 years away. There are too many other needs on the national agenda. These countries need an interim plan that will initiate basic conservation steps. They need to match this plan with a tourism plan that promotes their World Heritage Site as magnets for only limited tourism. Such a plan of action would help conserve the sites for future generations, allow access and appreciation among the present generations. Such a plan of action would help generate income for the national economy without endangering the national patrimony. In the future, World Heritage Sites may become the high-priced, hard-to-get-into attractions in the tourism world. (ICOMOS 1993: 3–4)

However, a difficult balancing act will need to be undertaken:

> The World Heritage convention requires that nations not only protect, conserve and rehabilitate World Heritage Sites; it also requires that these sites

with respect to tourism. The Convention states that a site is to remain open to visitors so that heritage identities can be strengthened in the public mind. The obligation to promote World Heritage sites is complemented by an obligation to protect these sites; however, promotion often threatens the site protection. Under the Convention, protection should take precedence over promotion, as is indicated in the full title of the Convention (Drost 1996). Nevertheless, World Heritage sites offer many practical advantages to the tourism industry as they possess many of the features that create a successful tourism attraction. World Heritage listing offers a clear and recognisable brand with an international profile (Buckley 2002; Hall and Piggin 2002). The listing processes identifies the characteristics that makes the site

Plate 6.4 Acropolis, Athens, Greece. Accorded World Heritage status, the Acropolis is under substantial pressures from both visitor impact and the affects of air pollution.

Plate 6.5 Smelter turned museum, Roros, Norway. This award winning museum interprets the industrial heritage of the World Heritage site to visitors.

be given a function in the life of the community. The point is not to place these treasures under lock and key but to make them safely part of the fabric of life. There is a dilemma here that re-emphasises the need for balance: old sites, residents, new numbers of visitors. (ICOMOS 1993: 4)

The tension between the global and the local, between different conceptions of use and value, operating within the context of the Convention has probably been seen more in federal systems, such as Australia and Canada, which accentuates the political goals of different levels of governance, than anywhere else. Indeed, few arrangements of international and domestic law can have been so misunderstood and distorted as the operation of the WHC in Australia in the 1980s (e.g. Hall 1992a; 2006d). 'Insofar as calculation is possible, Australia has probably had more litigation and political challenges to the Convention than all other states party to the Convention combined' (Suter 1991: 4). In commenting on the 1983 Franklin Dam case, Davis (1984: 186) noted that it was

> apparent that many politicians and the lay public had a rather confused view of what the World Heritage Convention entailed and how the nomination procedure operated. In particular few people appeared to know what Australian institutions were involved in World Heritage activities and how such bodies related to UNESCO in Paris.

Nevertheless, it can be noted that similar controversy occurred in New Zealand in the case of the nomination of South Westland to the WHL with respect to perceptions that local land was going to be under UNESCO control and concerns over the lack of recognition of local cultural values (Hall and Piggin 2002).

The local impact of World Heritage listing is in fact substantial – it proscribes appropriate and inappropriate activities in terms of maintenance of the integrity of the World Heritage values, it requires the conduct of a management plan while, with respect to natural values, section 44(b)(vi) of the Operational Guidelines states that the site 'should have adequate long-term legislative, regulatory or institutional protection. The boundaries should include sufficient areas

immediately adjacent to the area of outstanding universal value in order to protect the site's heritage values from direct effects of human encroachment and impacts of resource use outside of the nominated area' (UNESCO 1999). Nevertheless, as already noted above, international law cannot be enforced in the same manner as domestic law, because nations can only rarely be compelled to perform their legal obligations. Instead, the moral obligations that accrue to members of the international community and the norms of international relations are usually sufficient to gain compliance in most areas of international law. Unfortunately, this may mean that with respect to the implementation of international agreements, whether they be hard or soft international law, there may be substantial differences as to how different countries with different sets of institutional arrangements proceed with implementation, an issue that we will return to in Chapter 10.

The case of the World Heritage Convention serves to demonstrate that international agreements, policies and laws act both to directly affect local land use as well as circumscribe the planning and policy processes that are occurring at the local level (see also Chapter 10). Many hard international laws, as with a number of global conservation conventions, typically have spatial outcomes which are clearly discernible, e.g. the creation or recognition of a reserve such as a national park, while others are not so immediately visible, such as those which affect business practice. Nevertheless, they are real, they exist and they may have enormous implications for tourism planning and policy. The next section will look at some of these connections at the supranational level.

The supranational scale

The scope of supranational tourism policy and planning has grown substantially in recent years (Timothy 2003; Hall 2005a). The increased internationalisation of the world's economy and policy making has led to the development of regional trade alliances and groupings, e.g. NAFTA and APEC, while international groupings have developed in all manner of human affairs. Indeed one of the outcomes of economic globalisation has been not only increased awareness of the importance of the local but also increased attention to regional groupings of nations within which problems, which are now recognised as being international in scope (e.g. economic development, pollution, natural resource management), can be addressed. Tourism has also been strongly influenced by the development of such international bodies. However, the scope of such organisations is substantial, ranging from government membership only (e.g. ASEAN) through to public–private partnerships, e.g. Baltic Sea Tourism Commission, and fully international non-government organisations, e.g. ECPAT (also operating as Childwise in some jurisdictions). Furthermore, the goals of supranational organisations may range from being solely concerned with tourism, e.g. the Pacific Asia Tourism Association, through to a policy portfolio of which tourism is only a small part, e.g. the European Union. Nevertheless, the actions of such organisations may be extremely significant in tourism policy and planning terms. While policy and planning occurs at the supranational level, the effects of policy decisions will often be enacted at the local level, leading to significant outcomes for the processes of tourism development and for local communities. This section will discuss two examples of tourism within supranational organisations, the European Union and the Organization of American States.

The European Union

The European Union is frequently regarded as the most developed form of supranational organisation in the world today (Held *et al.* 1999). Tourism is an area of great economic significance to the European Union. In 2005 about 900 million holiday trips, almost evenly distributed between short (one to three nights) and long holidays (four and more nights) were made by EU tourists. Tourism expenditure and receipts were nearly in balance for the EU as a whole. Expenditure stood at €235.6 billion, while receipts

from tourism stood at €232.6 billion (Eurostat 2007). Although Europe's market share, in terms of both arrivals and revenue, of international tourism is tending to diminish in relation to other world regions, notably the Asia-Pacific region, Europe is still a major force in world tourism, with increased ease of travel between the EU member countries encouraging greater integration and therefore ongoing tourism growth. In 2005, 87.5 per cent of all nights spent in collective accommodation were spent by either residents of the country (59.1 per cent) or by residents of other EU member states (28.4 per cent) (Eurostat 2007). According to the European Commission tourism in Europe creates more than 4 per cent of the EU's GDP, with about 2 million enterprises employing about 4 per cent of the total labour force, representing approximately 8 million jobs. 'When the links to other sectors are taken into account, the contribution of tourism to GDP is estimated to be around 11% and it provides employment to more than 12% of the labour force (24 million jobs)' (Commission of the European Communities 2006: 2).

Although the European Parliament has been relatively slow in establishing policies for tourism relative to other economic, social and environmental areas of interest, partly as a result of not being included in considerations of the first European Treaties, the extent of EU involvement in tourism is not as insubstantial as may be suggested by the comments of the UNWTO Secretary-General quoted earlier in this chapter. As HOTREC, the organisation that represents hotels, restaurants and cafés in Europe, has argued with respect to discussions of a new European Treaty since the mid-1990s,

> the presence or not of the word tourism in the Treaties has had no influence whatsoever on the applicability to the sector of measures on VAT, protection of the consumer, protection of the environment and social affairs, which are based on specific articles of the Treaties relating to these issues. (2003: 1)

Indeed, the EU has a substantial impact on tourism development in Europe if not by direct virtue of tourism-specific policies then by a wide range of other measures, with HOTREC identifying over 250 EU measures that directly impact on the EU's hospitality and tourism industry (Corbalan *et al.* 2005). These measures have been developed in a number of Directorates-General (DG) of the European Commission, including Agriculture (farm and rural tourism), Environment (impact assessment, climate), Transport (Single European Sky) and Enterprise (entrepreneurship and innovation policy) among others (Corbalan *et al.* 2005).

The responsibility for tourism policy in the European Commission lies with the Tourism Unit of DG Enterprise. The European Parliament has a Committee for Tourism and Transport. There is also a European Parliament intergroup for tourism, which brings together members of the European Parliament who share an interest in tourism issues.

Tourism has become a significant part of EU planning and policies for a number of reasons (Commission of the European Communities 2006):

* Tourism is now recognised as an important economic activity (D. Hall 2004).
* The transnational character of some tourism businesses has necessitated the development of a European-wide policy framework.
* The cultural impacts of tourism have raised concerns over the retention of cultural identity while at the same time attempting to promote the concept of Europe.
* The movement of pollution across national boundaries and the possible movement of capital to locate where environmental standards and costs are lowest. Indeed the environmental dimensions of tourism have developed as a major EU concern in the tourism area (European Commission 1995; Bramwell *et al.* 1996; Church *et al.* 2000).
* Concerns over the social dimensions of poverty and unemployment, particularly in disadvantaged regions, give impetus to the use of tourism as a tool for employment generation and economic development at a regional level (Jenkins *et al.* 1998; D. Hall 2004; D. Hall *et al.* 2006).

Nevertheless, as early as the early 1980s, the European Parliament and the Council had adopted resolutions concerning the development of a policy for tourism. However, the EU's first tangible action in favour of tourism was the Council Decision of 21 December 1988 declaring 1990 the 'European Year of Tourism' (EYT). The objective of the EYT was to exploit the integrating role of tourism in the creation of a citizens' Europe and to stress the economic and social importance of the tourism sector (EU 1998: Sec. 8).

In 1994 the European Court of Auditors based in Luxembourg carried out a horizontal audit of tourist policy and the promotion of tourism. On the occasion of its first on-the-spot audit at the Commission, the Court found that there had been serious irregularities, leading to the suspension of two members of DG XXIII's staff (DG XXIII is responsible for enterprise, trade, tourism and social economy policy), and that the Commission had not released any information on this matter. However, the report by the Court (EU 1998) provides a valuable account of EU tourism, particularly with respect to expenditure and problems of coordination.

In 2006 the Commission of the European Communities released a communication with respect to a renewed European tourism policy, the main aim of which is 'to improve the competitiveness of the European tourism industry and create more and better jobs through the sustainable growth of tourism in Europe and globally' (4). The extent to which tourism is a multi-level governance field within the European Union can be seen by the Commission's statement 'Partnerships amongst all involved stakeholders are . . . necessary at every level of the decision-making process related to tourism. Partnerships must be a central component of action at all levels (European, national, regional and local; public and private)' (2006: 4).

EU tourism measures can be divided into direct measures that are provided for in the general budget and indirect measures in which tourism plays an instrumental role towards the realisation of other objectives. However, in the late

1990s it was estimated that the financial volume of the direct measures represents less than 1 per cent of total EU expenditure on tourism (EU 1998). The importance of tourism in relation to indirect expenditure is primarily reflected in EU funds allocated to implement regional development and social cohesion policies (Commission of the European Communities 2006). As the EU has enlarged so the extent of regional disparities within the Community has also expanded. In response to problems of regional disparity the EU established a series of 'structural' funds, e.g. the European Regional Development Fund (ERDF), the Cohesion Fund and Community Support Frameworks, many of which have been utilised for tourism development purposes (Commission of the European Communities 2006). Many of the programmes conducted under the structural funds arrangements provide a direct link from the EU to the local level of governance. In addition there is direct European Investment Bank (EIB) financing (individual loans and loans from global loans) in the tourism and leisure field (D. Hall *et al.* 2006).

Under the EU monies are being reallocated for development purposes as a result of policies that are being pursued at the supranational level and which, in turn, interact with policy settings at the national and regional level. Tourism planning at the local level in the EU member states is therefore clearly embedded within institutional arrangements and interests at higher levels. Indeed the power to act is also constrained by the authority that lies not only at the national and regional level, but also at the supranational level of the EU. To many people living in the EU area such a statement may be regarded as reasonably self-evident given the very visible range of EU regulations and development programmes. However, supranational institutions also play an important role in areas where the supranational organisation does not have the degree of legislative power accorded to it by member states, which is the case for the EU. The next section will look at the role that the Organization of American States plays in tourism planning and policy in the Americas.

The Organization of American States and tourism planning and policy

The American parallel to the European Union is the Organization of American States (OAS). The OAS is the world's oldest regional organisation, dating back to the First International Conference of American States held in Washington, DC, from October 1889 to April 1890, which approved the establishment of the International Union of American Republics. The Charter of the OAS was signed in Bogota in 1948 and entered into force in December 1951. The Charter was subsequently amended by a number of protocols. As of 2007 the OAS has 35 member states (although Cuba has been suspended from participation since 1962) with Permanent Observer status granted to 59 states and the EU. The basic purposes of the OAS are:

- to strengthen the peace and security of the continent;
- to promote and consolidate representative democracy, with due respect for the principle of non-intervention, to prevent possible causes of difficulties and to ensure the pacific settlement of disputes that may arise among the member states;
- to provide for common action on the part of those states in the event of aggression;
- to seek the solution of political, juridical and economic problems that may arise among them;
- to promote, by cooperative action, their economic, social and cultural development;
- to achieve an effective limitation of conventional weapons that will make it possible to devote the largest amount of resources to the economic and social development of the member states.

In the Declaration of Principles and in the Plan of Action from the 1996 Miami summit the OAS also agreed to establish the Free Trade Area of the Americas, in which barriers to trade and investment will be progressively eliminated, and to guarantee sustainable development and conserve the natural environment for future generations.

A body with similar functions within the OAS to the EU Tourism Unit within the Entrepreneurship Directorate-General of the European Commission is the Tourism Unit, which is responsible for matters directly related to tourism and its development in the hemisphere. The Unit was created in June 1996, in recognition of the growing importance of tourism in the hemisphere, and in order to strengthen the tourism group of the Organization of American States and its activities. The functions of the Unit are to:

- provide support to member states in the area of tourism services as they relate to trade, competitiveness and sustainable development;
- provide support to other areas of the General Secretariat engaged in activities related to tourism;
- formulate, evaluate and execute technical cooperation projects in the area of tourism and sustainable growth and development;
- facilitate the exchange of information and promote public/private sector cooperation in the area of tourism as it relates to trade;
- conduct research and analysis of the tourism sector and its relationship with trade;
- provide support to the Inter-American Tourism Congress, the main forum for formulating hemispheric tourism policy;
- collaborate with international, regional and sub-regional bodies as well as non-governmental organisations and the private sector in the area of tourism.
- identify and promote best practices in the use of information and communication technologies and Internet-based resources to enhance the competitive performance of small and medium enterprises (OAS 2007).

At a development and land-use planning level the Unit has been responsible for a range of technical cooperation activities and projects within the developing countries of the region. Indeed the Unit is directly charged with facilitating and supporting national and regional tourism development programmes and activities, and promoting mechanisms for external support and horizontal collaboration between member states. The Unit's activities include programmes relating to hotel quality systems, security, disaster preparedness, tourism capacity building, sustainable development and ecotourism. Even though the tourism activities of the OAS are tiny when compared to the EU what is significant is the extent to which decisions and undertakings at the supranational level with respect to tourism planning and development will have a regional and local impact. Similarly, the resolutions of the conferences and meetings of the OAS, although being examples of soft international law, may have substantial influence on overall international policy direction. For example, the Declaration of San José from the XVII Inter-American Travel Congress, San José, Costa Rica (OAS 1997) referred to sustainable development as an important element in tourism but, as with the WTO, also makes reference to the significance of public–private partnerships and trade liberalisation. The Final Act and Declaration of Guatemala City of the 2003 XVIII Inter-American Travel Congress in Guatemala covered similar fields but also emphasised the importance of security and the need to prevent trafficking for sex tourism. In addition an annex for a 'Plan of Action for Sustainable Tourism Development in Collaboration with the Private Sector' emphasised multi-layered governance when it reported on an initiative to 'promote horizontal and multilateral cooperation with the support of international, regional and sub-regional organizations and in particular the OAS' (OAS 2003). Such measures become important stepping stones in the world of international diplomacy and negotiation towards more formal agreements while, with the gradual development of a free trade zone throughout the Americas, tourism is also being signalled as a significant component of international trade in the area through such measures as an 'open-sky' policy with respect to international aviation.

Summary

This chapter has discussed some of the issues of governance and institutional arrangements surrounding tourism planning and policy making at the international and supranational level. It has concentrated on the organisational component so as to illustrate the role and influence of hard and soft international law on the various levels of governance that lie below the international scale. Examples have also been provided of the activities of the UNWTO, the EU and the OAS as well as the role of international conservation law through the World Heritage Convention. The key theme of the chapter has been the extent to which outcomes at the local scale, what most people conceive of tourism planning in terms of land use, are often the outcome of policy and planning decisions that have occurred at the international and supranational scale of governance. It should be noted that the relationship is not just top down. There is also a flow of information, influence and desire to affect outcomes between stakeholders from the local through to the global. However, such flows do not mean that supranational and international organisations are democratic in the same sense that there is a direct connection between individual voting behaviour and the capacity to change a government within a democratic state. The EU is the one exception to this. Instead, their power is 'given' to them by the national state. The next chapter will look at the national level in this ongoing process of relationship and interaction.

Questions

1. What are the implications of differences between 'hard' and 'soft' international law for tourism planning and policy?
2. How does international trade policy, particularly with respect to services, affect tourism?
3. How has the development of international conservation and environmental law affected tourism planning and policy?
4. Identify the various international and supranational tourism organisations of which your country is a member. Discuss their significance for tourism planning and policy.
5. What are the key features of the concept of 'governance'?

Important websites and recommended reading

Websites

UNESCO World Heritage Centre:
http://whc.unesco.org/

Tourism Section: Organization of American States:
http://www.oas.org/tourism/

World Travel and Tourism Council:
http://www.wttc.travel/

UN World Tourism Organization:
http://www.world-tourism.org/

Association of South East Asian Nations (ASEAN) Secretariat:
http://www.aseansec.org/

Europa: The European Union online:
europa.eu/

Recommended reading

1. Pierre, J. and Peters, B.G. (2000) *Governance, Politics and the State,* Macmillan, London.

   Provides an excellent account of the issues of participation in tourism and how this relates to sustainability, ethical and quality of life concerns.
2. Rhodes, R.A.W. (1997) *Understanding Governance: Policy Networks, Governance, Reflexivity and Accountability,* Open University Press, Buckingham.

   A highly influential work with respect to notions of governance and their connection to networks.
3. Aa, B.J.M. van der, Groote, P.D. and Huigen, P.P.P. (2004) 'World heritage as NIMBY: the case of the Dutch part of the Wadden Sea', *Current Issues in Tourism* 7(4–5): 291–302.

   Examination of the influence of an international agreement at a local level that also raises significant issues with respect to implementation (see Chapter 10).
4. Fyall, A. and Leask, A. (eds) (2006) *Managing World Heritage Sites,* Butterworth Heinemann, Oxford.

Edited text that provides a broad range of perspectives on World Heritage.

5. Harrison, D. and Hitchcock, M. (eds) (2005) *The Politics of World Heritage,* Channelview, Clevedon.

   A useful collection of papers that deal with some of the policy and planning dimensions of World Heritage at the local level.

6. Pease, K.S. (2003) *International Organizations: Perspectives on Governance in the Twenty-First Century,* 2nd edn, Pearson Education, Upper Saddle River, New Jersey.

   Introductory text to contemporary issues in governance at the international level.

7. Timothy, D.J. (2003) 'Supranationalist alliances and tourism: insights from ASEAN and SAARC', *Current Issues in Tourism,* 6(3): 250–66.

   Study of Asian supranational bodies and their involvement in tourism.

8. Church, A., Ball, R., Bull, C. and Tyler, D. (2000) 'Public policy engagement with British tourism: the national, local and the European Union', *Tourism Geographies,* 2(3): 312–36.

   A good paper on the linkages between policies at multi-level scales of governance.

9. Hall, C.M. (ed.) (2007) *Pro-poor Tourism,* Channelview, Clevedon.

   A collection of papers from a special issue of *Current Issues in Tourism* that detail pro-poor tourism policies and their impacts at various scales. Includes several papers that are critical of the pluralistic assumptions of the governance concept.

10. Peters, B.G. and Pierre, J. (2001) 'Developments in intergovernmental relations: towards multi-level governance', *Policy and Politics,* 29(2): 131–5.

    Useful article on multi-level governance.

11. Coles, T. and Hall, C.M. (eds) (2008) *International Business and Tourism: Global Issues, Contemporary Interactions,* Routledge, London.

    Book provides an International Business Studies perspective on tourism.

7 Tourism planning and policy at the national and sub-national level

Chapter objectives

After reading this chapter you will:

- Have developed working definitions of the state and government
- Appreciate some of the key roles of government with respect to tourism
- Understand the significance of sub-national government actors with respect to tourism
- Understand the significant impact of non-tourism institutions and policies on tourism and the difficulties this may create with respect to the effectiveness of tourism policy and planning.

Although processes of globalisation are dramatically affecting the role of the state in contemporary society, any comments that the state is dead are well and truly premature. As the previous chapter indicated, international and supranational organisations are clearly playing a major role in tourism planning and policy. However, although international law provides some basis for regulation and organisational authority, it carries nowhere near the weight of domestic law, particularly with respect to how laws are enforced. Undoubtedly, pressures for free trade, an apparent desire for smaller government in many western democracies (witnessed through reduced government intervention in the economic and the public spheres and a move away from the collective consumption of social services) and the reawakening of interest in regional governance have all given impetus to the possible claim that the role of the state has declined. Instead, we should perhaps note that the role of the state has changed, as it has always been doing, in relation to global economic, political and social processes (Bianchi 2002; McDavid and Ramajeesingh 2003) and domestic political interests (Whitford *et al.* 2001). Yet the state is still extremely significant.

The state can be conceptualised as a set of officials with their own preferences and capacities to effect public policy, or in more structural terms as a relatively permanent set of *political institutions* operating in relation to civil society (Nordlinger 1981). The term 'state' encompasses the whole apparatus whereby a government exercises its power. It includes elected politicians, the various arms of the bureaucracy, unelected public/civil servants, and the plethora of rules, regulations, laws, conventions and policies that surround government and private action. The main institutions of the state include the elected legislatures, government departments and authorities, the judiciary, enforcement agencies, other levels of government, government–business enterprises and corporations, regulatory authorities, and a range of para-state organisations, such as labour organisations (Hall and Jenkins 1995). Although the boundaries of the state are becoming increasingly blurred in many jurisdictions as emphasis is increasingly placed on the creation of public–private partnerships and reducing government intervention in the economy it should be noted that the state still sets the regulatory framework within which public and private activity occurs (Dredge and Jenkins 2007).

The functions of the state will affect tourism planning, policy and development to different degrees. This chapter will discuss the various roles that government assumes in tourism and their effect on tourism policy, the organisation of government involvement in tourism, the changing nature of intergovernmental relations, and the increasing significance of sub-national governments in tourism planning and policy at both the international and domestic level.

The role of government in tourism

Although tourism is often regarded as a private sector activity, government agencies at all levels of the state have been pursuing tourism as an economic development tool in most developed countries since the 1960s. Government helps shape the economic framework for the tourism industry (although international economic factors relating to exchange rates, interest rates and investor confidence are increasingly important), helps provide the infrastructure and educational requirements for tourism, establishes the regulatory environment in which business operates, and takes an active role in promotion and marketing. In addition, tourism may be politically and economically appealing to government because it can potentially give the appearance of producing results from policy initiatives in a short period of time in terms of visitor numbers and/or employment generation (Hall 1998b; Sharpley and Telfer 2002). For example, the European Union argued that 'The importance of tourism in a region's development is due in particular to its job-creating capacity, to its contribution to the diversification of economic regional activities and to various indirect effects of expenditure by tourists' (EU 1998: Sec. 74).

A number of roles of government in tourism can be identified, although there will be variation from place to place in terms of the extent to which they apply. The forerunner to the UNWTO, the International Union of Travel Organisations (1974), in their discussion of the role of the state in tourism identified five areas of public sector involvement in tourism: coordination, planning,

legislation and regulation, entrepreneur, and stimulation (also see Jenkins and Henry 1982; Mill and Morrison 1985). To this may be added two other functions, a social tourism role, and a broader role of interest protection (Hall 1994). A discussion on these eight roles of government in tourism follows.

Coordination

As discussed in Chapter 5 coordination is an extremely significant concept in tourism planning and policy (e.g. Allmendinger *et al.* 2002; Gunn with Var 2002; Swart 2005). Coordination is necessary both within and between the different levels of government in order to avoid duplication of resources between the various government tourism bodies and the private sector, and to develop effective tourism strategies. Given the large number of public organisations that have an interest in tourism matters one of the main challenges for government is being able to bring the various organisations and agencies together to work for common policy objectives. Furthermore, in several jurisdictions government has often served to help coordinate private sector activities as well.

Although considerable attention has been given to the importance of a coordinated government approach to tourism, many policy statements and commentators have failed to indicate exactly what is really meant by the concept. As noted in Chapter 5 the need for coordination remains one of the great truisms of tourism. Nevertheless, just because a concept resists easy definition does not mean that it does not have policy significance. For example, the federal government White Paper on Australia's mid- to long-term tourism strategy (Australian Government 2003) justified the restructuring of tourism agencies by the need for improved coordination: 'Amalgamating existing entities to form a new structure will also help to improve coordination and effectiveness in achieving the *Tourism Australia* vision' (Australian Government 2003: 3).

Also in many instances demands from stakeholders for improved coordination actually means closer relationships between government, and publically funded tourism bodies in particular, and the tourism industry. Such public–private partnerships (Wettenhall 2003) can be seen clearly in the structure of many government tourism agencies around the world where a publically funded organisation has a governing board of individuals that represent industry interests. At one level this may be regarded as a good thing as it may promote greater efficiency in tourism marketing and promotion and hopefully ensure that there is greater cooperation in achieving common economic goals. The opposite perspective would say that the relationship between industry and the public tourism bodies is so close that policy making may be extremely narrow in perspective and be closed to policy alternatives, particularly with respect to the wider public. In addition, although public–private partnerships may deliver efficiency gains and service improvements in some circumstances, such benefits may involve substantial political and democratic costs (Flinders 2005) as the notion of stakeholder has been narrowly defined to be 'industry' rather than a broader approach that would suggest 'community'.

Planning

As stated in the first chapter, public planning for tourism occurs in a number of forms (e.g. development, infrastructure, land and resource use, promotion and marketing); institutions (e.g. different government organisations) and scales (e.g. national, regional, local and sectoral). In several nations, such as Israel, and in several regions, notably the island states of the Pacific (Hall and Page 1997), national tourism development plans have been drawn up in which government identifies which sectors of the industry will be developed, the appropriate rate of growth and the provision of capital required for expansion. Throughout many parts of the world regional tourism development plans are also a common government initiative, particularly where such regions are seeking to utilise tourism as a response to problems of economic restructuring (Jenkins *et al.* 1998; Dredge and Jenkins 2007). However, in many western countries, such as

Australia and Canada, many governments now develop national or regional tourism strategies rather than development plans. This is not just an exercise in semantics as the notion of a strategy is a reflecting of the development of the concept of governance and its application to tourism, as in such situations a strategy tends to place a far greater emphasis on public–private partnership arrangements.

Nevertheless, while planning is recognised as an important element in tourism development, the conduct of a plan or strategy does not by itself guarantee appropriate outcomes for stakeholders, particularly as issues of implementation and the policy–action relationship need to be addressed (Pforr 2001). Indeed, as has already been noted, one of the major problems for public tourism planning is the extent to which tourism-specific agencies, which usually have a very limited legislative base of responsibility, have the authority to direct other government organisations to meet tourism-specific policy goals (e.g. Fennell and Dowling 2003).

Legislation and regulation

Government has a number of legislative and regulative powers that directly and indirectly impinge on tourism. Government involvement in this area ranges from authority on passport and visa matters through to environmental and labour relations policy. However, substantial issues for tourism often emerge because of the extent to which tourism policy needs to be integrated with other policy areas. With the possible exception of island microstates, which are highly economically dependent on tourism, tourism policy tends to be only a relatively minor area of government policy initiatives. Nevertheless, policy decisions undertaken in other policy jurisdictions, e.g. economic policy, and environmental and conservation policy, may have substantial implications for the effectiveness of policy decisions undertaken in tourism. For example, general regulatory measures such as industry regulation, environmental protection and taxation policy will significantly influence the growth of tourism (Hall 1998b).

The level of government regulation of tourism tends to be a major issue for the various components of the tourism industry (Shaw and Williams 2004). Undoubtedly, while industry recognises that government has a significant role to play, particularly when it comes to the provision of infrastructure, marketing or research, the predominant argument by industry throughout most of the world is that the industry must be increasingly deregulated. However, government simultaneously calls for increased regulation of tourism, especially with respect to the desire for environmental protection (e.g. Bramwell and Alletorp 2001), and, increasingly, human rights and social justice, especially with respect to the rights of indigenous peoples (e.g. Hall and Brown 2006).

The very nature of the tourism industry and the mobility of individuals means that there is a regulatory vacuum in which government must operate in order to establish clear guidelines. Given this situation, for example in the case of the environment, conservation groups will often seek the extension of government regulation to ensure that tourism remains 'controlled', particularly in environmentally and politically sensitive areas such as national parks or the coastal zone. In many cases, especially when tourism firms are using the environment as part of their branding and competitive strategy, the regulatory conflict is perhaps not so much whether controls should be in place but rather what the nature of the controls should be, with industry often seeking to place the locus of control on themselves, e.g. self-regulating, while conservationists will usually seek to have control placed in a government body, such as an environmental protection authority, which is distinct from the tourism industry (Hall 2005a).

Government as entrepreneur

Government has long had an entrepreneurial function in tourism. Governments not only provide basic infrastructure, such as roads and sewage, but may also own and operate tourist ventures including hotels and travel companies. Governments at all levels have had a long history of involvement in promoting tourism through bureaus, marketing ventures, development of transport networks through national airline and rail systems, and the provision of loans to private industry for specific tourism-related developments. The provision of infrastructure, for instance, is a widely accepted task of public authorities and one that can greatly facilitate tourism development and may even be used as a means of encouraging development in certain areas. However, the entrepreneurial role of government in tourism is changing in a climate in which less government intervention is being sought. This has meant the development of increasing public–private arrangements in tourism-related redevelopment projects and the conduct of such developments on a commercial basis where substantial direct economic return is being sought for government authorities rather than development occurring for the notion of a wider public good.

The role of the state as entrepreneur in tourism development is closely related to the concept of the 'devalorisation of capital'. The 'devalorisation of capital' (Damette 1980) is the process by which the state subsidises part of the cost of production, for instance by assisting in the provision of infrastructure or by investing in a tourism project where private venture capital is otherwise unavailable. In this process what would have been private costs are transformed into public or social costs. The provision of infrastructure, particularly transport networks, is regarded as crucial to the development of tourist destinations. There are numerous formal and informal means for government at all levels to assist in minimising the costs of production for tourism developers. Indeed, the offer of government assistance for development is often used to encourage private investment in a particular region or tourist project; for instance through the provision of cheap land, tax breaks or government-backed low-interest loans. For example, in India several states have created tourism development corporations for the purpose of encouraging tourism development and investment. The Tourism Corporation of Gujarat, for example, developed a tourism plan that included several tax concessions for investors, such as exemption from luxury tax, sales tax, electricity duty, turnover tax and entertainment tax, and long-term loans from state institutions. This, in part, has helped to address the negative image of India overseas as a tourist destination and limitations on foreign direct investment for tourism prior to the government's economic liberalisation measures in the 1990s (Chaudhary 1996).

Stimulation

Similar to the entrepreneurial role is the action that government can take to stimulate tourism development. Governments can stimulate tourism in three ways. First, financial incentives such as low-interest loans or a depreciation allowance on tourist accommodation. For example, the creation of incentives to encourage foreign investment in the tourism sector has been closely tied to the creation of new tourism development bodies at the state level in India. Concessions at the state level have also been matched by central government fiscal incentives for tourism projects, including income tax exemptions on 50 per cent of the profits from foreign exchange earnings, exemption on the remaining 50 per cent if the amount is reinvested in new tourism projects, and exemption on import duty on imports for hotel projects. In an effort to use tourism as a tool for regional development, the Indian federal government has explicitly sought to encourage regional tourism development by providing interest subsidies on term loans from eligible financial institutions for hotels in cities other than main centres such as Mumbai (Bombay), Delhi, Calcutta and Chennai (Madras), with higher rates of subsidy available for hotel development in designated tourist areas and heritage hotels. The provision of financial incentives for tourism by the Indian central government in the 1990s is indicative of not only increased attention by government to tourism's potential for generating employment and foreign exchange, but also the wider deregulation of the Indian economy to provide for competition and foreign investment. For example, in the accommodation sector the federal government now allows foreign management and up to 51 per cent foreign ownership of hotels (Hall and Page 1999b).

A second aspect of government stimulation of tourism is through sponsoring research for the general benefit of the tourism industry rather than for specific individual organisations and associations. In the case of countries such as Australia, Canada, New Zealand and the United States, for example, statistical information may be available to individuals for free or at a relatively low cost from either specific tourism agencies or from government statistical offices.

The third dimension of the stimulation role is that of marketing and promotion, generally aimed at generating tourism demand, although it can also take the form of investment promotion aimed at encouraging capital investment in tourism attractions and facilities. However, such is the size of the role government plays in promotion that it is usually recognised as a separate function.

Tourism promotion

> marketing of inbound tourism in large measure has the market failure and public good characteristics that indicate private sector under-provision and justify public sector support via government funding of marketing activity. (Access Economics 1997: 29)

One of the main activities of government is the promotion of tourism through tourism marketing campaigns. Tourist commissions and agencies have the task of identifying potential target markets, the best methods of attracting them and, once they want to buy the tourist product, where to direct them. Furthermore, as well as encouraging visits by foreign travellers, tourism promotion agencies will sometimes attempt to retain as many domestic tourists as possible through the conduct of domestic marketing campaigns in order to ensure the minimum of 'leakage' from outside of the national, state or regional tourism system.

Given calls for smaller government in western society since the early 1980s, there have been increasing demands from government and economic rationalists for greater industry self-sufficiency by industry in tourism marketing and promotion (e.g., Jeffries 1989). The political implications of such an approach for the tourism industry are substantial. As Hughes (1984: 14) noted, 'The advocates of a free enterprise economy would look to consumer freedom of choice and not to governments to promote firms; the consumer ought to be sovereign in decisions relating to the allocation of the nation's resources.' Such an approach means that lobbyists in the tourism industry may be better shifting their focus on the necessity of government intervention to issues of externalities, public goods and merit wants rather than employment and the balance of payments (Hall 1994; Dredge and Jenkins 2007). 'Such criteria for government intervention have a sounder economic base and are more consistent with a free-enterprise philosophy than employment and balance of payments effects' (Hughes 1984: 18). However, the conduct of government involvement in tourism promotion is as much a legacy of effective political lobbying as it is the conduct of economic rationalism, if not more so (Craik 1990, 1991a, 1991b; Jenkins 2001; Tyler and Dinan 2001; Dredge and Jenkins 2007).

Generic destination promotion funded by industry tends to benefit all sectors of the tourism industry and becomes a form of 'public good'. Therefore, the question of 'freeloaders' arises, i.e. those tourism firms that benefit from destination promotion even though they have not financially supported it. However, the freeloader or freerider problem can be regarded as rational business behaviour in the absence of some form of government intervention in tourism promotion. As Access Economics (1997: 29) observed:

> There will be a strong incentive for individual producers of tourism/travel services to minimalise their contribution to cooperative marketing, or even not to contribute at all, and other private sector producers have no power to coerce such producers and the beneficiaries of tourism activity, anyway.

Given the supply-side fragmentation of tourism and the substantial degree of market failure that exists with respect to generic destination promotion, governments may need to determine the most appropriate form of government intervention in order to fulfil their tourism planning and policy goals. In the Australian context,

Access Economics (1997) reviewed a number of different forms of intervention including:

- forcing businesses to pay a funding levy;
- 'user pays'/cooperative funding systems;
- levies on foreign exchange earnings;
- making government funding conditional on industry funding;
- levies on tourism investment;
- funding from a passenger movement charge;
- a bed tax;
- funding out of consolidated revenue;
- funding out of a possible Goods and Services Tax (GST) [similar to VAT] that emerges from tax reform measures.

After examining the different potential forms of government intervention, Access Economics concluded that the most appropriate form of government intervention is the appropriation of funds from consolidated revenue funds through budget processes. Several reasons were put forward for this conclusion:

- the inability to capture the benefits of generic marketing activity is severe in the light of the fragmented nature of the tourism industry;
- levies, user pays charges and business tax arrangements, including bed taxes, will institutionalise the 'freerider' or 'freeloader' problem;
- the benefits of successful generic promotion as a travel destination are dispersed across the community.

One of the more unusual features of tourism promotion by government tourism organisations is that they have only limited control over the product they are marketing, with very few governments actually owning the goods, facilities and services that make up the tourism product. This lack of control is perhaps testimony to the power of the public good argument used by industry to justify continued maintenance of government funding for destination promotion. However, it may also indicate the political power of the tourism lobby, such as industry organisations (Hall and Jenkins 1995; Jenkins 2001; Dredge and Jenkins 2007) to influence government tourism policies.

Social tourism

Social tourism can be defined as tourism relationships and phenomena resulting from participation in travel by economically weak or otherwise disadvantaged elements of society. Social tourism involves the extension of the benefits of holidays to economically marginal groups, such as the unemployed, single-parent families, pensioners and the handicapped (Hazel 2005). The International Bureau of Social Tourism defines social tourism as meaning 'the totality of relations and phenomena deriving from the participation in tourism of those social groups with modest incomes – participation which is made possible or facilitated by measures of a well defined social character' (Haulot 1981: 208).

According to Murphy (1985: 24) 'Social tourism has become a recognized component and legitimate objective for modern tourism. By extending the physical and psychological benefits of rest and travel to less fortunate people it can be looked upon as a form of preventative medicine.' Haulot (1981: 212) further extended this perspective by noting that: 'Social tourism . . . finds justification in that its individual and collective objectives are consistent with the view that all measures taken by modern society should ensure more justice, more dignity and improved enjoyment of life for all citizens.' However, the desire of conservative elements in society to reduce the extent of government intervention in economic and private life and focus on individual as opposed to public interest has meant a substantial decline in support for social tourism around the world in recent years (Hall and Brown 2006).

Government as public interest protector

The final role that government plays in tourism is that of interest protector. Although not necessarily tourism specific, such a role will have major implications for the development of tourism policy. Indeed, public tourism planning, particularly from the community and sustainable approaches in which equity is a major consideration, serves as an arbiter between competing interests. The defence of local and minority interests has traditionally occupied much government activity, particularly as government has had the role of balancing various interests and values in order to meet national or regional public interests, rather than narrow, sectional, private interests, such as that of a specific industry like tourism. This does not, of course, ignore the fact that various tourism interests are often represented within the structure of government, particularly under the guise of public–private partnership (Bramwell and Lane 2000; Jenkins 2001). 'Statutory authorities and a myriad of state agencies were established to protect sectional groups, to represent key interests in the policy process, and to protect the social order via welfare provisions to many sections of business and society in general' (Davis *et al.* 1993: 26). Nevertheless, tourism policy needs to be considered as being potentially subsumed beneath a broader range of government economic, social, welfare and environmental policies. Ideally, policy decisions will reflect a desire to meet the interests of the relevant level of government, e.g. national, provincial/state, or local, rather than the sectionally defined interests of components of the tourism industry (Hall 1994), although in reality the interest groups have generally come to dominate the tourism policy process (Pforr 2001; Tyler and Dinan 2001).

The issue of government as protector of the common or public interest lies at the heart of questions surrounding the role of government in tourism planning. It also causes us to question the democratic nature of planning and policy making – the extent to which planning and policy decisions are open to public scrutiny and debate and therefore provide for such decisions to be seen as legitimate in the public sphere. As Saul (1995: 115–16) states,

> Democracy is simply about the nature of legitimacy and whether the repository of that legitimacy – the citizens – are able to exercise the power its possession imposes upon them. We are having great difficulty today exercising the power of legitimacy. It has . . . shifted away into other hands.

One of the great ironies of the growth of the culture of place marketing, which extols the virtues of competition and choice (Kotler *et al.* 1993), is the manner in which debate over representation and redevelopment of place is often denied (Dredge and Jenkins 2003). Throughout much of the western world, in order to ensure that urban leisure and tourism development projects are carried out,

> local authorities have had planning and development powers removed and handed to an unelected institution. Effectively, an appointed agency is, in each case, replacing the powers of local government in order to carry out a market-led regeneration of each inner city. (Goodwin 1993: 161)

Harvey (1989a: 7) in an influential essay, described place competition and marketing as 'the new entrepreneurialism' which has, as its centrepiece, the concept of 'public–private partnership' in which a traditional local boosterism (see Chapter 3) is integrated with the use of local, regional and national government powers to seek to attract external sources of funding, direct investments or employment sources. However, such partnerships often do not include all members of a community: those who do not have enough money, are not of the right lifestyle, or simply do not have sufficient power, are ignored (Sunley 1999). For example, in referring to urban redevelopment in Derwentside in the United Kingdom, Sadler (1993: 190) argued:

> The kind of policy which had been adopted – and which was proving increasingly ineffective even in terms of its own stated objectives – therefore rested not so much on a basis of rational choice, but rather was a simple reflection of the narrow political and intellectual scope for alternatives. This restricted area did not come about purely or simply by chance, but had been deliberately encouraged and fostered.

'The question immediately arises as to why people accede to the construction of their places by such a process' (Harvey 1993). In many cases they do not. Communities may resist such change (Singh *et al.* 2003). However, while victories in short-term battles may save the physical fabric of inner-city communities, this will not usually win the war. The social fabric will usually change through gentrification and touristification of many areas leaving only heritage façades. Furthermore,

the very 'rules of the game' by which planning and development decisions are made will often favour business over community interest groups (Hall and Jenkins 1995; Tyler and Dinan 2001). Indeed, Harvey also notes that resistance has not checked the overall process of place competition. A mixture of coercion and co-optation centred around maintenance of real estate values, assumptions regarding employment and investment generation, and an assumption that growth is automatically good, has led to the creation of local growth coalitions, in which

> Coercion arises either through interplace competition for capital investment and employment (accede to the capitalist's demands or go out of business; create a 'good business climate' or lose jobs) or more simply, through the direct political repression and oppression of dissident voices (from cutting off media access to the more violent tactics of the construction mafias in many of the world's cities). (Harvey 1993: 9)

Such changes in government's role as interest protector has major implications for tourism and sustainability (Lansing and Vries 2007). As Blowers (1997: 36) noted,

> In the UK the long period of privatisation, deregulation, cuts in public expenditure and attacks on local government have resulted in a 'democratic deficit' – a dispersal of power to unelected quangos and business interests – and have led to unsustainable developments.

A critique also reflected in the work of Müller (2006) on literary tourism in southern Sweden and in the comments of Haughton and Hunter (1994: 272):

> The unregulated market approach, being relatively amoral, can allow individuals to be immoral. The ethical dimension is important since the market does not provide a sufficient basis for the resolution of the profound moral issues which face us every day; it can play a part in avoiding distorted decision making by individuals and organizations, but alone it cannot reconcile all of the environmental problems facing society.

If government is meant to occupy the role of general interest protector and, more particularly, if public tourism planning is meant to protect the interests of the wider community rather than just

National travel and tourism competitiveness

In 2007 the World Economic Forum (WEF) launched a Travel and Tourism Competitiveness Index (TTCI) that covered 124 countries around the world. The WEF's competitiveness studies are 'aimed at contributing to a better understanding of why some countries grow prosperous, while others are left behind' (WEF 2007: xiii). According to the WEF (2007: xiii) their TTCI 'aims to measure the factors and policies that make it attractive to develop the [travel and tourism] sector in different countries'. The WEF TTCI was produced in collaboration with Booz Allen Hamilton, the International Air Transport Association (IATA), the UNWTO, and the WTTC with feedback also provided by 'a number of key companies that are industry partners in the effort' (2007: xiii): Bombardier, Carlson, Emirates Group, Qatar Airways, Royal Jordanian Airlines, Silversea Cruises, Swiss International Airlines and Visa International. Data was obtained from publically available sources (i.e. IATA, ICAO, UNWTO, WTTC, UNESCO) and the results of a survey 'carried out among CEOs and top business leaders in all economies covered by our research – these are the people making the investment decisions in their respective economies' (WEF 2007: xiv).

The WEF TTCI is best on 13 'pillars' of travel and tourism competitiveness:

1. Policy rules and regulations
2. Environmental regulation
3. Safety and security
4. Health and hygiene
5. Prioritisation of travel and tourism
6. Air transport infrastructure
7. Ground transport infrastructure
8. Tourism infrastructure
9. ICT infrastructure
10. Price competitiveness in the T&T industry
11. Human resources
12. National tourism perception
13. Natural and cultural resources.

The 13 'pillars' were then in turn organised into three sub-indexes: regulatory framework (categories 1–5 above), business environment and infrastructure (categories 6–10 above), and human, cultural and natural resources (categories 11–13 above). The hard data and executive survey data used to derive competitiveness scores are illustrated in Table 7.1. Table 7.2 shows the world's top tourism destinations for 2004 (as determined by UNWTO figures) and their relative ranking and scores for the WEF TTCI. According to Blanke and Chiesa (2007) the correlation between the log of international tourist arrivals per 1,000 population in 2005 and the score given in the WEF TTCI was 0.77 while the correlation between the log of international tourism receipts (US\$) per 1,000 population in 2005 and the score given in the WEF TTCI was 0.84.

Undoubtedly, such rankings and scores will be given substantial emphasis by the media and by government and the tourism industry even though the basis by which they are developed is empirically highly questionable. Nevertheless, the WEF's scores reflect a significant policy interest in contemporary tourism and business. For example, according to some economic analysts, 'the critical issue for regional economic development practitioners to grasp is that the creation of competitive advantage is the most important activity they can pursue' (Barclays 2002 cited in Bristow 2005). Peak tourism bodies such as the UNWTO and the WTTC have embraced the competitiveness concept through a number of their programmes. For example, the UNWTO states interests in 'competitive tourism education systems' and 'competitive destinations', while the WTTC operates a competitiveness monitor on its website that 'indicates to what extent a country offers a competitive environment for Travel & Tourism development'. However, despite the influence of the concept on tourism policies of the national and local state the concept has been subject to relatively little critique, nor has there

▶

Table 7.1 'Hard' and executive survey data used to derive scores for the WEF (2007) Travel and Tourism Competitiveness Index

Pillar	Hard data elements	Executive survey data elements
Policy rules and regulations	Visa requirements	Foreign ownership restrictions
	Openness of bilateral air service agreements	Property rights
		Rules governing foreign direct investment
Environmental regulation		Stringency of environmental regulation
		Clarity and stability of environmental regulations
		Government prioritisation of sustainable travel and tourism
Safety and security		Business cost of terrorism
		Reliability of police services
		Business cost of crime and violence
Health and hygiene	Physician density	Government efforts to reduce health risks from pandemics
	Access to improved sanitation	
	Access to improved drinking water	
Prioritisation of travel and tourism	Travel and tourism government expenditure	Government prioritisation of the travel and tourism industry
	Travel and tourism fair attendance	Effectiveness of marketing and branding to attract tourists
Air transport infrastructure	Available seat kilometres	Quality of air transport infrastructure
	Departures per 1,000 population	International air transport network
	Airport density	
	Number of operating airlines	
Ground transport infrastructure		Road infrastructure
		Railroad infrastructure
		Port infrastructure
		Domestic transport network
Tourism infrastructure	Hotel rooms	
	Presence of major car rental companies	
	ATMs accepting Visa cards	

▶

Table 7.1 (continued)

Pillar	Hard data elements	Executive survey data elements
Information and communications technology infrastructure	Internet users	Extent of business Internet use
	Telephone lines	
Price competitiveness in the travel and tourism industry	Ticket taxes and airport charges	Extent and effect of taxation
	Purchasing power parity	
	Fuel price levels	
Human resources	Primary education enrolment	Quality of the education system
	Secondary education enrolment	Local availability of specialised research and training services
	HIV prevalance	Extent of staff training
	Malaria incidence	Hiring and firing practices
	Tuberculosis incidence	Ease of hiring foreign labour
	Life expectancy	
National tourism perception	Tourism openness	Attitude towards tourists
		Recommendation to extend business trips
Natural and cultural resources	Number of World Heritage sites	Business concern for ecosystems
	Carbon dioxide damage	
	Nationally protected areas	
	Risk of malaria and yellow fever	

Source: Derived from Blanke and Chiesa (2007) 'The travel and tourism competitiveness index: assessing key factors driving the sector's development', in World Economic Forum, *The Travel and Tourism Competitiveness Report 2007: Furthering the Process of Economic Development*, World Economic Forum, Geneva, pp. 3–26. Reproduced with permission.

been a substantive discussion of the philosophical and ideological underpinnings of such a concept. Instead competition, whether it be as a tourism destination or in a wider sense of regional competitiveness, is usually portrayed as a 'given' and what places 'must' do. Yet as Turner (2001: 40) noted with respect to the language of competitiveness, it 'provides a rosy glow of shared endeavour and shared enemies which can unite captains of industry and representatives of the shop floor in the same big tent'. More particularly in relation to meta-political narratives, competitiveness is a discourse that 'provides some shared sense of meaning and a means of legitimising neo-liberalism

rather than a material focus on the actual improvements of economic welfare' (Bristow, 2005: 300).

Although competitiveness is a significant policy goal there is still substantial confusion 'as to what the concept actually means and how it can be effectively operationalised . . . policy acceptance of the existence of regional competitiveness and its measurement appears to have run ahead of a number of fundamental theoretical and empirical questions' (Bristow, 2005: 286). This is especially the case in tourism, where there is already substantial evidence of the role of price competitiveness as a major determinant in tourism flows and where its parameters are clearly defined

▶

Table 7.2 Relationships between international tourism arrivals for countries by rank and WEF competitiveness rankings

Rank 2004	Country	International tourist arrivals (million)	Competi-tiveness index rank	Competi-tiveness index score	Regulatory framework rank	Environment and infrastructure rank	Human, cultural and natural resources rank
1	France	75.1	12	5.23	13	5	28
2	Spain	52.4	15	5.18	25	7	19
3	USA	46.1	5	5.43	33	1	12
4	China	41.8	71	3.97	78	61	93
5	Italy	37.1	33	4.78	42	30	32
6	UK	27.8	10	5.28	21	5	10
7	Mexico	20.6	49	4.38	48	57	50
8	Turkey	16.8	52	4.31	53	63	48
9	Germany	20.1	3	5.48	6	3	6
10	Russian Federation	19.9	68	4.03	100	49	65
11	Austria	19.4	2	5.54	3	12	1
12	Canada	19.2	7	5.31	15	4	16
13	Malaysia	15.7	31	4.80	27	27	57
14	Ukraine	12.5	78	3.89	76	73	89
15	Poland	13.7	63	4.18	63	62	60
16	Hong Kong	13.7	6	5.33	4	14	14
17	Greece	14.0	24	4.99	20	32	15
18	Hungary	12.2	40	4.61	26	51	51
19	Thailand	10.1	43	4.58	41	35	59
20	Portugal	11.6	22	5.05	11	22	30

Sources: Derived from WTO (2006a,b) World's Top Tourism Destinations (absolute numbers) (http://www.world-tourism.org/facts/menu.html); WEF (2007).

(Dwyer *et al.* 2000a, 2000b). However, more general notions of regional or destination competitveness are categories that Markusen (1999: 870) described as 'fuzzy concepts': 'characterizations lacking conceptual clarity are difficult to operationalize. In some cases, no attempt is made to offer evidence at all. Elsewhere, evidence marshaled is highly selective. Methodology is little discussed'. For example, with reference to the key question of what are the determinants of place competitiveness Deas and Giordano (2001) argued that the literature tends to offer a one-size fits all or 'checklist' approach to identifying the relevant determinants of competitiveness, even though inadequate empirical research has been conducted as to the relative significance of such factors. Similarly, Malecki (2002: 941) commented with respect to city competitiveness, 'all of

▶

short-term sectoral tourism interests, then increasing attention also needs to be given to the manner in which the institutional arrangements of government involvement in tourism are organised (Healey 1999) and the instruments by which government intervenes to achieve tourism planning and policy goals.

The organisation of government involvement in tourism

As has already been noted several times in this book, the tendency to privatise and commercialise functions that were once performed by government, which has been almost universal in western nations since the late 1970s, has substantially affected the nature of many national governments' involvement in the tourism industry (Hall and Jenkins 1995; Jenkins 2000; Araujo and Bramwell 2002; Dredge and Jenkins 2003; Priskin 2003; Lovelock and Boyd 2006). According to Davis *et al.* (1993: 24) three principal economic reasons for this trend can be identified: 'governments are interested in reducing the dependency of public enterprises on public budgets, in reducing public debt by selling state assets, and in raising technical efficiencies by commercialisation'. However, the economic reasons are themselves shrouded in political rationales that relate to broader philosophical perspectives regarding the question of what are the appropriate roles for the state and the individual within society (Freestone *et al.* 2006). Ideology therefore has practical effect in the design of government institutions and their tasks.

As readers would be aware, there are many different organisational structures for government involvement in tourism in the countries around the world. The organisational structures used by governments develop over time in relation to a number of factors (including political philosophies) as to the appropriate role of the state, national traditions of public administration, the nature of the political system, and values and interests in the bureaucratic and policy process (Figure 7.1). New government departments may be established as part of the growth in the activity and influence of government, particularly as new demands, interests or planning problems, such as environmental concerns, reach a prominent position on the political agenda. As Mercer (1979: 107) noted:

> The setting up of entirely new government departments, advisory bodies or sections within the existing administration is a well established strategy on the part of governments for demonstrating loudly and clearly that 'something positive is being done' with respect to a given problem. Moreover, because public service bureaucracies are inherently conservative in terms of their approach to problem delineation and favoured mode of functioning . . . administrative restructuring, together with the associated legislation, is almost always a significant indicator of public pressure for action and change.

Tourism has come to occupy a number of different positions in government administrative structures in different parts of the world. Tables 7.3 and 7.4 illustrate the institutional arrangements for government involvement in tourism in New Zealand. In general terms, the institutional arrangements for tourism in New Zealand are

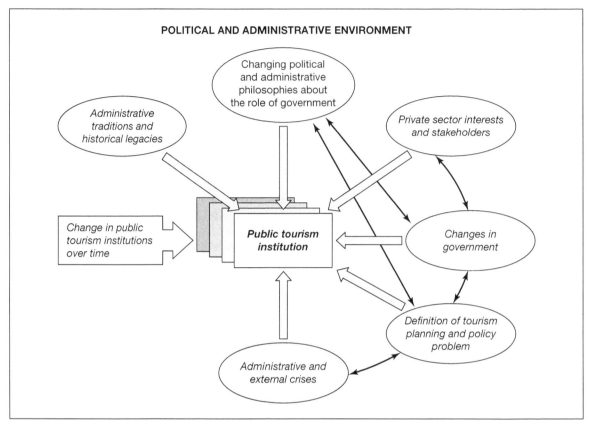

POLITICAL AND ADMINISTRATIVE ENVIRONMENT

Changing political and administrative philosophies about the role of government

Administrative traditions and historical legacies

Private sector interests and stakeholders

Change in public tourism institutions over time

Public tourism institution

Changes in government

Definition of tourism planning and policy problem

Administrative and external crises

Figure 7.1 Factors leading to the design of government tourism institutions, their authority and tasks

similar to other national jurisdictions in that there is a small core group of primary agencies directly responsible for tourism and a large number of secondary agencies that although having direct involvement in tourism have another administrative and/or policy area as their main focus. Not listed, but still significant, are those departments and agencies that indirectly affect tourism through their policies and the legislation for which they are responsible. For example, Departments of Finance and Treasury affect the overall economic environment within which tourism occurs through their setting of exchange and interest rates and by their policies on such matters as foreign investment.

The New Zealand example also illustrates the great problem surrounding coordination of tourism policy and planning for tourism in that there is a plethora of government stakeholders in

policy development in terms of different departments and agencies, responsible ministers, and legislative bases for action. In order for more than the simplest policy settings to be achievable in this policy environment it becomes apparent that agencies will need to develop a series of positive interorganisational relationships in which common goals can be agreed upon and in which information flow is maximised for coordination to occur. Such a situation is extremely difficult. Indeed, it may partially explain why effective tourism policy development has been so difficult in many national jurisdictions (Hall and Jenkins 1995). Instead, in many western nations the policy function of tourism at the national government level has been reduced at the expense of a narrower promotion function. For example, in countries as geographically dispersed as Australia, Austria, Canada, New Zealand and the

Table 7.3 Institutional arrangements for government involvement for tourism in New Zealand

Agency	Principal roles*	Enabling legislation	Responsible minister	Principal tourism-related functions
Primary agencies				
Ministry of Tourism (A Ministry within the Ministry of Economic Development)	Policy Operations	None, but administers several Acts: New Zealand Maori Arts and Crafts Institute Act 1963; New Zealand Tourism Board Act 1991; Tourist and Health Resorts Control Act 1908.	Tourism	Provides policy advice to the Minister of Tourism and works with other government departments on key tourism policy issues. Work also includes advising on and evaluating government investment in tourism, carrying out tourism research and assisting with major events. Manages 150 ha. Crown-owned land on which thermal springs are located and for which the Minister of Tourism is responsible.
Tourism New Zealand (New Zealand Tourism Board (NZTB)) (Crown agency)	Marketing Policy	New Zealand Tourism Board Act 1991	Tourism	Ensures that New Zealand is marketed as a visitor destination to maximise long-term benefits to New Zealand; develops implements and promotes strategies for tourism; and adapts government and industry on the development, promotion, implementation of those strategies.
Department of Conservation (DOC)	Policy Operations Regulation	Conservation Act 1987	Conservation	Management of land in the conservation estate to achieve conservation objectives; gives effect to the principles of Treaty of Waitangi; advocates conservation; education; provision of visitor services and visitor centres; maintains historic and cultural heritage; and liaises with stakeholders.
Secondary agencies				
Conservation				
Ministry for the Environment	Policy Regulation	Environment Act 1986	Environment	Advises government on all aspects of environmental administration; assists in the promotion of sustainable management; administers the Resource Management Act.
New Zealand Conservation Authority	Policy	Conservation Act 1987	Conservation	Advises government on DOC policy and activities; applies conservation management strategies and plans and National Park Management Plans.
Conservation Boards	Policy	Conservation Act 1987	Conservation	Advises New Zealand Conservation Authority (NZCA) and regional conservators on policy and concessions.

▲

Table 7.3 (continued)

Agency	Principal roles*	Enabling legislation	Responsible minister	Principal tourism-related functions
New Zealand Historic Places Trust	Regulation Operations Policy	Historic Places Act 1993	Conservation	Protects and manages historic and cultural heritage through advocacy, policy advice and direct management.
Fish and Game New Zealand	Regulation Operations Policy	Conservation Act 1987	Conservation	An angler and gamebird hunter organisation that has a statutory mandate to manage freshwater sportsfish fisheries and gamebird hunting. Coordinates the management, enhancement and maintenance of sportsfish and game, through policy, advocacy and management.
Antarctica New Zealand (Crown entity)	Policy Operations Regulation Information Infrastructure	New Zealand Antarctic Institute Act 1996	Foreign Affairs and Trade	Specialist agency responsible for developing, managing and administering New Zealand's activities in Antarctica and the Southern Ocean, including the Ross Sea. Undertakes scientific and conservation activities as well as monitoring tourism activities.
Employment, business, trade and economic development				
Ministry of Maori Development – Te Puni Kokiri	Policy Information	Ministry of Maori Development Act 1991	Maori Affairs	Mainly provides analysis and policy advice to increase Maori achievement within the tourism sector, and monitors other agencies' delivery of outcomes for Maori.
Department of Internal Affairs – Local Government and Community Branch, Local Government	Operations Policy Information		Internal Affairs Local Government Community and Voluntary Sector	Advises and informs community groups and organisations; provides funding through Lottery Grants Board, also includes Local Government Policy Unit. Although not tourism specific the Department is also where the Ministry of Civil Defence and Emergency Management sits in terms of government organisation. The Department is also responsible for the issuing of passports to New Zealand citizens.
Department of Labour – Employment Relations	Operations Policy Information Regulation		Labour	Employment relations, minimum wage, immigration/working holiday schemes.
Ministry of Agriculture and Forestry	Policy Information		Agriculture	Promotes rural diversification, including farm tourism.

Organisation	Function	Legislation	Portfolio	Description
Ministry of Foreign Affairs and Trade	Policy, Information		Foreign Affairs, Trade	Fosters international links involving tourism, including international expositions; inputs into tourism policy decisions affecting broader diplomatic considerations, e.g. Antarctic tourism policy; international agreements, treaties and trade relations. The Ministry also provides travel advisories.
Ministry of Economic Development	Policy, Operations, Information		Economic Development, Industry and Regional Development, Commerce, Small Business, Energy, Consumer Affairs	The Ministry of Economic Development works across the public sector to advise on, coordinate and align activities that stimulate economic development. Tourism-related responsibilities and activities not included within the Ministry of Tourism include funding for major events; Kiwi-made campaign; consumer and business rights and responsibilities; economic development, innovation and small business activities; energy strategy.

Public health and public safety sector

Organisation	Function	Legislation	Portfolio	Description
Public Health Group – Ministry of Health	Policy, Operations	Health Act 1956	Health	Manages and regulates activities including those affecting public health.
Occupational Safety and Health Service – Department of Labour	Regulation, Policy	Occupational Safety and Health Act 1992	Labour	The prevention of harm to employees at work and visitors to workplaces.
New Zealand Police	Operations, Regulation		Police	Protection of the public from criminal activity; traffic service compliance; search and rescue coordination.

Transport and transport safety sector

Organisation	Function	Legislation	Portfolio	Description
Ministry of Transport	Policy	Transport Act 1962	Transport	Provides advice and information relating to the promotion of safe, sustainable transport at reasonable cost; sets government framework for the transport sector; is the lead department for government policy on external aviation links.
Transit New Zealand (Crown agency)	Operations, Policy, Information	Transit New Zealand Act 1989	Transport	Controls and manages state highways; includes guideline roads in national parks and conservation reserves; also controls signage.
Civil Aviation Authority (Crown agency)	Policy, Regulation	Civil Aviation Act 1990	Transport	Controls and monitors safety and security in civil aviation, including provision of safety and security information, and policy advice to government.

Table 7.3 (continued)

Agency	Principal roles*	Enabling legislation	Responsible minister	Principal tourism-related functions
Land Transport Safety Authority (Crown agency)	Operations Regulation Policy	Land Transport Act 1993; Transport Services Licensing Act 1989	Transport	Promotes land transport safety; includes monitoring safety standards, education programmes, licence and regulation of passenger services industry.
Maritime Safety Authority (Crown agency)	Regulation	Maritime Transport Act 1994; Marine Pollution Act 1974	Transport	Promotes and monitors standards for safe shipping and the protection of the marine environment.
Airways New Zealand (Airways Corporation of New Zealand) (Crown agency)	Operations	Certified by the Civil Aviation Authority under the Civil Aviation Act 1990	Transport	Sole-provider status to deliver air traffic control and advisory services in national and international airspace, encompassing area control, approach control and flight information services.
Border security				
New Zealand Customs Service	Regulation	Customs and Excise Act 1996	Customs	Ensures smooth passage of people and products in and out New Zealand; controls prohibited or restricted products; agent for New Zealand Immigration Service at boom control points, such as airports.
Immigration New Zealand Service (part of Department of Labour)	Operations Policy	Enforces immigration law and regulations under the Immigration Act 1987	Immigration	Processes visa applications for people wanting to stay for longer than three months in New Zealand.
Ministry of Agriculture and Forestry (Quarantine Service, Biosecurity New Zealand)	Policy Operations	Biosecurity Act 1993	Agriculture	Manages risks associated with introduction of unwanted organisms, including inspection of aircraft in compliance with New Zealand Customs. Biosecurity New Zealand is responsible for the implementation of the national Biosecurity Strategy developed in 2003.

Organisation	Role	Legislation	Portfolio	Description
Aviation Security Service (Crown agency)	Operations	Section 80 Civil Aviation Act 1990; also Aviation Crimes Act 1972, Civil Aviation (Offences) Regulations 1997; these give effect to New Zealand's obligations as a signatory of Annex 17 of the Chicago Convention 1944	Transport	Responsible for aviation security, including passenger and baggage screening.
Recreation activities				
Ministry of Fisheries	Policy Regulation	Fisheries Act 1996	Fisheries	Manages New Zealand's fisheries, including recreational fishing.
Sport and Recreation New Zealand	Policy Operations	Sport, Fitness and Leisure Act 1987	Sport	Promotes sport, recreation, physical activity and excellence in high-performance sport; major initiatives include development of events with NZTB to promote events tourism.
Information and research				
Department of Statistics	Information	Statistics Act 1975	Statistics	Gathers statistical information about New Zealand tourism, including international arrivals and departures, and accommodation statistics; helped establish a Tourism Satellite Account.
Foundation for Research, Science and Technology (Crown agency)	Information	Foundation for Research, Science and Technology Act 1990	Research, Science and Technology	Allocates money from the Public Good Science Fund for research, including tourism research.
General				
Department of Internal Affairs	Policy Regulation	Local Government Act 1974	Local Government	Administers the Local Government Act 1974, which empowers local government to provide various services including infrastructure development; also administers Casino Control Act 1990.

* *Roles*: Infrastructure – Infrastructure development and provision; Information – Information provision and research; Marketing – Marketing and promotion; Operations – Direct land/asset management and/or service provision; Policy – Policy development and analysis, including sector development; Regulation – Managing compliance with legislation.

Table 7.4 Tourism responsibilities of local government agencies in New Zealand

Agency	Role	Primary acts	Functions
Territorial local authorities	Operations Policy Infrastructure Regulation Information Marketing	Local Government Act 2002 Resource Management Act 1991	Integrated management of the effects of the use, development and protection of land and associated natural and physical resources of the district. Also involved in economic development, local government-owned attractions (e.g. art galleries and museums) and the management of visitor information services.
Regional councils	Operations Policy Infrastructure Regulation Information	Local Government Act 1974 Resource Management Act 1991	Integrated management of natural and physical resources.
Regional tourism organisations (RTO)	Marketing Information Policy		Marketing and promotion of areas within New Zealand, international marketing usually undertaken in conjunction with the NZTB; provide information to operators and visitors. Funding base is usually from local authorities although some RTOs also have a membership base.

United Kingdom the policy function has come to be reduced in recent years, often with a split of government departments into separate agencies responsible for promotion and policy respectively. Such an institutional split has raised interesting issues in terms of encouraging sustainable tourism. If promotion and policy are separated how can promotion be seen to be set within sustainable tourism goals? In the short term increasing government funds for promotion at the expense of other functions may be welcomed by industry. However, it may also imply a lack of attention to other aspects of the roles of government in tourism including broader planning and policy functions that look beyond the short-term goal of attracting more tourists and attempt to deal with the long-term task of planning for sustainable development.

Given the complex situation that surrounds government involvement in tourism, issues of interorganisation relationships are therefore an extremely significant component of the tourism planning and policy system. Some of these issues will be dealt with in more detail in the next chapter. However, interorganisational relations occur not just horizontally, *within* the same level of government, but also vertically, *between* the different levels of government. The previous chapter noted how international and supranational policy actors influenced tourism planning and policy at the national, regional and local level. However, the relationship is clearly two-way. Member countries of the international institutions will also be attempting to influence the policy directions of those organisations in an attempt to meet national policy goals. For example, countries such as Australia, Canada, New Zealand and the United States have been trying to encourage the development of increasingly freer trade in the Asia-Pacific region, including trade in services and foreign investment, through APEC by using diplomatic methods to influence APEC agreements. Similarly, the various countries of the EU can be readily seen to be attempting to influence EU policy decisions and settings in order to meet their own national interests.

However, as the scope of international relations has increased in light of the expansion of global interdependence so the role of sub-national government (e.g. provincial, state and regional governments) has also increased in the international sphere. The emergence of international policy areas such as sustainable development, human rights, environmental pollution, migration, international trade flows and tourism in recent years has meant that, unlike traditional diplomatic/strategic/security concerns, these 'new' policy areas are intermistic in nature, that is, they are 'simultaneously, profoundly and inseparably both domestic and international' in character (Manning 1977: 309). The actions of sub-national actors in the international sphere, also described as paradiplomacy (Soldatos 1993) and constituent diplomacy (Kincaid 1990), is readily apparent in the tourism field, particularly in federal systems where states and provinces compete with each other not only for tourists but also for investment. For example, in Australia nearly all the states and territories have offshore offices from which they try and attract tourists, a situation that has led to confusion in the marketplace at times (Australian Government Committee of Inquiry Into Tourism 1987); while states and territories have also opposed any efforts to coordinate activities by which investment might be attracted for fear of losing out on investment to other states: 'The Northern Territory Government does not see a significant role or need for the co-ordination of foreign tourist development between the States, including the Northern Territory, by the Commonwealth Government' (Northern Territory Government submission quoted in Senate Standing Committee on Environment, Recreation and the Arts 1992: 248). Similarly, the Canadian provinces compete aggressively in their marketing in the United States, while the US states promote themselves separately in Canada.

The interdependence of local, national and international communities at a level 'that is far greater than any previously experienced' (Rosenau 1990: 17) has led to a situation in which leaders of sub-national governments have become 'acutely aware of the influence which international actors . . . can have on the economic well-being of their constituencies'

(Fry 1986: 301). The success of their leaders in attracting investment, trade and tourism can contribute both to economic development and employment generation and to increasing their chances for re-election. Nevertheless it is important to note that the international activities of sub-national governments are not simply the result of proactive policy settings. Provincial/state government subsidies are now subject to scrutiny under free trade regimes because of the possibility that they could be considered trade distortions. Therefore provincial/state governments may seek defensive positions with respect to their policy choices. In addition, environmental and social policies at the state/provincial level may also come under international scrutiny, particular with respect to transborder and regional policy issues.

The area of transnational relations, 'direct interactions between agencies (government sub-units) of different governments where those agencies act relatively autonomously from central government control' (Keohane and Nye 1976: 4) is therefore becoming of increasing importance in tourism policy and planning, particularly as regions seek to attract increasing amounts of international visitors in a complex and competitive market. Two types of transgovernment relations may be distinguished: first, where the sub-national government is a primary actor whereby it engages directly in international relations, e.g. through direct international promotion. Second, where the sub-national government is a mediating actor and seeks to affect international relations by attempting to influence the central government in its policy deliberations and actions for the purpose of promoting 'general policies that are beneficial to local conditions in such areas as trade and foreign investment' (Hocking 1986: 484), e.g. trade policy and targeted international tourism promotion. Further, it should be noted that increasingly it is not just provincial/state governments which are playing such an international role, but also cities (e.g. see Cohn and Smith 1995). For example, in the case of tourism, cities are increasingly lobbying to host international events, such as the Olympics and international expositions, and also competing to be able to attract international investment for tourism infrastructure, such as conference and exhibition centres and sports stadia (see Chapter 6).

The growing importance of sub-governments in international tourism has significant implications not only for international relations but also for the domestic relations between central and regional governments. The increasing activity of regional and municipal activity in tourism promotion and planning may create substantial tensions between different levels of government and further increase the difficulties that exist in coordinating government activities. Different state levels tend to have different sets of objectives to achieve via tourism development. Similarly, Williams and Shaw (1988: 230) observed that in the study of tourism 'policy formation is made more complex because the aims of the local state may diverge from those of the central state'. For example, in the Australian situation, the federal government has not taken an active role in direct national tourism planning in a statutory setting because of the constitutional and political difficulties that it would face and instead has focused on the development of national tourism strategies in which the national government assumes more of a coordination role (e.g. Department of Tourism 1992; Office of National Tourism 1997a, b; Australian Government 2003, 2004, 2005). Tourism-related land-use planning initiatives have occurred at the state level where responsibilities for statutory planning is more clearly defined. At times this has meant substantial conflicts between federal and state policy in a number of areas, such as resort and tourism infrastructure development in World Heritage areas. Nevertheless, the federal government still assumes a significant role in the tourism planning process at all levels of government through the provision of tourism marketing, promotion and research services; and direct funding for local tourism planning and visitor management programmes in such areas as ecotourism and rural tourism (Dredge and Jenkins 2007; Hall 2007a).

Similar conflicts between central and state/provincial government have occurred in Canada and the United States. In the case of Canada,

Sister city relationships as a sub-national tourism policy tool

Formal international partnerships based on the social, economic and political relationships between cities and towns have existed since the 1920s. Today, such relationships are commonly known as twinning or sister city relationships. The establishment of such relationships is a policy mechanism that many cities and towns are increasingly pursuing. With places becoming more competitive in a globalised economy the benefits that are being recognised through tourism and trade opportunities encourage the development of such links.

In September 1965 US President Dwight D. Eisenhower founded the sister cities programme to foster the promotion of world peace. Through their involvement in the programme, he believed that individuals from all levels of society could play a part in global diplomatic relations: 'the sister-city program is an important resource to the negotiations of governments in letting people themselves give expression of their common desire for friendship, goodwill and co-operation for a better world for all' (Boomerang Box 2003). From its beginnings as part of the *National League of Cities,* the now independent non-profit organisation *Sister Cities International* (SCI) has grown so that by 2007 700 communities in the United States had developed sister city relationships with nearly 2,000 cities in 134 countries. Similar patterns of growth have been recorded elsewhere. New Zealand had 140 sister city, twinning or friendship relations as of 2005 and Sister Cities New Zealand promotes the fact that these contacts are worth close to NZ$55 million a year in tourism and cultural exchange dollars alone (New Zealand Institute of Economic Research 2003). Indeed an analysis of the vision statements of official sister city organisations from across the globe reveals how the emphasis of these relationships has broadened from Eisenhower's founding objectives to take on a more commercial focus. *Sister Cities New Zealand* says the aim of such relations 'is to foster international understanding and friendship and to encourage exchange of education, culture and sport, and to promote, where possible, tourism and trade' while the *Australian Sister Cities Association* 'continues to regard economic benefit as not only a legitimate outcome of sister city relationships, but it can also be a legitimate reason to establish these relationships' (Australian Sister Cities Association 2004: 2).

In order to identify the nature and role of sister city relationships a survey was conducted of all 74 territorial authorities in New Zealand, where the majority of controlling bodies of New Zealand sister city relationships are based. A 90 per cent response rate was achieved (67 replies). These responses showed that:

> 66 per cent of territorial authorities have at least one sister city (n = 44);
> 34 per cent of territorial authorities do not have any sister city relationships (n = 23).

Japan is the main country with which linkages are established, followed by North America and Australia. Asia is increasing in importance with substantial growth in connections with China and Korea and, to a lesser extent, Taiwan. Such shifts also reflect the changing patterns of New Zealand trade and tourism.

The majority of cities have one relationship (42 per cent), with a third having two sister cities and 16 per cent with three; 13 per cent have four or more. Relationships were formed from the 1960s onwards with the number formed since the early 1990s levelling off and with no significant increase in overall numbers of relationships since the 1980s apparent, although the mix of countries has changed with a stronger Asian focus.

There is substantial variation in the management of sister city relationships. One-quarter of respondents did not know who initiated their sister city linkage. The most common person cited was the mayor, followed by an interest group or being approached

▶

from an overseas city. Within cities various people are responsible for their sister city relationship, primarily city council staff, with some totally community driven. Few cities have established a department or administrative section responsible for sister city relationships.

Factors that were important to the territorial authorities in New Zealand when forming a sister city relationship included:

- world peace/friendship, educational links and cultural links;
- professional and personal contacts;
- tourism is growing in importance;
- business and trade links are starting to become valued with half of the respondents indicating that here, too, there is potential for this aspect of sister city relationships to increase;
- in past years sister city affiliations emphasised cultural matters and the linkage of cities that had similar names, geography or heritage. These factors are not now considered so important.

Local authorities also identified reasons for not forming sister city relationships. These revolved around small population sizes, councils seeing no benefits from such relationships, the view that only the Mayor and council benefits and the belief that rates should be spent on services within the district. Lack of resources and community backing needed to make such a linkage a success were also cited. The importance of factors related to the formation of sister city relationships to New Zealand cities is illustrated in Table 7.5.

With respect to formal strategic planning in relation to sister city linkages the research indicated that nearly half of the cities had not implemented formal goals and objectives. Where formal goals had been set, for example in sister city agreements, methods that were used to meet the specified goals and objectives were exchanges and regular contact between the two municipalities (95 per cent), school-to-school contacts (90 per cent), sister city committees (75 per cent) and regular meetings (75 per cent). Many local governments also stated that social organisations were used to achieve these goals and objectives. Similarly, many authorities did not have a formal evaluation procedure for the effectiveness of sister city relations. Nearly half of all New Zealand relationships are not evaluated – 41 per cent of respondents who had established goals and objectives did not have any evaluation methods in place, while 8 per cent did not know what evaluation methods (if any) were in place. Of those that did use some form of evaluation, committees, regular meetings and feedback letters were the most prominent evaluation means.

As noted elsewhere in this chapter local policies are becoming more focused on providing economic development opportunities in their jurisdiction. The consequence of this for sister city relationships, as seen in the New Zealand experience, is that 'from the initial "international friendship" concept the sister cities' movement has grown into a more complex arrangement that involves incorporation at the broader processes of "globalisation"' (O'Toole, K. 2000: 45). Kevin O'Toole (2000, 2001) identified three interlinking principles that have emerged in the evolution of sister city links in Australia and which appear to apply to New Zealand and other developed countries. First of all, when such partnerships initially came into fruition, the objectives of partners were mainly 'associative', that is, these relations were along the broad aims of international friendship, cultural exchange and general international awareness. From here 'reciprocative' objectives were realised as sister cities began to take part in sporting, cultural, educational and professional exchanges with their international counterparts. With the 1970s involvement in sister city relationships began to have a more 'commercial' focus as local governments started to emphasise local economic development. That is not to say that the earlier 'associative' and 'reciprocative' goals were laid aside. Rather, local authorities sought to take advantage of the trusting, well-established relationships to help them pursue policies for economic growth in their communities: 'the end product is that local governments are looking to reconfigure pre-existing social and cultural relationships into economic ones' (O'Toole, K. 2001: 406). However,

▶

Table 7.5 The importance of factors related to the formation of sister city relationships to New Zealand cities

Factor	Very important (%)	Quite important (%)	Important (%)	Not so important (%)	Not important (%)	Not applicable (%)
Similar geographical attributes (n = 84)	8	5	29	25	25	8
Professional and personal contacts (n = 86)	14	24	48	5	3	3
Existing exchange programmes (n = 83)	17	17	19	12	14	21
Similar city size/ planning features (n = 84)	7	10	14	27	25	17
Identical city name (n = 82)	4	4	0	8	18	66
Heritage/migrant links (n = 83)	6	6	13	10	28	37
Business and trade opportunities (n = 82)	24	14	25	23	7	7
Educational links (n = 82)	27	22	33	6	7	5
Tourism growth (n = 84)	22	18	39	17	2	2
Sporting links (n = 83)	9	11	28	22	18	12
Cultural links (n = 83)	24	20	34	12	5	5
World peace/ friendship (n = 85)	31	24	15	14	11	6

as the New Zealand survey results indicated, there is clearly a need to ensure that this is done in a strategic and systematic manner if this is to be undertaken effectively.

Sister Cities International:
http://www.sister-cities.org/

The Council of European Municipalities and Regions Twinning Network:
http://www.ccre.org/
Sister Cities New Zealand:
http://www.sistercities.org.nz/
Sister Cities of Christchurch:
http://www.christchurch.org.nz/SisterCities/

Source: Michael Hall and Fiona McKay.

improved coordination between the provinces and Tourism Canada came about through greater emphasis on joint promotion exercises and greater private sector involvement. In the United States the direct tourism promotion and policy role of the federal government is extremely weak in comparison with the states. Where the federal government does play a significant role in tourism is in relation to the large expanses of federal land tied up in national parks, national monuments, and Forest Service and Bureau of Land Management lands. However, local, state and national governments often come into conflict over land use practices on federal lands as different stakeholders seek to influence various policy levels.

One of the outcomes of the desire to reduce the role of government in western society has been a devolution of responsibilities from central government to state/provincial and/or local government; in some cases a withdrawal by central government from the policy area and/or sector has resulted in the vacuum being filled by regional or local government and/or the private sector. For example, many transport systems have been privatised while heritage sites once managed by a national authority have become the responsibility of local government or community groups.

The changing role of government has also led to greater attention to the instruments or means by which government is able to achieve its planning and policy goals. For example, the Austrian National Tourism Organization (ANTO), or Österreich Werbung, which includes the country's federal and provincial governments, was restructured in 1997 in order to streamline the decision-making process and improve the cost effectiveness of marketing and promotional programmes, with a resultant drop in administrative and other fixed costs from 57 per cent in 1995 to less than 50 per cent of ANTO's total budget in 1998 (World Tourism Organization 1998g).

In line with the national constitution, Austria's nine provincial governments are responsible for tourism development in their respective provinces, while the federal government coordinates tourism policy across the country. One of the major focuses of Austrian tourism policy is the development of small and medium-sized tourism enterprises (SMTEs). In addition to the aim of providing a more favourable overall framework for tourism development through the restructuring process, the Austrian government has been developing instruments, such as the use of subsidies, to support SMEs. These include:

- promotion of participation and risk capital, since the Austrian tourism industry suffers from a high share of foreign capital for investment financing as a result of the low equity capital available;
- promotion of consultation and training measures in tourism facility design, in order to help develop a more varied tourism plant;
- promotion of cooperation – this is intended to show that the creation of voluntary groups and networks provide synergies that improve marketing efficiency;
- implementation of pilot projects in the field of cooperation – this can include multiple distribution channels, destination management schemes, or even joint offers and joint brand development (WTO 1998g).

The emphasis given by the Austrian government to the role of cooperation in tourism development highlights the role given to public–private partnerships and stakeholder collaboration in tourism planning as opposed to command planning approaches. Nevertheless, there is a wide range of instruments available for planners to achieve their objectives (see Chapter 10). Furthermore, as government withdraws more from direct intervention in the economy, so the role of persuasion, argument and the creation of partnerships with various stakeholder groups becomes all the more important. It is to these processes that the next chapter will now turn.

Summary

This chapter has examined a number of issues with respect to tourism planning and policy at the national and sub-national level. It has identified the various roles that government and the state play in tourism, with particular reference to the appropriateness of those roles and the role that public planners may pay with respect to attempting to meet the public interest. The chapter also discussed the organisational aspects of government involvement in tourism. Although there are many institutional means and forms by which government involvement in tourism is expressed, it was argued that at the broad level government involvement has been shifting from a developmental to a promotional role. This has corresponded with a change in the role of the central state and increasing importance of the local state expressed through the activities of sub-national governments (state, provincial and municipal governments). Such a shift also means that increasing attention needs to be given to domestic and, increasingly, international inter-organisational relationships in tourism planning and policy. Finally, the chapter discussed some of the instruments by which governments achieve their policy goals as part of the tourism planning process. The next chapter further continues the emphasis on relational aspects of tourism planning with a focus on the destination level of tourism.

Questions

1. What are the main roles of government in tourism? Discuss the extent to which they are given effect in your country at the national and local level.

2. What is the most equitable approach to funding tourism promotion?

3. Identify the manner by which the institutional arrangements for government involvement in tourism in your country are organised in terms of primary and secondary agency responsibility. How does this set of arrangements differ from the New Zealand situation (Table 7.3)?

4. Why have tourism-related sub-national government actors become more important in international relations?

Important websites and recommended reading

Websites

British Tourist Authority: www.visitbritain.com/

Canadian Tourism Commission: http://www.corporate.canada.travel/en/ca/

Finnish Tourist Board: http://www.mek.fi/

Greek National Tourism Organisation: http://www.gnto.gr/

Japan National Tourism Organisation: http://www.jnto.go.jp/eng/

New Zealand Tourism Ministry: http://www.tourism.govt.nz/

Singapore Tourism Board: www.visitsingapore.com/

Tourism Australia: www.tourism.australia.com/

Visit Sweden: http://www.visitsweden.com/

Recommended reading

1. Caffyn, A. and Jobbins, G. (2003) 'Governance capacity and stakeholder interactions in the development and management of coastal tourism: examples from Morocco and Tunisia', *Journal of Sustainable Tourism*, 11(2/3): 224–45.

   A good general introduction to issues of regional development in developed countries.

2. Sharpley, R. and Telfer, D. (eds) (2002) *Tourism and Development: Concepts and Issues*, Channel View Publications, Clevedon.

   Provides an overview of development issues in tourism.

3. Whitford, M., Bell, B. and Watkins, M. (2001) 'Indigenous tourism policy in Australia: 25 years of rhetoric and economic rationalism', *Current Issues in Tourism*, 4(2–4): 151–81.

An excellent historic overview of tourism policy and therefore how it has changed over time.

4. McDavid, H. and Ramajeesingh, D. (2003) 'The state and tourism: a Caribbean perspective', *International Journal of Contemporary Hospitality Management*, 15(3): 180–3.

   Discusses the role of the state in tourism within a specific geographical context.

5. Hall, C.M. and Jenkins, J.M. (1995) *Tourism and Public Policy*, Routledge, London.

   Seminal theoretical work with respect to state tourism policies.

6. Dredge, D. and Jenkins, J. (eds) (2007) *Tourism Planning and Policy*, John Wiley, Brisbane.

   Discusses tourism policies and planning in an Australian context.

7. Church, A. and Coles, T. (eds) (2007) *Tourism, Power and Space*, Routledge, London.

Edited work that has several chapters on the connection of power arrangements to tourism policy and planning.

8. *Current Issues in Tourism* (2001) Special edition on Tourism Policy Making: Theory and Practice, 4(2–4).

   The special edition has several articles of relevance to tourism policy and planning in addition to the Whitford *et al.* article noted above.

9. Hall, C.M. (2006) 'Policy, planning and governance in ecotourism,' in S. Gössling and J. Hultman (eds), *Ecotourism in Scandinavia*, CABI, Wallingford, 193–206.

   Examines a specific policy domain at the national level in the Nordic countries.

10. Hall, C.M. and Williams, A. (2008) *Tourism and Innovation*, Routledge, London.

    Examines the role of the state in tourism-related innovation systems at a national and sub-national level.

8 Planning destinations: competition and cooperation

Chapter objectives

After reading this chapter you will:

- Have developed an understanding of key concepts: network, cluster and trust
- Appreciate some of the key questions with respect to notions of destination competitiveness
- Understand some of the main controls, tools and techniques of destination growth management
- Understand the role of cooperation in bringing stakeholders together towards common goals
- Appreciate that in many instances the establishment of trust and positive social relationships takes time.

Destinations are the focal point for much tourism research. Metelka (1990: 46) defines a destination as the 'geographic location to which a person is traveling', with Gunn (1994: 107) equating the idea of a destination to that of a 'travel market area'. Similarly, Medlik (1993: 148) defines a tourism destination as:

> Countries, regions, towns or other areas visited by tourists. Throughout the year their amenities serve their resident and working populations, but at some or all times of the year they also have temporary users – tourists. How important any geographical unit is as a tourism destination, is determined by three prime factors: attractions, amenities and accessibility, which are sometimes called tourism qualities of the destination.

More recently, Papatheodorou (2006: xv) defined a tourism destination as 'a geographical area of variable territorial scale, where tourism is a predominant activity both from a demand-side (i.e. tourists) and a supply-side (i.e. infrastructure and employment) perspective'.

Nevertheless, defining what actually constitutes a destination is highly problematic (Davidson and Maitland 1997), with the term often being equated with that of a 'resort' (Vukonic 1997) and also being applied at a number of different spatial scales and scale of governance. Smith (1995) provides a number of ways in which regionalisation may be identified in tourism research through such measures as cartographic regionalisation, perceptual regionalisation, cognitive mapping, functional regionalisation and destination zone identification. Drawing on the work of Gunn (1979), Smith (1995: 199) identified a number of criteria that might be applied in the identification of destination zones:

- The region should have a set of cultural, physical and social characteristics that create a sense of regional identity.
- The region should contain an adequate tourism infrastructure to support tourism development. Infrastructure includes utilities, roads, business services and other social services necessary to support tourism businesses and to cater to tourists' needs.
- The region should be larger than just one community or one attraction.
- The region should contain existing attractions or have the potential to support

the development of sufficient attractions to draw tourists.

- The region should be capable of supporting a tourism planning agency and marketing initiatives to guide and encourage future development.
- The region should be accessible to a large population base. Accessibility may be by road, scheduled air passenger service, or cruise ships.

Nevertheless, despite the value of such an approach, precise boundaries will still be difficult to identify, a problem that has been long identified with respect to the problem of identifying regional characteristics. For example, as Grigg (1967: 478) observed, if a region, such as described by the term destination, 'is thought to be a real entity then it must be presumed to have clear and determinable limits'. Moreover, from a public planning perspective it should also be noted that perceptual regions or destination zones may run over different government boundaries, making land-use planning and even tourism promotion extremely difficult as it raises the potential for conflicts between different government jurisdictions. In attempting to overcome such difficulties, Davidson and Maitland (1997: 4) defined destinations in terms of 'a single district, town or city, or a clearly defined and contained rural, coastal or mountain area' that share a number of characteristics:

- a complex and multidimensional tourism product based on a variety of resources, products, services and forms of ownership;
- other economic and social activities, which may be complementary to or in conflict with the various aspects of tourism;
- a host community;
- public authorities and/or an elected council with responsibility for planning and management;
- an active private sector.

Davidson and Maitland's approach towards tourism destinations is useful as it highlights the complexity of destinations. Although some tourism marketers and promoters and, perhaps,

even planners may sometimes seem to propose otherwise, a destination is not just another 'product' or 'commodity'. Destinations are not just places of tourism consumption, they are also places in which people live, work and play and to which they may have a strong sense of attachment and ownership, what is usually described as a 'sense of place' – a term that is used to refer to the subjective, personal and emotional attachments and relationships people have to a place (Cresswell 2004). In many cases, people might only consciously notice the unique qualities of places when they are away from them, when a place is being rapidly altered, or when a place is being represented or marketed and promoted in a way they do not relate to. From this perspective, senses of place are extremely important when examining the effects of tourism development on a location as tourism-related changes may lead to changes in sense of place, possibly then leading to resentment towards tourism and even visitors (Cooper and Hall 2008). Therefore, if there is serious intent with respect to making places sustainable we need to pay attention to such concepts as sense of place that will be part of a feeling of well-being and quality of life (see Chapter 2), and treat them as the complex set of relationships and networks they are. As Hewison argued,

> the time has come to argue that commerce is *not* culture, whether we define culture as the pursuit of music, literature or the fine arts, or whether we adopt Raymond Williams' definition of culture as "a whole way of life". You cannot get a whole way of life into a Tesco's trolley or a V & A Enterprises shopping bag. (1991: 175)

Similarly, Goodwin (1993: 149) observed, regions are:

> more than a simple coherence of production and consumption (and even this is never guaranteed). It is a complex collection of individuals and communities, which in certain instances develop particular regional and local cultures, formed by social relations and practices outside of capital's narrow logic. Together these movements and cultures can be important in helping to sustain or to destroy the coherence of a particular place. The 'building' and 'revolutionising' of an urban landscape is thus never

just physical and economic: it is also social, cultural and political, and changes in these processes can play a vital role in easing economic transformation and helping to form a new round of coherence . . .

The promotion of new urban images, of new lifestyles and of new 'city myths', is often a necessary prelude to the establishment of new urban economies. Importantly, however, the formation of these new images themselves is an issue of challenge and contestation, an issue which is often fought through particular political agencies and institutions.

For some, places are now commodities to be produced and consumed. The competitive ethos of the marketplace has become translated into a burgeoning 'place market'. 'The primary goal of the place marketer is to construct a new image of the place to replace either vague or negative images previously held by current or potential residents, investors and visitors' (Holcomb 1993: 133), in order to effectively compete with other places within the constraints of a global economy for a share of mobile international cultural, human, intellectual and financial capital (Hall 2005a).

This chapter discusses tourism planning at the local or destination level. It first discusses the nature of place competition within a global economy before going on to examine the ways in which places manage themselves in terms of growth management strategies and cooperate in order both to compete more effectively and deal with conflict.

Destinations and places

Although destinations have long promoted themselves to potential visitors, there has been a qualitative change in the nature of place promotion since the early 1980s when shifts to reduce the role of the state in a globalising economy, otherwise known as 'Thatcherism' (United Kingdom), 'Reaganomics' (United States) and 'Rogernomics' (New Zealand), occurred (Hall 2005a). Within the tourism, geography and marketing literature, the concepts of 'place marketing' (e.g. Madsen 1992) also sometimes described as 'selling places' (e.g. Burgess 1982; Kearns and Philo 1993), 'geographical marketing' (e.g. Ashworth and Voogd 1988) or 'reimaging strategies' (Roche

1992; Hall 1994), have arisen to describe this new phenomenon. As Ashworth and Voogd (1988: 65) argue, the process of place marketing reflects a

> paradigm structuring the way the complex functioning of cities is viewed . . . [as] many urban activities operate in some kind of a market . . . in which a planned action implies an explicit and simultaneous consideration of both the supply-side and the demand-side . . . [and] such an approach has implications for . . . the way the cities are managed.

Although the notion of place marketing was initially applied in the urban context (Page and Hall 2003), the concept has increasingly come to be used to described place promotion in rural regions as well (Butler *et al.* 1998).

One of the main reasons for the attention given to place as a focus of academic, government and industry interest is the process of globalisation, whereby geographical transformations are now being brought about through the international restructuring of capitalist economies and the consequent changes to the nature and role of cities and regions as they seek to attract ever more mobile investors and customers. Similarly, in a highly influential book Kotler *et al.* have argued that 'In a borderless economy, [places] will emerge as the new actors on the world scene' (1993: 346). According to Kotler *et al.* (1993) we are living in a time of 'place wars' in which places are competing for their economic survival with other places and regions not only in their own country but throughout the world.

> All places are in trouble now, or will be in the near future. The globalization of the world's economy and the accelerating pace of technological changes are two forces that require all places to learn how to compete. Places must learn how to think more like businesses, developing products, markets, and customers. (Kotler *et al.* 1993: 346)

The profound changes to the global economic and cultural system – technological diffusion, decreasing cost and increasing speed of transportation, increasing diffusion of information, and declining barriers to trade – that are generally characterised under the heading of 'globalisation', have tremendous implications for tourism

Plate 8.1 Darling Harbour redevelopment, Sydney, Australia. The Darling Harbour redevelopment established a major leisure/tourism/retail in the inner city in an effort to renew a run-down dockyard area.

planning (Hall 2005a). As has been indicated in the emphasis placed by this book on systems, relationships and the multi-scale nature of tourism planning and policy, 'These changes express themselves both in the relationship of individual cities to each other and to the system of which they form a part; and also in the internal structure of the city' (P. Hall 1995: 3). 'Major cities of the world are becoming increasingly linked – by global networks of telecommunications, computers and air transport' (Brotchie *et al.* 1995: vi). While cities and places are in increased competition with each other they are correspondingly more linked and entwined with each other's fates than ever before. Furthermore, although there is no formal theory of location for 'high-touch industries' such as the arts, leisure and entertainment sectors, which are regarded as integral to the development of 'creative economies' (Florida 2002), they

> have a close symbiotic relationship with the more specialised non-mass segments of the tourist industry, notably business tourism and cultural tourism. Only rarely, and only in the mass tourist sector, can

entirely new urban spaces be created for this complex of industries. (Hall 1995: 8)

Although it is also argued that 'this sector is the most vulnerable to globalised third world competition exploiting the potential offered by long-haul jets and lower labour costs' (P. Hall 1995: 7–8). Similarly, according to Kotler *et al.* (1993: 18), the

> marketplace shifts and changes occur far faster than a community's capacity to react and respond. Buyers of the goods and services that a place can offer (i.e. business firms, tourists, investors, among others) have a decided advantage over place sellers (i.e. local communities, regions, and other places that seek economic growth).

Kotler *et al.* (1993: 18) refer to the need for places to adopt a process of 'strategic place marketing' for urban and regional revitalisation in order to design a community 'to satisfy the needs of its key constituencies'. Such a process embraces four interrelated core activities:

1. designing the right mix of community features and services;

Plate 8.2 Docklands redevelopment, London, England. The massive redevelopment of London's docklands has led to substantial changes in the area's economic and social mix.

2. setting attractive incentives for the current and potential buyers and users of its goods and services;
3. delivering a place's products and services in an efficient, accessible way;
4. promoting the place's values and image so that the potential users are fully aware of the place's distinctive advantages (1993: 18).

'Place marketing means designing a place to satisfy the needs of its target markets. It succeeds when citizens and businesses are pleased with their communities, and meet the expectations of visitors and investors' (Kotler *et al.* 1993: 99). Various investments can be made in a place to 'improve livability, investibility, and visitability', a process made up of the four components of place:

1. place as character
2. place as a fixed environment
3. place as a service provider
4. place as entertainment and recreation (Kotler *et al.* 1993: 100).

From all of this the reader may well ask, so how is strategic place marketing any different from the strategic tourism planning process discussed earlier in this book? In many ways they are clearly similar. However, there is one fundamental difference when we look towards public tourism planning that is attempting to develop sustainable forms of tourism development, and that is the notion of seeking to meet a public interest through equitable programmes and policies. In objectifying place as a commodity, as within the empiricist tradition of the majority of marketing studies, with the exception of social marketing, the people constituting place have often been placed outside of the place marketers and the tourism developer's frame of reference. As Hudson (1988: 493–4) recognised:

> [T]he point is that for these people the locality is *not just* a space in which to work for a wage but a place where they were born, went to school, have friends and relations etc.; places where they are socialised human beings rather than just the commodity labour-power and, as a result, places to which they have become deeply attached. These localities are places that have come to have socially endowed and shared meanings for people that touch on all aspects of their lives and that help shape who they are by virtue of where they are.

In commodifying place as a product that can be revitalised, advertised and marketed, places are presented not so much

> as foci of attachment and concern, but as bundles of social and economic opportunity *competing* against one another in the open (and unregulated) *market* for a share of the capital investment cake (whether this be the investment of enterprises, tourists, local consumers or whatever). (Philo and Kearns 1993: 18)

Plate 8.3 Crown Casino, Melbourne, Australia. The development of the casino complex was aimed not only at redeveloping the waterfront area but also in promoting a more exciting image of the city.

Harvey (1989c) sees four different competitive elements for cities attempting to restructure themselves:

1. competition within the spatial division of labour;
2. competition within the spatial division of consumption;
3. competition for command functions;
4. competition for redistribution.

The 'terrain of thinking' about local economic policies and political forms has therefore been shifted, so that a range of local institutions 'now internalise the idea that the interests of a place are best served by lifting the "dead hand" of regulation and by opening it to the sway of market forces' (Philo and Kearns 1993: 19). Although it is not usually acknowledged in the mainstream business and tourism literature the desire for such competitiveness emerges from within what is described as neoliberal thought. Neoliberalism promotes market-led economic and social

restructuring that produces, among other things, a more general orientation of economic and social policy to the private sector's 'needs'. In the case of tourism, the fusion of urban entrepreneurialism with the neoliberal political agenda has provided the ideological justification for place competitive reimaging strategies, including the hosting of mega-events and the construction of public–private infrastructure such as sports stadia, convention centres and waterfront redevelopments (Peck and Tickell 2002; Hall 2005a). Neoliberalism promotes market-led economic and social restructuring that produces, among other things, a more general orientation of economic and social policy to the private sector's 'needs' (Jessop 2002). In the case of regional development this has typically meant the development of structures and powers of governance that are opaque and unaccountable to public stakeholders and participation (Owen 2002). Neoliberalism therefore structures ideas about and the objectives set for community development, definitions of the public

Plate 8.4 Waterfront redevelopment Dublin, Ireland. Old dock areas have been converted into integrated office/retail/entertainment/leisure spaces.

good and definitions of citizenship that 'create wider distinctions than ever before between the "citizen" and the "consumer" and which of these ought to be the focal point of urban public life' (Lowes 2004: 71). Indeed, in relation to meta-political narratives, competitiveness is a discourse that 'provides some shared sense of meaning and a means of legitimizing neo-liberalism rather than a material focus on the actual improvements of economic welfare' (Bristow 2005: 300).

As discussed in Chapter 4, theories are also policies (Hall and Jenkins 1995). Academic, government and industry arguments as to the role of the local state are intimately related. As discussed previously, the institutional arrangements for tourism are increasingly based around the notions of privatisation and deregulation, twin processes that supposedly promote the operation of so-called 'market forces' and hence greater competitiveness. Much of the infrastructure of urban and regional government has been or is under pressure to be privatised or corporatised. 'Where public agencies were once seen as an essential part of the

solution to any urban crisis, they are now viewed as part of the problem itself' (Goodwin 1993: 148). However, it is ironic that Kotler *et al.*'s (1993) discussion of strategic place marketing fails to address the means by which the citizenry can actually participate in the place marketing process to decide how their city or region should be presented to consumers, if at all. Within this context, normative assumptions about equal individual access to power and decision making pervade much of the marketing literature. Yet, clearly, individuals do not have equal access to power and decision making. Business interest groups tend to dominate the tourism policy-making process (Hall and Jenkins 1995; Dredge and Jenkins 2007), while growth coalitions dominate much urban redevelopment (see the discussion in Chapter 7 on the role of government as public interest protector).

This is not to deny that concepts of productivity are not useful tools. However, there is the difficulty in translating a concept that was developed at the firm level to the destination or regional level (see also Chapter 7). At the firm

Plate 8.5 New opera house and waterfront development, Copenhagen, Denmark.

level there is a reasonably clear meaning for competitiveness that relates to a common unit – the firm – engaged in comparable activities – competing (surviving and growing) in a market, which therefore allows competitiveness to be conceived of in output-related indicators and metrics (Malecki 2004; Bristow 2005). Indeed, for Porter (1985, 1990) firm competitiveness is a proxy for productivity. Perhaps more significantly for the discourse on regional competitiveness Porter (2002: 3) has also argued that regional competitiveness and productivity are equivalent terms: 'A region's standard of living (wealth) is determined by the *productivity* with which it uses its human, capital, and natural resources. The appropriate definition of competitiveness is *productivity*.'

Porter's role is important because of the extent to which he 'has successfully branded, transformed and exported his diagnosis of how regions may improve their competitiveness to development agencies and governments all over the world' (Bristow 2005: 288). Porter, along with others (e.g. Kotler *et al.* 1993) contributed to the idea that places, regions and destinations are equivalent to firms in competing for various forms of capital as well as market share in an increasingly competitive global economy. Porter

argued that government creates the market conditions that allow firms to exploit each regional economy's competitive advantage with productivity in a region being a reflection of what firms 'choose to do in that location' (2002: 3), with competitiveness ultimately depending on 'improving the microeconomic foundations of competition' (2002: 5). Porter identified four sets of factors as interrelated elements of the microeconomic business environment's contribution to productivity: demand conditions, including local demand; the context for firm strategy and rivalry, particularly local conditions that contribute to open local competition, efficiency and investment; factor (input) conditions, which refers to high-quality, specialised inputs available to firms; and related and supporting industries in the form of local suppliers and clusters (Porter 2002: 6). Given the focus of Porter and others who espouse the concept of regional competitiveness it is therefore not surprising that 'the region' and 'the destination' have become a focal point of economic policy as well as being regarded as a crucible of economic development and wealth generation (e.g. Ritchie and Crouch 2000, 2003; Dwyer and Kim 2003). Nevertheless, there are differences. For example, Dwyer *et al.* (2000a, b)

Plate 8.6 Clarke Quay, waterfront redevelopment, Singapore.

provide an excellent discussion of national destination competitiveness, but on the empirical basis of price. Perhaps more comparably, Storper (1997: 264) defines regional competitiveness as 'the capability of a region to attract and keep firms with stable or increasing market shares in an activity, while maintaining stable or increasing standards of living for those who participate in it'. Although this approach is related to the same global competitiveness perspective of Porter and others, it is also strongly influenced by national and international policy discourses (Malecki 2004; Bristow 2005; Gibson and Klockner 2005). Importantly, unlike Porter, Storper (1997) asserts that regional competitiveness and regional prosperity are interdependent rather than equivalent notions and avoids equating regional competitiveness with productivity.

A number of key points can be highlighted with respect to the regional competitiveness literature (Martin and Sunley 2003; Bristow 2005; Martin 2005; Hall 2006f) (Table 8.1 details some of the factors that have been identified as significant with respect to regional competitiveness):

- There is no single theoretical perspective that captures the full complexity of the notion of 'regional competitiveness' or 'destination competitiveness'. Instead there are three basic conceptions of regional or destination competitiveness that focus on regions as sites of export specialisation, regions as source of increasing returns, regions as hubs of knowledge.
- In one sense, regional competitiveness has to do with the ability of a region to generate sufficient levels of exports (to other regions or overseas) to sustain rising levels of income and full employment of its resident population. But the productivity of locally oriented economic activity is also important with respect to non-traded services.
- The notion of regional competitiveness is as much about qualitative factors and conditions (such as untraded networks of informal knowledge, trust and social capital) as it is about quantifiable attributes and processes (such as interfirm trading, patenting rates and labour supply). This has consequent implications for the empirical measurement and analysis of regional competitiveness.
- The competitiveness of a region resides both in the competitiveness of its constituent individual firms and their interactions, and in its wider social, economic, environmental, institutional and public attributes and assets.

Table 8.1 Outline of regional factors of competitiveness

Infrastructure and accessibility	Human resources	Productive environment
• Transport infrastructure	• Demographic trends	• Entrepreneurial culture
• Housing and property infrastructure	• Migration trends	• Sectoral specialisation
• Educational infrastructure	• Cultural openness	• Innovation capacity
• Information and communication technology infrastructure	• Knowledge and skills levels	• Governance and institutional capacity
• Quality of place		• Availability of capital
• Location relative to market		• Internationalisation
		• Sectoral concentrations and activities
		• Nature of competition and cooperation

- The sources of regional competitiveness may originate at a variety of geographical scales, from the local, through regional, to national and even international. There is no natural, predefined 'regional' unit at which issues of competitiveness are best theorised or analysed.
- The causes of competitiveness are usually attributed to the effects of an aggregate of factors rather than the impact of an individual factor. Therefore the possibility of isolating correlation coefficients is limited (Martin 2005).

The fact that not everyone can win does not mean that competition is without value. There are both benefits and problems inherent in place competition, of which tourism is clearly a significant part. However, within regional development, tourism is usually seen as part of an imitative 'low-road' policy in contrast to 'high-road' knowledge-based policies (Table 8.2). According to Malecki (2004: 1103)

> The disadvantages of competition mainly concern the perils that low-road strategies build so that no strengths can prevail over the long term, which presents particular difficulties for regions trying to catch up in the context of territorial competition based on knowledge.

Low-road strategies are focused on 'traditional' location factors such as land, labour, capital, infrastructure and locational advantage with respect to markets or key elements of production as well as direct state subsidies to retain firms: more intangible factors, such as intellectual capital and institutional capacity are secondary (see Table 8.3). Low-road strategies are generally regarded as being tied into property-oriented growth strategies linked to the packaging of the place product, reimaging strategies and the gaining of media attention. For example, investment in infrastructure such as meeting and convention facilities, sports stadia, event facilities, entertainment and shopping is often similar from city to city because they are aimed at the same markets with few places being able to 'forgo competition in each of these sectors' (Judd 2003: 14). In contrast to the low-road approach, Malecki (2004) argues that a high-road approach of genuine entrepreneurship and innovation through the development of learning regions is possible although it is a much more difficult path to follow. There is a case for regional innovation and knowledge economies that utilise agglomeration economies, institutional learning, associative governance, proximity capital and interactive innovation (Cooke 2002). Regional infrastructure,

Table 8.2 Low-, middle- and high-road regional competitiveness strategies

Low road Zero sum	Middle path Growth enhancing	High road Network enhancing
Place promotion	Education and training	Internal networks
Capturing mobile investment, firms and capital	Fostering entrepreneurship	External (non-local) networks
Subsidised investment and means of production, e.g. sites and premises	Helping and mentoring new firms and entrepreneurs	Benchmarking assessments
Focus on visitors on the basis of numbers	Investment in infrastructure	Investing in superstructure
	Business advice	Transport links, especially airline and airfreight links
	Reducing uncertainty	Information and communications links
	Coordination	Scanning globally for new knowledge

Sources: After Cheshire and Gordon (1998); Malecki (2002, 2004); Hall (2007b).

Table 8.3 Key factors in the success of regional tourism development (measured in terms of numbers of visitors)

- The nature of demand/the market
  - age, population, income, education, time
  - length of stay and pattern of expenditure
- Lack of destination alternatives/competition
- Management/composition/adaptability of local labour force
- Positive attitudes of local communities towards tourism and second-home development
- Appropriate state intervention, including infrastructure provision and land use strategies
- Attractiveness/amenity values
- Low cost
- Ease of accessibility
  - distance from population centres
  - distance from main transport routes
  - travel ease
  - travel time
  - travel distance

Source: Adapted from Hall (1995).

both hard (communications, transport, finance) and soft (knowledge, intellectual capital, trustful labour relations, mentoring, worker-welfare orientation), is required in order to encourage innovation rather than adaption (Malecki 2004).

However, the soft infrastructure of learning, knowledge and interaction is difficult to control and measure. Similarly, the cognitive aspects of a regional innovation system are also particularly difficult to influence in a short space of time, particularly when one is faced with a long history of particular 'ways of doing' in business that shape perceptions of competition and cooperation. As Malecki (2004: 1108) noted, 'The objectives are less sporadic or ephemeral than permanent, incremental and focused on long-term development.' This therefore raises political problems for politicians and growth coalitions that are often geared towards demonstrating competitive success in relation to election cycles. Yet the higher road, with its focus on the construction of 'territorially rooted immobile assets' (Brenner 1998: 15–16) of an innovative culture and learning region takes considerably longer to achieve than the periodicity of local and national election cycles. Indeed, it is often much easier to build an innovation centre or science park as symbols of local innovation

Plate 8.7 Whistler, British Columbia, Canada. This resort development has grown into a permanent, thriving community that has a strong growth management strategy in order to maintain quality of life for residents and quality of attraction for visitors.

than it is to create an intense bundle of communication and interaction between firms and institutions. Therefore those places that do not attain high-road competitiveness quickly are then in danger of shifting back to low-road strategies of regional competitiveness. Such points are extremely important for understanding the economic development potential of tourism. The suggestion that tourism is part of a low-road approach, i.e. a competitive basis in which regions are production sites where the determinants of competitiveness often lie in the field of basic infrastructure and accessibility (such as low-cost sites, absence of congestion, affordable housing and the availability of human resources at reasonable costs) (Martin 2005) may raise fundamental issues about the role of tourism as a means of economic development. In the same way that there is a difference between sustainable tourism and sustainable development so a competitive tourism industry or a competitive destination needs to be seen as qualitatively different from that of a competitive region. Such a perspective does not mean that tourism is unimportant, or does not have a part to play in high-road

strategies. It certainly does, as high-road strategies emphasise connectivity, through transport and aviation as well as communication linkages and diasporic networks, and high levels of amenity that may also attract visitors as well as be important for residents. However, these are strategies in which tourism is a subsidiary element of a knowledge-based economy rather than a strategy in itself. Tourism in this sense is clearly seen as a subset of a broader understanding of human mobilities (Hall 2005a). Indeed, as Doel and Hubbard (2002: 263) argue, policy makers need to 'replace their place-based way of thinking with a focus on connectivity, performance and flow'. Yet just as importantly they also need to develop a far greater understanding of what competition actually means.

Changing places, changing thinking

The focus on the local, on cities and regions, has led to changes in thinking about how places operate. As Brotchie *et al.* (1995: 442) observed, there has been a shift in thinking in urban planning and policy theory from macro-analysis to micro levels of analysis,

> from the notion that cities are strong, collectively organised systems to ideas that cities are composed of many groups and individuals in competition, betraying great diversity but also great adaptability, acting locally but generating organisation and order which is manifest at more global scales through the urban hierarchy.

Such sentiments apply equally well to rural areas. Brotchie *et al.*'s comment illustrates the need to perceive what is happening at the local level in the context of what is happening at the sub-national, national and international scales. As has been previously noted, the relationships that drive the tourism planning process are horizontally and vertically connected within the different scales of governance. This means that in focusing on local processes that give rise to the aggregates we observe new approaches to 'organised complexity' (Batty 1995: 470). However it must be noted that, as the field of place marketing indicates, the capacity to think globally, act locally does not necessarily lead to sustainable conclusions. Nevertheless, realisation of the embedded set of relations between local, regional, national and global processes does have substantial value. For example, in the age of ecology and global environmental issues we increasingly recognise the transborder nature of economic and environmental problems. Indeed there may be significant shortcomings attached to the inappropriate use of traditional planning methods, such as local land-use control, including:

- the absence of a comprehensive planning framework;
- the predominance of municipal self-interest and the lack of a mechanism to allocate undesirable but socially necessary land uses to optimal sites;
- the inherent inability of local governments to address larger environmental questions.

As Cullingsworth (1997: 125) observed, 'Local governments are severely limited in their ability to manage urban growth. The issues are essentially regional in character. Restraints in one area may simply result in development pressures

moving elsewhere in the region.' In such cases resolution of growth issues then moves to another scale, i.e. state or provincial. In response to such problems growth management emerged in North America in the early 1990s as a highly important approach not only to urban development but the management of tourist destinations as well (Gill and Williams 1994; Gill 1998, 2000; Singh *et al.* 2003; Harrill 2004), with many of its elements now adopted throughout the world.

Ideally, growth management includes both the promotion of development and the protection of land against development.

> Growth management is inherently a governmental process which involves many interrelated aspects of land use. The process is essentially coordinative in character since it deals with reconciling competing demands on land and attempting to maximize locational advantages for the public benefit (Cullingsworth 1997: 149–50).

Several elements of growth management can be identified:

- consistency among government units – ensuring that different agencies share similar policy goals, values and instruments;
- concurrency – requiring infrastructure to be provided in advance or concurrent with the new development;
- containment of urban growth – the substitution of compact development for urban sprawl;
- provision of affordable housing – so as to ensure social equity;
- broadening of growth management to embrace economic development – the 'managing to grow' aspect;
- protection of natural systems, including land, air and water; and a broadened concern for viability of the regional economy (after DeGrove and Miness 1992; Stein 1993; Murphy and Murphy 2004).

Gill (1998, 2000) has noted that in the case of much tourism resort development it is only after the resort has established itself as a tourist destination that the challenge of addressing the needs of residents is considered. 'While clearly this post-hoc consideration of residents' needs seems inappropriate, economic considerations in developer-driven resort projects seem, at least in the past, to have dictated such an approach' (Gill 1998: 106). Nevertheless, emerging longer-term visions of resort and destination viability linked to the recognition that good resorts and destinations are good communities may lead to more integrated approaches in which residents' needs as well as those of the tourist are considered to be of equal or even greater importance.

Growth management is a systematic impact management strategy which demands an integrated sharing of ideas between citizens and managers in order to fulfil quality of life goals that should be marked via a series of indicators. Such a process is not easy as it requires the identification and reconciliation of the different values of stakeholders regarding ideal conditions (Jamal et al. 2002). 'Conflicts over natural resources are rarely exactly what they seem. What appears to be a simple collision of purposes is usually a combination of issues, past history, personalities, and emotions' (Amy 1987 in Millar and Aiken 1995: 628). As Cullingsworth (1997: 150) noted,

Acceptability across the spectrum on interests is the key characteristic of successful growth management policies. Securing of this acceptability is difficult, enormously time consuming, and fraught with political problems. Moreover, it is an ongoing process: the determination of land uses, the timing of development, the coordination of development with the provision of infrastructure all involve continuing debate and planning, the achievement of consensus, and the provision of adequate finance. In short, growth management is a major part of the continuing process of government.

The tourism industry needs to be sensitive to the needs of the local community and must, in the long term, be accepted by it if it is to maintain economic sustainability for extended time horizons (Gunn with Var 2002). This requires an understanding of the mechanisms by which tourism can become a part of the community rather than something that is imposed on it. Ongoing collaborative planning between stakeholders in tourist destinations is surprisingly rare, given attention to community-based tourism planning in the tourism literature, but is

becoming an increasingly important component of strategic tourism planning (Jamal and Getz 1995, Murphy and Murphy 2004; see also Chapter 5). However, some resort communities in North America (e.g. Aspen, Colorado; Lake Tahoe, Nevada; Whistler, British Columbia), Europe and elsewhere around the world have turned to growth management practices as a means to establish more integrated tourism planning and development approaches (Gill and Williams 1994; Gill 2000; Clark et al. 2006), often under the guise of 'smart growth' or 'sustainable' strategies. As Landis et al. (2002: 5) commented with respect to the relationship between 'smart growth' and 'growth management' in general:

Smart growth, with its emphasis on bottom-up, locally appropriate, and proactive planning is *in*, while growth management, with its reputation for top-down planning and blunt regulation is *out*. In reality, of course, smart growth is simply the newest adaptation of growth management (which is itself an adaptation of growth control), albeit with a more incentive- and project-based focus.

The establishment of a monitoring system is a vital aspect of growth management strategies as not only does it provide details by which progress towards desirable futures can be benchmarked, it also details a series of indicators that serve to provide a basis for informed community stakeholder debate about such futures. As Williams and Gill (1994: 184) commented, 'Community involvement in establishing desirable conditions is perhaps the single most important element of growth management.' Table 8.4 provides a number of examples of community management-based indicators of tourism impact that can be used in growth management planning strategies for resort communities. They may also be used outside of resort communities, but where this occurs some of the indicators may not be causally linkable just to the effects of tourism although they will still be valuable indicators with respect to the quality of life overall for a community. Furthermore, there is a significant tension with respect to the selection of indicators because at one level you need to select indicators that meet the specific requirements of the location but you also need indicators that can be used across destinations

Table 8.4 Examples of community management-based indicators of tourism impact in resort communities

Community management objective	Indicators of impact
Population stabilisation	Out-migration levels
	In-migration levels
	Age/gender structure
Employment change	Direct job creation
	Indirect job creation
	Employment levels
	Job retention levels
	Job displacement levels
	Job satisfaction
	Labour force structure
Income change	Person/household income levels
	Inflation levels
	Tax revenue levels
	Direct economic impact
	Indirect economic impact
Community viability enhancement	Infrastructure levels
	Public service levels
	Housing availability
	Employee housing availability
	Resident attitudes
	Educational levels
	Health levels
Welfare/social services	Health/social service/education access and distribution
	Recreation activity access and distribution
Cultural enhancement	Cultural facility access
	Cultural event frequency
	Resident attitudes
Conservation improvement	Pollution levels
	Indicator species
	Measures of biodiversity
	Conservation practices
	Cultural feature damage
	Environmental maintenance costs
Amenity enhancement	Levels of crowding density
	Privacy access
	Visual amenity satisfaction

and locations if you are seeking to be engaged in benchmarking processes. Indicators to reflect desired conditions and use should ideally:

- be directly observable;
- be relatively easy to measure;
- reflect understanding that some change is normal, particularly in ecological systems, and be sensitive to changing use conditions (see also Chapter 2);
- reflect appropriate scales (spatial and temporal) (see also Chapter 4);
- have ecological, bio-regional or watershed boundaries, not just institutional or administrative boundaries;
- encompass relevant structural, functional and compositional attributes of the ecosystem;
- include social, cultural, economic and physical parameters;
- reflect understanding of indicator function/type (e.g. baseline/reference, stress, impact, management, system diagnostic);
- clearly relate to vision, goals and objectives;
- be understood by stakeholder groups with respect to both their implementation and understanding of what indicator data actually means;
- be amenable to management.

The evaluation of destination capacities, which is often a component of growth management, parallels project-based planning that is a common feature of tourist development. For example, the Shankland Cox partnership, a British-based planning consultancy, identified four basic studies regarded as essential in the preparation of a comprehensive plan for any tourism development:

1. the tourist market: its origin, form, needs, rate of growth and competition for it;
2. the physical capacity of the area: its ability to absorb the requirements of tourism in terms of its natural attractions, infrastructure and economic resources;
3. the socio-economic impact on local communities migration, housing and social infrastructure for the support population;
4. the environmental capacity of the area: the limits imposed upon tourist development to protect the quality of the area in terms of

landscape, townscape, tranquillity and culture (Mills 1983: 132).

Project-based planning probably represents one of the most immediate faces of tourism planning for most members of the general public. However, the efficacy and effectiveness of project planning will depend on the emphasis given to its various elements by developers and the receptiveness of planning authorities to its usefulness as a planning tool, particularly in relation to broader local and regional planning measures. Furthermore, while such planning may be described as comprehensive in terms of the range of dimensions it covers, it cannot be described as 'integrated' in that it does not provide for linkages and relationships with stakeholders in terms of the formulation, development, implementation and evaluation of the tourism planning process. Finally, project-based planning tends to be a 'one-shot' study that, although valuable for establishing baseline data, does not become part of an ongoing assessment and evaluation of tourism's affects on the destination, and the community stakeholders' selection of desired futures.

The involvement of people in the planning and decision-making processes that affect their community is extremely important: such activity is likely to foster sustainable outcomes, as participants will then be more likely to regard themselves as stakeholders in the implementation of programmes (Murphy and Murphy 2004). Nevertheless, governments will also need to use a range of instruments by which growth management policies can be implemented; different categories include:

- policy and assessment;
- impact analyses;
- regulatory systems (environment controls, development right transfers, restrictive covenants, zoning uses, quota systems, development/building permits, utility connections);
- capital expenditures;
- revenue systems (exactions, tax and fee systems).

Table 8.5 presents a selection of growth management tools and techniques, while Table 8.6

Table 8.5 Characteristics of local growth controls and management techniques

Implementation tool	Policy object	Comprehensive or limited in scope?	Development control or impact mitigation?	Primarily formal or ad hoc measures?	Primary level of required regulatory enactment
Traditional zoning	Land supply, land use, building intensity and environmental quality	Comprehensive	Control	Depends on ease of rezoning	Local
Subdivision regulations	Lot quality	Comprehensive	Control	Formal	Local
Impact analyses	Social and economic externalities	Comprehensive	Both	Ad hoc	State/national
Environmental assessment and review	Environmental externalities; Development intensity	Comprehensive	Both	Formal and ad hoc	State/national
Indicators	Policy development; Impact monitoring	Comprehensive (ideal)	Both	Ad hoc	Local
Information services	All aspects of development	Comprehensive (ideal)	Both	Ad hoc	Local
Infrastructure financing districts	Public service costs	Limited	Mitigation	Formal	Local
Development impact fees	Public service cost; Externalities	Limited	Mitigation	Formal	Local
Conditional use permit	Land, environmental and building quality	Limited	Both	Ad hoc	Local
Specific and area plans	All aspects of development	Limited	Both	Formal	Local
Planned unit development	All aspects of development	Limited	Both	Formal	Local
Moratoria (and creative go-slows)	All aspects of development	Limited	Both	Ad hoc	Local
Adequate public facilities ordinances	Public cost externalities	Both	Mitigation	Formal	Local
Development agreements	Land supply, building intensity and environmental controls	Limited	Both	Ad hoc	Local
Environmental zoning	Environmental externalities	Limited	Control	Mostly formal	Local
Urban service boundary	Land and building supply	Comprehensive	Control	Formal	Local
Urban limit line/growth boundary	Land and building supply; Public service costs	Comprehensive	Control	Formal	Local

Table 8.5 (continued)

Implementation tool	Policy object	Comprehensive or limited in scope?	Development control or impact mitigation?	Primarily formal or ad hoc measures?	Primary level of required regulatory enactment
Annual population or housing cap	Building supply	Comprehensive	Primarily control	Formal	Local
Annual commercial space cap	Building supply	Limited	Primarily control	Formal	Local
Annexation limits	Land supply	Comprehensive	Control	Formal and ad hoc	Local
Sphere-of-influence boundary adjustments	Land supply	Limited	Control	Formal and ad hoc	Local
Development exactions	Public service costs (including land/capital/facility dedications); Low-income housing provision agreements	Limited	Mitigation	Ad hoc	Local
Linkage fees	Public service costs; Externalities	Limited	Mitigation	Formal	Local
Urban design and heritage preservation contracts	Townscape and heritage conservation	Limited	Control	Formal	State/local
Agricultural land preservation contracts	Farmland and landscape conservation; Economic diversification	Limited	Control	Formal	State/local
Inclusionary zoning	Private externalities	Limited	Mitigation	Formal	Local
Land banking	Public externalities	Limited	Control	Formal	Local
Property exchange	Public externalities	Limited	Control	Ad hoc	Local
Transfer of development rights	Building quality (intensity)	Limited	Control	Formal	Local
Purchase of development rights	Public service quality (open space)	Limited	Control	Ad hoc	Local
Conservation easements	Public service quality (open space)	Limited	Control	Ad hoc	Local
Land trusts	Private and public benefits	Limited	Mitigation	Ad hoc	Local

Sources: Kelly (1993); Schiffman (1995); Landis *et al.* (2002).

Table 8.6 Potential tourism development specific growth management strategy options

Direct strategies	Indirect strategies
Activity restrictions	*Physical alterations*
• restrict:	• provide guidelines for:
– type of use and behaviours	– architectural design
– length of stay	– development
– timing of activity	– landscape design
	– access to infrastructure
	– capacity
Zoning	*Information dispersal*
• separate incompatible:	• disseminate appropriate behaviour information
– activities	• advertise alternate locations
– land uses	• distribute low-impact activity guidelines
– tourist groups	• distribute codes of ethics for tourists, residents, tourism operators
– resident/tourist groups	
Use rationing	*Economic incentives*
• limit use of:	• create:
– specific facilities/sites	– differential user-fee structures
– access routes	– differential utility fees
• provide reservation use only	
Economic incentives	
• create:	
– specific visitor fees and taxes	

illustrates potential direct and indirect tourism-specific growth management strategy options. However, it must be recognised that there is no universally appropriate 'one-size-fits-all' strategy available for managing growth in tourism destinations. Each planning strategy that is used will have system-wide effects (Pendall 1999, 2000; Warner and Molotch 2000; Carruthers 2002). For example, restricting urban growth may increase the price of the local housing market. In a US nationwide study of local land-use regulations, housing production, and community economic and demographic characteristics, Pendall (2000) found strong correlations between building cap programmes and large-lot zoning, reduced rental housing construction, and lowered proportions of poorer and black and Hispanic residents. Other planning measures such as urban growth boundaries, adequate public facilities ordinances and temporary building moratoria were not found to affect rental housing construction or racial composition. In some cases planning measures that improve the amenity and quality of life and therefore the attractiveness of a location may also serve to create displacement effects as house prices increase. Because wealthy communities are more likely to adopt local growth control and management measures than poorer ones, it is hard to determine whether the higher quality of life in such communities is due to controls or because of higher levels of income (Landis *et al.* 2002). Indeed, this last observation raises all kinds of questions about the efficacy of growth control and management, as it may mean that unless carefully thought through and integrated with other policy measures growth control and management programmes may have consequences beyond immediate environmental and personal quality of life considerations.

At the destination level strategies, tools and techniques are usually selected according to local characteristics, the nature of the planning problem and the acceptability of such instruments. Nevertheless, the above discussion of growth management and the changing thinking surrounding how to manage changing places does highlight the role of stakeholder relationships and collaboration in tourism planning and it is to these lynchpins of strategic tourism planning that we shall now turn.

Relationships and networks

This book has continually stressed the relational aspects of tourism planning. The metaphor of relational webs and social and economic networks provides a useful descriptive way of capturing a conception of relational social dynamics that exist in tourism planning and, of course, everyday life. Spatial planning systems provide a framework to manage the various connections between networks that co-exist in a locality. Governance, in terms of the management of the common affairs of political communities, i.e. the public interest, may serve to sustain or transform relational webs. Increasingly, the role of the public tourism planner is to assist in the development and maintenance of networks, whether it be for reasons of tourism development (Jamal and Getz 1995), management of valued sites (Hall and McArthur 1998), or the maintenance of agency or planning support through the development of relations with stakeholders and the wider public (Margerum 1999; Margerum and Whitall 2004).

Networking refers to a wide range of cooperative behaviour between otherwise competing organisations and between organisations linked through economic and social relationships and transactions. Current government interest in networking stems from the view that the networked firm appears to be an important component of both successful national economies and of highly performing regional economies (e.g. Malecki 2004) and may offer considerable potential to assist in cushioning the effects of economic restructuring, particularly in rural and peripheral areas (e.g. Butler *et al.* 1998; Jansson and Müller 2007).

Networks are a distinct, hybrid mode of coordinating economic activity that are alternatives to organisation by markets or within firms (hierarchical transactions). Networks involve firms of all sizes in various combinations; they can be locally or internationally based, can occur at all stages of the value chain, and they range from highly informal relationships through to contractual obligations. Network development has received enormous attention in both academic and government circles in recent years. However, networking is not a new phenomenon and has long been a hallmark of innovative organisations because of the central importance of external collaboration with users and external sources of expertise, even if the expression 'network' was not used.

Networks can be defined as arrangements of interorganisational and personal cooperation and collaboration (see Table 8.7). Such collaboration occurs, for example,

> where firms cooperate in production and marketing, to exchange know-how and market intelligence, to jointly train their employees, to develop research capacities and new markets, to purchase raw materials in bulk, to share equipment and infrastructure, and so on. If the collaborators also compete in input and product markets – as is often the case – networks are said to encompass the cooperative elements of otherwise competitive relationships.
> (Bureau of Industry Economics (BIE) 1991b: 5)

Similarly, in a much-cited work, Powell notes that in networks:

> Transactions occur neither through discrete exchanges nor by administrative fiat, but through networks of individuals or institutions engaged in reciprocal, preferential, mutually supportive actions. Networks can be complex: they involve neither the explicit criteria of the market, nor the well-organised routines of the hierarchy. A basic assumption of network relationships is that parties are mutually dependent upon resources controlled by

Table 8.7 Organisational and personal dimensions of the network construct in tourism

Network dimension	Interorganisational	Personal
Actors	Organisations: private (e.g. firm), public (e.g. tourism ministry), public–private (e.g. tourism promotion board), non-government organisation (e.g. environmental group)	Individuals, copreneurs, entrepreneurs
Type of link	Formal	Informal
Common categorisations	Economic transactions, economic network, marketing network, vertical network, horizontal network	Social network, social relationships, communication

Source: Hall, C.M. (2005a) *Tourism: Rethinking the Social Science of Mobility,* Prentice Hall, Harlow. Reprinted with permission.

another, and that there are gains to be had by the pooling of resources. In network forms of resource allocation, individual units exist not by themselves, but in relation to other units. These relationships take considerable effort to establish and sustain, thus they constrain both partners' ability to adapt to changing circumstances. As networks evolve, it may become more economically sensible to exercise voice rather than exit. Benefits and burdens come to be shared . . . Complementarity and accommodation are the cornerstones of successful production networks (1990: 78).

Network relationships are of great significance for tourism promotion. For example, with respect to Baltic Sea tourism destinations World Tourism Organization Chief of Quality of Tourism Development, Henryk Handszuh, commented, the region's

> tourism image must be strengthened, enhanced and, to the extent possible, coordinated. Coordination here does not mean any formal intervention, but identifying and working towards common objectives by tourism enterprises in the region and by their support bodies in the public and private sectors. (WTO 1998h)

Similarly, Buhalis and Cooper (1998: 338) observed that networking will allow SMTEs to:

- pool their resources in order to increase their competitiveness;
- draw up strategic management and marketing plans;
- reduce operating costs;
- increase their know-how.

Despite increasing recognition of the significance of networks there is an absence of a common set of factors for describing and explaining the development of networks, as the conditions that give rise to network formation are quite diverse. Network arrangements have multiple causes and varied 'historical trajectories' (Powell 1990: 323):

> in some cases, the formation of networks anticipates the need for [network] form of exchange; in other situations, there is a slow pattern of development which ultimately justifies the form; and in still other circumstances, networks are a response to the demand for a mode of exchange that resolves exigencies that other forms are ill-equipped to handle.

Nevertheless, several classifications of network relationships have been developed. For example, the BIE (1991a, b) developed an institutional categorisation (e.g. firm, government), while Powell (1990) developed a classification scheme that emphasised the reasons why the network came into being. Several different types of interorganisational linkages can be recognised (after Harper 1993). Table 8.8 illustrates the different types of networks, with examples taken from the field of wine tourism (Hall *et al.* 1997). One of the most significant aspects of all four types of networks is that not only do they

Table 8.8 Network categorisations – using wine tourism examples

Interorganisational relationship		Example
Dyadic linkage	Formed when two organisations find it mutually beneficial to collaborate in achieving a common goal.	A joint venture between a winery and a tour company to promote winery visitation.
Organisation sets	Interorganisational linkages that refer to the *clusters* of dyadic relations maintained by a *focal* organisation.	A visitor information centre or wine tourism organisation develops individual relationships with wineries so as to provide tourists with information on each winery.
Action sets	A coalition of *interacting* organisations that work together in order to achieve a specific purpose.	A visitor information centre and the wineries in a region come together to produce a regional wine tourism promotional campaign.
Networks	Used here in a narrow formal sense, refers to a group of organisations that share common organisational ties and can be recognised as a *bounded* interorganisational system.	A federation or association of wine tourism organisations, e.g. the Movimento del Turismo del Vino (Italy) or the European Council of Wine Regions (Assembleia das Regioes Europeias Viticolas).

Source: After Hall *et al.* (1997).

represent flows of corporate information, e.g. research and promotion, but, from a tourism perspective, they may also represent flows of tourists on the ground. In other words, the economic and social characteristics of networks parallel the flow of goods and services including tourists. Communicative relationships therefore affect economic and political relationships (Figure 8.1).

From the perspective of government, such flows are particularly attractive as they represent a potential enhancement of the multiplier effect of tourist spending, particularly in rural and peripheral areas, thereby enhancing regional economic development processes. Furthermore, from a policy perspective, networking is attractive because it reflects a middle ground that reflects the contemporary focus on developing public–private partnerships. However, network formation may be difficult in areas where there are information gaps about the perceived benefits of such linkages (Hall *et al.* 1997).

Two industry areas that have been the focus of considerable national and regional government attention because of their income-generating capacities and economic development potential are the food (including wine) and tourism industries (e.g. AusIndustry 1996; Hall *et al.* 2003; Hall 2004d; Hall and Mitchell 2008). However, despite a broad awareness by policy makers of the potential linkages that exist between the wine and tourism industries there appears to be only a gradual increase in understanding of the nature of food and wine tourism among industry stakeholders, a situation which may substantially limit the ability and, therefore, potential benefits of creating linkages between the two industries.

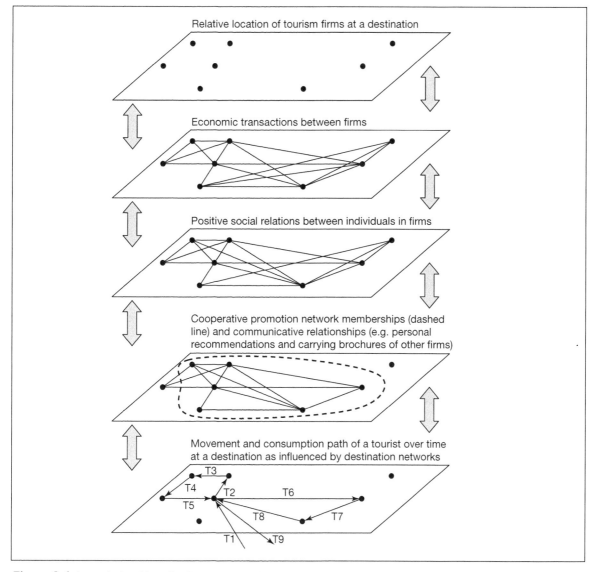

Figure 8.1 Interrelationships of different forms of network relationships at a destination and relationship to tourist consumption

Source: Hall, C.M. (2005a) *Tourism: Rethinking the Social Science of Mobility*, Prentice Hall, Harlow. Reproduced with permission.

In a study of the New Zealand wine industry, Hall and Johnson (1997) reported that approximately 85 per cent of wineries were open for cellar door sales. Indeed, many of the smaller wineries could not survive without them as visitors contribute to both direct sales by purchase at the winery and indirectly by placing themselves on mail order lists and purchasing wine upon their return home. Yet many wineries did not see themselves as dealing with 'tourists' and/or excursionists and therefore as part of the tourism industry.

Hall and Johnson (1997; see also Hall *et al.* 1997) in their survey reported a range of approaches by wineries in their relationships towards tourism. For example, in responses to questions about their attitudes towards tourism, three Hawke's Bay wineries, on the east coast of the North Island of New Zealand, commented:

'Overseas tourists are not as interested in wineries, wine buying, wines. They have not in general, come to the region because of the wines . . . This could be a pointer for the promotion of the region.'

'Do you mean overseas or local visitors?'

'Generally tourists don't buy much wine but are time consuming for staff.'

There were similar reactions from two Canterbury (South Island) wineries: 'Not at this stage – but more money spent on wine promotion instead of administration would be good', and 'I don't really support tourism – most countries I have travelled to which are heavily tourist orientated were ruined countries.' In a reflection of a widely held attitude among over half of those interviewed, a Martinborough (South Island) winery stated: 'As I don't consider being a tourist operator I am in the business of selling my wine, all the rest is carried out by us to welcome people to us.' A statement supported by another local winery:

Our small business is to grow and make wine for sale to customers, whether they are 'tourists' or not. I am coordinator of group visits for the wineries that are prepared to take groups – 5 or 6 at present date. Many groups are not interested at all in wine and groups often only buy 1–6 bottles between them. None of us, if truthful, consider ourselves to be tourist orientated as we are very small establishments and tourism is an extra expense just at present and time consuming without extra (unpaid!) staff.

Nevertheless, in Marlborough, a region in the South Island of New Zealand that has some of the strongest relationships between the wine and tourism industries, with a high proportion of wineries offering cellar door sales, the response was much more positive (Hall and Johnson 1997). Following are two responses which are representative of the comments received from the region:

'Here in Marlborough we are fortunate that most wineries and tourism operators work together well.'

'Need to look at generating greater volumes of tourists through Marlborough & attempt to cater all seasons. I believe most tourists are intimidated by the atmosphere of some wineries – need to bring these people into a "comfort zone" – in addition – EDUCATE! – people seek information constantly – need to provide professional quality, varied levels of education – improve their awareness and comfort with the wine industry.'

In an extremely supportive statement about wine tourism in the region, one winery commented,

Although we do not undertake cellar door sales [and] tastings we still see ourselves as part of the tourism industry. Tourism promotion is important to regional wine industries [and] to all small local vineyards . . . We belong to a wine marketing group (sub group of a wine growers [association]) which produces a winery map, undertakes displays [and] could in future mount food and wine events. (Hall and Johnson 1997)

Indeed several responses, even from those who had otherwise been negative about tourism, recognised the value of relevant cooperative relationships and networks. For an example, a Marlborough winery called for 'relationship marketing with parallel industries – arts, music, food, etc.'. Similarly, a Martinborough (North Island) winery called for 'linkage of wineries to events held in area – golf tournaments, cycle tours, flower and garden shows, music and entertainments', with another observing a 'lack of cooperative element within the wineries of the region'. Finally, a Central Otago (South Island) winery noted that New Zealand wineries were 'just babies at wine tourism compared with Australia – need local and central government financial assistance to get further down track'.

The range of responses received by Hall and Johnson (1997) is reflective of the partial industrialisation of tourism discussed in Chapter 4 (Leiper 1989; 1990b). Although, as students of tourism, we can recognise that many segments of the economy may benefit from tourism, it is only those organisations with a direct relationship to tourists and/or who actually *perceive* their customers as tourists which become actively involved in fostering tourism development or in marketing. For example, there are many other businesses, such as food suppliers, petrol stations and retailers (sometimes described as 'allied industries'), and as the discussion above notes, wineries, that also benefit from tourists but which do not readily identify themselves as part of the tourism industry (Hall 1998b). Therefore, in most circumstances, unless there is a clear financial motive for wine businesses to create linkages with tourism businesses it will often require an external inducement, such as the establishment by government at no or minimal cost to individual businesses, of new network structures that link the wine and tourism sectors.

In the case of New Zealand several wine and food tourism networks were established at both regional and national levels in the ten years since the national wine tourism survey was first undertaken. Activities that have taken place have included national wine tourism conferences, regional wine tourism seminars and workshops. Just as importantly national strategies and working groups have been established in order to try and bring the different sectors together, with arguably a high degree of success. This does not mean that all wineries are members of such networks, nor that all wineries are positive towards tourism, but there has been a significant positive shift in attitudes towards wine-related tourism (Michael 2007; Hall and Mitchell 2008).

In several parts of the world such organisations have been established with government or external assistance. All Australian state governments have established organisations specifically to facilitate and coordinate the development of wine tourism. Similarly, network development is an important component of European wine tourism initiatives. Many of the European wine trails and routes are developed with the assistance of the Europäische Weinstrassen (European Council of Wine Routes), incorporated within the European Council of Wine Regions (Assembleia das Regioes Europeias Viticolas), which

was created within the framework of the Dyonisos multimedia network of European wine-producing regions. The network was established in 1992 with European Community support and now encompasses more than 60 European wine regions (Hall and Macionis 1998). According to the Europäische Weinstrassen, winetrails are, 'the best framework for cooperative work between government, private enterprises and associations, the tourism industry, wine and the local council' in encouraging regional development and job creation. In addition, from the perspective of individual producers,

> an opportunity exists for the winegrower to establish advantageous connections and a strategically important means of obtaining trade in high quality produce which encourages the development of direct sales and levels of awareness, and consolidates the image of products as well as creating a loyal consumer market. (translated from Europäische Weinstrassen, nd, in Hall and Macionis 1998)

The issue of government or external intervention, such as European Union funding, to directly promote networking arrangements raises a number of issues, including: if networks are so overwhemingly positive in their effects, why do they not arise spontaneously without government intervention? And, what advantages do public tourism planners and policy makers have in identifying profitable opportunities for increased interorganisational networking that market participants do not have? (Harper 1993). The BIE (1991a, b) identified four potential roles for government in the development of networks:

1. disseminating information on the opportunities created by networks;
2. encouraging cooperation within industries through industry associations;
3. improving existing networks between the private sector and public sector agencies involved in research and development, education and training;
4. examining the effects of the existing legislative and regulatory framework on the formation, maintenance and breakup of networks relative to other forms of organisation, such as markets and firms.

In the case of wine tourism, government has directly utilised the first three roles in the creation of specific organisations and/or the provision of funding for research, education, cooperative strategies and mechanisms, and information provision. The BIE (1991a, b) considered information gaps to be a major factor in the impairment of network formation. Indeed the discussion above indicates substantial negative attitudes towards tourism by wineries, whereas tourism organisations tend to be far more positive towards the wine industry (Hall *et al.* 1997; Hall and Macionis 1998), a situation that is extremely supportive of Leiper's (1989) concept of tourism's partial industrialisation. However, some negative responses by wineries towards linkages with the tourism industry may not be entirely misplaced: some wineries, by virtue of their market and/or their location, may receive little direct benefit from tourism – for example if they do not have cellar door sales or, in the case of some major companies, see their direct customers as being wholesale and retail outlets (Hall *et al.* 1997; Hall and Mitchell 2008).

In order to maximise the potential contribution of network development to regional economies it becomes essential that network relationships move from dyadic linkages and organisation sets (such as those which typically exist when the wine tourism organisations are first established) to action sets and formal networks. Indeed, there is already considerable encouragement for such a move given the development of regional wine tourism associations in Europe, North America and Australasia (Michael 2007; Hall and Mitchell 2008). Yet, for such networks to be sustained it is important that they be internally driven rather than government maintained. To argue, as do Morris and King (1997), that 'The opportunities abound. It is simply a matter of being sufficiently entrepreneurial to explore the options and work with others to create tourism products that are unique and provide contributing SMEs with a competitive advantage' is inadequate. Wineries, particularly in those areas that are not major tourist destinations, require substantial persuasion and information

provision so as not only to illustrate the potential benefits of linkages between wine and tourism but also to dispel myths about what constitutes tourism, particularly the belief that domestic excursionists to the cellar door are not tourists (Hall 2004d; Hall and Mitchell 2008). The task for the tourism planner is then to use argument and persuasion in attempting to encourage the development of networks. Not every network will succeed and it should also be recognised that networks, as with any organisational structure which is goal driven, will also go through an organisational life cycle. Moreover, not every business in a given region will want to become part of a network. Nevertheless, great things can still be accomplished through the establishment of such networks that can achieve more by operating in cooperative arrangements than could possibly be achieved by a single business.

Notions of collaboration, coordination and partnership are closely related within the network paradigm. The nature of such linkages exists on a continuum ranging from 'loose' linkages to coalitions and more lasting structural arrangements and relationships. Mandell (1999) identifies a continuum of such collaborative efforts as follows:

- linkages or interactive contacts between two or more actors;
- intermittent coordination or mutual adjustment of the policies and procedures of two or more actors to accomplish some objective;
- ad hoc or temporary task force activity among actors to accomplish a purpose or purposes;
- permanent and/or regular coordination between two or more actors through a formal arrangement (e.g. a council or partnership) to engage in limited activity to achieve a purpose or purposes;
- a coalition where interdependent and strategic actions are taken, but where purposes are narrow in scope and all actions occur within the participant actors themselves or involve the mutually sequential or

simultaneous activity of the participant actors;

- a collective or network structure where there is a broad mission and joint and strategically interdependent action. Such structural arrangements take on broad tasks that reach beyond the simultaneous actions of independently operating actors.

Indeed, allied to the spatial dimension of the network paradigm is the emphasis given to clusters. Networks and the associated concept of clusters are being seen as increasingly important to peripheral regions and network development and collaboration has received substantial attention in recent years (e.g. Rosenfeld 1997; Waits 2000; Michael 2007). In areas that may suffer from a relative lack of human capital, and intellectual capital in particular, networks may offer substantial value in knowledge development as well as for cooperative marketing (Jansson and Müller 2007).

Industry clusters exist where there is loose geographic concentration or association of firms and organisations involved in a value chain producing goods and services and innovating. A cluster is defined as a concentration of companies and industries, in a geographic region that are interconnected by the markets they serve and the products they produce, as well as by the suppliers, trade associations and educational institutions with which they interact (Porter 1990). Such exporting chains of firms are the primary 'drivers' of a region's economy, on whose success other businesses, such as construction firms, for example, depend in terms of their own financial viability. An industry cluster includes companies that sell inside as well as outside the region, and also supports firms which supply raw materials, components and business services to them. These clusters form 'value chains' that serve as one of the fundamental units of competition in the global economy. Firms and organisations involved in clusters are able to achieve synergies and leverage economic advantage from shared access to information and knowledge networks, supplier and distribution chains, markets and marketing intelligence, competencies, and resources in a specific locality.

The cluster concept focuses on the linkages and interdependencies among actors in value chains. Although one of the lessons of cluster development programmes around the world 'is that there is no precise, "right" (one size fits all) formula for developing industry clusters' (Blandy 2000: 80), a number of factors have been recognised as significant in the development of clusters and the associated external economy which serves to reinforce the clustering process (Hall 2005a; Michael 2007). These include:

- the life cycle stage of innovative clusters;
- government financing and policies;
- the skills of the region's human resources;
- the technological capabilities of the region's research and development activities;
- the quality of the region's physical, transport, information and communication infrastructure;
- the availability and expertise of capital financing in the region;
- the cost and quality of the region's tax and regulatory environment; and
- the appeal of the region's lifestyle to people that can provide world-class resources and processes.

Hall (2004d) identified several other factors that may be significant in cluster and network success:

- spatial separation – the existence of substantial spatial separation between elements of a cluster that inhibit communication;
- administrative separation – the existence of multiple public administrative agencies and units within a region;
- the existence of a 'champion' to promote the development of a network;
- the hosting of meetings to develop relationships.

However, also critical, as Rosenfeld (1997: 10) observed, is the ' "current" of a working production system . . . often embedded in professional, trade and civic associations, and in informal socialization patterns . . . The "current" depends on norms of reciprocity and sufficient levels of trust to encourage professional interaction and collaborative behaviour'. In light of the significance of trust as a factor in cluster and network development, Rosenfeld (1997: 10) redefined clusters as, 'A geographically bounded concentration of interdependent businesses with active channels for business transactions, dialogue, and communications, and that collectively shares common opportunities and threats'. Importantly, this definition asserts that 'active channels' are as important as 'concentration', and without active channels even a critical mass of related firms is not a local production or social system and therefore does not operate as a cluster. Without such active channels it is extremely unlikely that the various firms in a region, large or small, can actively cooperate in order to achieve regional aims. As Hall (2005a: 180–1) noted,

> without sufficient social capital, the co-location of firms may at times lead to a lack of social exchange as often as it does to a positive sharing of knowledge and ideas unless the firms are seen to have some shared interests on which they communicate.

Therefore, network creation and collaborative arrangements can take time to establish and to develop trust between participants, especially if they come from different sectoral or cultural backgrounds, a situation that is also reflective of the way in which relational approaches to tourism planning may be able to assist in conflict resolution in tourism.

Conflict in destination development

Opposition to the growth of tourism in an area or the establishment of specific tourism developments often arises because access to common resources, e.g. scenic qualities, water, air, public resources (the commons) is coveted by other users with different, often incompatible interests (Adams *et al.* 2003). Opposition is often multifaceted and based on a range of concerns that may range from opposition on macro-level

environmental (e.g. habitat destruction, air and water pollution and alterations in scenic values), social (e.g. loss of low-income housing, loss of sense of place, breakdown of communities and lack of employment opportunities to locals) and economic (e.g. failure to purchase locally, localised inflation and increases in rents and government taxes) grounds to micro-level concerns which arise from jealousy and envy (e.g. see Sharpley and Telfer 2002; Hall and Boyd 2005; Jansson and Müller 2007). Moreover, many of these elements are combined with respect to how residents' sense of place is affected by tourism development. 'People demonstrate their sense of place when they apply their moral or aesthetic discernment to sites and locations' (Tuan 1974: 235) and, as noted earlier in the chapter, people may only consciously notice the unique qualities of their place when they are away from it or when it is being rapidly altered.

Change is a normal part of the human experience. However tourism, as with much of modernity, may serve to hasten rates of change above those that are 'comfortable' for many people. New buildings, new economic structures and, perhaps most significant of all, influxes of new people – the tourists and the people who serve them – can serve to dramatically alter the web of relations that residents have with place, and therefore substantially affect tourism development and planning as well. As Millar and Aiken (1995: 620) commented,

> Conflict is a normal consequence of human interaction in periods of change, the product of a situation where the gain or a new use by one party is felt to involve a sacrifice or changes by others. It can be an opportunity for creative problem solving, but if it is not managed properly conflict can divide a community and throw it into turmoil.

Tourism planners therefore typically have to find accommodation between various stakeholders and interests in tourism development in an attempt to arrive at outcomes that are accepted by stakeholders including the wider community (Bramwell and Lane 2000; Lovelock 2002).

Conflict resolution is a process of value change that attempts to manage disputes through negotiation, argument and persuasion by which conflict is eliminated or at least minimised to the extent that a satisfactory degree of progress is made by the interested stakeholders. Substantial attention has long been given to issues of conflict resolution in the field of resource and environmental management (e.g. Mitchell 1989); however, relatively little attention to such issues has been forthcoming in tourism, a somewhat surprising situation given the extent to which research on tourism destination development and the environmental and social impacts of tourism have highlighted the extent to which dissatisfaction often arises with tourism by residents (e.g., Singh *et al.* 2003).

Conflict resolution can take a number of forms, ranging from information exchange to mediation involving a neutral third party, through to binding arbitration in which a decision-making function is mutually given to a third party by the affected stakeholders. In all such situations two primary objectives will be sought. First, an agreed definition of resource use. Second, the creation of a working relationship between the affected parties which will provide for effective implementation of the resource use agreement and ongoing monitoring, evaluation and procedural mechanisms for dealing with new problems that might emerge.

Conflict resolution and mediation is clearly an integral component of sustainable tourism development with the assumption that the various groups and interests involved have doubts about their ability to achieve objectives. For example, Ostrom (1990) noted the following interrelated factors of sustainable development at the community level:

- clearly defined boundaries;
- harmony between appropriation and provision rules and local conditions;
- participation by all interested parties in changes that may affect them;
- accountable monitoring;
- graduated sanctions administered by an accountable authority;
- low cost and readily accessible mechanisms for conflict resolution;

- recognition by governments of the rights to organize;
- for those regimes that are part of large systems of governance, appropriate licensing provisions, monitoring, enforcement, conflict resolution and organisational arrangements.

Much conflict resolution, particularly in terms of land-use planning, is based on the interests of the stakeholders engaged in conflicts. Such a process of consultation and bargaining assumes that stakeholders have clearly defined specific interests that are amenable to negotiation. According to Millar and Aiken (1995) the following are the necessary conditions for resolving an interest-based conflict:

- the parties to the conflict identify themselves and are represented;
- all parties can agree on the 'facts';
- there is an urgent need for all parties to arrive at an agreement;
- the parties want to resolve the matter as soon as possible;
- all parties are willing to be flexible;
- all parties can be certain that the other parties will abide by the agreement once it is defined.

However, such interest-based approaches only work effectively in a limited range of situations; for example when there are only a limited number of parties to the resolution process. As Powell (1990: 326) noted with respect to the creation of networks, 'The more homogenous the group, the greater the trust, hence the easier it is to sustain network-like arrangements.' Therefore, the likelihood of interest-based approaches working can be expected to fall as:

- the number of stakeholders increases;
- the size of social groups increases;
- the membership of social groups becomes more unstable;
- stakeholders become more geographically dispersed;
- the diversity of participants increases.

Similarly, such an approach will work best in relation to a single project, issue or small site; the more complex the conflict becomes the more difficult will be the possibilities for resolving conflicts based on interests. More significantly, an interest-based approach may do little to resolve conflicts and antagonisms that are rooted in deep-seated differences in values, ideologies and philosophies, 'for as long as the initial motives, understandings, and interests remain, so too will the conflict' (Millar and Aiken 1995: 621) – for example, as often seems to exist between conservation groups and developers in tourism in areas of perceived high environmental value. Conflict management therefore needs to be able to develop structures that can deal with fundamental value differences in terms of issues of:

- *Appropriateness* – how appropriate is a certain type of development or use of technology in an area given its wider impacts?
- *Property rights* – what are the respective rights of neighbouring land uses and the rights of individual property owners in relation to wider public rights?
- *Governance* – who sets the rules and regulations under which the parties operate and how are they enforced and changed?

Fundamental value differences are clearly not unique to tourism-related development; however, little effort has been made to transfer the experience of conflict resolution in other areas of resource management and use to the complex set of stakeholder attitudes and relations that usually surround tourism (e.g. Schusler *et al.* 2003). Legal regulation is not sufficient to resolve value conflict in tourism planning and development. While 'winners' and 'losers' can be determined through legal processes, fundamental value conflict can continue and possibly be made worse as 'losers' come to feel even further alienated from the 'rules of the game' that set the structures within which conflict resolution may occur (Hall and Jenkins 1995). For example, 'the agenda is often the subject of intense debate since some parties will work hard to add or delete issues of special concern' (Susskind and Madigan 1984: 185). It is necessary, therefore, to seek to resolve

or manage conflict at a deeper level than that represented through mere legal solutions. This deeper level is best recognised as that of 'trust'.

Trust

Embedded in the continuation of a mutually satisfying relationship is a dialogue of trust. While trust is a future-oriented concept, it is based on past performance. Ongoing interactions and flows of information over time have built up a bond of confidence that anticipated outcomes can be relied upon to be achieved. This is a significant departure from transaction cost economics, which assumes that the agent within the principal/agent relationship is not to be trusted. As Millar and Aitken (1995: 623) recognised, 'it is a general rule of all agreements that the formal particulars are only effective to the extent that the working relationship is based on trust'.

Trust is one of the basic elements of understanding cooperation and conflict among stakeholders in the tourism planning process (Bramwell and Lane 2000). Trust is 'confidence in the reliability of a person or system, regarding a given set of outcomes or events', which is based on 'faith in the probity or love of another, or in the correctness of abstract principles' (Giddens 1990: 34). It is the glue that holds communities and societies together. Trust creates the potential for voluntary collective action through fostering the assurance necessary for individuals to commit towards a common goal (Stein and Harper 2003).

Trust is a 'collective attribute' based on the relationships between people within a larger social system rather than just the individual recipients. Trust is therefore a set of social expectations, including broad social rules of fair, right and taken-for-granted assumptions over common understandings that are shared by everyone involved in economic and social exchange. Coleman (1990) acknowledges that the relationship between two actors may well be conditional on the placement of trust on other related actors.

The withdrawal of trust by one actor potentially has a domino effect on the system of interactions. Significantly, Coleman likens this to a grid effect with highly sensitive configurations predisposed to breaking down at a single weak point. For networks, then, the performance and position of the weakest element is important to the functioning of the total network.

Where trust is absent, cooperative or voluntary collective action is impossible, particularly in 'commons' situations that rely on the 'curbing of opportunistic impulses toward individual exploitation' (Millar 1996: 207). Trust therefore provides for a sufficient number of reciprocal and cooperative actions to occur such that there will be a greater return to all stakeholders than would be forthcoming through individual exploitation (Brann and Foddy 1987). Trust requires a sufficiently common set of values between stakeholders in order to operate. Therefore attention in much conflict resolution and management in tourism development needs to be given to the social and political context within which development occurs and value conflict arises (Jamal *et al.* 2002). To place the observations of Millar and Aitken (1995: 623–624) within a tourist context:

> In conflict situations, the social component is critical. The main purpose of [tourism] is to produce and ultimately sell a product, but in conflict situations we must be more concerned with how the local society and resource base are organized to accept such production . . . communities exist within a web of kinship, physical interdependency, and social obligation, and in this context, [tourism] cannot be separated from the social issues of property and morality.

For example, Millar and Aitken (1995) have identified that in many communities faced with new patterns of resource development and use there is a two-part morality of neighbourliness in which, while there is a recognition that everyone has the right to make a living, there is also a belief that everyone who is affected by developments should have the right to be consulted. Where such consultation does not occur and where sufficient resentment is reached, extra-legal means may be used to oppose new developments, including damage or destruction of property.

In the majority of societies the turmoil that may be created by such developments has clear limits of political and social acceptability. When these limits are reached then government action and intervention become the order of the day, particularly as government usually seeks to minimise conflict and encourage consensus. However, the institutional arrangements of government, particularly at higher levels, may be at odds with conflict resolution at the community level. Not because government necessarily wants to be, indeed new government structures may be established so as to try to promote conflict resolution, but because the inherently bureaucratic nature of government is often at odds with the social characteristics of a community. For example, as Bingham (1986: 115) recognised,

> A general problem, particularly for public agencies and corporations, is that often the individuals with decision-making authority who can speak for the organization are not the same as those with specific technical expertise on the issues. Also, in large organizations, it is often not possible for the policy makers to spend their time to be present personally in all negotiations.

> Operating within the community setting, the ethics of a bureaucracy can lead to mistrust and conflict. In a community, heterogeneity and autonomous decision-making, not conformity, are the hallmarks; custom and tradition, not just law and rational arguments, ar\e the guiding principles. (Millar and Aitken 1995: 626)

For example, in an oft-cited study of public participation in natural resource management, Sewell and Phillips (1979) found that the managing agency provided pragmatic, agency-oriented objectives while the community had a broader set of objectives for being involved in consultation. Specifically, the objectives from the management agency point of view were to develop programmes with broad public acceptance, enhance performance and improve the image of the agency. In contrast, Sewell and Phillips found the objectives from the community's point of view were to influence the design and implementation of policy and reduce the power of bureaucracy and its planners.

While public participation is seen as a standard tourism planning mechanism to deal with controversial issues, it should be noted that simply the hosting of a public meeting – a common consultation strategy – for example, will not by itself make it more likely that conflicts will be resolved. Indeed they may well lead to even greater conflict between parties and serve to reinforce rather than change positions and come closer to agreement.

> Public meetings may help to identify conflicts, but they cannot resolve or manage them. While it is true they allow everyone to have his or her say, the root causes . . . are often neglected. In the end, the government is often left with the task of sorting out what it considers to be the relevant facts. (Millar and Aiken 1995: 627)

The problem has often been a focus on the technique – the public meeting – rather than the process and the creation of social relations and what the hoped-for outcome of the process actually is (Umemoto and Suryanata 2006). Too often processes have been interest based rather than values based. However, if long-term agreement and common ground between stakeholders is sought then attention must be given to the values of those who are involved in the conflict (Millar and Yoon 2000). Public meetings, as with some other forms of public participation, may help in the identification of conflicts and opinions but they do not of themselves manage or resolve them (Hall and McArthur 1998). Smith (1992), for example, recommended that decision-making processes be structured around four principles:

1. real and regular consultation – which seeks to be inclusive of all stakeholders and that begins early in any decision-making process;
2. development of a common information base;
3. action plans that also involve multiple stakeholders – while more costly in terms of time and often money, savings can be gained in the longer term as parties to any agreement reduce the cost of regulation.

Action plans should also seek to encourage ongoing dialogue in order to encourage further cooperation and anticipate difficulties in implementation and/or possible future potential conflict;
4. the use of a variety of effective mechanisms including mediation and zoning.

If the equity component of sustainability is to be treated seriously then it therefore becomes vital that tourism planning, and public participation as a component of tourism planning, addresses values and people's perception of the 'truth' rather than just be geared to short-term interest management which deals with the 'facts' as seen by the makers of the rules of the tourism planning game.

This does not mean that community-based tourism planning will automatically lead to either sustainable tourism development or even a reduction in the amount of conflict surrounding tourism development. Instead, a local focus allows for the dynamics of the planning process to be altered as stakeholders face their interdependencies at a place-specific level. However, we should not romanticise the local, as so often seems to be the case in discussions of tourism planning. As Millar and Aiken (1995: 629) recognised,

> Communities are not the embodiment of innocence; on the contrary, they are complex and self-serving entities, as much driven by grievances, prejudices, inequalities, and struggles for power as they are united by kinship, reciprocity, and interdependence. Decision-making at the local level can be extraordinarily vicious, personal, and not always bound by legal constraints.

Nevertheless, a community-based approach does provide the possibility that the necessity to consult over the use of shared resources and the needs of neighbours opens the way to conflict resolution. Perhaps more significantly, with a reduction in the extent of formal government procedures, a community-based process of management and conflict resolution may provide an informality in personal relationships between stakeholders by which trust is able to develop.

Classifying policy

One of the most influential approaches to classifying public policy has been that of Lowi (1972). According to Lowi classification 'reveals the hidden meanings and significance of the phenomena, suggesting what the important hypotheses ought to be concerned with' (1972: 299). Because the content of a policy implies particular outcomes, this results in particular responses from those affected which in turn have an impact on debate in terms of decision making as well as the implementation process (see Chapter 10) as the choice of policy mechanism constrains the selection of implementation tools. To Lowi, such classification also leads to the identification of discrete areas of politics, each area characterised by its own political structure, policy process, elites and group relations,

and power structures and policy-making processes that differ according to the type of issue they deal with (Jenkins 1978). These four areas were identified by Lowi as distributive, constituent, regulative, and redistributive (see Table 8.9). Although Lowi's approach has been criticised for failing to account for the emergence of new and innovative public policies and new issues in agenda setting, as well as the problem of classifying a policy when its attributes cross policy boundaries (Jenkins 1978) the approach has nevertheless been extremely influential.

The Lowi approach was reinterpreted by Anderson (1994) who substituted constituent policy with a category of self-regulatory policy. However, in using the Lowi typology 'self-regulatory policy' is really just a

Table 8.9 Classification of policy types

Policy type	Characteristics of the policy	Characteristics of the policy arena	Policy examples	Policy and regulatory instruments
Distributive	Collective public provision	Consensual	Research grants; general tax reduction	Incentives
Redistributive	Relation between costs and benefits obvious	Conflict; polarisation between winners and losers; ideologically driven	Labour market policy; economic assistance programmes	Imposed by state
Regulative	Legal and institutional norms for behaviour	Changing coalitions according to the distribution of costs and benefits	Consumer protection, occupational health and safety, environmental protection	Varied: imposed by the state, persuasion, self-regulation (allowed by the state)
Constituent	Public–private partnerships; institutional norms	Specific policy networks, especially sub-governments	Setting up of a new agency; new procedures; allowing self-regulation	Imposed by the state

Sources: After Lowi (1972); Heinelt (2005).

▶

subset of regulatory policy and can be interpreted as having been allowed by the state and is a form of constituent policy in that it is usually the result of the activities of public–private partnership. The nature of each policy classification is set out below.

Regulatory policy refers to the placement of restrictions and limits on the actions of individual persons or organisations. Regulatory provisions may include restrictions on movement for either political or environmental reasons, restrictions on land use or resource protection laws (Parker 1999). Self-regulatory policy is a subset of regulatory policy in that it refers to controls on the behaviour of identified groups or individuals but is undertaken by the regulated group or non-government organisation. Self-regulation may be utilised as a government policy as a form of public–private partnership so as to reduce its own costs or to satisfy the demands and needs of particular producer groups to reduce their compliance costs. However, it is only as effective as the extent to which compliance with regulatory standards is actually sought.

Constituent policy refers to the development of specific policies to meet the interests of specific groups. Such policies are often developed through public–private partnerships but may also be developed with respect to the issue networks surrounding particular policy concerns such as the environment or security. Examples of constituent policies include the development of new agencies or organisations with specific constituent developed mandates.

Distributive policies involve the distribution of benefits to particular groups in society. Parker (1999: 320) argues that distributive policy is 'fundamentally promotional in nature and governments rely heavily upon it to stimulate the tourism and ecotourism industries', although he also gives examples such as the use of investment tax credits, accelerated depreciation, leasing of property, subsidisation and market support as exogenous distributive policies that are typically used to attract investment.

Redistributive policies are specific policies to move the distribution of wealth or other resources from one group in society to another. This may be undertaken on the basis of income levels, wealth, class, ethnicity or region. For example, in the 1980s ecotourism was conceived as a means of improving the level of economic well-being of otherwise marginal communities in peripheral areas. More recently, the notion of pro-poor tourism has become increasingly significant as it reflects a policy idea that tourism can be used as a targeted means of redistribution of wealth through encouraging consumers to undertake certain tourism activities in specific locations that require poverty reduction strategies (Hall 2007d).

Summary

This chapter has reviewed some of the contemporary processes within which places find themselves being turned into destinations via the process of place marketing. The chapter has also highlighted the set of interrelationships that exist within destinations which the tourism planner seeks to understand and manipulate in order to achieve certain goals and outcomes. (I realise that some readers may be upset by the use of the word 'manipulation', but that is what we try to do in social settings in order to achieve our objectives, even if these are something like more sustainable planning outcomes.) Competitiveness and regional development, networks, clusters and conflict resolution are four spheres in which the tourism planner is extremely active in working with relationships with planning stakeholders. In this setting, 'spatial and environmental planning, understood relationally, becomes a practice of building a relational capacity which can address collective concerns about spatial co-existence, spatial organisation and the qualities of place' (Healey 1997: 69). Tourism planners are therefore more often than not in these more entrepreneurial times involved in 'link-making' work between stakeholders, establishing relationships through the social glue of trust.

Relational resources can be regarded as a form of social capital. Collaborative or relational planning approaches focus attention on the relational webs and networks in which we live our lives. 'The challenge is to make sense of a multiplicity of claims for attention arising from the different relational webs which each actual and potential participant brings to the public arena' (Healey 1997: 67). Creating and maintaining dialogue therefore becomes a critical role of the tourism planner. The planner will typically be involved in direction setting, which refers to the articulation by stakeholders of the values and interests that guide their individual pursuits in order to appreciate a common sense of purpose and direction, and the establishment of equitable ground rules for participation and negotiation between interests.

> Procedural issues can include deciding whether to allow the use of alternate representatives, selecting meeting sites, scheduling meetings, handling confidential information, using outside experts, deciding how to handle relations with the media, and determining whether agreements will be put in writing and, if so, in what form. (Bingham 1986: 106)

The revitalisation and planning of place requires more than just the development of product and image. The re-creation of a sense of place is a process that involves the formulation of planning and design strategies based on conceptual models of places and regions which are, in turn, founded on notions of civic life and the public realm as part of sustainability (Berke 2002) and the idea of planning as debate and argument. Unfortunately, such models have only limited visibility within the place-marketing and tourism realms, as tourism and place planning is often poorly conceptualised with respect to participatory procedures (Dredge and Jenkins 2007), while the institutional arrangements for many of the public–private partnerships for urban redevelopment actually exclude community participation in decision-making procedures (Talen 2000).

Policy visions, whether they be for places or for industries, typically fail to be developed in the light of oppositional or critical viewpoints. Place visions tend to be developed through the activities of industry experts rather than the broad populace, perhaps because the wider public's vision for a place may not be the same as some segments of business. Community involvement is undertaken through opinion polls, surveys or SWOT analyses rather than through participatory measures (e.g. Hall *et al.* 1997; Hall and McArthur 1998;

Dredge and Jenkins 2007). Nevertheless, cities and regions

> will be re-imagined in democratic forms only by creating the conditions for the emergence of a genuinely public, political discourse about their future, which should go beyond the conformist platitudes of the "visions" formulated by the new breed of civic boosters and municipal marketers. (Bianchini and Schwengel 1991: 234)

A call unfortunately ignored by many involved in destination planning.

To enable the facilitation of public discourse it is vital that tourism planners become actively engaged in the places that they seek to plan. Tourism planning is therefore a combination of formal and informal theory (common sense). For example, in conflict management nothing is more valuable and productive than meeting face to face (Amy 1987). Nevertheless, we also have to be able to imagine different possibilities and futures. As Morgan (1986: 331) commented, 'The images or metaphors through which we read organizational situations help us describe the way organizations are, and offer clear ideas over the way they could be.' 'Our different languages and discourses provide vocabularies of metaphors and reference points. Our understandings are shaped by and filtered through our thoughtworlds, our cultural systems of meaning' (Healey 1997: 65). In this we have to understand and appreciate other people's values and perspectives as well as our own, the way in which they change over time, and the fact that our own perspectives may be ignored or even regarded as 'wrong'.

Tourism planning is imperfect. 'Local-level development is an uncomfortable and often painful process, requiring that new community-based decision-making structures be defined and experimented with' (Millar and Aiken 1995: 640). Nevertheless, the very diversity of values and interests that make the tourism planner's life difficult at times is also a great strength, as the existence of a diversity of social groups and their values can also offer sources of resilience, resistance and innovation in changing times. One of the planner's tasks may be, therefore, to find ways of enhancing the institutional capacities and qualities of place, and it is to this task that the next chapter will turn.

Questions

1. How can place marketing approaches more effectively incorporate community perception and ownership of place?
2. What are the key elements of growth control and management and how can they be applied to tourism?
3. To what extent can conflict resolution be regarded as a process of value change?
4. How can the equity component of sustainable development best be addressed?
5. What are the necessary conditions for resolving conflict?
6. Using the different categories of networks identified in Table 8.8 identify different tourism network relationships in your destination.
7. Table 8.5 described the characteristics of local growth controls and management techniques as they are usually applied in North America. To what extent are such controls and techniques used where you live and what level of government is responsible for their regulatory basis?

Recommended reading

1. Michael, E.J. (2007) *Micro-clusters and Networks: The Growth of Tourism*, Elsevier, Oxford.

   A good introduction to issues of clusters and networks in tourism.

2. Sharpley, R. and Telfer, D. (eds) (2002) *Tourism and Development: Concepts and Issues*, Channel View Publications, Clevedon.

   Good introductory account of various dimensions of tourism and development.

3. Cresswell, T. (2004) *Place: A Short Introduction*, Blackwell, Oxford.

   Excellent introduction to concepts of place.

4. Ritchie, J.R.B. and Crouch, G.I. (2003) *The Competitive Destination: A*

Sustainable Tourism Perspective, CABI, Wallingford.

   Influential book on destination competitiveness.

5. Dwyer, L. and Kim, C. (2003) 'Destination competitiveness: determinants and indicators', *Current Issues in Tourism*, 6(5): 369–414.

   Useful paper on destination competitiveness that was originally developed within a Korean context.

6. Martin, R. and Sunley, P. (2003) 'Deconstructing clusters: chaotic concept or policy panacea?', *Journal of Economic Geography*, 3: 5–35.

   Extremely good critique of the cluster concept particularly in relation to the work of Porter.

7. Florida, R. (2002) *The Rise of the Creative Class, and How It's Transforming Work, Leisure, Community and Everyday Life*, Basic Books, New York.

   Influential book on the role of the 'creative classes' in urban development.

8. Gill, A. (2000) 'From growth machine to growth management: the dynamics of resort development in Whistler, British Columbia', *Environment and Planning A*, 32(6): 1083–1103.

   Excellent article that records the changes in development approach at Whistler Resort in Canada.

9. Carruthers, J.I. (2002) 'The impacts of state growth management programmes: a comparative analysis', *Urban Studies*, 39: 1959–82.

   Evaluates growth management programmes in the United States.

10. Warner, K. and Molotch, H. (2000) *Building Rules: How Local Controls Shape Community Environments and Economies*, Westview Press, Boulder.

   Excellent book on the implications of planning controls on communities and places.

9 Planning sites: sustainable design

Loved buildings are the ones that work well, that suit the people in them, and that show their age and history. All it takes is keeping most everything that works, most everything that is enjoyed, much of what doesn't get in the way, and helping the rest evolve. That goes better if the place is neither owned nor maintained by remote antagonists, because they distance the building from its users. What makes a building learn is its physical connection to the people within . . . an adapted state is not an end state. A successful building has to be periodically challenged and refreshed, or it will turn into a beautiful corpse. (Brand 1997: 209)

Chapter objectives

After reading this chapter you will:

- Appreciate some of the key questions with respect to the application of sustainable design principles to tourism development
- Appreciate the significance of adaptive capacities and systems
- Understand the relational aspects of the concept of authenticity
- Understand the elements that make up the site planning panarchy.

As several chapters in the book have already noted, many people think of tourism planning in terms of land use. The book has argued that while land use is a major role, the theories, thinking and assumptions behind such planning traditions require much more analysis if we are to envisage

sustainable place futures which involve tourism. In order to conceptualise and imagine sustainable futures we have advocated a multi-scaled, systems-based approach to tourism planning that emphasises the relational nature of planning and, perhaps, provides a more accurate mental representation of the way in which human–environment interaction actually works. Sustainability is, after all, basically an ecological concept (Holling 2001). 'Seeing nature whole, understanding interrelationships and connections between human and non-human life, must, therefore, begin with the places where most people live' (Hough 1995: 25). This chapter looks briefly at some of the implications of such an approach with respect to design issues in tourism and the way an improved understanding of material change may also lead us to develop more sustainable places.

An ecological approach

The previous chapters have moved down the different levels of tourism planning and policy analysis from the international through to the local. This chapter looks at site-level operations and the interconnections between the site and its urban and regional context. Although tourism facilities and 'resorts do not belong to the category in which much of contemporary debate on architecture is centred' (Beng 1995: 6), recognition of such relationships are, of course, not new. The field of urban ecology has long stressed such relationships. An environmental view is an essential component of the economic, engineering, political and design processes that shape cities, with the problems facing the larger regional context of the countryside often having their roots in cities, particularly with respect to their ecological footprint (see Chapter 2); 'solutions must, therefore, also be sought there' (Hough 1995: 6) (see also Keil 2003; Hinchcliffe and Whatmore 2006). Indeed, increasingly places are being considered as a form of 'civic ecosystem' in which the interaction of buildings and other forms of infrastructure with each other in a given environmental context gives rise to collectively made physical forms, or what is often described as vernacular architecture that is representative of place. These emergent forms can be described as built species and civic ecosystems. Built species are lineages handed down over time because their association between built form and social practices retains cultural coherence. Civic ecosystems emerge from interactions among built forms within the physical and conceptual environment, and have the coherence and resilience characteristic of complex adaptive systems (Childs 2001).

According to Hough (1995: 20), 'The nature of design is one of initiating purposeful and beneficial change, with ecology and people as its indispensable foundation.' The principles of design that he advocates are reflective of the systems and relational approaches advocated through this book (see also Alexander *et al.* 1977, 1987; Alexander 1979). Indeed one has only to reflect on the relationship between ecology and economics in terms of its original Greek root – *oikos* – 'the management of the household so as to increase its value to all members of the household over the long run' (Daly and Cobb 1989: 138) – to appreciate the ecological foundations of economic development, something which is often forgotten in contemporary development practices. Perhaps we should also note that *domus* meant 'house' in an expanded sense, which included the people within the walls, not just the physical structure, thereby also reinforcing the significance of the social dimension of development.

The notion of *oikos* is also implicit in the concept of sustainability. According to Donella Meadows (as cited in Beatley and Manning 1997: 1),

The problem of the 21st century is how to live good and just lives within limits, in harmony with the earth and each other. Great cities can rise out of cruelty, deviousness, and a refusal to be bounded. Liveable cities can only be sustained out of humility, compassion, and acceptance of the concept of enough.

In Chapter 2 we identified the concept of ecological footprint to measure the impact of individual, organisational and collective consumption. This measure was extremely valuable in identifying the extent to which over-consumption, including the impacts of travel and tourism, is leading to undesirable environmental and social change. However, while consumption – particularly of transport – is the major contributor to our overall tourism footprint (see Chapter 2), it can be still be influenced by design and self-selection (Moos *et al.* 2006).

To Hough (1995) three principles underlie good site design:

1. *Process* – 'The tendency to view phenomena as static events, frozen in time, is a root cause of the aesthetic dilemmas that we face. When nature is seen as a continuum, the argument of what is beautiful or what is less so in the landscape becomes, if not meaningless, then of a very different order of meaning' (Hough 1995: 18–19).
2. *Diversity* – in ecological terms diversity implies health. In the urban setting, 'Diversity makes social as well as biological sense . . . since the requirements of an infinitely diverse urban society implies choice' (Hough 1995: 23).
3. *Connectedness* – as the systems approach stresses, everything is ultimately connected to everything else. To understand a local place, therefore, requires an understanding of its larger context, including not only the economic, social and political context but also the environmental context such as 'the watershed and bio-region in which it lies' (Hough 1995: 24).

Therefore, given these ecological principles, 'One of the fundamental tasks of reshaping the city is to focus on the human experience of one's home places; to recognize the existence and the latent potential of natural, social and cultural environments to enrich urban places' (Hough 1995: 26). As we noted in the previous chapter with respect to the concept of 'sense of place', over time communities develop a complex web of perceptions and attitudes as to what is appropriate and compatible with 'their' space, which may be substantially affected by tourism development. This human ecology is intimately connected with people's relationship with their environment and changes that may occur. Therefore such linkages and relationships need to be made visible in the tourism planning process in order to minimise negative impacts.

> Much of our daily existence is spent in surroundings designed to conceal the processes that sustain life and which contribute, possibly more than any other factor, the acute sensory impoverishment of our living environment . . . visibility is essential in economic and political terms . . . policies should capitalize on the visibility of the environmental consequences of human actions in the process of daily living. (Hough 1995: 30)

The loss of linkage is a significant theme in tourism, whether it be environmental relationships or culture-driven relationships such as notions of authenticity (Cohen 2007; Hall 2007c; Pearce 2007). According to Beng (1995: 6), 'The production of tourist architecture distorts both time and place. There is a tendency to homogeneity behind the false fronts.' The loss of historically rooted places, including the attempt to depoliticise them, 'decontextualising them and sucking out of them all political controversy – so as to sell . . . places . . . to outsiders who might otherwise feel alienated or encounter encouragements to political defiance' (Philo and Kearns 1993: 24), appears commonplace in tourism. Heritage centres and historical anniversaries typically serve to flatten and suppress contested views of history. However, the presentation of one-dimensional views of the past to the tourist and the community is also encountered at the destination and resort level. For example, in the case of tourism, history and ethnicity in Monterey, Norkunas (1993) argues that the rich and complex ethnic history of Monterey is almost completely absent in the 'official' historic tours

and the residences available for public viewing. In Monterey, as in many other parts of the world, heritage is presented in the form of the houses of the aristocracy or elite (see Hirsh 2002; Hanna and Del Casino 2003; Hanna et al. 2004). 'This synopsis of the past into a digestible touristic presentation eliminates any discussion of conflict; it concentrates instead on a sense of resolution. Opposed events and ideologies are collapsed into statements about the forward movement and rightness of history' (Norkunas 1993: 36). Narratives of labour, class and ethnicity are typically replaced by romance and nostalgia. Overt conflict, whether between ethnic groups, classes or, more particularly, in terms of industrial and labour disputes, are either ignored or glossed over in 'official' tourist histories (see also Chiang 2004). The overt conflict of the past has been reinterpreted by local elites to create a new history in which heritage takes a linear, conflict-free form. In the case of Monterey, the past is reinterpreted through the physical transformation of the canneries (see also Chiang 2004).

> Reinterpreting the past has allowed the city to effectively erase from the record the industrial era and the working-class culture it engendered. Commentary on the industrial era remains only in the form of touristic interpretations of the literature of John Steinbeck. (Norkunas 1993: 50–51)

The homogenisation and standardisation of 'public' life and space as a result of tourism and hospitality developments, sometimes referred to as Disneyfication (Relph 1976, 2000) or McDonaldisation (Ritzer 1996), is a major criticism of tourism and contemporary cultural processes. Indeed, at first glance it might be assumed that place marketing, with its enthusiastic embrace of place, its appeal to the supposedly unique attractions of particular locations, and its passionate text, should be anything but homogenising (Torres and Momsen 2005).

> Yet ultimately, the deconstructed discourses of the packed newly post-industrial cities replicate the same images, amenities, and potentials and contain the same silences with respect to poverty, race and blight. The pastiche of upscale places is contextless: presumably intentionally so, since the

Authenticity

One of the most intriguing things about the continued focus on authenticity in tourism (e.g. Cohen 2007; Pearce 2007) is that for all the supposed growth in interest in the 'authentic' (e.g., Boyle 2004; Yeoman *et al.* 2007), it is also readily apparent that there is a growing preponderance of the fake or 'inauthentic' attractions or locations which does not necessarily detract people from visiting them. Fakery is the replication of environmental and/or social meaning through the manipulation of appearances, actions or experiences. Yet replication is not intrinsically bad; what is important is the different experiential depth (i.e. historical depth, spatial depth, cultural depth, environmental depth, educational depth) between the original and the replication (Hall 2007c). Time is also an extremely significant factor in people's understanding of authenticity. As Brand (1997: 23) observed with respect to how buildings are perceived and experienced, 'Age plus adaptivity is what makes a building come to be loved. The building learns from its occupants, and they learn from it.' In many cases replication is the only way that someone may be able to gain understanding or experience of the original. Therefore, inauthenticity emerges out of the very attempt to retain authenticity. Instead, a crisis of authenticity occurs when there is a deliberate attempt to deceive through fakery, reproduction or simulation and a breakdown of trust occurs between the consumer and the producer. Replication or simulation is not intrinsically immoral unless there is deception. As Dovey (1985: 39) suggests, people 'can accept all kinds of faked things and perhaps even learn to love them so long as they are not deceived by those things'.

However, in all of the discussion over authenticity an argument can be made that the concept should not even be used with respect to things and places at all. Authenticity is experiential, in that it is derived from the property of connectedness of the individual to the perceived, everyday world and environment, and the processes that created it and the consequences of one's engagement with it. From such a perspective anywhere, or anything, can provide the connectedness that leads to authenticity as authenticity is not intrinsically dependent on location. Nevertheless, place – in the sense of everyday lived experiences and relations – does matter. Of course this may well mean that rather than the high-yielding authentic tourist supposedly in search of 'authentic tourism experiences' that many national and regional tourism marketing organisations appear to dream of in their marketing strategies (e.g. Tourism Western Australia, Visit Scotland, Industry Canada) the most authentic tourist is likely to be someone visiting friends and relations or going to the cottage because of the relational and connected nature of that experience (Hall 2007c).

fashionable fern bars are often in not-yet-completely gentrified neighbourhoods. The time of places marketed is present and future. The only past that matters is the packaged past of the heritage industry (Holcomb 1993: 141).

Diversity and the recognition of linkages and relationships are often not being acknowledged, let alone maintained in such circumstances, thereby potentially affecting the long-term viability of such locations. In contrast, planners influenced by their knowledge of the significance of ecological systems for urban sustainability 'seek a design language whose inspiration derives from making the most of available opportunities; one that re-establishes the concept of multi-functional, productive and working landscapes that integrate ecology, people and economy' (Hough 1995: 31).

What might such a design language look like? One strong possibility is in the idea of adaptive architecture, which is in itself related to the concept of adaptive systems. An adaptive system is one in which the system tends to move through four recurring phases, referred to as adaptive cycles. The four phases are rapid growth,

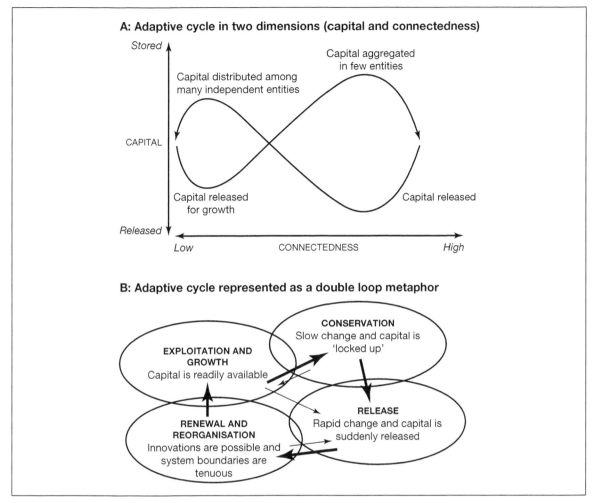

Figure 9.1 Metaphors of adaptive cycles

Sources: After Holling (2001) and Resilience Alliance (2007).

conservation, release and reorganisation, followed again by rapid growth (Holling 2001) (Figure 9.1). The application of adaptive systems to tourism has only occurred since the late 1990s and then primarily in connection to sustainability and the conceptualisation of tourism systems (e.g. Hunter 1997; Farrell and Twinning-Ward 2004, 2005; Picken 2006; Harrison 2007).

Brand (1997), expanding on the work of Duffy (1990), argues that buildings should not be conceived of as unchanging architecture, rather they should be seen as several layers or hierarchies of longevity of different built compo-

nents. Brand identified six hierachies of change which, in turn, we can locate within the local, regional, national and international contexts discussed earlier in this book (Figure 9.2). The six Ss of layered change in a building are:

1. *Site* – refers to the geographical setting and the legally defined property boundaries. Site can be an extremely long-lasting influence on urban form, in particular as witnessed in the extent to which the street pattern for the cores of many present-day cities in Europe and the Middle East have been in existence

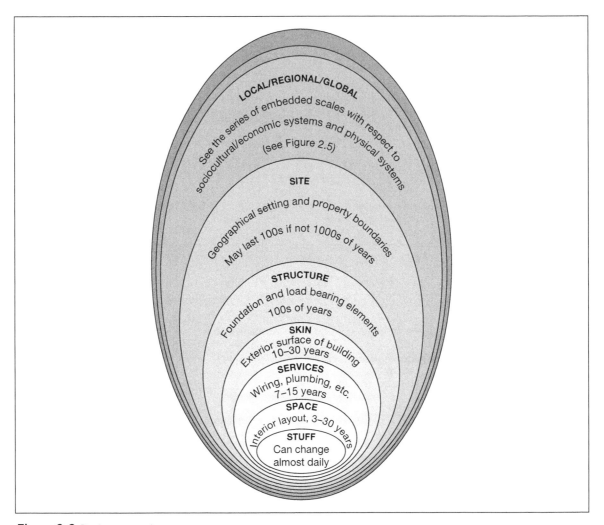

Figure 9.2 Design panarchy

for many hundreds, and in some cases thousands, of years.

2. *Structure* – refers to the foundation and load-bearing elements of buildings, which may also last hundreds of years.

3. *Skin* – this is the exterior surface of the building that changes according to fashion, technologies and maintenance needs, often measured in tens of years.

4. *Services* – refers to such things as the wiring, plumbing, air conditioning, heating, ventilation, elevators and so on. These are often replaced within 7–15 years.

5. *Space* – this is the interior layout and refers to such things as the location of walls and doors. Rates of change here may vary from approximately 3 years in commercial buildings to 30 years in residential properties.

6. *Stuff* – refers to furniture and personal belongings that may be relatively mobile.

The hierarchies of change are the basis of socio-economic and biophysical systems over various scales. When combined with the adaptive cycle of each hierarchy they form what is known as a panarchy (Holling 2001). Each level operates at its own pace of change, protected from above by slower, larger levels but invigorated from below by faster, smaller cycles of innovation. The whole panarchy is therefore both creative and conserving. In the case of the design of tourism infrastructure as well as existing resource use the layering of change helps define how buildings and places relate to people:

> Organizational levels of responsibility match the pace levels. The building interacts with individuals at the level of stuff; with the tenant organization (or family) at the Space plan level; with the landlord via the Services (and slower levels) which must be maintained; with the public via the Skin and entry; and with the whole community through city or county decisions about the footprint and volume of the structure and restrictions on the Site. The community does not tell you where to put your desk or your bed; you do not tell the community where your building will go on the Site (unless you're way out in the country). (Brand 1997: 17)

Most interaction is within the same level of pace of change. 'The dynamics of the system will be dominated by the slow components, with the rapid components simply following along' (O'Neil *et al.* 1986: 98). Nevertheless, interaction and influence is a two-way process. Indeed, it is at times of major change in a system that the quick processes appear most to influence the slow. However, as Brand (1997: 18) records, 'Slow is healthy. Much of the wholesome evolution of cities can be explained by the steadfast persistence of Site.' The pattern of ownership of land and property is extremely important for the way in which places change. Small lots allow for ongoing fine-grain change as opposed to the sudden wholesale change that can occur with large parcels of land (Moudon 1982). The more owners the more gradual and adaptive will be the change.

> Small lots will support resilience because they allow many people to attend directly to their needs by designing, building and maintaining their own environment. By ensuring that property remains in many hands, small lots bring important results: many people make many different decisions, thereby ensuring variety in the resulting environment. And many property owners slow down the rate of change by making large-scale real estate transactions difficult (Moudon 1986: 188).

Such an observation has many significant implications for the way in which tourism development is managed, particularly in urban areas. Appropriate and sustainable tourism development may well mean relatively gradual small-scale change with the inclusion of large numbers of stakeholders as opposed to large-scale developments with limited numbers of 'owners' of the project. While the large-scale project may well be a grand gesture which politicians and boosters support by virtue that they are seen to be 'doing something', the more unspectacular gradual change is likely to be more sustainable. For example, in the case of Vancouver in British Columbia, Canada, the gradual redevelopment of Granville Island by the Canadian federal government as a mixed use area that maintained associations with traditional waterfront businesses, e.g. chandlers, boat repairs and moorings, as well as providing for new uses such as a hotel, markets, bookshops and theatres, has proven to be a far more sustainable development with respect to environmental and social factors than the large-scale development of other parts of the former dock area through the hosting of the 1986 Expo (McCullough 1996; Gourley 1998). Over a decade later, many parts of the former Expo site were still undeveloped.

According to Brand (1997: 23) good urban design is respect for what came before: 'Age plus adaptivity is what makes a building come to be loved. The building learns from its occupants, and they learn from it'. Similarly, Jacobs (1993: 245) recognised that 'Old ideas can sometimes use new buildings. New ideas must come from old buildings.' From this position the preservation movement has been one of the great design revolutions, which has had substantial implications for tourism, particularly with respect to conveying place identity. Consistent representations of place rely on built species (Childs 2001) that are the design lineages handed down over time because their association between built form and social practices retains cultural coherence and are understood as vernacular architecture. Such vernacular material is integral to place, as Glassie (1968: 33) observed, 'a search for pattern in folk

Plate 9.1 Granville Island, Vancouver, British Columbia, Canada. This redevelopment has worked because it retained a diverse economic, social and cultural base, provided opportunities to small businesses, and was developed through a series of incremental steps.

material yields regions, where a search for pattern in popular material yields periods'.

'Preservationists have a philosophy of time and responsibility that includes the future' (Brand 1997: 90). In this sense, the preservation movement is creating a form of intergenerational equity through the maintenance and adaptive re-use of buildings and structures from one generation to another, while also contributing to substantial economic and energy savings. For example, 'even extensive rehabilitation (services, windows, roof) typically costs 3 to 16 per cent less than demolishing and replacing an old building' (Rypkema 1992: 27), while preservation can also help conserve the 'embodied energy' of buildings and reduce the solid-waste burden of demolition (Rathje and Murphy 1992). Life cycle assessment (LCA) is an increasingly important dimension in assessing the environmental quality of any product (Figure 9.3), including the physical infrastructure on which tourism depends. Meijkamp (1994) indicated that LCAs reveal that the major environmental impact of a product often lies not in the production but in the use. This observation particularly applies for products that process energy and materials when used (e.g. transport). However, with respect to preservation and recycling of existing buildings and infrastructure cultural, environment and aesthetic arguments only go so far; economic issues tend to remain at the forefront of site preservation.

In many places the greatest impact of tourism is through the effect that tourism development can have on real estate values, although such effects are generally little discussed in terms of their impacts on sustainability. According to Brand:

> Nearly everything about real estate estranges buildings from their users and interrupts any form of sustained continuity. A triumph of abstraction, real estate operates distant from the daily life of building use, distant from the real. The 'real' in 'real estate' derives from *re-al* – 'royal' – rather than *res* – 'thing' which is the root of 'reality'. Realty is in many ways the opposite of reality.

Plate 9.2 Cement works, Granville Island. The retention of industrial use adds to the attractiveness of the development as it is a 'living' community.

Plate 9.3 Development of post Expo derelict land, Vancouver. This parcel of prime waterfront land less than 100 m from Granville Island lay derelict post Expo 1986 for 15 years with condominium development only completed in 2005.

Life cycle analysis

Life cycle thinking is critical to design. Until the middle of the twentieth century consumer durables were generally viewed as investments and, within reasonable cost boundaries, were designed to last as long as possible. Since then, however, planned obsolescence, the deliberate curtailment of a product's lifespan, has become common place, driven by, for example, a need for cost reductions in order to meet 'price points,' the convenience of disposability, and the appeal of fashion (Cooper 2005: 57).

Life cycle analysis is a tool that is increasingly being used to assess the environmental impacts of product systems and services over the lifespan of the product in order to encourage more sustainable forms of production and consumption (UNEP 2004). LCA accounts for the emissions and resource uses during the production (including extraction and manufacturing), distribution, use and disposal of a product over its lifespan (Figure 9.3). The approach has developed out of research on energy demand (including that embodied in the product) and uses physical process analysis and economic input–output analysis as its key features. The results of LCAs can also be used to inform consumer decision making with respect to the environmental impacts of different types of products, i.e. the relative costs and benefits of different types of heating, but are more widely being used to influence policy makers and planners who seek to encourage sustainable consumption (ecolabelling). The marketing 'product life cycle' is different but relevant as it refers to the period between the point of introduction on to the market and the point at which it is removed. If products are made more durable or given a longer lifespan there are obvious implications for production and business behaviour.

LCAs usually consist of three analytical steps. First, the actual determination of the processes involved in the life cycle of a product. Second, the determination of environmental pressures (i.e. emissions, pollution, resource use) over the life cycle. Third, the assessment of environmental impacts in order to identify impact indicators. In addition to which, ISO (1997) adds two procedural steps, goal and scope definition (planning the LCA) and interpretation. Goal and scope definition are important as they may help determine the relative importance of different types of impact, such as whether energy use should be prioritised over reduced waste and as to whether use of a product should be included as well as production, distribution and disposal. (For example, consider the implications of evaluating the greenhouse gas equivalent emissions of a Boeing 747 or an Airbus A300 with and without the use phase!) In effect this is a question of system boundaries.

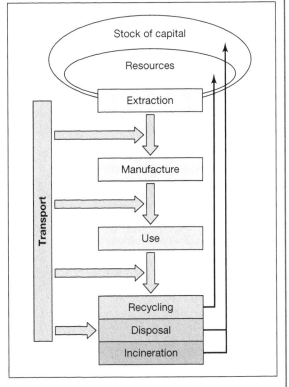

Figure 9.3 Life cycle assessment

An LCA is therefore seeking to construct a causal link between production processes, production products and the associated environmental stress. This is usually done by either: (1) dividing the amount of emissions and/or resource use by the total number of products produced over a given period of time (attributional analysis); or (2) identifying the marginal impacts of production, i.e. in the case of electricity generation where the emissions of old plant may be significantly different from new plant. In the basic attributional model, LCA can be represented by a set of linear equations:

$$I_{LC} = CS(I - A)^{-1}y$$

Where

I_{LC} is the life cycle impact, expressed as a vector of impact indicators for different impact categories;

y is the vector representing the functional unit;

$I - A$ represents the matrix of production, use, and disposal processes, i.e. recycling or incineration, that constitute the product life cycle;

S represents the table of emissions factors per unit process; and

C is the table of characterisation factors per impact category.

The flows in the matrix $I - A$ that described the production technology can represent either physical or economic flows. Hertwich (2005) integrated the use of LCA with input–output analysis to review research on household energy consumption and CO_2 emissions and while registering significant differences in mobility as a component of annual per capita energy use by household between countries (8 per cent in India, 36 per cent in the United States he noted significant difficulties in undertaking comparative studies because many of the original studies were not fully comparable in terms of methods, activities included in the assessment, indicators, nomenclature, results, and how capital is treated:

> Many input–output studies do not include the emissions connected to aviation and ocean transport, because the consumption of so-called 'bunker fuels' is commonly not included in the national environmental accounts, and these emissions are not accounted for under the Kyoto protocol. (Hertwich 2005: 4679)

In addition he identified the need for the evaluation of rebound effects – the secondary behavioural effect produced by a primary technical or quality measure (usually a technical improvement) – which, in part, offsets the initial effect of the primary measure. Such effects are extremely significant in the transportation field in relation to the cost of fuel and consequent changes in behaviour, while also in transportation and tourism research there is clear evidence of a time rebound effect as access to faster transport has meant that the radius of action or space–time prism of tourism mobility expands but the total travel time remains roughly constant (see Hall 2005a).

All that is sold melts into cash. Real estate turns buildings into money, into fungible units devoid of history and therefore of learning (1997: 87).

Rapid changes in real estate value are extremely dangerous to the lives of buildings and places. Substantial increases or decreases in value can dramatically affect land-use development strategies as well as municipal charges placed on residents and owners. Tourism development is often used by cities in conjunction with private sector partners to try to improve real estate values. However, such developments may have ripple effects across the social and economic fabric of the city: for example, through the hosting of mega-events such as the Olympics or through the construction of flagship developments and retail/leisure/tourism complexes often associated with waterfronts, the development of stadia and/or convention and exhibition centres (Smyth 1994; Page and Hall 2003). Moreover, the overall long-term impacts of large-scale tourism developments on a destination are often ignored in the planning process despite the role that such events and facilities clearly play in urban redevelopment strategies. If there are no lasting benefits and no identifiable economic opportunity costs from urban redevelopment programmes, then we are left with the proposition of Bourdieu (1984): 'the most successful ideological effects are those which have no words' (quoted in Harvey 1989b: 78).

The function of a flagship development is then 'reduced to inducing social stability, assuming the generated experience is sustainable for enough people over a long period and is targeted towards those who are potentially the harbingers of disruption what is the purpose of marketing the city?' (Smyth 1994: 7). (See Table 9.1 on lessons of flagship developments.)

Property-led urban regeneration has had some success in terms of localised economic regeneration, 'but it has not provided a solution to the problem of urban regeneration, even during the property boom of the mid- and late-1980s' (Smyth 1994: 12). Urban and regional regeneration must be therefore seen as a long-term activity in which diversity and relationships are enhanced not minimised (Pike *et al.* 2006; Cochrane 2007). As Worpole (1991: 145) observed:

> A town centre in which it is no longer possible to buy a pint of milk, a tin of paint, a fishing rod, a ball of wool, a bicycle tyre, or get a pair of shoes mended – and there are many such towns in Britain – will be in serious trouble in the future, when mobile companies and populations start relocating again and look for self-reliant towns and cities that exhibit an economic and cultural dynamic and its associated quality of life.

A diverse base not only protects the local population from the extremes of recession and external decision making, but also attracts and helps retain inward investment. As Jane Jacobs (1965: 162) argued with respect to the role of diversity within an urban system (an equally valid point holds with tourism systems):

> So long as we are content to believe that city diversity represents accident and chaos, of course its erratic generation appears to represent a mystery. However, the conditions that generate city diversity are quite easy to discover by observing places in which diversity flourishes and studying the economic reasons why it can flourish in these places. Although the results are intricate and the ingredients producing them may vary enormously, this complexity is based on tangible economic relationships which, in principle, are much simpler that the intricate urban mixtures they make possible.

However, diversity also implies adopting policies of inclusiveness and equity in planning

Table 9.1 Lessons of flagship developments

- Flagship developments require an overt marketing strategy.

- Flagship developments require management of the policy formulation, implementation and evaluation process.

- The strategy and management may be project, area and/or city based.

- Marketing concerns the creation and bringing together of supply and demand factors in an implicit exchange in the urban context.

- Success is not contingent upon public versus private finance or initiation.

- Design and planning should arise from the social relations of residents, businesses and organisations in the affected areas and those envisaged for the area.

- Economic benefits do not trickle down to the disadvantaged.

- All organisations must take responsibility for the impact of their development on others in order to make the market work, as well as for moral reasons.

- Political legitimacy and economic necessity will increasingly demand the participation of the local residents and other interests in the policy and development process in order to help maintain social stability, create a 'saleable' urban 'product' and create new development markets within the urban economy.

- Participation may produce benefits for all parties, yet it will be a politicised process, the balance of the benefits being the object of conflict and the outworking of transforming city lives and economies.

- Participation is essential to the transformation of the urban economy and of relations within it and is a key management issue.

- Management must identify techniques and means to facilitate and accelerate the policy and the development process, rather than closing down the process. The management approach must be one of serving not controlling.

Source: Adapted from Smyth (1994: 259–60).

strategies. Yet the results can be extremely bene-ficial, as Harvey (1989b: 14) noted, 'If everyone, from punks and rap artists to the "yuppies" and the haute bourgeoise can participate in the pro-duction of social space, then all can at least feel some sense of belonging to that place.' Although, according to Smyth (1994: 242)

> planners tend to fear diversity and their ability to control it. Postmodernism is ostensibly trying to cre-ate diversity, yet this frequently results in efforts to create a 'sense of place', a local identity, which squeezes out the most disadvantaged in terms of labour market opportunities and geographically through planning and development decisions.

Indeed Hughes (1993: 162) went on to note that the hosting of a mega-event, such as the Olympics, may even disturb 'the "normal" devel-opment of tourism and other activity', with the possibility that they are 'a distraction from the pursuit of a more fundamental development strategy that will ensure long-term sustainable growth' – a comment that reflects the 'low-road' economic development strategies noted in the previous chapter (Malecki 2004). In these situa-tions, higher-use value of existing buildings, facil-ities and structures should be encouraged in order to reflect and serve long-term value, with tourism obviously being a major mechanism to provide for this. According to Brand (1997: 80), 'The degree of institutionalization of real estate value over use value is odious enough as an invasion of privacy, but it also prevents buildings from exer-cising their unique talent for getting better with time.' Similarly, Jacobs has commented,

> Time makes the high building costs of one genera-tion the bargains of a following generation. Time pays off original capital costs, and this depreciation can be reflected in the yields required from a build-ing. Time makes certain structures obsolete for some enterprises, and they become available to others. Time can make the space efficiencies of one generation the space luxuries of another generation. One century's building commonplace is another century's useful aberration (1993: 247).

Nevertheless, the ideas of preservation – space planning, scale, mutability, adaptivity, materials, functional tradition and originality – may also be applied to new construction and development.

'Hindsight is *better* than foresight. That's why evo-lutionary forms such as vernacular building types always work better than visionary designs such as geodesic domes. They grow from experience rather than from somebody's forehead' (Brand 1997: 188). Attention to the vernacular also high-lights the role that process plays in design.

'An organic process of growth and repair must create a gradual sequence of changes, and these changes must be distributed evenly across every level of scale' (Alexander *et al.* 1975: 68), while, according to Hough (1995: 19),

> Design and maintenance, based on the concept of process, become an integrated and continuing man-agement function, rather than separate and distinct activities, guiding the development of the human-made landscape over time.

Indeed, in terms of creating options for future use, one of the tenets of sustainability, Lynch (1972: 115) writes of 'future preservation': 'Our most important responsibility to the future is not to coerce it but to attend to it. Collectively, [such actions] might be called "future preservation", just as an analogous activity carried out in the present is called historical preservation'. In tourism, notions akin to that of future preser-vation are generally found in the area of eco-tourism and local development, rather than in mainstream large-scale tourism development. For example, Matthews (1998) argued that tourism developments in high latitude regions

> can only be truly sustainable, that is, supportable where there is a framework based on the (relatively simple) parameters of
>
> * researching local historical models for design elements;
> * utilisation of appropriate materials;
> * the selection of either (or both) of the basic design tenets of integrated or camouflaged design; and
> * design by local partnership with consultants and advisors who have either no, or reduced voting rights.

Stadia, festival marketplaces and convention centres are often constructed with the likelihood of relatively short-term periods of use in the order of 15–30 years before they are replaced. Such patterns of development have little in

Plate 9.4 Adaptive use of vernacular design for a hotel complex, near Lillehammer, Norway. Use of traditional design principles, such as earth roofs, is energy efficient, environmentally friendly and fits into the region's natural and cultural landscape.

Plate 9.5 Leisure, culture and tourism adaptive reuse, Christchurch, New Zealand. The old University of Canterbury buildings are now integral to the city's cultural precinct as the Arts Centre. The buildings house performance space, arts and crafts retailers, community groups, cafés and a thriving market at weekends.

common with the comments of one of the founders of the preservation movement: 'When we build, let us think that we build forever. Let it not be for present delight, nor for present use alone; let it be such work as our descendants will thank us for' (Ruskin 1989: 186). For Lynch, future preservation not only implies longer-term thinking in construction but also that such buildings are favoured because of the way in which they contribute to a sense of place and a city's 'wholeness'. 'Longevity and evanescence gain savor in each other's presence . . . We prefer a world that can be modified progressively, against a background of valued remains, a world in which one can leave a personal mark alongside the marks of history' (Lynch 1972: 38–39). However, longevity has no chance without serious Structure:

> A building's foundation and frame should be capable of living 300 years. That's beyond the economic lifetime of any of the players. But construction for longlife is what invites the long-term tampering it takes for a building to reach an adapted state (Alexander in Brand 1997: 194)

which is also often described as representing something which is 'authentic' of that place. Yet this does not mean that a building is frozen in time. Indeed, Hewison's (1987) frequently cited scathing attack on Britain's heritage industry, which still held 20 years on, was not because he considered some things were not worth preserving but because the focus on heritage appeared to exclude the potential for new possibilities and innovations that would continue the life of the heritage in question in response to the world around it rather than being 'frozen in time'. As Beng (1995: 218) observed with respect to the design of resort developments in south-east Asia,

> historicism can be avoided if the design has been based on the generational principles of the past rather than on acknowledged forms and symbols. The continued regeneration of traditional forms or literal, kitsch variants of past models, no matter how sensually or carefully crafted, can only at its best, result in the stagnation of the operational idea of tradition. At its worse, it debases both itself and the past model.

> To change is to lose identity; yet to change is to be alive . . . buildings partially resolve the paradox by offering the hierarchy of pace – you can fiddle with the Stuff and Space plan all you want while the Structure and Site remain solid and reliable. (Brand 1997: 167)

In seeking to extend the lifespan of tourism developments can there be any planning principles that can support some of the design principles discussed above? The answer is a definite yes and seeks to place some of the principles already discussed with respect to regional and local planning at the site level. One of the clearest planning principles is that of consultation. Brand (1997), for example, notes that in addition to failing to understand the faster areas of change in a building and the urban environment, many architects, planners and developers are image and fad driven and often fail to consult with the users. This failure to interrelate is also recorded by Moreno (1989) who noted the lack of post-occupancy evaluation by architects of the people who occupied their buildings.

At the level of policy greater attention can also be given by planners to the conflict between use value and market (exchange) value (Hall 2005a). As Brand (1997: 73) observed, 'Every building leads three contradictory lives – as habitat, as property, and as component of the surrounding community.'

> A building is the interface between two human organizations – the intense group within and the larger, slower, more powerful community outside. The building's Site, Structure, Skin, and the connection to its Services are all shaped by the community at large . . . What you see on the street is the product of the unending conflict between the organizations inside and outside – buildings pretending to fit in or defying fitting in (Brand 1997: 73).

Planning legislation and regulation through land-use controls are extremely significant in determining the life of buildings. However overzealous, control-oriented planning also has the potential 'to defeat every imaginable future problem, that any possibility of life, spontaneity, or flexible response to unanticipated events is eliminated' (Garreau 1991: 453). While providing broad frameworks, planning needs to be both responsive to stakeholder needs and flexible enough to allow places to evolve and change to meet the local needs. As Krier (1984 in Brand 1997: 79) noted, 'Functional zoning is not an innocent instrument; it has been the most effective means in destroying the infinitely complex social and physical fabric of pre-industrial urban communities, of urban democracy and culture.' In design, as in planning,

> at each level of scale, it is those actually using the space who understand best how it can be made/altered to have the character of being conducive to the work, and this group should be given sole control over that space. (Alexander in Brand 1997: 173)

Brand (1997) advocates what he describes as 'subsumption architecture', meaning that a bottom-up decision-making process is used for design and planning. Such an approach is reflective of much of the community-based approach in tourism planning and the desire for greater equity for stakeholders in sustainable tourism strategies.

Summary

Sustainability stimulates thinking about durability. While many natural tourist attractions are relatively durable, many human-made attractions are not, while the infrastructure that surrounds much of the tourism industry also has a relatively short lifespan. Responsibility and adaptivity are keys to the survival of buildings (Alexander *et al.* 1987) because of the ways in which they are responsive to the immediate users and the wider community. They are allowed to evolve.

> You cannot predict or control adaptivity. All you can do is make room for it – room at the bottom. Let the mistakes happen small and disposable . . . Adaptivity is a fine grained process. If you let it flourish, you get a wild ride, but you also get sustainability for the long term. You'll never be over-specified at the wrong scale. (Brand 1997: 174)

However, evolution is generally built of a series of small changes by which adaption is made to the environment. 'Authenticity can perhaps be

viewed as the attainment of an integrated, unstrained totality derived from . . . meaningful dialectical relationships between . . . different contexts' (Beng 1995: 218). Rapid, large-scale adaptations may work in the short term but in the long term they are the least easy to change as environmental conditions again change.

> Instant-gratification, universal-standard buildings *are* corrupting. What is called for is the slow moral plastic of the 'many ways' diverging, exploring, insidiously improving. Instead of discounting time, we can embrace and exploit time's depth. Evolutionary design is healthier than visionary design. (Brand 1997: 221)

In a similar fashion, Hough (1995: 21) writes of the principle of least effort as a guiding element in urban design:

> The greatest or the most significant results that spring from an undertaking usually come from the least amount of effort and energy expended rather than the most. It involves the idea that from minimum resources and energy, maximum environmental, economic and social benefits are available. It also involves the idea of doing things small, since it suggests that making small mistakes is infinitely preferable to making very large ones. Over time small mistakes can be adapted to social and environmental conditions; large ones may last indefinitely.

The interactions between cycles in a panarchy (see Figure 9.2) combine learning with continuity. As Holling (2001) emphasises, an analysis of this process can help clarify what sustainable development means. According to Holling (2001) sustainability is the capacity to create, test and maintain adaptive capability whereas development is the process of creating, testing and maintaining opportunity. Combining the two into 'sustainable development' thus refers to the goal of creating opportunities and fostering adaptive capabilities.

In thinking about sustainable design and site level issues of tourism planning, one can consider Brand's (1997: 49) statement that 'the product of careful continuity is love'. Unfortunately, many site developments designed for tourist consumption or to support tourism are not loved. In part this has been a failure of architects, politicians and planners to place such developments in a relevant local context. However, it also reflects the failure to appreciate the role of process and adaptive change. Such developments are also not sustainable.

Questions

1. What are the three principles that underlie good site design? How might they be applied to tourism?
2. What are the six Ss of layered change in a building? Examine how they might be applied to a tourism development of your choice.
3. How do rates of change and patterns of ownership affect the sustainability of tourism developments?
4. In what way is the use of old buildings for heritage tourism purposes a form of intergenerational equity?

Recommended reading

1. Brand, S. (1997) *How Buildings Learn: What Happens After They're Built,* Phoenix Illustrated, London.

   Brand's book was developed in conjunction with a TV series of the same name that is well worth viewing and is likely to be available through architecture libraries.

2. Hough, M. (1995) *Cities and Natural Process,* Routledge, London and New York.

   Influential book with respect to urban form and sustainability.

3. Smyth, H. (1994) *Marketing the City: The Role of Flagship Developments in Urban Regeneration,* E & FN Spon, London.

   An extremely good account of the problems encountered with flagship redevelopments, but the book has never received as much attention in the tourism literature as it probably deserves.

4. Alexander, C., Neis, H., Anninou, A. and King, I. (1987) *A New Theory of Urban Design,* Oxford University Press, New York.

   Extremely influential book on urban design that is extremely relevant to tourism because of its focus on adaptivity.

5. Childs, M.C. (2001) 'Civic ecosystems', *Journal of Urban Design,* 6(1): 55–72.

   Application of some of the notions of adaptive systems.

6. Moos, M., Whitfield, J., Johnson, L.C. and Andrey, J. (2006) 'Does design matter? The ecological footprint as a planning tool at the local level', *Journal of Urban Design,* 11(2): 195–224.

   Discussion of the potential of design to contribute to a reduction in the ecological footprint (see Chapter 2).

10 Implementation and instruments: policy and implementation as two sides of the same coin

Chapter objectives

After reading this chapter you will:

- Have developed a working definition of implementation
- Appreciate some of the key questions with respect to the implementation of tourism plans and policies
- Understand the three main approaches to implementation studies.

Although an extremely significant area of planning and policy analysis (Saetren 2005) implementation has only received limited study in the tourism field. Although it is often noted as a decision-making issue or noted in a flow chart of the planning process, it is seldom analysed, and rarely theoretically informed in terms of policy literature (e.g. see Go *et al.* 1992; Berry and Ladkin 1997; Zhang *et al.* 2002). Mazmanian and Sabatier (1983: 20) define implementation as 'the carrying out of basic policy decisions, usually incorporated in a statute but which can also take the form of implementation executive orders or court decisions'. For L.J. O'Toole (2000: 266) policy implementation is 'what develops between the establishment of an apparent intention on the part of government to do something or to stop doing something, and the ultimate impact in the world of action'. Implementation therefore implies a linkage between policy and action (Barrett and Fudge 1981). A working definition of implementation can be taken from the seminal work in the field by Pressman and Wildavsky (1979: xxi)

in which implementation, 'may be viewed as a process of interaction between the setting of goals and actions geared to achieve them'. However, in order to avoid an 'implementation gap' or 'deficit' – the degree of variation between intended and actual results – just having a goal-setting statement will almost certainly not be enough as many issues arise in achieving the actions required (Treuren and Lane 2003), including:

- What resources and incentives (time, money, expertise) are required?
- Are institutional arrangements appropriate?
- Is there sufficient authority to successfully implement?
- Does there need to be a change to regulations or legislation?
- If there are multiple agencies involved and/or private or non-government partners how will efforts be coordinated and how do we ensure that every party understands the goals in the same way?
- Can all actors and stakeholders be included in the process and are they committed to the implementation process?
- Are policies written in such a way that makes them actionable?
- How accountable are actors?
- How transparent is the process?

Indeed, the difficulties of implementation have long been recognised; to refer to Pressman and Wildavsky again,

> Our working definition of implementation will do as a sketch of the earliest stages of the program, but the passage of time wreaks havoc with efforts

to maintain tidy distinctions . . . In the midst of action the distinction between the initial conditions and the subsequent chain of causality begins to erode . . . The longer the chain of causality, the more numerous the reciprocal relationships among the links and the more complex implementation becomes. (1979: xxi)

This chapter examines some of the issues with respect to the implementation of policies and plans in a tourism context. The chapter commences with an example of implementation issues in tourism before providing a discussion of different approaches to implementation drawn from the policy studies field.

The problem of implementation

One of the recurrent themes of this book is the extent to which tourism policy, planning and governance has become multi-layered. What were once domestic issues have now become international concerns and, to a lesser extent, the reverse has also occurred, with some international concerns now receiving a local focus. Environmental-related policy serves as a good example of this. The locus of environmental policy making has shifted slowly and inexorably upwards to supra-national and international fora generating new institutional forms and constraints, and new patterns of politics. Yet as discussion over such issues as tourism and climate change has evidenced there is often a clear disjoint between what happens at the international scale in terms of legislative and policy agreement and what happens at the national or even regional scale (Gössling and Hall 2006). Arguably one of the most studied areas in tourism with respect to the implementation of an international agreement is the World Heritage Convention where the political issues surrounding the nomination and management of sites have been shown to be substantial despite the existence of an international convention that is seen as one of the pinnacles of global conservation efforts (Harrison and Hitchcock 2005). Therefore the Convention, which has been discussed elsewhere in the book (see Chapter 6) provides a good opportunity to examine implementation in multi-level governance. As Jordan (1995: 1) commented, 'while there are many insightful commentaries on the negotiation of international environmental agreements, we know a good deal less about how and to what extent they are actually implemented in domestic contexts'.

Implementing the World Heritage Convention

As of early 2007 World Heritage had a total of 830 sites listed under its Convention. These include 644 cultural, 162 natural and 24 mixed properties in 138 State Parties (see Chapter 6). Although the vast majority of World Heritage Sites are protected at the national level under existing national legislation, which may in turn be complemented by regulation at a regional or local level, nations have not adopted any standard legislative or regulatory approach to ensure that their obligations to the Convention are met. Instead, there is a vastly different array of regulatory and institutional instruments that State Parties utilise depending on the nature of the heritage to be protected and national legal and institutional arrangements. These may range from national park acts, conservation legislation and heritage law through to planning ordinances and policy statements. To complicate the picture even further in some State Parties a number of the legal instruments that are used to help preserve WHC values and particular sites are derived from local or regional legislative authority even though the actual nomination must be undertaken through the national government as the State Party to the Convention.

In a study of the implementation of the Convention, van der Aa (2005) noted that while most World Heritage Sites have some degree of local or national legal protection, designation does not necessarily lead to an increase in legal protection under domestic law. Of the 64 sites he studied only 39 per cent (25 sites) received further protection under law although, as van der Aa observed, in certain situations increased protection may be a precursor to nomination so as to assure the World Heritage Committee that a site has suitable protected status so as to enable appropriate management strategies.

There is also no common planning or management approach although UNESCO does provide a set of implementation guidelines and provide a framework within which conservation practice can be benchmarked and good practices developed. Nevertheless, this means that there is no common approach to developing participatory structures in the nomination and management process for affected people and businesses that live and operate in the area affected by nomination or declaration (see Harrison and Hitchcock 2005). This may be significant as World Heritage listing is not universally supported, with some stakeholders opposing nominations or the boundaries of nominated sites particularly if they believe that it may restrict land use or development options (e.g. van der Aa *et al.* 2004; Putra and Hitchcock 2005).

Examples of the differences in implementation of obligations under the World Heritage Convention can be illustrated by reference to the British and Australian experience; countries that, although having similar legal systems and substantial cultural and political commonalities, have adopted significantly different approaches to institutional implementation (see Hall 2006e for a fuller discussion of World Heritage implementation in the two countries from which the present discussion is derived).

In Australia World Heritage has been the subject of the introduction of specific legislation. Although this approach may seem logical to a reader with respect to implementing an international treaty it is actually unusual as an approach as most countries utilise existing legislation. In part this approach may be a response to World Heritage listing in Australia in the 1980s and 1990s arguably being more controversial than in any other country because it has become part of debates on economic development and the relative conservation and economic values of an area, as well as discussion over state and national government rights and powers within the Australian federal system. (For a discussion on heritage in Australia see Jones and Shaw 2007.)

In the late 1970s and early 1980s there was considerable national debate over the proposed construction of a hydroelectric dam in the wilderness areas of south-west Tasmania. The Tasmanian state government supported the construction of the dam while the national government under the conservative Liberal–National Party coalition opposed it but would not seek to overrule the state in court as it regarded land-use decision making as a state right. However, in 1983 the Labor Party won the federal election and immediately passed regulations under the National Parks and Wildlife Conservation Act 1975 and passed the World Heritage Properties Conservation Act 1983 in order to prohibit the construction of the dam in an area of World Heritage quality, with the Act also being applicable to other World Heritage Sites. Subsequent uses of the Act allowed the Australian federal government to protect other World Heritage Sites and potential sites from state government actions, such as with respect to the rainforests of northern Queensland.

Another change of national government in 1996 with the election of a Liberal–National Party federal government led to the development of new institutional approaches to World Heritage. In November 1997 a Heads of Agreement on Commonwealth and State Roles and Responsibilities for the Environment (Council of Australian Governments 1997) was signed by all heads of federal and state government and by the Australian Local Government Association. Part I of the Agreement states that, 'The Commonwealth has a responsibility and an interest in relation to meeting the obligations of the *Convention for the Protection of the World Cultural and Natural Heritage*'. A new Act governing the Commonwealth's responsibilities with respect to World Heritage, as well as other significant environmental and heritage matters of national interest were also introduced (see Aplin 2007 for a broader discussion of heritage conservation under the Act). The Environment Protection and Biodiversity Conservation Act 1999 came into force from 16 July 2000, arguably further enhancing the management and protection of Australia's World Heritage properties. Some of the key dimensions introduced by the Act included:

- greater up-front protection for World Heritage properties;
- a modified assessment and approvals process;
- application of consistent World Heritage management principles for all World Heritage properties regardless of location; and
- a new set of Commonwealth (federal)/state government arrangements.

Following the legal precedents set in the 1980s the 1999 Act protects all Australian properties that are inscribed on the World Heritage List; where a site has been nominated for, but not yet inscribed on, the World Heritage List; and where, even though a site has not been nominated to the List, the Minister believes that the property contains World Heritage values that are under threat. The Act regulates actions that will, or are likely to, have a significant negative impact on the World Heritage values of a declared property, including those actions that occur outside the boundaries of a World Heritage Site. Actions that are taken in contravention of the Act can attract a civil penalty of up to Aus.$5.5 million, or a criminal penalty of up to seven years imprisonment.

Regulations pursuant to the Act (Environment Protection and Biodiversity Conservation Regulations 2000) outline the Australian World Heritage management principles for the management of natural heritage and cultural heritage (Table 10.1). The regulations also state that at least one management plan must be prepared for each declared World Heritage property, which contains a number of specific elements that must be included (Table 10.2) as well as the environmental impact assessment and approval process. Under the regulations the assessment of an action that is likely to have a significant impact on the World Heritage values of a property occurs whether the action is inside the property or not. The assessment process should identify the World Heritage values of the property that are likely to be affected by the action; examine how the World Heritage values of the property might be affected; and provide adequate opportunities for public consultation. Finally, the regulations state that 'An action should not be approved if it would be inconsistent with the protection, conservation, presentation or transmission to future generations of the World Heritage values of the property' (reg. 10.3.04) with monitoring of compliance with respect to actions also identified under the regulations. Nevertheless, as Aplin (2007: 20) notes, despite Australia generally having a

> robust system of identification, conservation, and management of heritage . . . heritage does often play second fiddle to other concerns, and there is a

Table 10.2 Legally required elements of management plans for a declared Australian World Heritage property

(a) state the World Heritage values of the property for which it is prepared;

(b) include adequate processes for public consultation on proposed elements of the plan;

(c) state what must be done to ensure that the World Heritage values of the property are identified, conserved, protected, presented, transmitted to future generations and, if appropriate, rehabilitated;

(d) state mechanisms to deal with the impacts of actions that individually or cumulatively degrade, or threaten to degrade, the World Heritage values of the property;

(e) provide that management actions for values, which are not World Heritage values, are consistent with the management of the World Heritage values of the property;

(f) promote the integration of Commonwealth, state or territory and local government responsibilities for the property; and

(g) provide for continuing monitoring and reporting on the state of the World Heritage values of the property; and

(h) be reviewed at intervals of not more than seven years.

Source: Environment Protection and Biodiversity Conservation Regulations (2000): regulation 10.01, Schedule 5.

great deal of scope for political interference and over-ruling of decisions by the heritage agencies, especially on the interface between heritage and planning.

In contrast to the well-developed legislative and regulatory framework developed for World Heritage in Australia, the United Kingdom does not have specific World Heritage legislation. Instead, in England planning policies were changed in 1994 so as to protect World Heritage properties from inappropriate development (Rutherford 1994; Wainwright 2000). No additional statutory controls follow from the inclusion of a UK site in the World Heritage List beyond those that already exist with respect to planning, conservation and heritage. Under the Policy Guidance from the Office of the Deputy Prime Minister each local authority, as well as other interested parties, such as other public authorities, property owners, developers, amenity bodies and all members of the public, have to recognise the implications of World Heritage designation as well as other statutory designation, in the formulation of

specific planning policies for protecting these sites and include these policies in their development plans. Policies should reflect the fact that all these sites have been designated for their outstanding

universal value, and they should place great weight on the need to protect them for the benefit of future generations as well as our own. Development proposals affecting these sites or their setting may be compatible with this objective, but should always be carefully scrutinised for their likely effect on the site or its setting in the longer term. Significant development proposals affecting [WHS] will generally require formal environmental assessment, to ensure that their immediate impact and their implications for the longer term are fully evaluated. (Office of the Deputy Prime Minister 2005: para. 2.23)

Nevertheless, inclusion of a site on the World Heritage List

highlights the outstanding international importance of the site as a key material consideration to be taken into account by local planning authorities in determining planning and listed building consent applications, and by the Secretary of State in determining cases on appeal or following call-in. (Office of the Deputy Prime Minister 2005: para. 2.22)

For example, this has occurred with respect to an application to engage in mining activities near Hadrian's Wall (Rutherford 1994). Such an approach means that in the United Kingdom development projects that affect World Heritage sites, 'should always be carefully scrutinized for their likely effect on the site or its setting in the longer term' (Cookson 2000: 698) before planning approval can be given. Unlike the Australian legislative and regulatory context, the UK planning guidance with respect to World Heritage specifically refers to the World Heritage Committee's *Operational Guidelines for the Implementation of the World Heritage Convention* (first produced in 1978 and regularly revised) as a document that local authorities should refer to with respect to the planning and management of World Heritage Sites. (Although in Australia the guidelines may be referred to with respect to management practice there is no regulatory requirement to do so.) In addition, local planning authorities are encouraged to work with owners and managers of properties within World Heritage Sites within their jurisdiction, and with other agencies, to ensure that comprehensive management plans are developed. According to the planning guidance (Office of the Deputy Prime Minister 2005) these plans should:

* appraise the significance and condition of the site;
* ensure the physical conservation of the site to the highest standards;
* protect the site and its setting from damaging development and;
* provide clear policies for tourism as it may affect the site.

Both Australian and British World Heritage Sites, although often attracting controversy, are generally regarded as well managed. Yet there are substantial differences in legislative and regulatory approach and, correspondingly, in the nature of public consultation and participation in the listing process and what follows after listing. Such a situation reflects van der Aa's (2005: 140) observation that, 'most actors involved in the [World Heritage Convention] – UNESCO, countries and stakeholders of world heritage sites alike – have been able to use the convention for their own purposes'. However, more significantly for the purposes of the present chapter it

illustrates some aspects of the complex nature of implementation:

* Different layers of governance have different sets of powers and institutional arrangements.
* Decisions made at one level of governance may be interpreted differently at another, with the 'scope' of interpretation ranging as a result of legal, political and economic factors and capacities.
* Policy agreement at one level of governance may be opposed at another.
* One area of policy concern may become entwined with other policy arenas and sets of interests.
* Outcomes from the same policy objective may be sought via different instruments.

Selection of planning and policy implementation instruments

Table 10.3 illustrates the range of planning and policy instruments that are available to government to give effect to tourism policy and planning objectives. The various measures range from voluntary instruments through to highly coercive mechanisms such as removal of property rights by compulsion. However, there is no one 'perfect' instrument or measure to solve planning and policy problems. Multiple instruments are often used and even these will result in 'imperfect' solutions. Selman's (1992: 10) comments with respect to environmental planning instruments therefore apply equally well with respect to tourism,

> this inherent variety [of instruments] is instructive . . . as it confirms that there is no single panacea for the regulation of natural resources, but rather a menu of potential mechanisms which may be selected according to the nature of the issue at stake and their political acceptability.

Although the selection of a policy instrument (Table 10.3) is contingent on the problem that is to be managed and the political acceptability of

Table 10.3 Tourism planning and policy instruments

Categories	Instruments	Examples
Regulatory instruments	1. Laws	Planning laws can give considerable power to government to encourage particular types of tourism development through, for example, land-use zoning, which determines desirable and undesirable land uses.
	2. Licences, permits, consents and standards	Regulatory instruments can be used for a wide variety of purposes especially at local government level, e.g. restraining undesirable uses, setting materials standards for tourism developments, or they can be used to set architectural standards for heritage streetscapes or properties.
	3. Tradeable permits	Often used in the United States and, increasingly, in Europe to limit pollution or resource use. However, the instrument requires effective monitoring for it to work.
	4. Quid pro quos	Government may require businesses to do something in exchange for certain rights, e.g. land may be given to a developer below market rate, the development is of a particular type or design or there is a guaranteed period of occupancy or use.
	5. Removal of property rights	In order to achieve planning outcomes, such as the development of tourism infrastructure or the removal of inappropriate land uses, government may remove property rights (freehold or leasehold ownership) either on the market or through compulsory acquisition.
Voluntary instruments	1. Information and education	Expenditure on educating the local public, businesses or tourists to achieve specific goals, e.g. appropriate tourist or industry behaviour.
	2. Volunteer associations and non-governmental organisations	Government support of community tourism organisations is very common in tourism. Support may come from direct grants, tax benefits and/or by provision of office facilities. Examples of this type of development include local or regional tourist organisations, heritage conservation groups, mainstreet groups, tour guide programmes, or the establishment of industry associations and networks, including sectoral networks, e.g. farmstay, bed and breakfast, adventure tour operator and winery associations; and regional tourism operator networks.
	3. Technical assistance	Government can provide technical assistance and information to business with regard to planning and development requirements, including the preparation of environmental and social impact statements.
	4. Argument and persuasion	Government may seek the cooperation of stakeholders by persuading them that certain patterns of behaviour or conduct are appropriate for furthering common interest of stakeholders and/or self-interest.
Expenditure	1. Expenditure and contracting	This is a common method for government to achieve policy objectives as the government can spend money directly on specific activities; this may include the development of infrastructure, such as roading, or it may include mainstreet beautification programmes. Contracting can be used as a means of supporting existing local businesses or encouraging new ones.
	2. Investment or procurement	Investment may be directed into specific businesses or projects, while procurement can be used to help provide businesses with a secure custom for their products.

Instrument		Description
	3. Public enterprise	When the market fails to provide desired outcomes, governments may create their own businesses, e.g. rural or regional development corporations' enterprise boards. If successful, such businesses may then be sold off by private sector.
	4. Public–private partnerships	Government may enter into partnership with the private sector in order to develop certain products, locations or regions. These may take the form of a corporation that has a specific mandate to attract business to a certain area for example.
	5. Monitoring and evaluation	Government may allocate financial resources to monitor rural economic, environmental and socio-economic indicators. Such measures may not only be valuable to government to evaluate the effectiveness and efficiency of tourism planning and development policies and objectives but can also be a valuable source of information to the private sector as well.
	6. Promotion	Government may spend money on promoting a region to visitors either with or without financial input from the private sector. Such promotional activities may allow individual businesses to reallocate their own budget by reducing expenditures that might have been made on promotion.
Financial incentives	1. Pricing	Pricing measures may be used to encourage appropriate behaviour, market segments and/or to stimulate or reduce demand, e.g. use of particular walking trails through variations in camping or permit costs.
	2. Taxes and charges	Governments may use these to encourage appropriate behaviours by individuals and businesses, i.e. pollution charges. Taxes and charges, e.g. passenger or bed taxes, may also be used to help fund infrastructure development, e.g. regional airports, or help fund regional tourism promotion.
	3. Grants and loans	Seeding money may be provided to businesses to encourage product development, business relocation, and/or to encourage the retention of heritage and landscape features. Grants and loans may also be used to provide for business retention in marginal economic areas.
	4. Subsidies and tax incentives	Although subsidies are often regarded as creating inefficiencies in markets they may also be used to encourage certain types of behaviour with respect to social and environmental externalities, e.g. heritage and landscape conservation, that are not taken into account by conventional economics. Subsidies and tax incentives are one of the most common methods to establish or retain tourism businesses, especially in peripheral and rural areas.
	5. Rebates, rewards and surety bonds	Rebates and rewards are a form of financial incentive to encourage individuals and businesses to act in certain ways. Similarly, surety bonds can be used to ensure that businesses act in agreed ways; if they do not then the government will spend the money for the same purpose.
	6. Vouchers	Vouchers are a mechanism usually used to affect consumer behaviour by providing a discount on a specific product or activity, e.g. to shop in a specific centre or street.
Non-intervention	1. Non-intervention (deliberate)	Government deciding not to directly intervene in sectoral or regional development is also a policy instrument, in that public policy is what government decides to do and not do. In some cases the situation may be such that government may decide that policy objectives are being met so that their intervention may not add any net value to the rural development process and that resources could be better spent elsewhere.

Sources: After Hall (1998b); Hall and Jenkins (1998).

the approach used there are a number of criteria by which different planning and policy instruments can be evaluated:

- An instrument must be capable of attaining its objective in a reliable and consistent fashion, while being adaptable to changing circumstances over time and sensitive to differences in local conditions. (This is a measure of effectiveness.)
- The instrument should be judged against costs relative to desired outcomes and the costs of other instruments. (This is a measure of efficiency.)
- An instrument should be equitable in its impact across the target population of actors, i.e. of firms, organisations and/or individuals.
- Compliance costs need to be factored in to policy considerations.
- An instrument should be politically acceptable, easy to operate and as transparent and understandable as possible.
- An instrument should be compatible with other policy approaches.

Nevertheless, even given the undertaking of a comprehensive evaluation of policy and planning instruments to achieve a desired policy objective, it should be noted that the selection is ultimately a political decision. However, implementation is not just an issue of selection of policy instrument. As per Figure 1.4, in order to open up the black box of policy, planning and implementation we also need to understand the role of institutional arrangements that surround policy and implementation as well as the allocation of power within policy systems (see Reed and Gill 1997 for a discussion of institutional arrangements and power with respect to agencies in British Columbia). It is also important to see policy and implementation as being inseparable because, as Jordan and Richardson (1987: 238) observed, there are 'probably more policies which are never introduced because of the anticipation of resistance, than policies which have failed because of resistance'.

Power is not evenly distributed within a community and some groups and individuals have the ability to exert greater influence over the tourism development and planning process than others through the access to financial resources, expertise, public relations, media, knowledge and time to put into contested situations (Church and Coles 2007). For example, in many developed countries indigenous groups often do not have the same financial and technical capacities to engage in policy debate and lobbying as non-indigenous business interests. Pforr's (2006) analysis of tourism administration and decision making in Australia's Northern Territory highlighted the extent to which Aboriginal groups had only limited influence on the use of Aboriginal images and representations while simultaneously being encouraged to use tourism as a mechanism of economic development for the Territory as a whole. Indeed Aboriginal Australians, as with those of many other developed countries such as Canada, Finland, New Zealand, Norway, Sweden and the United States, have historically not had the capacity to control tourism development. As Langton and Palmer (2003) noted, 'while there has been Indigenous participation in the tourism industry in Australia since at least the 1900s . . . it was usually non-Indigenous people who dictated the way in which Aboriginal people participated in the industry'. Such a situation reflects the importance of the 'rules of the game' that surrounds planning, policy and implementation. As Schattsneider (1960: 71) commented,

> All forms of political organisation have a bias in favour of the exploitation of some kinds of conflict, and the suppression of others, because organisation is the mobilisation of bias. Some issues are organised into politics while some others are organised out.

Indeed such concerns are inseparable from the task of 'doing implementation', because

> any attempt to develop implementation theory must face the difficulty – once it moves away from the attempt to develop checklists of pitfalls for the implementation process . . . of becoming involved with the wide range of questions which have been raised in relation to policy making and in the study of organisations. (Ham and Hill 1994: 115)

Tourism and the 'rules of the game' for First Nations in British Columbia

In February 2007 the Honourable David Emerson, Canadian Federal Minister of International Trade and Minister for the Pacific Gateway and the Vancouver-Whistler Olympics, spoke before delegates at an Aboriginal Business Summit, hosted by the Four Host First Nations Society, of the 2010 Winter Games. Minister Emerson's address, entitled 'Aboriginal participation in the 2010 Winter Games: celebrating history, arts, culture and business', focused on the Canadian government's support of Aboriginal participation and its desire to promote Aboriginal business opportunities related to the 2010 Winter Games. According to Minister Emerson,

> The active and ongoing involvement of Aboriginal People in these Games is a key priority for Canada's New Government . . . The vision and the leadership of the Four Host First Nations recognized very early on that the Vancouver 2010 Winter Games represented a tremendous opportunity for their communities, and for all First Nations, Inuit, and Métis peoples. (Canadian Heritage 2007)

The enthusiasm of the federal minister to promote First Nations tourism has also been reflected by his provincial counterparts. For example, the provincial government has been promoting the benefits of the 2010 Winter Olympic Games for First Nations peoples including a programme to boost 'Aboriginal tourism'.

> As we invest in First Nations by creating new opportunities, one of our priorities is to ensure that we are matching skills training with areas of greatest need in our economy – clearly tourism is one of those. There are enormous openings emerging in Aboriginal tourism as we prepare for the Olympics and we are working to support these. This new program will help build management and administrative skills for First Nations and enhance the entrepreneurial spirit that every successful industry needs. (Ministry of Advanced Education and Treaty Negotiations Office 2004a)

At the same time that the provincial government promotes its investment in aboriginal tourism (see Ministry of Advanced Education and Treaty Negotiations Office 2004b) it is also

> building a New Relationship with First Nations founded on the principles of mutual respect, recognition and reconciliation of Aboriginal rights. The goal is to ensure Aboriginal people share in the economic and social development of British Columbia, in line with government's five great goals for a golden decade. (Office of the Premier 2006)

However, at the same time that economic partnership is being encouraged the nature of the political partnership has been substantially altered.

In 2002 the province's Liberal government initiated a referendum on Native land claims based on the argument that it was required to secure a new public mandate for a new set of negotiating principles. In an analysis of the referendum Rossiter and Wood (2005) argued that the government and its supporters employed a discourse centred on a private property ethic/neoliberal logic in order to justify the exercise. Given the community and collective property ethic attached to Native land ownership such a shift in the treaty process therefore needed to be understood as a contest over the terms of citizenship and not simply as a conflict over land resources (Rossiter and Wood 2005), and tourism was deeply embedded in such processes as a result of both recreation and parks being explicitly mentioned in the referendum as well as tourism being noted as an area of First Nations economic development.

Under the 2002 referendum initiated by the Campbell Liberal government ballots were mailed to the British Columbian electorate, asking voters to indicate their support for the following statements with a simple 'yes' or 'no':

- Private property should not be expropriated for treaty settlements.

▶

- The terms and conditions of leases and licenses should be respected; fair compensation for unavoidable disruption of commercial interests should be ensured.
- Hunting, fishing and recreational opportunities on Crown land should be ensured for all British Columbians.
- Parks and protected areas should be maintained for the use and benefit of all British Columbians.
- Province-wide standards of resource management and environmental protection should continue to apply.
- Aboriginal self-government should have the characteristics of a local government, with powers delegated from Canada and British Columbia.
- Treaties should include mechanisms for harmonising land-use planning between Aboriginal governments and neighbouring local governments.
- The existing tax exemptions for Aboriginal people should be phased out (Elections BC 2002).

The limiting of options in referenda, for example, is a classic example of non-decision making when electors are given a number of options with respect to development or other proposals. In the case of the 2002 British Columbia referendum on Native land claims, the wording of the referendum was described as 'amateurish' by the Angus Reid polling company, 'but the basic message was that it was unjust to put the rights of a minority group to the vote of a majority and that the questions being asked were designed to garner a 'yes' vote' (Rossiter and Wood 2005: 360). Indeed, a yes vote was the result with voters responding 'yes' to the various questions with a range of 84.52 per cent (Question 1) to 94.50 per cent (Question 4), with over 20,000 votes not being considered as they did not meet the requirements of the Treaty Negotiations Referendum Regulation (Elections BC 2002). Such 'spoiled' ballots were likely to be protest votes as a result of a campaign by the Union of BC Indian Chiefs. Elections BC also received letters and written comments that

> expressed concern that there was no mechanism to cast a 'protest vote', or to have a means of influencing the outcome of the referendum other than to vote Yes or No . . . Similar concerns that there is not a 'none of the above' option on election ballots have also been expressed by voters. (2002: 7, 8)

However, just as importantly, only 35.8 per cent of registered voters actually returned ballots.

In this situation the provincial government has changed the 'rules of the game' for Aboriginal peoples in British Columbia by simultaneously denying 'the complexity that lies behind First Nations' assertions of land title and rights to self-government' while indicating a desire to attract investment 'within the logic of neo-liberalism. As is demonstrated by the "Aboriginal tourism" program' (Rossiter and Wood 2005: 365).

Aboriginal Tourism Association of British Columbia: http://www.aboriginalbc.com/

First Nations Summit: http://www.fns.bc.ca/

British Columbia Treaty Commission: http://www.bctreaty.net/

Approaches to implementation

Although there is a substantial body of literature on implementation within the policy and planning fields (Saetren 2005), approaches to implementation can broadly be categorised into three approaches: 'top down', 'bottom up' and 'interactive' (Table 10.4). However, it should be emphasised that the approaches do have significant overlap and are not necessarily applied in a discrete fashion (Sabatier 1986).

Top down

Top-down approaches suggest that there is a policy hierarchy in which policies are introduced at the 'top' by decision makers and then implemented by those at the 'bottom' of the hierarchy. Such an approach also suggests that it is clearly possible to distinguish between policy and implementation. This approach is often represented in undergraduate management and tourism texts, where they discuss the strategic planning process in which

Table 10.4 Approaches to implementation

Issue	Top-down 'rational' models	Bottom-up models	Interactional, network and governance models
Exemplar studies/ key works	Van Meter and Van Horn (1975); Sabatier (1986)	Pressman and Wildavsky (1979); Sabatier (1986); Ham and Hill (1994)	Barrett and Fudge (1981); Rhodes (1981, 1990, 1994)
Policy themes	Hierarchy, control, compliance	Complexity, local autonomy, devolved power	Networks, governance, steering, bargaining, exchange and negotiation
Policy aims	To improve perform-ance (achieve the top's goals)	To explain what actually happens as policies are implemented	To explain how policy is the product of bargaining between interests; to understand the nature of contemporary governance
Policy standpoint	Top: policy makers; legislators; central government	Bottom: implementers, 'street level bureaucrats' and local officials	Where negotiation and bargaining take place
Primary focus	Effectiveness: to what extent are policy goals actually met?	What influences action in an issue area?	Bargained interplay between goals set centrally and actor (often local) innovations and constraints
Breadth of focus	Relatively narrow: tends to concentrate on a single legislative policy area	Broad: starts with a policy problem and examines the actors and processes that cluster around it	Fairly broad: analyses the coalition of interests that come together to bargain out policy and its direction
View of non-central (initiating) actors	Passive agents or potential impediments	Potentially policy innovators or problem shooters	Tries to account for the behaviour of all those who interact in the implementation of policy
Distinction between policy formulation and implementation	Actually and conceptually distinct; policy is made by the top and implemented by the bottom	Blurred distinction: policy is often made and then remade by individual and institutional policy actors	Policy–action continuum: policy seen as a series of intentions around which bargaining takes place
Policy perspective	Policy is an independent variable: a starting point and a benchmark	Policy is dependent upon the interaction between actors at the local level	Policy is dependent upon a process of bargaining
Administrative discretion	Can and should be controlled by sanctions and incentives (discretion creates policy 'drift' and failure)	Cannot or should not be controlled: it helps to get things done when objectives are complex and problems uncertain and changing	Generally good: it helps to get things done when objectives are complex and problems uncertain and changing
Criterion of success	When outputs/ outcomes are consistent with a priori objectives	Achievement of actor (often local) goals	Difficult to assess objectively
Implementation gaps/deficits	Occur when outputs/ outcomes fall short of a priori objectives	'Deficits' are a sign of policy change, not failure. They are inevitable	All policies are modified as a result of negotiation (there is no benchmark)

▶

Table 10.4 (continued)

Issue	Top-down 'rational' models	Bottom-up models	Interactional, network and governance models
Reason for implementation gaps/deficits	Good ideas poorly executed	Bad ideas faithfully executed	'Deficits' are inevitable as abstract policy ideas are made more concrete
Solution to implementation gaps/deficits	Simplify the implementation structure; apply inducements and sanctions	'Deficits' are inevitable	'Deficits' are inevitable
Policy outputs and outcomes	Fairly predictable (if the implementation process is properly structured)	Fairly unpredictable: depends on actor (often local) interaction	Fairly unpredictable: depends on bargaining
Research methodology	Deductive: starts with a model of what should happen, then compares it with reality	Essentially inductive: starts with empirical observations of what actually happens then aggregates these into single observations and theories	Deductive/inductive

Sources: Derived from Van Meter and Van Horn (1975); Pressman and Wildavsky (1979); Barrett and Fudge (1981); Rhodes (1981, 1990, 1994, 1997); Sabatier (1986); Ham and Hill (1994); Jordan (1995); Schofield (2001).

there is a clear division or dichotomy between the implementation and policy concepts. An exemplar of such an approach was Van Meter and Van Horn (1975: 448) who argued that '[w]e should emphasise that the implementation phase does not commence until goals and objectives have been established by prior policy decisions. It takes place only after legislation has been passed and funds committed'. Such an approach is often designed to provide advice on how measures could succeed by providing policy prescriptions that may include such things as providing more direct mechanisms, having clearer policies and objectives, and improving the overall structure of the process. From such a perspective policy is regarded as being 'owned' by those at the top (Ham and Hill 1994). For example, Mazmanian and Sabatier (1983) argued that studies of implementation should address four central questions:

1. To what extent are the outputs or outcomes of the implementation process consistent with the objectives enunciated in the original statute?
2. Were the objectives successfully attained? Over what period of time?
3. What factors affected policy outcomes or caused the goals to be modified?
4. How was the policy reformulated over time in the light of experience?

Mazmanian and Sabatier (1983) and Sabatier (1986) then went on to specify a series of six conditions for the effective implementation of policy:

1. Policy objectives should be clear and consistent.
2. Causal assumptions embodied within the policy must be correct.
3. Legal and administrative structures must be sufficient to keep discretion within organisational bounds.
4. Implementing agents must be skilled and committed.

5. There must be support from interest groups and other critical policy actors.
6. There must be no major socio-economic upheavals or disturbances.

However, the approach has been criticised on a number of counts.

- Testing a set of conditions for effective implementation against what actually happens provides very little explanation as to the policy and implementation process itself. Obviously, almost any policy would benefit from more funds and greater interest group/stakeholder support!
- Policy making does not occur in a vacuum. It is not easy to isolate a policy from the influences of other policies. For example, in the case of tourism we have pointed out in earlier chapters that policies are often layered on top of each other at different levels of governance as well as existing in conjunction with a range of other policies that although not explicit tourism policies affect tourism phenomenon. What Majone (1989) would describe as a crowded 'policy space'.
- By focusing only on one policy or piece of legislation there is a danger in accrediting everything that happens with respect to action in the policy area within the policy implementation structure in question when other factors or actors may be more significant. For example, Sabatier (1986) refers to a study of pollution control in Holland which concluded that the reduction in emissions were an unintended consequence of governmental energy policies and changes in the relative cost of fuels rather than pollution control legislation per se.
- The bottom is not always compliant to the top and may have considerable autonomy in its own right (Barrett and Fudge 1981). In addition, deviation at the bottom may actually be appropriate so as to give better effect to the intentions of policies and ensure they meet local conditions rather than effectively actioning a policy but then not achieving the desired outcomes.

Bottom up

The bottom-up approach describes a range of literature which emphasises that policy, legislation and regulation developed by those at the top is poorly connected to what actually happens on the ground (Majone and Wildavsky 1979; Pressman and Wildavsky 1979; Sabatier 1986; Ham and Hill 1994) and that greater attention needs to be given to the action dimension of implementation as, in one sense, this is where policy is really 'made'. This approach therefore focuses on a much more complex process of policy action and reaction. However, it can be described as bottom up because of the importance of the behaviours and motivations of the actors responsible for implementation as well as the constraints and structures within which they operate. This approach has some resonance with the community dimension in tourism planning and the consequent emphasis on public and stakeholder participation (i.e. Ioannides 1995; Singh et al. 2003). Sabatier (1986) noted that those with a bottom-up perspective are more likely to start with a policy problem that requires a policy response than with the goals of the top-level decision makers. Furthermore, the approach also suggests that a policy will usually be given effect through a number of public, private and non-government organisations rather than a single organisation, a point that has become increasingly important given the growth of public–private partnerships as described in previous chapters. Rather than a focus on implementation failure, as per the top-down perspective, the bottom-up approach 'accepts the difficulties faced by those at the bottom, applauds their attempts to overcome them, and notes the very positive contribution that they can make to the better delivery of services' (Jordan 1995: 13). However, the approach has several criticisms:

- Some authors (i.e. Sabatier 1986) disagree with the lack of distinction between policy formulation and implementation because it fails to separate the influence and roles of elected officials (democratic accountability) and public servants (administrative discretion) as well as the notion of policy as something that can be evaluated, which means that there is nothing to differentiate analyses of implementation from analyses of policy. In other words implementation and policy are two sides of the same coin. However, it should be noted that for those with a bottom-up rather than a top-down perspective such a situation is not an issue.

- The bottom may actually not have that much discretion with respect to some policies because of the way that some policies can be structured.
- The normative perspectives of a bottom-up approach as to how policy implementation *actually* occurs should not necessarily be interpreted as being how it *should* occur.

Interactional approaches

A third approach to examining implementation is that provided by what can be described as interactional perspectives which emphasise the complex process of negotiating and bargaining between policy actors at all levels of the policy and planning process (Barrett and Fudge 1981). This approach has been enormously influential and underlies much of the development of notions of governance as a way of describing how policies are steered through numerous actor networks (see Chapter 6 in particular) (Callahan 2007), which although sometimes described as an additional approach to policy and implementation (e.g. Carlsson 2000) shares a sufficient intellectual and policy heritage so as to be integrated for the purpose of the present discussion. Barrett and Fudge's (1981) political perspective on the implementation process was that policy 'bargaining' continued as a seamless web rather than as part of a discrete process (Ingram 1989). Barrett and Fudge (1981) argue that there is a false dichotomy between the bottom-up and top-down approaches and that both operate simultaneously in that implementation is top down to the extent that legislation and regulations constrain the power of those below but that it is also bottom up, with lower level policy actors taking 'decisions which effectively limit hierarchical influence, pre-empt top decision making, or alter policies' (Barrett and Fudge 1981: 25). Barrett and Fudge also make the important point that bargaining over specific policies takes place within a much broader set of institutional arrangements (formal legal frameworks, political culture and behavioural norms) or 'rules of the game', or as they describe it 'negotiated order'. Therefore, 'specific issues may be haggled over, but within broader limits. The limits themselves will vary both in and over time, and are themselves subject to negotiation in relation to the wider social setting' (1981: 24).

The Barrett and Fudge (1981) approach was arguably almost too fluid with respect to the implementation process. Therefore the work of Rhodes (1981) with respect to the power relationships and interaction between different levels of government – and the associated concepts of networks and subgovernments – arguably found greater appeal because it provided a comprehensive framework with which to understand relationships between policy actors.

Rhodes (1997) suggests that policy networks are characterised by:

- interdependence between the organisations involved;
- continual interaction between the membership that exchanges resources and negotiates shared purposes;
- interactions that are governed by the 'rules of the game' and which develop trust;
- a significant degree of autonomy from state intervention.

Rhodes (1988, 1990) identified several different types of network that varied along five key dimensions: the constellation of interests; membership; vertical interdependence; horizontal interdependence; and the distribution of resources. Five different configurations of networks – ranging from highly integrated stable policy communities with a relatively small number of members to the relatively fluid affiliation of an issue network with a relatively large number of members – were articulated by Rhodes, showing the different levels of interdependency between actors in the network: issue network, producer network, intergovernmental network, professional network, territorial network and policy community. Rhodes' work is significant in terms of understanding policy implementation in tourism not only because of its contribution with respect to the overall issue of governance but also because it indicates that there is a series of fluid linkages between policy actors who operate within a policy sector or with respect to a planning issue. It emphasises that implementation is best understood as a component of the whole policy and planning process. In this there are considerable similarities between the notion of a policy community and Sabatier's (1987) work on policy learning and advocacy coalitions (Sabatier refers to policy subsystems). However, one of the criticisms of the network approach is that it offers a pluralistic understanding of the policy process in which emphasis is placed on the visible dimensions of the policy and implementation process rather than the role in which structure can influence individual agency. For example, pluralism does not offer an adequate explanation for the way policy initiatives, such as privatisation of state assets, both reflect existing inequalities and become structured into the operation of social institutions, thus ensuring a policy regime that tends to become entrenched and resistant to further change (Collyer 2003).

Summary

It should now be readily apparent that implementation is complex both empirically and theoretically. Each approach to understanding implementation not only asks different questions but also sees problems and solutions within the policy and implemention process in different dimensions as well. Such an observation reinforces Conley and Moote's (2003) findings with respect to the evaluation of the collaborative natural resource management in the United States. As they noted, evaluative criteria show commonalities as well as differences, but that evaluation approaches will necessarily vary with the evaluation's intent, the type of collaborative effort being evaluated, and the values of the evaluator. Perhaps most significantly they emphasise that not only should the management process be transparent but so too should evaluators make explicit their standards for comparison, criteria and methods in order to clarify the nature of an evaluation and facilitate the transferability of their findings (Sinclair 2006).

As discussed earlier in this book theory choice is ultimately driven by the questions posed and answers sought by the analyst. Questions such as the relationship between policy goals and outputs and outcomes can be well handled by top-down approaches, which is probably reflective of much of the writing on implementation in the tourism field. However, questions regarding whether the outputs and outcomes were appropriate to the policy problem need to be dealt with by other approaches that lie beyond the narrow confines of the top down approach. Indeed the utilisation of comprehensive models of the policy and implementation process are vital if students of tourism planning and policy are actually going to understand how decisions are made, policies formulated and plans implemented. The value of implementation studies should therefore be seen not just in terms of being able to describe the gap that exists between the ideal and reality but in being able to illustrate the very real struggles that exist between actors, often at different levels, with respect to policy and planning as well as the potential policy and planning choices that are never taken.

Questions

1. What effect may multiple levels of governance have on implementation of international or national policies?

2. Why does the selection of theory influence the perceptions of planning problems with respect to implementation studies?

3. What are the main characteristics of the three different approaches to implementation?

4. Evaluate the application of tourism policy instruments (Table 10.3) in your country. What criteria have you developed and why?

Important websites and recommended reading

Websites

Journal of Planning Literature:
http://jpl.sagepub.com/

Journal of Planning Education and Research:
http://intl-jpe.sagepub.com/

Planning Theory (journal):
http://plt.sagepub.com/

Current Issues in Tourism:
http://www.multilingual-matters.net/cit/

Journal of Sustainable Tourism:
www.multilingual-matters.net/jost/

Tourism Geographies:
http://www.tandf.co.uk/journals/titles/14616688.asp

Recommended reading

1. Saetren, H. (2005) 'Facts and myths about research on public-policy implementation: out-of-fashion, allegedly dead, but still very much alive and relevant', *Policy Studies Journal*, 33(4): 559–82.

   An overview of the implementation field that provides a useful literature source.

2. Pressman, J.L. and Wildavsky, A.B. (1979) *Implementation: How Great Expectations in Washington are dashed in Oakland; Or, Why it's amazing that federal programs work at all, this being a saga of the Economic Development Administration as told by two sympathetic observers who seek to build morals on a foundation of ruined hopes*, 2nd edn, University of California Press, Berkeley.

   The classic work in the field. Worth looking at for the title alone! Second and later editions have excellent postscript contributions.

3. Dudley, G., Parsons, W., Radaelli, C.M. and Sabatier, P. (2000) 'Symposium: theories of the policy process', *Journal of European Public Policy*, 7(1): 122–40.

This fascinating debate on public policy processes provides a valuable discussion on perspectives of top-down, bottom-up and interactive-based approaches to policy and implementation within the European context.

4. Barrett, S. (2004) 'Implementation studies: time for a revival? Personal reflection on 20 years of implementation studies', *Public Administration*, 82(2): 249–62.

   A paper that is also part of a special symposium issue on implementation and policy studies. The review discusses how public policy planning has been influenced by public sector reforms since the early 1980s. The article raises three important points that are reflected throughout all four papers in the symposium issue: (1) the analytical difficulties of understanding the role of bureaucratic discretion and motivation; (2) the problem of evaluating policy outcomes; and (3) the need to focus upon micro-political processes that occur in public sector organisations.

5. Zhang, Q.H., Chong, K. and Jenkins, C. (2002) 'Tourism policy implementation in mainland China: an enterprise perspective', *International Journal of Contemporary Hospitality Management*, 14(1): 38–42.

   Although limited in its reference to the policy studies literature the article provides a good case study of some of the issues associated with policy implementation in a tourism context.

6. Majone, G. (1989) *Evidence, Argument and Persuasion in the Policy Process*, Yale University Press, New Haven.

   Remains one of the best guides for analysts and planners with respect to their potential to influence implementation and policy.

7. Harrison, D. and Hitchcock, M. (eds) (2005) *The Politics of World Heritage: Negotiating Tourism and Conservation*, Channelview, Clevedon.

Study of World Heritage issues that highlights, although often without direct acknowledgement, the problems of multi-layered governance, policy and implementation.

8. Reed, M.G. and Gill, A.M. (1997) 'Tourism, recreational, and amenity values in land allocation: an analysis of institutional arrangements in the postproductivist era', *Environment and Planning A*, 29(11): 2019–40.

   Excellent study of the effects of institutional arrangements on implementation.

9. Dredge, D. (2006) 'Policy networks and the local organization of tourism', *Tourism Management*, 27(2): 269–80.

   One of the few studies of policy networks in tourism.

10. Conley, A. and Moote, M.A. (2003) 'Evaluating collaborative natural resource management', *Society and Natural Resources*, 16(5): 371–86.

    Excellent article on the issues associated with evaluation as part of the policy-implementation cycle.

11 Conclusions and reflections: thinking sustainable planning

Chapter objectives

After reading this chapter you will:

- Have reflected further on individual roles and capacities in tourism planning
- Appreciate the role of reflexivity
- Considered the likelihood of sustainable planning having been achieved.

Sustainability is an overarching value or collection of values that we increasingly find being enacted in legislation, regulations, institutional arrangements and planning processes at different scales around the globe. 'Sustainability' is also an 'ecological word' (Meier 1995: 454). 'Global thinking must become a framework for local action, since the two are inextricably linked' (Hough 1995: 286). Any approach to sustainable tourism planning needs to be based on sound ecological principles. This means not just an appreciation of the physical environment but also a deeper understanding of the economic, social, political and physical systems of which tourism is a part.

One of the key principles of systems thinking is that of the principle of requisite variety (Ashby 1956): in order to control or plan systems, towards some explicit goal, there must be as much variety in the controller as there is in the system itself. Such a situation lays a clear challenge to the student of tourism. What capacities do we possess to be able to understand the system we are interacting with and trying to direct along

certain paths? This book has argued that our capacities are increased by an improved understanding of the process nature of planning and our role within it. Planning is not rational. It is highly political. The goal of sustainability is not a given. It is a contested concept that as students of tourism we need to be arguing for. The field of planning therefore represents an ongoing effort to interrelate conceptions of the qualities of places with notions of the social processes of 'shaping' and 'representing' places through the articulation, development and implementation of policies (see Healey 1997).

Tourism planning must also be theory rich in order to be effective in the long term so that it can adapt to its own environment. A focus on techniques at the expense of understanding different theories on the way in which planning operates, their assumptions and intended contributions, denies students a deeper understanding of planning problems. Moreover, it limits their own capacity to adapt to a rapidly changing environment and the challenges it brings. As Morgan (1986: 336) argued,

> Many practical people believe that theory gets in the way of practice and that, by and large, theorizing is a waste of time. But there is a great fallacy in this way of thinking. For in recognizing how taken-for-granted images or metaphors shape understanding and action, we are recognizing the role of theory. Our images or metaphors *are* theories or conceptual frameworks. Practice is never theory-free, for it is always guided by an image of what we are trying to do. The real issue is whether or not we are aware of the theory guiding our action.

Tourism planning, within the policy analysis tradition that this book takes, is a style of governance which should involve strategic outlooks at the direction of public activity, and the attempt to interrelate different spheres of such activity. Planning is relational. Tourism planning may also serve to challenge forms of governance if stakeholder interests and values are not being met. Indeed, one of the biggest challenges facing tourism planners is the relevance of their work in terms of who benefits. As has been noted throughout, one of the tenets of sustainability is the idea of equity. However, the means by which such equity may be achieved in the context of tourism has been little discussed in the tourism literature (Dredge and Jenkins 2007).

Process and change are also major themes in tourism planning, perhaps increasingly so given the vagaries of global environmental, economic and social change (see also Gössling and Hall 2006). Innovative planning is especially prevalent in rapidly changing social systems. It is even more difficult to succeed in establishing effective organisational linkages among institutions engaged in innovative planning, although clearly where a massive effort for change is intended, as in the case of sustainable development, this is a necessary condition for the successful transformation of the system.

> The strategic problem is to identify the critical points for system transformation and to activate innovative planning at these points. But if a system is already undergoing rapid change, the importance of this strategic problem decreases sharply; for the system generates change automatically. (Friedmann 1973: 365)

Tourism planners therefore need to be able to understand the direction of those changes and attempt to influence and adapt to them accordingly. However, planning is not perfect, things do go wrong. Peter Hall (1992) outlined several reasons why planning goes wrong:

- knowledge about the planning environment may change rapidly;
- there are complex interrelationships between different levels of the planning system, and

between different elements of the planning system;
- values change over time;
- there are often difficulties in reconciling values;
- planning is political in character;
- trade-offs are made between the interests of different generations.

Planning measures also vary greatly in their effectiveness and ease of implementation, and attempted action over planning issues will often be frustrated by a lack of regulatory power. Perhaps nowhere more so than in any area such as tourism planning where legislative and regulatory control tends to lie outside of the tourism agency. Yet it is for this very reason that one of the most important planning skills is the capacity to combine persuasion, mediation and negotiation with regulation. Tourism planning is also increasingly collaborative in nature, unlike the old-fashioned command and control model (Selin 1998). Such a shift has dramatic implications not only in the development of theories and models of planning but also for the individuals involved as well. How well are planners able to adapt to roles of mediator and convenor that require different interpersonal skills? How well do you think you would be able to take on the role of a convener, 'lacking any formal authority but having the intent to form a collaboration', and using your 'credibility, influence, knowledge of the problem domain, knowledge of stakeholder interrelationships, and personal charisma to persuade stakeholders to participate'? (Wood and Gray 1991: 153).

A general theory of collaborative planning must be able to articulate the role of the collaborative planner in establishing, legitimising and guiding the collaborative alliance. However,

> no firm conclusions have yet been drawn as to how the convener uses various forms of authority to identify and persuade stakeholders to participate, which differences can be observed when conveners are responsive to stakeholder initiatives or are proactive in implementing their own ideas, or which specific roles conveners might play in helping organize the problem domain. (Wood and Gray 1991: 149)

Nevertheless, some significant factors may be identified (Gray 1989; Wood and Gray 1991); the convener/planner must:

- have the ability to identify stakeholders and then induce them to participate, often this power may be based on formal planning authority, although such powers only have a limited range of application in forming partnerships;
- have legitimacy among stakeholders;
- be perceived by stakeholders as having a fair and even-handed approach to the planning problem;
- appreciate the value of collaboration and possess the necessary interpersonal and communication skills that help establish the collaborative process and facilitate interaction between stakeholders;
- be responsive to the needs of stakeholders;
- be trusted.

In tourism planning there has often been far too much concentration on the techniques of planning without a look at the processes that are occurring. Nevertheless, despite the potential contribution of tourism planning towards more sustainable forms of tourism and the creation of sustainable places, planning 'should not claim the instant ability to solve complex problems'.

> It should not even necessarily claim unique expertise. It should certainly not claim to know what is good for people. Rather, it should be exploratory and instructive. It should aim to help communities think clearly and logically about resolving their problems, and in particular some of the more subtle underlying issues that concern such matters as equity and growth. It should try to examine alternative courses of action and trace through, as far as possible, the consequences of each of these for different groups of people in different places. It should not seek to avoid the difficult questions of who exercises political power on behalf of whom, and by what legitimacy. It should make recommendations, but it should not seek to impose prescriptions. It should claim modestly that planners may perhaps be more capable than the average person to conduct this kind of analysis, but not they are uniquely expert. In other words, it should aim to provide a resource for democratic and informed decision-making. This is

all planning can legitimately do, and all it can pretend to do. Properly understood, this is the real message of the systems revolution in planning and its aftermath'. (P. Hall 1992: 249–50)

Indeed, a critical concern must be that while it is possible for some locations to have excellent planning practices and policies which embrace sustainability and change, what of those places that do not? Experience with growth management suggests that growth is like toothpaste. If undesirable and unsustainable short-term developments are squeezed out of one location they will go to another. For example, Levine (1999) found that measures which either removed land from development or reduced development intensities served to displace both ownership and rental housing to less-controlled jurisdictions. In other words local sustainable solutions are valuable but the problems may just be shifted. Realisation of the problems of sustainable development (see Chapter 2) means that we are all in this together. Therefore sustainable tourism means having to be not just concerned about planning and policies in your jurisdiction but also being concerned and arguably seeking to influence what is happening elsewhere, particularly with respect to global initiatives (Gössling and Hall 2006).

Speaking truth to power

This book has emphasised the relational and, ideally, collaborative nature of tourism planning. In focusing on the interplay of substance and process it has made a departure from much of the existing focus of tourism planning on techniques, control and land use to attempt to provide a more integrative approach to the complexity of tourism planning problems. The book has also stressed the role of argument and persuasion in the planning process. Tourism planning is not value free. Neither is the tourism planner. Instead, tourism planning should be recognised as being value laden. However, this should be seen as a positive as it provides the planner with the relational resources with which to appropriately adapt and change in the global environment. Nevertheless, the argumentative turn in planning (Fischer and Forester 1993), the desire to 'speak truth to power' (Wildavsky 1987) will at times prove difficult. As Reade (1997: 71) comments:

> In every society there is a dominant ideology. There must be, for without this ideological support, the ruling class could not rule. What every ruling class does, however, is to persuade the population that the ideology that legitimates its rule is no ideology at all, but a set of factual statements about the objective nature of the world. It is *the others*, they tell us (i.e. those without power, and who want it) who peddle ideology. They themselves, our rulers tell us, are pragmatists and realists, their policies and actions reflect nothing but what, given the facts of the situation, common sense dictates, and in fact no reasonable human beings could do more than they are doing.

Yet, as public tourism planners we should be engaged in the notion of the public interest and the challenge of sharing spaces. The idea of a sustainable community is more than just the people who live in an area or a pleasant physical environment, it conveys an image of an integrated place world (*gemeinschaft*). The idea of a place-based community is both illusion and fact. Nevertheless, such illusions are extremely important as we are often as willing to take a stand for something which is an ideal – such as community, democracy or sustainability – knowing that although what we end up with is always imperfect, it is still worth fighting for. Table 11.1 outlines some characteristics of a sustainable community. They are characteristics which could probably not wholly apply to any community on the planet for an extended period of time but they are still important and desirable.

Table 11.1 The four characteristics of a sustainable community

Economic security

A more sustainable community includes a variety of businesses, industries and institutions that are environmentally sound (in all aspects), financially viable, provide training, education and other forms of assistance to adjust to future needs, provide jobs and spend money within a community, and enable employees to have a voice in decisions which affect them. A more sustainable community is also one in which residents' capital remains in the community and the surrounding region.

Ecological integrity

A more sustainable community is in harmony with ecological systems by minimising its ecological footprint by reducing and converting waste into non-harmful and beneficial outputs, reducing food and travel miles, and by utilising the natural ability of environmental resources for human needs without undermining their ability to function over time.

Quality of life

A more sustainable community recognises and supports people's sense of well-being, which includes a sense of belonging, a sense of place, a sense of self-worth, a sense of safety and security, a sense of connection with nature, and provision of goods and services that meet their needs, both as they define them and as can be accommodated within the ecological integrity of natural systems.

Empowerment and responsibility

A more sustainable community enables people to feel empowered and to take responsibility based on a shared vision, equal opportunity, transparency of planning and policy processes and governance structures, ability to access expertise and knowledge for their own needs, and a capacity to affect positively the outcome of decisions that affect them.

Sources: After *Wingspread Journal* (1996); Morgan (2004), Pike *et al.* (2006).

This book has noted the multiple layers of analysis within planning systems from the international to the site level. Clearly, within all of this, the individual actor in the tourism planning and policy-making process is important. In fact one of the things that has been missing from assessments of tourism planning is not only the role of the planner and analyst as actors in the planning and policy system but also their personal disposition, capacities and values. Organisational values and roles are significant but so to are the individual's values, actions and personalities. Ultimately how planning problems are defined and managed by individuals within organisations or as external actors is determined not just by regulatory factors and the role of different planning traditions in defining problems and solutions (Chapter 3), but also by an individual's planning orientation (Figure 11.1).

Planning orientation refers to the collection of personality and dispositional tendencies applied by individuals to formulate a plan to manage complex problem situations affecting such factors as perceived level of personal agency, action competence, judgement accuracy, goal orientation and risk assessment (see Strohschneider and Güss 1999; Stout *et al.* 1999; Weber and Hsee 2000; Donovan and Hafsteinsson 2006; Fortunato and Goldblatt 2006). Furthermore, the action competence concept should be applied not only to an individual's cognitive and motivational competencies necessary to solve problems or tasks and reach goals but also to the collection of action competencies and complementary dispositions that exist across different individuals that are necessary for tourism planning to be undertaken effectively by a group or institution. Therefore, in understanding planning processes consideration needs to be given to individually and collectively available planning skills, including:

- non-specific vocational competencies: literacy, numeracy, critical thinking abilities, planning orientation;
- specific tourism planning vocational competencies: domain-general and domain-specific knowledge, management

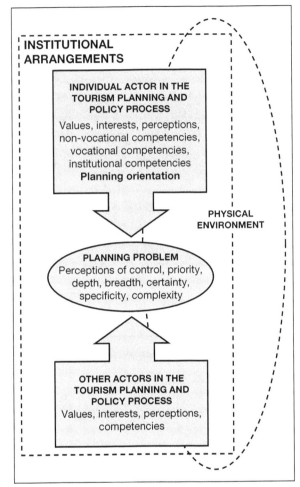

Figure 11.1 Planning orientations and the planning problem

competencies, problem definition and diagnostic competencies, argumentative and communicative competencies;
- institutional-specific competencies: institutional engagement, institutional identification and relational competencies with stakeholders.

In addition, awareness of different planning orientations and competencies in both individuals and groups perhaps also requires greater reflection on the cultural biases inherent in planning problem definition and planning processes and strategies. For example, there is considerable evidence that uncertainty avoidance – 'the extent to which the members of a culture feel threatened by uncertain or unknown situations' (Hofstede 2001: 161) varies between cultures, therefore influencing not only travel decision making but decision-making strategies in general. Hofstede's (2001) study indicated uncertainty avoidance in 53 countries with India and the United States showing weak uncertainty avoidance, whereas Brazil demonstrated high uncertainty avoidance.

Reflections

This book began with a personal observation and so will finish with one. The book has emphasised the complex, relational world in which we live. In my Master's thesis I quoted a wonderfully inspirational geographer by the name of Gilbert White as a kind of research credo:

> Speaking only as one individual, I feel strongly that I should not go into research unless it promises results that would advance the aims of the people affected and unless I am prepared to take all practicable steps to help translate the results into action. (White 1972: 102)

Some 20-plus years on from first using that quote, I find myself sitting at my desk at 2 am on a cool Christchurch morning writing the final sentences to this book and asking myself again if I still believe that credo. On reflection I can say I do. But my optimism as a student has been somewhat battered by the experiences of politics, universities and life.

Establishing and maintaining collaborative and stakeholder relationships can be extremely difficult. There are clearly some people we find it difficult to get on with, whether it be personality, ego, attitudes, value differences or sheer bloody-mindedness and stupidity (to put it kindly!). Yet as a collaborative planner one still has to try and do so, but I fully admit that this process is not easy and I would not pretend otherwise. Similarly, somewhat obviously by now, you would realise the extent to which I believe that argument, persuasion and transparency play such an important part in tourism planning and policy. This

book is part of those arguments. However, there is also a more public role that one can play in communicating ideas. Although at times you may be uninvited or excluded from the policy and planning process, at other times there may be opportunities to engage with it. But, as in all arguments, you win some and you lose some. Indeed, perhaps the hardest thing to accept is one's sometime inability to communicate ideas effectively and win policy and planning arguments or even become part of a debate that is often not transparent and occurs behind closed doors. Nevertheless, I still believe that tourism planning, and public planning in particular, potentially has a vital role to play.

The previous chapter noted the wonderful concept of adaptive systems. Perhaps this book is an example of adaptive academia. It is an attempt to understand the complexity of tourism planning and, from that, to also try to see how tourism and places can be made more sustainable in the broadest sense of the word – environmentally, economically and socially – the latter also including political aspects of sustainability with respect to openness and transparency in decision making with respect to the wider community, not just a select few, in the tourism industry, something that many government agencies fail to understand. This book is also part of a process, a staging post on a route to hopefully deeper understanding and better communicated observations on the nature and direction of tourism planning and policy. I do not think that systems thinking alone will guarantee people become more environmentally and socially aware in their actions and therefore more likely to support sustainable tourism strategies. People still have to make conscious decisions about their actions and endeavours. I am not sure if I believe any more that one act can change the world, although I do think we can still all influence it. Nevertheless, ideas are powerful things that reverberate throughout the web of relations within which we exist. The idea of sustainability – including participation and transparency in decision making, planning and policy – is a very powerful notion that is more important than ever before. It is to be hoped that book will make one small contribution towards that goal.

Questions

1. Does planning have to achieve 100 per cent of its objectives in order to be regarded as successful?
2. How effectively do you feel that you can 'speak truth to power' (Wildavsky 1987)?
3. What personal attributes do you think are required for a planner to more effectively advance more sustainable tourism outcomes?
4. Lew and Hall (1998) outlined five 'lessons' of sustainable tourism (see Chapter 3). To what extent are these lessons supported or not by the discussions and observations in this book and the contemporary tourism environment?

Important websites and recommended reading

Websites

Journal of Planning Literature:
http://jpl.sagepub.com/

Journal of Planning Education and Research:
http://intl-jpe.sagepub.com/

Planning Theory (journal):
http://plt.sagepub.com/

Current Issues in Tourism:
http://www.multilingual-matters.net/cit/

Journal of Sustainable Tourism:
www.multilingual-matters.net/jost/

Tourism Geographies:
http://www.tandf.co.uk/journals/titles/14616688.asp

Recommended reading

1. Pike, A., Rodríguez-Pose, A. and Tomaney, J. (2006) *Local and Regional Development,* Routledge, London.

   A good general introduction to issues of regional development in developed countries.

2. Dredge, D. and Jenkins, J. (eds) (2007) *Tourism Planning and Policy.* Wiley, Brisbane.

   Australian- and New Zealand-oriented textbook on tourism planning and policy.

3. Hall, D. and Brown, F. (2006) *Tourism and Welfare: Ethics, Responsibility and Sustained Well-Being,* CABI, Wallingford.

   Provides an excellent account of welfare issues in tourism and how this relates to sustainability, ethical and quality of life concerns.

4. Majone, G. (1989) *Evidence, Argument and Persuasion in the Policy Process,* Yale University Press, New Haven.

   Excellent book with respect to acting in and understanding policy and planning processes.

5. Hall, C.M. (2004) 'Reflexivity and tourism research: situating myself and/with others', in J. Phillimore and L. Goodson (eds) *Qualitative Research in Tourism: Ontologies, Epistemologies and Methodologies,* Routledge, London, 137–55.

   Discussion of role of reflexivity.

6. Hall, C.M. and Williams, A. (2008) *Tourism and Innovation,* Routledge, London.

   Examines the relationship between tourism and innovation.

Bibliography

Access Economics (1997) *The Economic Significance of Travel and Tourism and Is There a Case for Government Funding for Generic Tourism Marketing*, prepared by Access Economics, Tourism Council Australia, Property Council of Australia and Tourism Task Force, Canberra.

Ackoff, R.L. (1974) *Redesigning the Future*, John Wiley, New York.

Adams, W.M., Brockington, D., Gyson, J. and Vira, B. (2003) 'Managing tragedies: understanding conflict over common pool resources', *Science*, 302(5652): 1915–16.

Agrawala, S. (2007) *Climate Change in the European Alps: Adapting Winter Tourism and Natural Hazards Management*, OECD, Paris.

Alexander, C. (1979) *Timeless Way of Building*, Oxford University Press, New York.

Alexander, C., Silverstein, A., Ishikawa, S. and Abrams, D. (1975) *The Oregon Experiment*, Oxford University Press, New York.

Alexander, C., Ishikawa, S., Silverstein, M., Jacobson, M., Fiksdahl-King, I. and Angel, S. (1977) *A Pattern Language*, Oxford University Press, New York.

Alexander, C., Neis, H., Anninou, A. and King, I. (1987) *A New Theory of Urban Design*, Oxford University Press, New York.

Allaby, M. (1985) *The Oxford Dictionary of Natural History*, Oxford University Press, Oxford.

Allison, G. (1971) *The Essence of Decision*, Little & Brown, Boston.

Allison, G. and Zelikow, P. (1999) *The Essence of Decision*, 2nd edn, Longman, Boston.

Allmendinger, P. and Tewdwr-Jones, M. (eds) (2002) *Planning Futures: New Directions in Planning Theory*, Taylor & Francis, London.

Allmendinger, P., Barker, A. and Stead, S. (2002) 'Delivering integrated coastal-zone management through land-use planning', *Planning Practice and Research*, 17(2): 175–96.

Amy, D.J. (1987) *The Politics of Environmental Mediation*, Columbia University Press, New York.

Anderson, J.E. (1994) *Public Policymaking: An Introduction*, Houghton Mifflin, Dallas.

Anderson, L.T. (1995) *Guidelines for Preparing Urban Plans*, Planners Press, Chicago.

Andriotis, K. (2001) 'Tourism planning and development in Crete: recent tourism policies and their efficacy', *Journal of Sustainable Tourism*, 9(4): 298–316.

Aplin, G. (2007) 'Heritage protection in Australia: the legislative and bureaucratic framework', in R. Jones and B. Shaw (eds), *Geographies of Australian Heritages: Loving a Sunburnt Country*, Ashgate, Aldershot, 9–23.

Appreciative Inquiry Commons (2007) What is appreciative inquiry?, http://appreciative inquiry.case.edu/intro/whatisai.cfm [accessed 20 February 2007].

Araujo, L.M. de and Bramwell, B. (2002) 'Partnership and regional tourism in Brazil', *Annals of Tourism Research*, 29(4): 1138–64.

Archer, B.H. (1982) 'The value of multipliers and their policy implications', *Tourism Management*, 3: 236–41.

Arcoleo, D.P. (2001) Underneath appreciative inquiry, http://appreciativeinquiry.case.edu/research/bibCompletedDissertationsDetail.cfm?coid=807 [accessed 7 July 2006].

Arnstein, S. (1969) 'A ladder of citizen participation', *Journal of American Institute of Planners*, 35: 216–24.

Ashby, W.R. (1956) *Introduction to Cybernetics*, Methuen, London.

Ashby, W.R. (1966) *Design for a Brain: The Origin of Adaptive Behaviour,* Chapman & Hall, London.

Ashworth, G.J. and Tunbridge, J.E. (1990) *The Tourist Historic City,* Belhaven, London.

Ashworth, G.J. and Voogd, H. (1988) 'Marketing the city: concepts, processes and Dutch applications', *Town Planning Review,* 59(1): 65–80.

AusIndustry (1996) *Network News: AusIndustry Business Networks Program,* December, No. 6: 8.

Australian Government (2003) *Tourism White Paper: A Medium to Long Term Strategy for Tourism,* Commonwealth of Australia, Canberra.

Australian Government (2004) *Tourism White Paper Implementation Plan 2004,* Department of Industry, Tourism and Resources, Commonwealth of Australia, Canberra.

Australian Government (2005) *Achievement by Partnerships: Tourism Collaboration Intergovernmental Agreement,* Commonwealth of Australia, Canberra.

Australian Government Committee of Inquiry Into Tourism (1987) *Report of the Australian Government Committee of Inquiry Into Tourism,* Vol. 1, Australian Government Publishing Service, Canberra.

Australian Heritage Commission (1983) *Manual,* Australian Heritage Commission, Canberra.

Australian Sister Cities Association Inc. (2004) *Strategic Plan 2004–2007,* Australian Sister Cities Association Inc., Altona.

Barrett, S. (2004) 'Implementation studies: time for a revival? Personal reflection on 20 years of implementation studies', *Public Administration,* 82(2): 249–62.

Barrett, S. and Fudge, C. (1981) *Policy and Action,* Methuen, London.

Bates, G. (1983) *Environmental Law in Australia,* Butterworths, Sydney.

Batty, M. (1995) 'Cities and complexity: implications for modeling sustainability', in J. Brotchie, M. Batty, E. Blakely, P. Hall and P. Newton (eds), *Cities in Competition: Productive and Sustainable Cities for the 21st Century,* Longman Australia, South Melbourne, 469–86.

Baud-Bovy, M. and Lawson, F. (1977) *Tourism and Recreational Development,* The Architectural Press, London.

Bayliss, D. and Walker, G. (1996) 'Environmental monitoring and planning for sustainability', in S. Buckingham-Hatfield and B. Evans (eds), *Environmental Planning and Sustainability,* John Wiley, Chichester, 87–103.

Beatley, T. and Manning, K. (1997) *The Ecology of Place: Planning for Environment, Economy and Community,* Island Press, Washington DC.

Benckendorff, P.J. (2006) 'An exploratory analysis of planning characteristics in Australian visitor attractions', *Asia Pacific Journal of Tourism Research,* 11(1): 43–63.

Benckendorff, P.J. and Pearce, P.L. (2003) 'Australian tourist attractions: the links between organizational characteristics and planning', *Journal of Travel Research,* 42(1): 24–35.

Beng, T.H. (1995) *Tropical Resorts,* Page One Publishing, Singapore.

Bennett, R.J. and Chorley, R.J. (1978) *Environmental Systems: Philosophy, Analysis and Control,* Methuen, London.

Berke, P.R. (2002) 'Does sustainable development offer a new direction for planning? Challenges for the twenty-first century', *Journal of Planning Literature,* 17(1): 21–36.

Berry, S. and Ladkin, A. (1997) 'Sustainable tourism: a regional perspective', *Tourism Management,* 18(7): 433–40.

Bianchi, R.V. (2002) 'Towards a new political economy of global tourism', in R. Sharpley and D.J. Telfer (eds), *Tourism and Development: Concepts and Issues,* Channel View Publications, Clevedon, 265–99.

Bianchini, F. and Schwengel, H. (1991) 'Reimagining the city', in J. Corner and S. Harvey (eds), *Enterprise and Heritage: Crosscurrents of National Culture,* Routledge, London, 212–34.

Bingham, G. (1986) *Resolving Environmental Disputes: A Decade of Experience,* Conservation Foundation, Washington DC.

Blandy, R. (2000) *Industry Clusters Program: A Review,* South Australian Business Vision 2010, Government of South Australia, Adelaide.

Blank, U. (1989) *The Community Tourism Industry Imperative: The Necessity, The Opportunities, Its Potential,* Venture Publishing, State College, PA.

Blanke, J. and Chiesa, T. (2007) 'The Travel and Tourism Competitiveness Index: assessing key factors driving the sector's development', in World Economic Forum, *The Travel and Tourism Competitiveness Report 2007: Furthering the Process of Economic Development,* World Economic Forum, Geneva, 3–26.

Blowers, A. (1997) 'Environmental planning for sustainable development: the international context', in A. Blowers and B. Evans (eds), *Town Planning Into the 21st Century,* Routledge, London and New York, 34–53.

Board of the Millennium Ecosystem Assessment (2005) *Living Beyond Our Means: Natural Assets and Human Well-being, Statement from the Board,* World Resources Institute and the UN Environmental Programme, Washington, DC and Nairobi.

Bohm, D. (1980) *Wholeness and the Implicate Order,* Routledge & Kegan Paul, London.

Boomerang Box (2003) *Sister cities: friendship, goodwill and cooperation, a better world for all,* http://www.apl.com/boomerangbox/d2499.htm [accessed 10 May 2005].

Boyle, D. (2004) *Authenticity: Brands, Fakes, Spin and the Lust for Real Life,* Harper Perennial, London.

Bramwell, B. and Alletorp, L. (2001) 'Attitudes in the Danish tourism industry to the roles of business and government in sustainable tourism', *International Journal of Tourism Research,* 3(2): 91–103.

Bramwell, B. and Lane, B. (1993) 'Sustainable tourism: an evolving global approach', *Journal of Sustainable Tourism,* 1(1): 6–16.

Bramwell, B. and Lane, B. (eds) (2000) *Tourism Collaboration and Partnerships: Politics, Practice and Sustainability,* Channel View Publications, Clevedon.

Bramwell, B. and Sharman, A. (1999) 'Collaboration in local tourism policymaking', *Annals of Tourism Research,* 26(2): 392–415.

Bramwell, B., Henry, I., Jackson, G. and van der Straaten, J. (1996) 'A framework for understanding sustainable tourism management', in B. Bramwell, I. Henry, G. Jackson, A.G. Prat, G. Richards and J. van der Straaten (eds), *Sustainable Tourism Management: Principles and Practice,* Tilburg University Press, Tilburg, 23–71.

Brand, S. (1997) *How Buildings Learn: What Happens After They're Built,* Phoenix Illustrated, London.

Brann, P. and Foddy, M. (1987) 'Trust and the consumption of a deteriorating common resource', *Journal of Conflict Resolution,* 31: 615–30.

Brenner, N. (1998) 'Global cities, global states: global city formation and state territorial restructuring in contemporary Europe', *Review of International Political Economy,* 5: 1–37.

Bristow, G. (2005) 'Everyone's a 'winner': problematising the discourse of regional competitiveness', *Journal of Economic Geography,* 5: 285–304.

Britton, S.G. (1989) 'Tourism, capital, and places: a contribution to the geography of tourism', a paper prepared for the New Zealand Geographic Society Conference, 20–24 August, University of Otago, Dunedin.

Britton, S.G. (1991) 'Tourism, capital and place: towards a critical geography of tourism', *Environment and Planning D: Society and Space,* 9(4): 451–78.

Brotchie, J., Batty, M., Blakely, E., Hall, P. and Newton, P. (eds) (1995) *Cities in Competition: Productive and Sustainable Cities for the 21st Century,* Longman Australia, South Melbourne.

Buckley, R. (2002) *World Heritage Icon Value: Contribution of World Heritage Icon Branding to Nature Tourism,* Australian Heritage Commission, Canberra.

Buhalis, D. and Cooper, C. (1998) 'Competition or co-operation? small and medium-sized tourism enterprises at the destination', in E. Laws, B. Faulkner and G. Moscardo (eds), *Embracing and Managing Change in Tourism: International Case Studies,* Routledge, London, 324–46.

Bull, A. (1994) *The Economics of Travel and Tourism,* 2nd edn, Longman Australia, South Melbourne.

Bureau of Industry Economics (BIE) (1991a) *Networks: A Third Form of Organisation,* Discussion Paper 14, Bureau of Industry Economics, Canberra.

Bureau of Industry Economics (BIE) (1991b) 'Networks: a third form of organisation', *Bulletin of Industry Economics,* 10: 5–9.

Burgess, J. (1982) 'Selling places: environmental images for the executive', *Regional Studies,* 16: 1–17.

Burns, J.P.A. and Mules, T.L. (1986) 'A framework for the analysis of major special events', in J.P.A. Burns, J.H. Hatch, T.L. Mules (eds), *The Adelaide Grand Prix: The Impact of a Special Event,* The Centre for South Australian Economic Studies, Adelaide, 5–38.

Burns, P. (1999) 'Paradoxes in planning: tourism elitism or brutalism?', *Annals of Tourism Research,* 26(2): 329–48.

Burns, T. and Stalker, G.M. (1961) *The Management of Innovation,* Tavistock, London.

Burt, T. (2003) 'Scale: upscaling and downscaling in physical geography', in S.L. Holloway, S.P. Rice and G. Valentine (eds), *Key Concepts in Geography,* Sage Publications, London, 209–27.

Bushe, G.R. (1999) 'Advances in appreciative inquiry as an organisation development intervention', *Organisation Development Journal,* 17(2): 61–9.

Bushe, G.R. and Kassam, A.F. (2004) When is appreciative inquiry transformational? A meta-case analysis, http://www.gervasebushe.ca/aimeta.htm [accessed 16 March 2007].

Butcher, J. (2003) *The Moralisation of Tourism,* Routledge, London.

Butler, R.W. (1980) 'The concept of a tourist area cycle of evolution, implications for management of resources', *Canadian Geographer,* 24(1): 5–12.

Butler, R.W. (1990) 'Alternative tourism: pious hope or trojan horse', *Journal of Travel Research,* 28(3): 40–5.

Butler, R.W. (1991) 'Tourism, environment, and sustainable development', *Environmental Conservation,* 18(3): 201–9.

Butler, R.W. (ed.) (2006) *The Tourism Life Cycle,* 2 vols, Channelview Press, Clevedon.

Butler, R.W., Hall, C.M. and Jenkins, J. (eds) (1998) *Tourism and Recreation in Rural Areas,* John Wiley, Chichester.

Caffyn, A. and Jobbins, G. (2003) 'Governance capacity and stakeholder interactions in the development and management of coastal tourism: examples from Morocco and Tunisia', *Journal of Sustainable Tourism,* 11(2/3): 224–45.

Callahan, R. (2007) 'Governance: the collision of politics and cooperation', *Public Administration Review,* 67(2): 290–301.

Campbell, S. and Fainstein, S. (2003a) 'Introduction: the structure and debates of planning theory', in S. Campbell and S. Fainstein (eds), *Readings in Planning Theory,* 2nd edn, Blackwell, Oxford, 1–16.

Campbell, S. and Fainstein, S. (eds) (2003b) *Readings in Planning Theory,* 2nd edn, Blackwell, Oxford.

Canadian Heritage (2007) News release: Minister Emerson delivers keynote address at Tourism British Columbia 2010 Aboriginal Business Summit and unveils the Royal Canadian Mint's Four Host First Nations gold coin, Canadian Heritage, Vancouver, 2 February. http://www.canadianheritage.gc.ca/newsroom/index_e.cfm?fuseaction=displayDocument&DocIDCd=CDE061460.

Capra, F. (1997) *The Web of Life: A New Synthesis of Mind and Matter,* Flamingo, London.

Carlsson, L. (2000) 'Policy networks as collective action', *Policy Studies Journal,* 28(3): 502–20.

Carpenter, S.L. and Kennedy, W.J.D. (1988) *Managing Public Disputes: A Practical Guide to Handling Conflict and Reaching Agreements,* Jossey-Bass, San Francisco.

Carruthers, J.I. (2002) 'The impacts of state growth management programmes: a comparative analysis', *Urban Studies,* 39: 1959–82.

Carter, B. (2006) '"One expertise among many" – working appreciatively to make miracles instead of finding problems: using appreciative inquiry as a way of reframing research', *Journal of Research in Nursing,* 11(1): 48–63.

Cauley, D.N. (1993) 'Evaluation: does it make a difference?', *Evaluation Journal of Australasia,* 5(2): 3–15.

Chadwick, G. (1971) *A Systems View of Planning,* Pergamon Press, Oxford.

Chaudhary, M. (1996) 'India's tourism: a paradoxical product', *Tourism Management,* 17(8): 616–19.

Chiang, C.Y. (2004) 'Novel tourism: nature, industry, and literature on Monterey's Cannery Row', *Western Historical Quarterly,* 35(3).

Childs, M.C. (2001) 'Civic ecosystems', *Journal of Urban Design,* 6(1): 55–72.

Cheshire, P.C. and Gordon, I.R. (1998) 'Territorial competition: some lessons for policy', *Annals of Regional Science,* 32: 321–46.

Church, A. and Coles, T. (eds) (2007) *Tourism, Power and Space,* Routledge, London.

Church, A., Ball, R., Bull, C. and Tyler, D. (2000) 'Public policy engagement with British tourism: the national, local and the European Union', *Tourism Geographies,* 2(3): 312–336.

Clark, T., Gill, A. and Hartmann, R. (eds) (2006) *Mountain Resort Planning and Development in an Era of Globalization,* Cognizant Communication Corporation, New York.

Clawson, M. and Knetsch, J.L. (1966) *Economics of Outdoor Recreation,* Johns Hopkins University Press, Baltimore.

Clement, K., Bradley, K. and Hansen, M. (2004) *Environment and Sustainable Development Integration in the Nordic Structural Funds: An Appraisal of Programming Documents,* Nordregio, Stockholm.

Cochrane, A. (2007) *Understanding Urban Policy: A Critical Approach,* Blackwell, Oxford.

Coggins, G.C. and Wilkinson, C.F. (1981) *Federal Public Land and Resources Law,* Foundation Press, New York.

Cohen, E. (2007) 'Authenticity in tourism studies: *après la lutte',* *Tourism Recreation Research,* 32: in press.

Cohn, T.H. and Smith, P.J. (1995) 'Developing global cities in the Pacific Northwest: the cases of Vancouver and Seattle', in P.K. Kresl and G. Gappert (eds), *North American Cities and the Global Economy: Challenges and Opportunities,* Sage, Thousand Oaks, 251–85.

Coleman, J.S. (1990) *Foundations of Social Theory,* Belknap Press, Cambridge.

Colenutt, B. (1997) 'Can town planning be for people rather than property?', in A. Blowers and B. Evans (eds), *Town Planning Into the 21st Century,* Routledge, London and New York, 105–18.

Coles, T.E. (2006) 'Enigma variations? The TALC, marketing models and the descendants of the product life cycle', in R.W. Butler (ed.), *The Tourism Life Cycle: Conceptual and Theoretical Issues,* Channelview Publications, Clevedon, 49–66.

Coles, T., Duval, D. and Hall, C.M. (2004) 'tourism, mobility and global communities: new approaches to theorising tourism and tourist spaces', in W. Theobold (ed.), *Global Tourism,* 3rd edn, Heinemann, Oxford, 463–81.

Coles, T., Hall, C.M. and Duval, D. (2006) 'Tourism and post disciplinary enquiry', *Current Issues in Tourism,* 9(4–5): 293–319.

Collinson S. (1996) 'Visa requirements, carrier sanctions, safe third countries and readmission: the development of an asylum buffer zone in Europe', *Transactions of the Institute of British Geographers,* 21(1): 76–90.

Collyer, F.M. (2003) 'Theorising privatisation: policy, network analysis, class', *Electronic Journal of Sociology,* 7(3): http://www.sociology.org/content/vol7.3/01_collyer.html

Commission of the European Communities (2006) *Communication from the Commission. A Renewed EU Tourism Policy: Towards a Stronger Partnership for Europe,* COM(2006) 134 final, Brussels.

Commonwealth of Australia (1999) *Environment Protection and Biodiversity Conservation Act 1999,* Canberra.

Commonwealth of Australia (2000) *Environment Protection and Biodiversity Conservation Regulations, 2000,* Canberra.

Conley, A. and Moote, M.A. (2003) 'Evaluating collaborative natural resource management', *Society and Natural Resources,* 16(5): 371–86.

Cooke, K. (1982) 'Guidelines for socially appropriate tourism development in British Columbia', *Journal of Travel Research,* 21(1): 22–8.

Cooke, P. (2002) *Knowledge Economies: Clusters, Learning and Cooperative Advantage,* Routledge, London.

Cookson, N. (2000) *Archeological Heritage Law,* Barry Rose Law Publishers, Chichester.

Cooper, C. and Hall, C.M. (2008) *Contemporary Tourism,* Elsevier, London.

Cooper, T. (2005) 'Slower consumption: reflections on product life spans and the "throwaway society"', *Journal of Industrial Ecology,* 9(1–2): 51–67.

Cooperrider, D.L. (1986) 'Appreciative inquiry: toward a methodology for understanding and enhancing organizational innovation', unpublished doctoral dissertation, Case Western Reserve University, Ohio.

Cooperrider, D.L. and Srivastva, S. (1987) 'Appreciative inquiry in organisational life', in R. Woodman and W. Pasmore (eds), *Research in Organisational Change and Development,* JAI Press, Greenwich, 129–69.

Cooperrider, D.L. and Whitney, W. (2005) *Appreciative Inquiry: A Positive Revolution in Change,* Berrett-Koehler, San Francisco.

Coper, M. (1983) *The Franklin Dam Case,* Butterworths, Sydney.

Corbalan, S., Dresin, E. and Fuccella, F. (2005) *250 European Union Measures Affecting the Hotel, Restaurant and Café Sector,* HOTREC, Brussels.

Council of Australian Governments (1997) *Heads of Agreement on Commonwealth and State Roles and Responsibilities for the Environment,* Council of Australian Governments, Canberra.

Cowell, R. and Owens, S. (1997) 'Sustainability: the new challenge', in A. Blowers and B. Evans (eds), *Town Planning Into the 21st Century,* Routledge, London and New York, 15–31.

Craik, J. (1988) 'The social impacts of tourism', in B. Faulkner and M. Fagence (eds), *Frontiers in Australian Tourism: The Search for New Perspectives in Policy Development and Research,* Bureau of Tourism Research, Canberra, 17–31.

Craik, J. (1990) 'A classic case of clientelism: the Industries Assistance Commission Inquiry into Travel and Tourism', *Culture and Policy,* 2(1): 29–45.

Craik, J. (1991a) *Resorting to Tourism: Cultural Policies for Tourist Development in Australia,* Allen & Unwin, St Leonards.

Craik, J. (1991b) *Government Promotion of Tourism: The Role of the Queensland Tourist and Travel Corporation,* The Centre for Australian Public Sector Management, Griffith University, Brisbane.

Cresswell, T. (2004) *Place: A Short Introduction,* Blackwell, Oxford.

Cullingsworth, B. (1997) *Planning in the USA: Policies, Issues and Processes,* Routledge, London and New York.

Cupitt, D. (1987) *The Long Legged Fly: A Theology of Language and Desire,* SCM Press, London.

Current Issues in Tourism (2001) Special edition on Tourism Policy Making: Theory and Practice, 4(2–4).

Daly, H.E. and Cobb, J.B., Jnr (1989) *For the Common Good,* Beacon, Boston.

Damette, F. (1980) 'The regional framework of monopoly exploitation: new problems and trends', in J. Carney, R. Hudson and J.R. Lewis (eds), *Regions in Crisis,* Croom Helm, London.

Davidson, R. and Maitland, R. (1997) *Tourism Destinations,* Hodder & Stoughton, London.

Davis, B.W. (1984) 'How the World Heritage Convention works', *Environmental and Planning Law Journal,* 1: 196–8.

Davis, G., Wanna, J., Warhurst, J. and Weller, P. (1993) *Public Policy in Australia,* 2nd edn, Allen & Unwin, St Leonards.

de Kadt, E. (ed.) (1979) *Tourism: Passport to Development?,* Oxford University Press, Oxford.

Deas, I. and Giordano, B. (2001) 'Conceptualising and measuring urban competitiveness in major English cities: an exploratory approach', *Environment and Planning A,* 33: 1411–29.

DeGrove, J.M. and Miness, D.A. (1992) *The New Frontier for Land Policy: Planning and Growth Management in the States,* Lincoln Institute of Land Policy, Cambridge.

Delbecq, A.L. (1974) 'Contextual variables affecting decision-making in program planning', *Journal of the American Institute for Decision Sciences,* 5(4): 726–42.

Department of Tourism (Australia) (1992) *Tourism Australia's Passport to Growth: A National Tourism Strategy,* Commonwealth Department of Tourism, Canberra.

Department of Tourism (Australia) (1993) *Rural Tourism: Tourism Discussion Paper No. 1,* Commonwealth Department of Tourism, Canberra.

de-Shalit, A. (1997) 'Is liberalism environmentally friendly?', in R. Gottlieb (ed.), *The Ecological Community: Environmental Challenges for Philosophy, Politics and Morality,* Routledge, London, 82–103.

De Stefano, L. (2004) *Freshwater and Tourism in the Mediterranean,* WWF Mediterranean Programme, Rome.

Diamantis, D. (ed.) (2004) *Ecotourism: Management and Assessment,* Thomson, London.

Doel, M.A. and Hubbard, P.J. (2002) 'Taking world cities literally: marketing the city in a global space of flows', *City,* 6: 351–68.

Donovan, J.J. and Hafsteinsson, L.G. (2006) 'The impact of goal-performance discrepancies, self-efficacy, and goal orientation on upward goal revision', *Journal of Applied Social Psychology,* 36(4): 1046–69.

Douglas, D. (1992) 'Program evaluation and performance measurement in Queensland', in C. O'Faircheallaigh and B. Ryan (eds), *Program Evaluation and Per-formance Monitoring: An Australian Perspective,* Macmillan, South Melbourne, 19–34.

Dovey, K. (1985) 'The quest for authenticity and the replication of environmental meaning', in D. Seamon and R. Mugerauer (eds) *Dwelling, Place and Environment: Towards a Phenomenology of Person and Word,* Martinus Nijhoff Publishers, Dordrecht, 33–50.

Dowling, R.K. (1993a) 'Tourism planning, people and the environment in Western Australia', *Journal of Travel Research,* 31(4): 52–8.

Dowling, R.K. (1993b) 'Tourist and resident perceptions of the environment–tourist relationship in the Gascoyne region, Western Australia', *Geojournal,* 29(3): 243–51.

Dowling, R.K. (1997) 'Plans for the development of regional ecotourism: theory and practice', in C.M. Hall, J. Jenkins and G. Kearsley (eds), *Tourism Planning and Policy in Australia and New Zealand: Cases, Issues and Practice,* Irwin Publishers, Sydney, 110–26.

Downs, A. (1972) 'Up and down with ecology: the issue attention cycle', *The Public Interest,* 28: 38–50.

Dredge, D. (1999) 'Destination place planning and design', *Annals of Tourism Research,* 26: 772–91.

Dredge, D. (2006) 'Policy networks and the local organization of tourism', *Tourism Management,* 27(2): 269–80.

Dredge, D. and Jenkins, J. (2003) 'Destination place identity and regional tourism policy', *Tourism Geographies,* 5(4): 383–407.

Dredge, D. and Jenkins, J. (eds) (2007) *Tourism Planning and Policy,* John Wiley, Brisbane.

Dror, Y. (1973) 'The planning process: a facet design', in A. Faludi (ed.), *A Reader in Planning Theory,* Pergamon Press, Oxford, 323–43.

Drost, A. (1996) 'Developing sustainable tourism for World Heritage sites', *Annals of Tourism Research,* 23(2): 479–92.

Dudley, G., Parsons, W., Radaelli, C.M. and Sabatier, P. (2000) 'Symposium: theories of the policy process', *Journal of European Public Policy,* 7(1): 122–40.

Duffy, F. (1990) 'Measuring building performance', *Facilities,* May: 17.

Dunlop, A. (2003) *Tourism Services Negotiation Issues: Implications for Cariform Countries,* Caribbean Regional Negotiating Machinery, Barbados.

Dutton, I. and Hall, C.M. (1989) 'Making tourism sustainable: the policy/practice conundrum', *Proceedings of the Environment Institute of Australia Second National Conference,* Melbourne, 9–11 October.

Dwyer, L. and Kim, C. (2003) 'Destination competitiveness: determinants and indicators', *Current Issues in Tourism,* 6(5): 369–414.

Dwyer, L. Forsyth, P. and Rao, P. (2000a) 'The price competitiveness of travel and tourism: a comparison of 19 destinations', *Tourism Management,* 21(1): 9–22.

Dwyer, L., Forsyth P. and Rao, P. (2000b) 'Sectoral analysis of destination price competitiveness: an international comparison', *Tourism Analysis,* 5: 1–12.

Dye, T. (1992) *Understanding Public Policy,* 7th edn, Prentice-Hall, Englewood Cliffs.

Easton, D. (1953) *The Political System: An Inquiry into the State of Political Science,* Knopf, New York.

Easton, D. (1957) 'An approach to the analysis of political systems', *World Politics,* 9(3): 383–400.

Easton, D. (1990) *The Analysis of Political Structure,* Routledge, New York.

Edgell, D.L. (1990) *International Tourism Policy,* Van Nostrand Reinhold, New York.

Edwards, S.N., McLaughlin, W.J. and Ham, S.H. (1998) *Comparative Study of Ecotourism Policy in the Americas, Vol. III: USA and Canada,* Department of Resource Recreation and Tourism College of Forestry, Wildlife and Range Resources University of Idaho/Inter-Sectoral Unit for Tourism Organization of American States, Moscow.

Egan, T.M. and Lancaster, C.M. (2005) 'Comparing appreciative inquiry to action-research: OD practitioner perspectives', *Organisation Development Journal,* 23(2): 29–51.

Ekins, P. (1993) 'Making development sustainable', in W. Sachs (ed.), *Global Ecology: A New Arena of Conflict,* Fernwood Publications, Halifax, 91–103.

Elections BC (2002) *Referendum 2002: Report of the Chief Electoral Office on the Treaty Negotiations Referendum,* Elections BC, Victoria.

Elliot, J. (1997) *Tourism: Politics and Public Sector Management,* Routledge, London.

Elliott, C. (1999) *Locating the Energy for Change: An Introduction to Appreciative Inquiry,* International Institute for Sustainable Development, Winnipeg.

European Commission (1995) *Green Paper on Tourism,* DGXXIII European Commission, Brussels.

European Union (1998) *Special Report No 3/96 on Tourist Policy and the Promotion of Tourism, Together with the Commission's Replies,* Official Journal NO. C 017, 16/01/1997 P. 0001–0023, EUR-Lex: Document 397Y0116(01), Court of Auditors, Luxembourg, http:// europa.eu.int/eur-lex/en/ lif/dat/en_397Y0116_ 01.html [accessed 27 August 1998].

Eurostat (2007) *Inbound and Outbound Tourism in Europe,* Industry, Trade and Services, Population and Social Conditions, 52/2007, European Communities, Brussells.

Evans, B. (1997) 'From town planning to environmental planning', in A. Blowers and B. Evans (eds), *Town Planning Into the 21st Century,* Routledge, London and New York, 1–14.

Evans, N., Campbell, D. and Stonehouse, G. (2003) *Strategic Management for Travel and Tourism,* Butterworth-Heinemann, Oxford.

Fagence, M. (1979) *The Political Nature of Community Decision-making,* Planning Research Paper No. 1, Department of Regional and Town Planning, University of Queensland, St Lucia.

Farrell, B.H. and Twining-Ward, L. (2004) 'Reconceptualizing tourism', *Annals of Tourism Research,* 31(2): 274–95.

Farrell, B.H. and Twining-Ward, L. (2005) 'Seven steps towards sustainability: tourism in the context of new knowledge', *Journal of Sustainable Tourism,*

Fennell, D. and Dowling, R. (eds) (2003) *Ecotourism: Policy and Strategy Issues,* CABI, Wallingford.

Fischer, F. and Forester, J. (1993) *The Argumentative Turn in Policy Analysis and Planning,* UCL Press, London.

Flinders, M. (2005) 'The politics of public– private partnerships', *The British Journal of Politics and International Relations,* 7(2): 215–39.

Florida, R. (2002) *The Rise of the Creative Class, and How It's Transforming Work, Leisure, Community and Everyday Life,* Basic Books, New York.

Fortunato, V.J. and Goldblatt, A.M. (2006) 'An examination of goal orientation profiles using cluster analysis and their relationships with dispositional characteristics and motivational response patterns,' *Journal of Applied Social Psychology,* 36(9): 2150–83.

Freestone, R., Williams, P. and Bowden, A. (2006) 'Fly buy cities: some planning aspects of airport privatization in Australia', *Urban Policy and Research,* 24(4): 491–508.

Friedmann, J. (1959) 'Introduction', *International Social Science Journal,* 11(3): 327–34.

Friedmann, J. (1973) 'A conceptual model for the analysis of planning behaviour', in A. Faludi (ed.), *A Reader in Planning Theory*, Pergamon Press, Oxford, 344–70.

Fry, E.H. (1986) 'The economic competitiveness of the western states and provinces: the international dimension', *American Review of Canadian Studies*, 16(3): 301.

Fyall, A. and Leask, A. (eds) (2006) *Managing World Heritage Sites*, Butterworth-Heinemann, Oxford.

Gallie, W.B. (1955–56) 'Essentially contested concepts', *Proceedings of the Aristotelian Society*, 56: 167–98.

Garreau, J. (1991) *Edge City*, Doubleday, New York.

Gergen, K. (1985) 'The social constructionist movement in modern psychology', *American Psychologist*, 40: 266–75.

Gergen, K.J. (1991) *The Saturated Self: Dilemmas of Identity in Contemporary Life*, Basic Books, New York.

Getz, D. (1986) 'Models in tourism planning towards integration of theory and practice', *Tourism Management*, 7(1): 21–32.

Getz, D. (1987) 'Tourism planning and research: traditions, models and futures', paper presented at The Australian Travel Research Workshop, Bunbury, Western Australia, 5–6 November.

Getz, D. (1992) 'Tourism planning and destination life cycle', *Annals of Tourism Research*, 19: 752–70.

Getz, D. (1994) 'Resident's attitudes towards tourism: a longitudinal study in Spey Valley, Scotland', *Tourism Management*, 15(4): 247–58.

Getz, D. and Jamal, T.B. (1994) 'The environment-community symbiosis: A case for collaborative tourism planning', *Journal of Sustainable Tourism*, 2(3): 152–73.

Gibson, C. and Klocker, N. (2005) 'The "cultural turn" in Australian regional development discourse: neoliberalising creativity?', *Geographical Research*, 43(1): 93–102.

Giddens, A. (1984) *The Constitution of Society*, Polity Press, Cambridge.

Giddens, A. (1990) *The Consequences of Modernity*, Stanford University Press, Stanford.

Gill, A. (1998) 'Local and resort development', in R. Butler, C.M. Hall and J. Jenkins (eds), *Tourism and Recreation in Rural Areas*, John Wiley, Chichester, 97–111.

Gill, A. (2000) 'From growth machine to growth management: the dynamics of resort development in Whistler, British Columbia', *Environment and Planning A*, 32(6): 1083–1103.

Gill, A. and Williams, P.W. (1994) 'Managing growth in mountain tourism communities', *Tourism Management*, 15(3): 212–20.

Glassie, H. (1968) *Pattern in the Material Folk Culture of the Eastern United States*, University of Pennsylvania, Philadelphia.

Go, F., Milne, D. and Whittles, L. (1992) 'Communities as destinations: a marketing taxonomy for the effective implementation of the tourism action plan', *Journal of Travel Research*, 30(4): 31–7.

Goodwin, M. (1993) 'The city as commodity: the contested spaces of urban development', in G. Kearns and C. Philo (eds), *Selling Places: The City as Cultural Capital, Past and Present*, Pergamon Press, Oxford, 145–62.

Gössling, S. (2002) 'Global environmental consequences of tourism', *Global Environmental Change*, 12: 283–302.

Gössling, S. and Hall, C.M. (eds) (2006) *Tourism and Global Environmental Change*, Routledge, London.

Gössling, S. and Hultman, J. (eds) (2006) *Ecotourism in Scandinavia*, CABI, Wallingford.

Gössling, S., Hansson, C.B., Hörstmeier, O. and Saggel, S. (2002) 'Ecological footprint analysis as a tool to assess tourism sustainability', *Ecological Economics*, 43: 199–211.

Gourley, C. (1998) *Island in the Creek: The Granville Island Story*, Harbour Publishing, Vancouver.

Grant, S. and Humphries, M. (2006) 'Critical evaluation of appreciative inquiry', *Action-research*, 4(4): 401–18.

Gray, B. (1985) 'Conditions facilitating interorganizational collaboration', *Human Relations*, 38(10): 911–36.

Gray, B. (1989) *Collaborating: Finding Common Ground for Multiparty Problems*, Jossey-Bass, San Francisco.

Greenberg, G.D., Miller, J.A., Mohr, L.B. and Vladeck, B.C. (1977) 'Developing public policy theory–perspectives from empirical research', *American Political Science Review*, 71(4): 1532–43.

Grigg, D. (1967) 'Regions, models and classes', in R.J. Chorley and P. Haggett (eds), *Models in Geography*, Methuen, London, 461–510.

Gunn, C.A. (1977) 'Industry pragmatism vs tourism planning', *Leisure Sciences*, 1(1): 85–94.

Gunn, C.A. (1979) *Tourism Planning*, Crane Russak, New York.

Gunn, C.A. (1988) *Tourism Planning*, 2nd edn, Taylor & Francis, New York.

Gunn, C.A. (1994) *Tourism Planning*, 3rd edn, Taylor & Francis, Washington.

Gunn, C.A. with Var, T. (2002) *Tourism Planning: Basics, Concepts, Cases*, 4th edn, Routledge, New York.

Haggett, P. (1965) 'Scale components in geographical problems', in R.J. Chorley and P. Haggett (eds), *Frontiers in Geographical Teaching*, Methuen, London, 164–85.

Hales, D.F. (1984) 'The World Heritage Convention: status and directions', in J.A. McNeely and K.R. Miller (eds), *National Parks, Conservation and Development: The Role of Protected Areas in Sustaining Society*, Proceedings of the World Congress on National Parks, Bali, Indonesia, 11–12 October 1982, Smithsonian Institution Press, Washington, 744–50.

Hall, C.M. (1992a) *Wasteland to World Heritage: Conserving Australia's Wilderness*, Melbourne University Press, Carlton.

Hall, C.M. (1992b) *Hallmark Tourist Events: Impacts, Management and Planning*, Belhaven, London.

Hall, C.M. (1994) *Tourism and Politics: Policy, Power and Place*, John Wiley, Chichester.

Hall, C.M. (1995) 'Tourism and regional development: softening the blows of changing times', in *National Regional Tourism Conference*, Tourism Council Australia, Launceston.

Hall, C.M. (1998a) 'Historical antecedents of sustainable development and ecotourism: new labels on old bottles?', in C.M. Hall and A. Lew (eds), *Sustainable Tourism Development: Geographical Perspectives*, Addison Wesley Longman, Harlow, 13–24.

Hall, C.M. (1998b) *Tourism: Development, Dimensions and Issues*, 3rd edn, Addison Wesley Longman, South Melbourne.

Hall, C.M. (1999) 'Rethinking collaboration and partnership: A public policy perspective', *Journal of Sustainable Tourism*, 7(3/4): 274–89.

Hall, C.M. (2000) *Tourism Planning*, 1st edn, Prentice Hall, Harlow.

Hall, C.M. (2002) 'Travel safety, terrorism and the media: the significance of the issue-attention cycle', *Current Issues in Tourism*, 5(5): 458–66.

Hall, C.M. (2003a) 'Institutional arrangements for ecotourism policy', in D. Fennell and R. Dowling (eds), *Ecotourism: Policy and Strategy Issues*, CABI, Wallingford, 21–38.

Hall, C.M. (2003b) 'Tourism and temporary mobility: circulation, diaspora, migration, nomadism, sojourning, travel, transport and home', International Academy for the Study of Tourism (IAST) Conference, 30 June–5 July 2003, Savonlinna, Finland.

Hall, C.M. (2004a) 'Scale and the problems of assessing mobility in time and space', paper presented at the Swedish National Doctoral Student Course on Tourism, Mobility and Migration, hosted by Department of Social and Economic Geography, University of Umeå, Umeå, Sweden, October.

Hall, C.M. (2004b) 'Ecotourism policy', in D. Diamantis (ed.), *Ecotourism: Management and Assessment*, Thomson, London, 135–50.

Hall, C.M. (2004c) 'Reflexivity and tourism research: situating myself and/with others', in J. Phillimore and L. Goodson (eds), *Qualitative Research in Tourism: Ontologies, Epistemologies and Methodologies*, Routledge, London, 137–55.

Hall, C.M. (2004d) 'Small firms and wine and food tourism in New Zealand: issues of collaboration, clusters and lifestyles', in R. Thomas (ed.), *Small Firms in Tourism: International Perspectives*, Elsevier, Oxford, 167–81.

Hall, C.M. (2005a) *Tourism: Rethinking the Social Science of Mobility,* Prentice Hall, Harlow.

Hall, C.M. (2005b) 'Selling places: hallmark events and the reimaging of Sydney and Toronto', in J. Nauright and K. Schimmel (eds), *The Political Economy of Sport,* Palgrave Macmillan, London, 129–51.

Hall, C.M. (2006a) 'Space-time accessibility and the tourist area cycle of evolution: the role of geographies of spatial interaction and mobility in contributing to an improved understanding of tourism', in R.W. Butler (ed.), *The Tourism Life Cycle: Conceptual and Theoretical Issues,* Channelview Publications, Clevedon, 83–100.

Hall, C.M. (2006b) 'Tourism urbanization and global environmental change', in C.M. Hall and S. Gössling (eds), *Tourism and Global Environmental Change: Ecological, Economic, Social and Political Interrelationships,* Routledge, London, 142–56.

Hall, C.M. (2006c) 'Human mobility: barriers, constraints and "open borders"'; paper presented in the session on Regulatory Frameworks in Tourism: Mobilities, Policies and Governance, Tourism and Travel Research Association Conference, 18–20 June, Dublin.

Hall, C.M. (2006d) 'Policy, planning and governance in ecotourism,' in S. Gössling and J. Hultman (eds), *Ecotourism in Scandinavia,* CABI, Wallingford, 193–206.

Hall, C.M. (2006e) 'World Heritage, tourism and implementation: what happens after listing?', in A. Fyall and A. Leask (eds), *Managing World Heritage Sites,* Butterworth-Heinemann, Oxford, 18–32.

Hall, C.M. (2006f) 'Tourism and regional competitiveness,' paper presented at Cutting Edge Research in Tourism: New Directions, Challenges and Applications, 6–9 June, University of Surrey, Guildford.

Hall, C.M. (2007a) *Introduction to Tourism in Australia,* 5th edn, Pearson, South Melbourne.

Hall, C.M. (2007b) 'North–south perspectives on tourism, regional development and peripheral areas', in B. Jansson and D. Müller (eds), *Tourism in High-Latitude Peripheries: Space, Place and Environment,* CABI, Wallingford.

Hall, C.M. (2007c) 'Response to Yeoman *et al:* the fakery of "The authentic tourist"', *Tourism Management,* 28(4): 1139–40.

Hall, C.M. (ed.) (2007d) *Pro-poor Tourism,* Channelview, Clevedon.

Hall, C.M. and Boyd, S. (eds) (2005) *Nature-based Tourism in Peripheral Areas: Development or Disaster,* Channelview Publications, Clevedon.

Hall, C.M. and Butler, D. (1995) 'In search of common ground: reflections on sustainability, complexity and process in the tourism system', *Journal of Sustainable Tourism,* 3(2): 99–105.

Hall, C.M., Cambourne, B., Macionis, N. and Johnson, G. (1997) 'Wine tourism and network development in Australia and New Zealand: review, establishment and prospects', *International Journal of Wine Marketing,* 9(2/3): 5–31.

Hall, C.M. and Härkonen, T. (eds) (2006) *Lake Tourism: An Integrated Approach to Lacustrine Tourism,* Channel View Publications, Clevedon.

Hall, C.M. and Jenkins, J.M. (1995) *Tourism and Public Policy,* Routledge, London.

Hall, C.M. and Jenkins, J.M. (1998) 'The policy dimensions of rural tourism and recreation', in R. Butler, C.M. Hall and J. Jenkins (eds), *Tourism and Recreation in Rural Areas,* John Wiley, Chichester, 16–42.

Hall, C.M. and Jenkins, J.M. (2004) 'Tourism and public policy', in A. Lew, C.M. Hall and A.M. Williams (eds), *Companion to Tourism,* Blackwells, Oxford, 525–40.

Hall, C.M., Jenkins, J.M. and Kearsley, G. (eds) (1997) *Tourism Planning and Policy in Australia and New Zealand: Cases, Issues and Practice,* Irwin, Sydney.

Hall, C.M. and Johnson, G. (1997) 'Wine tourism in New Zealand: larger bottles or better relationships?', in J. Higham (ed.), *Trails, Tourism and Regional Development Conference Proceedings,* Centre for Tourism, University of Otago, Dunedin.

Hall, C.M. and Lew, A. (eds) (1998) *Sustainable Tourism: A Geographical Perspective,* Addison Wesley Longman, Harlow.

Hall, C.M. and Macionis, N. (1998) 'Wine tourism in Australia and New Zealand', in

R.W. Butler, C.M. Hall and J. Jenkins (eds), *Tourism and Recreation in Rural Areas*, John Wiley, Chichester, 267–98.

Hall, C.M. and McArthur, S. (1996) 'Strategic planning: integrating people and places through participation', in C.M. Hall and S. McArthur (eds), *Heritage Management in Australia and New Zealand: The Human Dimension*, Oxford University Press, Melbourne, 22–36.

Hall, C.M. and McArthur, S. (1998) *Integrated Heritage Management*, Stationery Office, London.

Hall, C.M. and Mitchell, R.M. (2008) *Wine Marketing*, Elsevier, Oxford.

Hall, C.M. and Page, S. (eds) (1997) *Tourism in the Pacific*, International Thompson Business Publishing, London.

Hall, C.M. and Page, S. (1999a) *The Geography of Tourism and Recreation*, Routledge, London.

Hall, C.M. and Page, S. (1999b) 'Developing tourism in South Asia: India, Pakistan and Bangladesh – SAARC and beyond', in C.M. Hall and S. Page (eds), *Tourism in South and South-east Asia: Critical Perspectives*, Butterworth-Heinemann, Oxford.

Hall, C.M. and Page, S. (2006) *The Geography of Tourism and Recreation: Space, Place and Environment*, 3rd edn, Routledge, London.

Hall, C.M. and Piggin, R. (2001) 'Tourism and World Heritage in OECD countries', *Tourism Recreation Research*, 26(1): 103–105.

Hall, C.M. and Piggin, R. (2002) 'Tourism business knowledge of World Heritage Sites: A New Zealand case study', *International Journal of Tourism Research*, 4: 401–11.

Hall, C.M., Sharples, E., Mitchell, R., Cambourne, B. and Macionis, N. (eds) (2003) *Food Tourism Around the World: Development, Management and Markets*, Butterworth-Heinemann, Oxford.

Hall, C.M. and Tucker, H. (eds) (2004) *Tourism and Postcolonialism*, Routledge, London.

Hall, D.R. (1991) 'Eastern Europe and the Soviet Union: overcoming tourism constraints', in D.R. Hall (ed.), *Tourism and Economic Development in Eastern Europe and the Soviet Union*, Belhaven Press, London, 49–78.

Hall, D.R. (ed.) (2004) *Tourism and Transition: Governance, Transformation and Development*, CABI, Wallingford.

Hall, D.R. and Brown, F. (2006) *Tourism and Welfare: Ethics, Responsibility and Sustained Well-being*, CABI, Wallingford.

Hall, D.R., Smith, M. and Marciszewska, B. (eds) (2006) *Tourism in the New Europe: The Challenges and Opportunities of EU Enlargement*, CABI, Wallingford.

Hall, P. (1982) *Urban and Regional Planning*, 2nd edn, Penguin, Harmondsworth.

Hall, P. (1992) *Urban and Regional Planning*, 3rd edn, Routledge, London.

Hall, P. (1995) 'Towards a general urban theory', in J. Brotchie, M. Batty, E. Blakely, P. Hall and P. Newton (eds), *Cities in Competition: Productive and Sustainable Cities for the 21st Century*, Longman Australia, South Melbourne, 3–35.

Ham, C. and Hill, M.J. (1984) *The Policy Process in the Modern Capitalist State*, Simon & Shuster, New York.

Ham, C. and Hill, M.J. (1994) *The Policy Process in the Modern Capitalist State*, 2nd edn, Prentice-Hall, New York.

Hammond, S. (1998) *The Thin Book of Appreciative Inquiry*, Thin Book Publishing Company, Plano.

Hanna, S.P. and Del Casino, V.J., Jnr (eds) (2003) *Mapping Tourism*, University of Minnesota Press, Minneapolis.

Hanna, S.P., Del Casino, V.J., Jnr, Selden, C. and Hite, B. (2004) 'Representing as work in "America's most historic city"', *Social and Cultural Geography*, 5(3): 459–81.

Hardin, G. (1968) 'The tragedy of the commons', *Science*, 162: 1243–48.

Harper, D.A. (1993) *An Analysis of Interfirm Networks*, NZ Institute of Economic Research, Wellington.

Harrill, R. (2004) 'Residents' attitudes toward tourism development: a literature review with implications for tourism planning', *Journal of Planning Literature*, 18(3): 251–66.

Harrison, D. (ed.) (1992) *Tourism and the Less Developed Countries*, Belhaven, London.

Harrison, D. (2007) 'Towards developing a framework for analyzing tourism phenomena: a discussion', *Current Issues in Tourism,* 10(1): 61–86.

Harrison, D. and Hitchcock, M. (eds) (2005) *The Politics of World Heritage,* Channelview, Clevedon.

Harvey, D. (1969) *Explanation in Geography,* Edward Arnold, London.

Harvey, D. (1989a) 'From managerialism to entrepreneurialism: the transformation in urban governance in late capitalism', *Geografiska Annaler,* 71B: 3–17.

Harvey, D. (1989b) *The Condition of Postmodernity: An Enquiry into the Origins of Cultural Change,* Basil Blackwell, Oxford.

Harvey, D. (1989c) *The Urban Experience,* Blackwell, Oxford.

Harvey, D. (1993) 'From space to place and back again: reflections on the condition of postmodernity', in J. Bird, B. Curtis, T. Putnam, G. Robertson and L. Tickner (eds), *Mapping the Futures: Local Cultures, Global Change,* Routledge, London and New York, 3–29.

Harvey, D.W. (1995) 'A geographer's guide to dialectical thinking', in A.D. Clift, P.R. Gould, A.G. Hoare and N.J. Thrift (eds), *Diffusing Geography: Essays for Peter Haggett,* The Institute of British Geographers Special Production Series 31, Blackwell, Oxford, 3–21.

Haughton, G. and Hunter, C. (1994) *Sustainable Cities,* Regional Policy and Development Series 7, Jessica Kingsley Publishers, London.

Haulot, A. (1981) 'Social tourism: current dimensions and future developments', *Tourism Management,* 2: 207–12.

Haywood, K.M. (1988) 'Responsible and responsive tourism planning in the community', *Tourism Management,* 9(2): 105–18.

Hazel, N. (2005) 'Holidays for children and families in need: an exploration of the research and policy context for social tourism in the UK', *Children and Society,* 19(3): 225–36.

Healey, P. (1992a) 'Planning through debate: the communicative turn in planning theory', *Town Planning Review,* No. 632: 143–62.

Healey, P. (1992b) 'A planner's day: knowledge and action in communicative perspective', *Journal of the American Planning Association,* 58(1): 9–20.

Healey, P. (1993) 'The communicative work of development plans', *Environment and Planning B: Planning and Design,* 20: 183–94.

Healey, P. (1996) 'The communicative turn in planning theory and its implication for spatial-strategy making', *Environment and Planning B: Planning and Design,* 23: 217–34.

Healey, P. (1997) *Collaborative Planning: Shaping Places in Fragmented Societies,* Macmillan Press, Basingstoke.

Healey, P. (1999) 'Institutionalist analysis, communicative planning, and shaping places', *Journal of Planning Education and Research,* 19(2): 111–21.

Heath, E. and Wall, G. (1992) *Marketing Tourism Destinations: A Strategic Planning Approach,* John Wiley, New York.

Heclo, H. (1974) *Modern Social Politics in Britain and Sweden,* Yale University Press, New Haven.

Heeley, J. (1981) 'Planning for tourism in Britain', *Town Planning Review,* 52: 61–79.

Heinelt, H. (2005) *Do Policies Determine Politics?* School for Policy Studies Working Paper Series Paper No. 11, School for Policy Studies, University of Bristol, Bristol.

Held, D., McGrew, A., Goldblatt, D. and Perraton, J. (1999) *Global Transformations: Politics, Economics, and Culture,* Polity and Stanford University Press, Cambridge.

Hertwich, E. (2005) 'Lifecycle approaches to sustainable consumption', *Environmental Science & Technology,* 39(13): 4673–84.

Hewison, R. (1987) *The Heritage Industry: Britain in a Climate of Decline,* Methuen, London.

Hewison, R. (1991) 'Commerce and culture', in J. Corner and S. Harvey (eds), *Enterprise and Heritage: Crosscurrents of National Culture,* Routledge, London, 162–77.

Hill, G. and Rosier, J. (1989) 'Seabird ecology and resort development on Heron Island', *Journal of Environmental Management,* 27: 107–14.

Hinchcliffe, S. and Whatmore, S. (2006) 'Living cities: towards a politics of conviviality', *Science as Culture,* 15(2): 123–38.

Hirsh, C.D. (2002) 'Green organizing in Austin, Texas: place-ballet and the rhetorical community, 1990–1999', *Ethnologies*, 24(1), http://www.erudit.org/revue/ethno/2002/v24/n1/006531ar.html.

HMSO (1994) *Sustainable Development: The UK Strategy*, Cm2426, HMSO, London.

Hocking, B. (1986) 'Regional governments and international affairs: foreign policy problems or deviant behaviour?', *International Journal*, 41: 484.

Hofstede, G. (2001) *Culture's Consequences: Comparing Values, Behaviors, Institutions, and Organizations Across Nations*, 2nd edn, Thousand Oaks, Sage.

Hogwood, B. and Gunn, L. (1984) *Policy Analysis for the Real World*, Oxford University Press, Oxford.

Holcomb, B. (1993) 'Revisioning place: de- and re-constructing the image of the industrial city', in G. Kearns and C. Philo (eds), *Selling Places: The City as Cultural Capital, Past and Present*, Pergamon Press, Oxford, 133–43.

Hollick, M. (1993) *An Introduction to Project Evaluation*, Longman Cheshire, South Melbourne.

Holling, C.S. (2001) 'Understanding the complexity of economic, ecological, and social systems', *Ecosystems*, 4(5): 390–405.

Hollinshead, K. (1992) ' "White" gaze, "red" people – shadow visions: the disidentification of "Indians" in cultural tourism', *Leisure Studies*, 11: 43–64.

HOTREC (2003) *Tourism in the Treaties, HOTREC Position Paper, Catania, 12 April 2003*, HOTREC, Brussels.

Hough, M. (1995) *Cities and Natural Process*, Routledge, New York.

Hudson, R. (1988) 'Uneven development in capitalist societies: changing spatial divisions of labour, forms of spatial organisation of production and service provision, and their impacts upon localities', *Transactions of the Institute of British Geographers*, 13(NS): 484–96.

Hughes, H.L. (1984) 'Government support for tourism in the UK: a different perspective', *Tourism Management*, 5(1): 13–19.

Hughes, H.L. (1993) 'Olympic tourism and urban regeneration', *Festival Management and Event Tourism*, 1: 157–62.

Hula, R.C. (1988) 'Using markets to implement public policy', in R.C. Hula (ed.), *Market-based Public Policy*, St Martin's Press, New York.

Hunter, C. (1997) 'Sustainable tourism as an adaptive paradigm', *Annals of Tourism Research*, 24(4): 850–67.

Hunter, C. and Green, H. (1995) *Tourism and the Environment: A Sustainable Relationship?*, Routledge, London.

ICOMOS (1993) *Cultural Tourism. Tourism at World Heritage Cultural Sites: The Site Manager's Hand Book*, The ICOMOS International Specialized Committee on Cultural Tourism, Sri Lanka National Committee of ICOMOS, Colombo.

Ingram, H. (1989) 'Implementation: a review and suggested framework', in N.B. Lynn and A. Wildavsky (eds), *Public Administration: The State of the Discipline*, Chatham House, Chatham, 462–80.

Innes, J. (1995) 'Planning theory's emergent paradigm: communicative action and interactive practice', *Journal of Planning Education and Research*, 58: 440–53.

Inskeep, E. (1987) 'Environmental planning for tourism', *Annals of Tourism Research*, 14: 118–35.

Inskeep, E. (1991) *Tourism Planning: An Integrated and Sustainable Development Approach*, Van Nostrand Reinhold, New York.

Inskeep, E. (1994) *National and Regional Tourism Planning*, Routledge, New York.

Ioannides, D. (1995) 'A flawed implementation of sustainable tourism: the experience of Akamas, Cyprus,' *Tourism Management*, 16(8): 583–92.

ISO (1997) *ISO 140140: Environmental Management–Life Cycle Assessment–Principles and Framework*, International Organization for Standardization, Geneva.

International Union for Conservation of Nature and Natural Resources (IUCN) (1980) *World Conservation Strategy*, with the advice, cooperation and financial assistance of the United Nations Environment Education (UNEP) and the World Wildlife Fund (WWF) and in collaboration with the Food and Agricultural Organization of the United Nations (FAO) and the United Nations Educational, Scientific and Cultural Organization (UNESCO), IUCN, Morges.

International Union of Official Travel Organizations (IUOTO) (1974) 'The role of the state in tourism', *Annals of Tourism Research,* 1(3): 66–72.

Jackson, J., Houghton, M., Russell, R. and Triandos, P. (2005) 'Innovations in measuring economic impacts of regional festivals: A do-it-yourself kit', *Journal of Travel Research,* 43(4): 360–7.

Jacobs, J. (1965) *The Death and Life of Great American Cities: the Failure of Town Planning,* Penguin, Harmondsworth.

Jacobs, J. (1993) *The Death and Life of Great American Cities,* Random House, New York.

Jacobs, M. (1991) *The Green Economy,* Pluto Press, London.

Jain, N. and Triraganon, R. (2003) *Community-based Tourism for Conservation and Development: A Training Manual,* The Mountain Institute and the Regional Community Forestry Training Center for Asia and the Pacific, Washington DC and Bangkok.

Jamal, T.B. and Getz, D. (1995) 'Collaboration theory and community tourism planning', *Annals of Tourism Research,* 22: 186–204.

Jamal, T.B., Stein, S.M. and Harper, T.L. (2002) 'Beyond labels: pragmatic planning in multi-stakeholder tourism–environmental conflicts', *Journal of Planning Education and Research,* 22(2): 164–77.

Jansson, B. and Müller, D. (eds) (2007) *Tourism in Peripheries: Perspectives from the Far North and South,* CABI, Wallingford.

Jeffries, D. (1989) 'Selling Britain: a case for privatisation?', *Travel and Tourism Analyst,* No. 1: 69–81.

Jenkins, C. and Henry, B. (1982) 'Government involvement in tourism in developing countries', *Annals of Tourism Research,* 9(4): 499–521.

Jenkins, J. (1993) 'Tourism policy in rural New South Wales – policy and research priorities', *Geojournal,* 29(3): 281–90.

Jenkins, J. (1997) 'The role of the Commonwealth Government in rural tourism and regional development in Australia', in C.M. Hall, J. Jenkins and G. Kearsley (eds), *Tourism Planning and Policy in Australia and New Zealand: Cases, Issues and Practice,* Irwin Publishers, Sydney, 181–91.

Jenkins, J. (2000) 'The dynamics of regional tourism organizations in New South Wales, Australia: history, structures and operations', *Current Issues in Tourism,* 3: 175–203.

Jenkins, J. (2001) 'Statutory authorities in whose interests? The case of Tourism New South Wales, the bed tax, and "the Games"', *Pacific Tourism Review,* 4(4): 201–18.

Jenkins, J., Hall, C.M. and Troughton, M. (1998) 'The restructuring of rural economies: rural tourism and recreation as a government response', in R. Butler, C.M. Hall and J. Jenkins (eds), *Tourism and Recreation in Rural Areas,* John Wiley, Chichester, 43–68.

Jenkins, W.I. (1978) *Policy Anaysis: A Political and Organizational Perspective,* St Martin's Press, New York.

Jessop, B. (2002) 'Liberalism, neoliberalism, and urban governance: a state-theoretical perspective', *Antipode,* 34: 452–72.

Johnston, R.J. (1991) *Geography and Geographers: Anglo-American Human Geography since 1945,* 4th edn, Edward Arnold, London.

Jones, R. and Shaw, B. (eds) (2007) *Geographies of Australian Heritages: Loving a Sunburnt Country,* Ashgate, Aldershot.

Jordan, A. (1995) *Implementation Failure or Policy Making? How do we Theorise the Implementation of European Union (EU) Environmental Legislation?* CSERGE Working Paper GEC 95-18, Centre for Social and Economic Research on the Global Environment, University of East Anglia and University College London.

Jordan, A. and Richardson, J. (1987) *British Politics and the Policy Process,* Allen & Unwin, London.

Judd, D.R. (2003) 'Building the tourist city: editor's introduction', in D.R. Judd (ed.), *The Infrastructure of Play: Building the Tourist City,* M.E. Sharpe, Armonk, 3–16.

Kast, E. and Rosenzweig, J.E. (1973) *Contingency Views of Organization and Management,* Science Research Associates, Chicago.

Kearney, E.P. (1992) 'Redrawing the political map of tourism: the European view', *Tourism Management,* March, 34–6.

Kearns, G. and Philo, C. (1993) 'Preface', in G. Kearns and C. Philo (eds), *Selling Places: The City as Cultural Capital, Past and Present,* Pergamon Press, Oxford, ix–x.

Keil, R. (2003) 'Urban political ecology', *Urban Geography,* 24(8): 723–8.

Kelly, E.D. (1993) *Managing Community Growth: Policies, Techniques and Impacts,* Praeger, Westport.

Keogh, B. (1990) Public participation in community tourism planning, *Annals of Tourism Research,* 17(3), 449–65.

Keohane, R.O. and Nye, J.S., Jnr (1976) 'Introduction: the complex politics of Canadian–American interdependence', in A.B. Fox, A.O. Hero Jnr and J.S. Nye Jnr (eds), *Canada and the United States: Transnational and Transgovernmental Relations,* Columbia University Press, New York, 4.

Kincaid, J. (1990) 'Constituent diplomacy in federal politics and the nation state: conflict and co-operation', in H.J. Michelmann and P. Soldatos (eds), *Federalism and International Relations: The Role of Subnational Units,* Oxford University Press, New York, 54–75.

Kooiman, J. (ed.) (1993a) *Modern Governance: New Government–Society Interactions,* Sage, London.

Kooiman, J. (1993b) 'Findings, speculations and recommendations', in J. Kooiman (ed.), *Modern Governance: New Governmment–Society Interactions,* Sage, London, 249–62.

Kooiman, J. (2003) *Governing as Governance,* Sage, London.

Kotler, P., Haider, D.H. and Rein, I. (1993) *Marketing Places: Attracting Investment, Industry, and Tourism to Cities, States, and Nations,* Free Press, New York.

Krippendorf, J. (1987) *The Holiday Makers: Understanding the Impact of Leisure and Travel,* Heinemann Professional Publishing, Oxford.

Kroll, M. (1969) 'Policy and administration', in F.J. Lyden, G.A. Shipman and M. Kroll (eds), *Policies, Decisions and Organisations,* Appleton-Century-Crofts, New York.

Landis, J., Deng, L. and Reilly, M. (2002) *Growth Management Revisited: A Reassessment of its Efficacy, Price Effects, and Impacts on Metropolitan Growth Patterns,* IURD Working Paper Series, University of California, Berkeley.

Langton, M. and Palmer, L. (2003) 'Modern agreement making and indigenous people in Australia: issues and trends', *Australian Indigenous Law Reporter,* 8(1): 1, http:// www. austlii.edu.au/au/journals/AILR/2003/1.html.

Lansing, P. and de Vries, P. (2007) 'Sustainable tourism: ethical alternative or marketing ploy?', *Journal of Business Ethics,* 72(1): 77–85.

Le Pelley, B. and Laws, E. (1998) 'A stakeholder–benefits approach to tourism management in a historic city centre: The Canterbury City Centre Initiative', in E. Laws, B. Faulkner and G. Moscardo (eds), *Embracing and Managing Change in Tourism: International Case Studies,* Routledge, London, 70–94.

Leiper, N. (1989) *Tourism and Tourism Systems,* Occasional Paper No. 1, Department of Management Systems, Massey University, Palmerston North.

Leiper, N. (1990a) *Tourism Systems: An Interdisciplinary Perspective,* Occasional Paper No. 2, Department of Management Systems, Business Studies Faculty, Massey University, Palmerston.

Leiper, N. (1990b) 'Partial industrialization of tourism systems', *Annals of Tourism Research,* 17: 600–5.

Lennon, J.J. (ed.) (2003) *Tourism Statistics: International Perspectives and Current Issues,* Continuum, London.

Levine, N. (1999) 'The effect of local growth controls on regional housing production and population redistribution in California,' *Urban Studies,* 36(12): 2047–68.

Levins, R. and Lewontin, R. (1985) *The Dialectical Biologist,* Harvard University Press, Cambridge.

Lew, A. and Hall, C.M. (1998) 'The geography of sustainable tourism: lessons and prospects', in C.M. Hall and A. Lew (eds), *Sustainable Tourism: A Geographical Perspective*, Addison Wesley Longman, Harlow, 199–203.

Lew, A., Hall, C.M. and Williams, A.M. (eds) (2004) *A Companion to Tourism*, Blackwell, Oxford.

Lewin, K. (1948) 'Action-research and minority problems', in G.W. Lewin (ed.), *Resolving Social Conflicts*, Harper & Row, New York.

Lickorish, L.J., Jefferson, A., Bodlender, J. and Jenkins, C.L. (1991) *Developing Tourism Destinations: Policies and Perspectives*, Longman, Harlow.

Lindberg, K. and McKercher, B. (1997) 'Eco-tourism: a critical overview', *Pacific Tourism Review*, 1: 65–79.

Lindblom, C.E. (1980) *The Policy-Making Process*, 2nd edn, Prentice-Hall, Englewood Cliffs.

Lovelock, B. (2002) 'Why it's good to be bad: the role of conflict in contributing towards sustainable tourism in protected areas', *Journal of Sustainable Tourism*, 10(1): 5–30.

Lovelock, B. and Boyd, S. (2006) 'Impediments to a cross-border collaborative model of destination management in the Catlins, New Zealand', *Tourism Geographies*, 8(2): 143–61.

Lovins, A.B., Lovins, L.H. and Hawken, P. (1999) 'A road map for natural capitalism', *Harvard Business Review*, May–June: 145–58.

Lowes, M. (2004) 'Neoliberal power politics and the controversial siting of the Australian Grand Prix Motorsport event in an urban park', *Society and Leisure*, 27(1): 69–88.

Lowi, T.A. (1972) 'Four systems of policy, politics and choice', *Public Administration Review*, 32(4): 298–310.

Ludema, J.D., Cooperrider, D.L. and Barrett, F.J. (2006) 'Appreciative inquiry: the power of the unconditional positive question', in P. Reason and H. Bradbury (eds), *Handbook of Action-Research*, Sage, London, 155–66.

Lukes, S. (2005) *Power: A Radical View*, 2nd edn, Palgrave MacMillan in association with the British Sociological Association, London.

Lyden, F.J., Shipman, G.A. and Kroll, M. (eds) (1969) *Policies, Decisions and Organizations*, Appleton-Century-Crofts, New York.

Lynch, K. (1972) *What Time Is This Place?*, MIT Press, Cambridge.

Lyster, S. (1985) *International Wildlife Law: An Analysis of International Treaties Concerned with the Conservation of Wildlife*, Grotius Publications, Cambridge.

Macbeth, J. (1997) 'Planning in action: a report and reflections on sustainable tourism in the ex-Shire of Omeo', in C.M. Hall, J. Jenkins and G. Kearsley (eds), *Tourism Planning and Policy in Australia and New Zealand: Cases, Issues and Practice*, Irwin Publishers, Sydney, 145–53.

Madsen, H. (1992) 'Place-marketing in Liverpool: a review', *International Journal of Urban and Regional Research*, 16(4): 633–40.

Majone, G. (1980a) 'The uses of policy analysis', in B.H. Raven (ed.), *Policy Studies Annual Review*, Vol. 4, Sage, Beverley Hills, 161–80.

Majone, G. (1980b) 'An anatomy of pitfalls', in G. Majone and E.S. Quade (eds), *Pitfalls of Analysis*, International Institute for Applied Systems Analysis/John Wiley, Chichester, 7–22.

Majone, G. (1989) *Evidence, Argument and Persuasion in the Policy Process*, Yale University Press, New Haven.

Majone, G. (1996) *Regulating Europe*, Routledge, London.

Majone, G. and Wildavsky, A. (1979) 'Implementation as evolution', in J. Pressman and A. Wildavsky, *Implementation*, 2nd edn, University of California Press, Berkeley, 177–94.

Malecki, E.J. (2002) 'Hard and soft networks for urban competitiveness', *Urban Studies*, 39: 929–45.

Malecki, E.J. (2004) 'Jockeying for position: what it means and why it matters to regional development policy when places compete', *Regional Studies*, 38(9): 1101–20.

Mandell, M.P. (1999) 'The impact of collaborative efforts: changing the face of public policy through networks and network structures', *Policy Studies Review*, 16(1), 4–17.

Manning, B. (1977) 'The Congress, the executive and intermestic affairs: three proposals', *Foreign Affairs*, 55: 309–25.

Margerum, R.D. (1999) 'Integrated environmental management: the elements critical to success', *Environmental Management,* 65(2): 151–66.

Margerum, R.D. and Whitall, D. (2004) 'The challenges and implications of collaborative management on a river basin scale', *Journal of Environmental Planning and Management,* 47(3): 407–27.

Markusen, A. (1999) 'Fuzzy concepts, scanty evidence, policy distance: the case for rigour and policy relevance in critical regional studies', *Regional Studies,* 33(9): 869–84.

Martin, R.L. (2005) *A Study on the Factors of Regional Competitiveness: A Draft Final Report for the European Commission Directorate-General Regional Policy,* Cambridge Econometrics, Cambridge and Ecorys-Neil, Rotterdam.

Martin, R. and Sunley, P. (2003) 'Deconstructing clusters: chaotic concept or policy panacea?', *Journal of Economic Geography,* 3: 5–35.

Mason, P. (2003) *Tourism Impacts, Planning and Management,* Butterworth-Heinemann, Oxford.

Mason, P. and Mowforth, M. (1996) 'Codes of conduct in tourism', *Progress in Tourism and Hospitality Research,* 2(2): 151–67.

Mathieson, A. and Wall, G. (1982) *Tourism: Economic, Physical and Social Impacts,* Longman, Harlow.

Matthews, L.D. (1998) 'Tourism developments in sensitive environments: the design of architectural/infrastructural elements, processes and solutions', paper presented at Harnessing the High Latitudes Conference, University of Surrey, Guildford, June.

Mazmanian, D. and Sabatier, P. (1983) *Implementation and Public Policy,* Scott Foresman, Glenview.

McConnell, S. (1981) *Theories for Planning,* Heinemann, London.

McCool, S.F. (1994) 'Planning for sustainable nature dependent tourism development: the limits of acceptable change system', *Tourism Recreation Research,* 19(2): 51–5.

McCullogh, M. (1996) *Granville Island: An Urban Oasis,* Canada Mortgage and Housing Corporation, Ottawa.

McDavid, H. and Ramajeesingh, D. (2003) 'The state and tourism: a Caribbean perspective', *International Journal of Contemporary Hospitality Management,* 15(3): 180–3.

McIntosh, R.W. and Goeldner, C.R. (1986) *Tourism: Principles, Practices, Philosophies,* 5th edn, John Wiley, New York.

McKercher, B. (1997) 'Benefits and costs of tourism in Victoria's Alpine National Park: Comparing attitudes of tour operators, management staff and public interest group leaders', in C.M. Hall, J. Jenkins and G. Kearsley (eds), *Tourism Planning and Policy in Australia and New Zealand: Cases, Issues and Practice,* Irwin Publishers, Sydney, pp. 99–110.

McLean, G.N. (1996) 'Action-research in OD: RIP?', *Human Resource Development Quarterly,* 7(1): 1–3.

McLoughlin, J.B. (1969) *Urban and Regional Planning: A Systems Approach,* Faber & Faber, London.

McMichael, D.F. and Gare, N.C. (1984) 'Keynote address: the Australian realm', in J.A. McNeely and K.R. Miller (eds), *National Parks, Conservation and Development: The Role of Protected Areas in Sustaining Society,* Proceedings of the World Congress on National Parks, Bali, Indonesia, 11–12 October 1982, Smithsonian Institution Press, Washington, 258–66.

Medlik, S. (1993) *Dictionary of Travel, Tourism and Hospitality,* 2nd edn, Butterworth-Heinemann, Oxford.

Meier, R.L. (1995) 'Sustainable urban ecosystems: working models and computer simulations for basic education', in J. Brotchie, M. Batty, E. Blakely, P. Hall and P. Newton (eds), *Cities in Competition: Productive and Sustainable Cities for the 21st Century,* Longman Australia, South Melbourne, 455–68.

Meijkamp, R. (1994) *Service Products and Consumer Behaviour: How to Make Consumer Behaviour Environmentally Friendly,* Green Product Design, Delft.

Mellish, L.E. (2000) *Appreciative Inquiry at Work,* Mellish & Associates, Brisbane.

Mellor, A. (1991) 'Enterprise and heritage in the dock', in J. Corner and S. Harvey (eds), *Enterprise and Heritage: Crosscurrents of*

National Culture, Routledge, London and New York, 93–115.

Mercer, D. (1979) 'Victoria's Land Conservation Council and the alpine region', *Australian Geographical Studies,* 17(1): 107–30.

Metelka, C.J. (1990) *The Dictionary of Hospitality, Travel and Tourism,* 3rd edn, Delmar Publishers, Albany.

Metsähallitus (Forest and Park Service) (2000) *The Principles of Protected Area Management in Finland: Guidelines on the Aims, Function and Management of State-owned Protected Areas,* Metsähallituksen luonnonsuojelulkaisuja Sarja B No.54. Metsähallitus – Forest and Park Service, Natural Heritage Services, Vantaa.

Meyer, W.B. and Turner II, B.L. (1995) 'The Earth transformed: trends, trajectories, and patterns', in R.J. Johnston, P.J. Taylor and M.J. Watts (eds), *Geographies of Global Change: Remapping the World in the Late Twentieth Century,* Blackwells, Oxford, 302–17.

Michael, E.J. (2007) *Micro-clusters and Networks: The Growth of Tourism,* Elsevier, Oxford.

Michael, S. (2005) 'The promise of appreciative inquiry as an interview tool for field research', *Development in Practice,* 15(2): 222–30.

Mill, R.C. and Morrison, A.M. (1985) *The Tourism System: An Introductory Text,* Prentice-Hall International, Englewood Cliffs.

Millar, C. (1996) 'The Shetland way: morality in a resource regime', *Coastal Management,* 24: 195–216.

Millar, C. and Aiken, D. (1995) 'Conflict resolution in aquaculture: a matter of trust', in A. Boghen (ed.), *Coldwater Aquaculture in Atlantic Canada,* 2nd edn, Canadian Institute for Research on Regional Development, Moncton, 617–45.

Millar, C. and Yoon, H. (2000) 'Morality, goodness and love: a rhetoric for resource management', *Ethics, Place and Environment,* 3(2): 155–72.

Millennium Ecosystem Assessment (MEA) (2005) *Ecosystems and Human Well-being: Synthesis,* Island Press, Washington DC.

Miller, G. and Twining-Ward, L. (2005) *Monitoring for a Sustainable Tourism Transition: The Challenge of Developing and Using Indicators,* CABI, Wallingford.

Mills, E.D. (1983) *Design for Holidays and Tourism,* Butterworths, London.

Ministry of Advanced Education and Treaty Negotiations Office (2004a) News Release: BC boosts tourism training, jobs for First Nations, Ministry of Advanced Education and Treaty Negotiations Office, 12 March, http://www2.news.gov.bc.ca/nrm_news_releases/2004MAE0006-000161.htm.

Ministry of Advanced Education and Treaty Negotiations Office (2004b) Backgrounder: Economic development opportunities for First Nations, Ministry of Advanced Education and Treaty Negotiations Office, 12 March, http://www2.news.gov.bc.ca/nrm_news_releases/2004MAE0006-000161-Attachment1.htm.

Mitchell, B. (1989) *Geography and Resource Analysis,* 2nd edn, Longman, Harlow.

Moore, C.W. (1986) *The Mediation Process: Practical Strategies for Resolving Conflict,* Jossey-Bass, San Francisco.

Moos, M., Whitfield, J., Johnson, L.C. and Andrey, J. (2006) 'Does design matter? The ecological footprint as a planning tool at the local level', *Journal of Urban Design,* 11(2): 195–224.

Morales-Moreno, I. (2004) 'Postsovereign governance in a globalizing and fragmenting world: the case of Mexico', *Review of Policy Research,* 21(1): 107–17.

Moreno, E.R.M. (1989) 'The many uses of postoccupancy evaluation', *Architecture,* April: 119–21.

Morgan, G. (1986) *Images of Organization,* Sage, Newbury Park.

Morgan, K. (2004) 'Sustainable regions: governance, innovation and scale', *European Planning Studies,* 12(6): 871–89.

Morris, R. and King, C. (1997) 'Cooperative marketing for small business growth and regional economic development: a case study in wine tourism entrepreneurship', in S.W. Kunkel and M.D. Meeks (eds), *The Engine of*

Global Economic Development, Proceedings of the 42nd World Conference International Council for Small Business, San Francisco, June, http://www.icsb.org/conferences/w97/papers/FullPapers/index.htm.

Moudon, A.V. (1982) 'Blocks, lots and houses, San Francisco', *Space and Society,* 22: 110–17.

Moudon, A.V. (1986) *Built for Change: Neighbourhood Architecture in San Francisco,* MIT Press, Cambridge.

Mowforth, M. and Munt, I. (2003) *Tourism and Sustainability: Development and New Tourism in the Third World,* 2nd edn, Routledge, London.

Mulford, C.L. and Rogers, D.L. (1982) 'Definitions and models', in D.L. Rogers and D.A. Whetten (eds), *Interorganizational Coordination,* Iowa State University Press, Ames.

Müller, D.K. (1999) *German Second Home Owners in the Swedish Countryside: On the Internationalization of the Leisure Space,* Kulturgeografiska institutionen, Umeå.

Müller, D.K. (2002a) 'German second home development in Sweden', in C.M. Hall and A.M. Williams (eds), *Tourism and Migration: New Relationships between Production and Consumption,* Kluwer, Dordrecht, 169–86.

Müller, D.K. (2002b) 'Reinventing the countryside: German second home owners in southern Sweden', *Current Issues in Tourism,* 5: 426–46.

Müller, D.K. (2002c) 'Second home ownership and sustainable development in Northern Sweden', *Tourism and Hospitality Research,* 3: 343–55.

Müller, D.K. (2004) 'Second homes in Sweden: patterns and issues', in C.M. Hall and D. Müller (eds), *Tourism, Mobility and Second Homes: Between Elite Landscape and Common Ground,* Channelview Publications, Clevedon, 244–60.

Müller, D.K. (2006) 'Unplanned development of literary tourism in two municipalities in rural Sweden', *Scandinavian Journal of Hospitality and Tourism,* 6(3): 214–28.

Murphy, P.E. (1985) *Tourism: A Community Approach,* Methuen, New York.

Murphy, P.E. (1988) 'Community driven tourism planning', *Tourism Management,* 9(2): 96–104.

Murphy, P.E. and Murphy, A.E. (2004) *Strategic Management for Tourism Communities,* Channel View Publications, Clevedon.

Nauright, J. and Schimmel, K. (eds) (2005) *The Political Economy of Sport,* Palgrave Macmillan, London.

Newsome, D., Moore, S. and Dowling, R. (2001) *Natural Area Tourism: Ecology, Impacts and Management,* Channelview Publications, Clevedon.

Newsome, D., Dowling, R. and Moore, S. (2005) *Wildlife Tourism,* Channelview Publications, Clevedon.

New Zealand Institute of Economic Research (2003) *The Economic Benefits of Sister City Relationships: Report to Sister Cities New Zealand,* New Zealand Institute of Economic Research (Inc.), Wellington.

Nichols, M., Stitt, B.G. and Giacopassi, D. (2002) 'Community assessment of the effects of casinos on quality of life', *Social Indicators Research,* 57(3): 229–62.

Nield, K. and Egan, D. (2003) 'The economic impact of tourism: a critical review', *Journal of Hospitality and Tourism Management,* 10(2): 170–7.

Nordlinger, E. (1981) *On the Autonomy of the Democratic State,* Harvard University Press, Cambridge.

Norkunas, M.K. (1993) *The Politics of Memory: Tourism, History, and Ethnicity in Monterey, California,* State University of New York Press, Albany.

O'Faircheallaigh, C. and Ryan, B. (eds) (1992) *Program Evaluation and Performance Monitoring: An Australian Perspective,* Macmillan, South Melbourne.

O'Neil, R.V., DeAngelis, D.L., Wade, J.B. and Allen, T.F.H. (1986) *A Hierarchical Concept of Ecosystems,* Princeton University Press, Princeton.

O'Toole, K. (2000) 'From mates to markets: Australian sister city type relationships', *Policy, Organisation and Society,* 19(3): 43–56.

O'Toole, K. (2001) '*Kokusaika* and internationalisation: Australian and Japanese sister city type relationships', *Australian Journal of International Affairs,* 55(3): 403–19.

O'Toole, L.J. (2000) 'Research on policy implementation: assessment and prospects', *Journal of Public Administration Research and Theory,* 10(2): 263–88.

Office of National Tourism (1997a) *Towards a National Tourism Plan: A Discussion Paper,* Office of National Tourism, Canberra.

Office of National Tourism (1997b) *Getting it Right for the Millennium,* report by Jon Hutchison to the Minister for Industry, Science and Tourism, Office of National Tourism, Canberra.

Office of the Deputy Prime Minister (2005) *Planning Policy Guidance 15: Planning and the Historic Environment,* Office of the Deputy Prime Minister, London.

Office of the Premier, British Columbia (2006) *News Release: $4 Million Preserves Haida Culture and Builds Tourism,* Office of the Premier/Skidegate Band Council, 13 July.

Ohmae, K. (1983) *The Mind of the Strategist,* Penguin Books, New York.

Olds, K. (1998) 'The housing impacts of mega-events', *Current Issues in Tourism,* (1): 2–46.

Ollman, B. (1993) *Dialectical Investigations,* Routledge, London.

Ophuls, W. (1977) *Ecology and the Politics of Scarcity,* W.H. Freeman, San Francisco.

Organization for Economic Cooperation and Development (OECD) (1974) *Government Policy in the Development of Tourism,* OECD, Paris.

Organization for Economic Cooperation and Development (OECD) (1999) *What is OECD?* http://www.oecd.org/about/general/index.htm [accessed 15 March 1999].

Organization for Economic Cooperation and Development (OECD) (2007) *About OECD,* http://www.oecd.org/about/0,2337,en_2649_201185_1_1_1_1_1,00.html [accessed 1 April 2007].

Organization of American States (OAS) (1997) *Declaration of San José,* XVII Inter-American Travel Congress, San José, Costa Rica, http://www.oas.org/EN/PROG/TOURISM/decla.htm [accessed 11 January 1999].

Organization of American States (OAS) (2003) Final Act XVII Inter-American Travel Congress, 18–20 June, Ciudad de Guatemala, Guatemala, OEA/Ser.K/III.19.1, TURISMO/doc.15/03, June, 2003, http://www.oas.org/tourism/home/documents/tourism/05/xviii_iatc_final_act_eng.pdf [accessed 1 April 2007].

Organization of American States Tourism Section (2007) *Background About Tourism Section,* http://www.oas.org/tourism/home/background.html [accessed 1 April].

Ostrom, E. (1990) *Governing the Commons: The Evolution of Institutions for Collective Action, The Political Economy of Institutions and Decisions,* Cambridge University Press, Cambridge.

Owen, K.A. (2002) 'The Sydney 2000 Olympics and urban entrepreneurialism: local variations in urban governance', *Australian Geographical Studies,* 40: 323–36.

Page, S. and Hall, C.M. (2003) *Urban Tourism Management,* Pearson Education, Harlow.

Papatheodorou, A. (2004) 'Exploring the evolution of tourism resorts', *Annals of Tourism Research,* 31(1): 219–37.

Papatheodorou, A. (ed.) (2006) *Managing Tourism Destinations,* Elgar Reference Collection, Cheltenham.

Parker, S. (1999) 'Ecotourism, environmental policy and development', in D.L. Soden and B.S. Steel (eds), *Handbook of Global Environmental Policy and Administration,* Marcel Dekker, New York, 315–45.

Pearce, D.G. (1989) *Tourism Development,* 2nd edn, Longman Scientific and Technical, Harlow.

Pearce, D.W. and Turner, R.K. (1990) *Economics of Natural Environments and the Environment,* Harvester Wheatsheaf, Hemel Hempstead.

Pearce, D.W., Barbier, E.B. and Markandya, A. (1988) *Sustainable Development and Cost-Benefit Analysis,* IIED/UCL London Environment Economics Centre, LEEC Paper 88–03.

Pearce, D.W., Markandya, A. and Barbier, E. (1989) *Blueprint for a Green Economy,* Earthscan, London.

Pearce, P.L. (2007) 'Persisting with authenticity: gleaning contemporary insights for future tourism studies', *Tourism Recreation Research,* 32: in press.

Pease, K.S. (2003) *International Organizations: Perspectives on Governance in the Twenty-First Century,* 2nd edn, Pearson Education, New Jersey.

Pechlaner, H. and Sauerwein, E. (2002) 'Strategy implementation in the alpine tourism industry', *International Journal of Contemporary Hospitality Management,* 14(4): 157–68.

Peck, J. (2001) 'Neoliberalizing states: thin policies/hard outcomes', *Progress in Human Geography,* 25(3): 445–55.

Peck, J. and Tickell, A. (2002) 'Neoliberalizing space', *Antipode,* 34: 380–403.

Peelle III, H.E. (2006) 'Appreciative inquiry and creative problem solving in cross-functional teams', *Journal of Applied Behavioral Science,* 42(4): 447–67.

Pendall, R. (1999) 'Do land-use controls cause sprawl?', *Environment and Planning B: Planning and Design,* 26: 555–71.

Pendall, R. (2000) 'Local land-use regulation and the chain of exclusion', *Journal of the American Planning Association,* 66: 125–42.

Peters, B.G. (1996) *The Future of Governing,* University Press of Kansas, Lawrence.

Peters, B.G. (1998) *Globalization, Institutions and Governance,* Jean Monnet Chair Paper RSC No 98/51, European University Institute, Florence.

Peters, B.G. and Pierre, J. (2001) 'Developments in intergovernmental relations: towards multi-level governance', *Policy and Politics,* 29(2): 131–5.

Pforr, C. (2001) 'Tourism policy in Australia's Northern Territory: a policy process analysis of its tourism development masterplan', *Current Issues in Tourism,* 4(2–4): 275–307.

Pforr, C. (2006) 'Tourism administration in the Northern Territory in the era of the Country Liberal Party governance 1978–2001', *Australian Journal of Public Administration,* 65: 61–74.

Phillips, P.A. and Moutinho, L. (2000) 'The strategic planning index: a tool for measuring strategic planning effectiveness', *Journal of Travel Research,* 38(4): 369–79.

Philo, C. and Kearns, G. (1993) 'Culture, history, capital: a critical introduction to the selling of places', in G. Kearns and C. Philo (eds), *Selling Places: The City as Cultural Capital, Past and Present,* Pergamon Press, Oxford, 1–32.

Picken, F. (2006) 'From tourist looking-glass to analytical carousels: navigating tourism through relations and context', *Current Issues in Tourism,* 158–170.

Pierre, J. and Peters, B.G. (2000) *Governance, Politics and the State,* Macmillan, London.

Pigram, J.J. (1990) 'Sustainable tourism-policy consideration', *Journal of Tourism Studies,* 1(2): 2–9.

Pike, A., Rodríguez-Pose, A. and Tomaney, J. (2006) *Local and Regional Development,* Routledge, London.

Pocock, D. (1997) 'Some reflections on World Heritage', *Area,* 29(3): 260–8.

Porritt, J. (1984) *Seeing Green,* Basil Blackwell, Oxford.

Porter, M.E. (1980) *Competitive Strategy: Techniques for Analyzing Industries and Competitors,* Free Press, New York.

Porter, M.E. (1985) *Competitive Advantage,* Free Press, New York.

Porter, M.E. (1990) *The Competitive Advantage of Nations,* Macmillan, London.

Porter, M.E. (2002) '*Regional foundations of competitiveness: issues for Wales',* paper presented at Future Competitiveness of Wales: Innovation, Entrepreneurship and Technological Change, Wales, 3 April, available at http://www.isc.hbs.edu/archive-speeches.htm.

Powell, W. (1990) 'Neither market nor hierachy: network forms of organization', in B. Straw and L. Cummings (eds), *Research in Organizational Behaviour,* Vol. 12, JAI Press, Greenwich, 295–336.

Preobrazhensky, V.S., Yu, A., Vedenin, A., Zorin, I.V. and Mukhina, L.I. (1976) *Current Problems of Recreational Geography,* XXIII International Geographical Congress, Moscow.

Preskill, H. and Catsambas, T. (2006) *Reframing Evaluation Through Appreciative Inquiry,* Sage, Thousand Oaks.

Pressman, J.L. and Wildavsky, A.B. (1979) *Implementation: How Great Expectations in Washington are dashed in Oakland; Or,*

Why it's amazing that federal programs work at all, this being a saga of the Economic Development Administration as told by two sympathetic observers who seek to build morals on a foundation of ruined hopes, 2nd edn, University of California Press, Berkeley.

Primozic, K., Primozic, E. and Leben, R. (1991) *Strategic Choices: Supremacy, Survival, or Sayonara*, McGraw-Hill, New York.

Priskin, J. (2001) 'Assessment of natural resources for nature-based tourism: the case of the Central Coast Region of Western Australia', *Tourism Management*, 22: 637–48.

Priskin, J. (2003) 'Issues and opportunities in planning and managing nature-based tourism in the Central Coast of Western Australia', *Australian Geographical Studies*, 41(3): 270–86.

Putra, N.D. and Hitchcock, M. (2005) 'Pure besakih: a World Heritage site contested', *Indonesia and the Malay World*, 33: 225–37.

Rakoff, S.M. and Schaefer, G.F. (1970) 'Politics, policy and political science: theoretical alternatives', *Politics and Society*, 1(1): 51–77.

Rathje, W. and Murphy, C. (1992) *Rubbish!*, HarperCollins, New York.

Reade, E. (1997) 'Planning *in* the future or planning *of* the future', in A. Blowers and B. Evans (eds), *Town Planning into the 21st Century*, Routledge, London, 71–103.

Reason, P. and Bradbury, H. (2006) 'Introduction: inquiry and participation in search of a world worthy of human aspiration', in P. Reason and H. Bradbury (eds), *Handbook of Action-Research*, Sage, London, 1–15.

Redclift, M. (1987) *Sustainable Development: Exploring the Contradictions*, Methuen, London.

Redclift, M. and Sage, C. (1994) 'Introduction', in M. Redclift and C. Sage (eds), *Strategies for Sustainable Development: Local Agendas for the Southern Hemisphere*, Wiley, Chichester, 1–16.

Reed, J., Jones, D. and Irvine, J. (2005) 'Appreciating impact: evaluating small voluntary organisations in the United Kingdom', *Voluntas: International Journal of Voluntary and Non-profit Organizations*, 16(2), 123–41.

Reed, M.G. (1997) 'Power relations and community-based tourism planning', *Annals of Tourism Research*, 24(3): 566–91.

Reed, M.G. and Gill, A.M. (1997) 'Tourism, recreational, and amenity values in land allocation: an analysis of institutional arrangements in the postproductivist era', *Environment and Planning A*, 29(11): 2019–40.

Rees, W.E. (1992) 'Ecological footprints and appropriated carrying capacity: what urban economics leaves out', *Environment and Urbanization*, 4(2): 121–30.

Rees, W.E. (1995) 'Achieving sustainability: reform or transformation?', *Journal of Planning Literature*, 9(4): 343–61.

Rees, W.E. (2000) 'Eco-footprint analysis: merits and brickbats', *Ecological Economics*, 32(3): 371–4.

Rees, W.E. (2001) 'Ecological footprint, concept of', in S. Levin (ed.), *Encyclopedia of Biodiversity*, Vol. 2, Academic Press, San Diego, 229–44.

Relph, E. (1976) *Place and Placelessness*, Pion, London.

Relph, E. (2000) 'Classics in human geography revisited: *Place and Placelessness*', *Progress in Human Geography*, 24(4): 613–19.

Resilience Alliance (2007) Key concepts, http://www.resalliance.org/564.php.

Rhodes, R.A.W. (1981) *Control and Power in Central–Local Government Relations*, Gower, Aldershot.

Rhodes, R.A.W. (1988) *Beyond Westminster and Whitehall*, Unwin Hyman, London.

Rhodes, R.A.W. (1990) 'Policy networks: a British perspective', *Journal of Theoretical Politics*, 2(3): 293–317.

Rhodes, R.A.W. (1994) 'The hollowing out of the state', *Political Quarterly*, 65(2): 138–51.

Rhodes, R.A.W. (1996) 'The new governance: governing without government', *Political Studies*, 44: 652–67.

Rhodes, R.A.W. (1997) *Understanding Governance: Policy Networks, Governance, Reflexivity and Accountability*, Open University Press, Buckingham.

Richter, L.K. (1989) *The Politics of Tourism in Asia*, University of Hawaii Press, Honolulu.

Ritchie, J.B.R. (1984) 'Assessing the impact of hallmark events: conceptual and research issues', *Journal of Travel Research*, 23(1): 2–11.

Ritchie, J.R.B. and Crouch, G.I. (2000) 'The competitive destination: a sustainability perspective', *Tourism Management*, 21(1): 1–7.

Ritchie, J.R.B. and Crouch, G.I. (2003) *The Competitive Destination: A Sustainable Tourism Perspective*, CABI, Wallingford.

Ritzer, G. (1996) *The McDonaldization of Society: An Investigation into the Changing Character of Contemporary Social Life*, Pine Forge Press, Newbury Park.

Roberts, N.C. and King, P.J. (1989) 'The stakeholder audit goes public', *Organizational Dynamics*, 17(3): 63–79.

Roche, M. (1992) 'Mega-events and micro-modernization: on the sociology of the new urban tourism', *British Journal of Sociology*, 43(4): 563–600.

Rosenau, J.N. (1990) *Turbulence in World Politics: A Theory of Change and Continuity*, Princeton University Press, Princeton.

Rosenfeld, S.A. (1997) 'Bringing business clusters into the mainstream of economic development', *European Planning Studies*, 5(1): 3–23.

Ross, G. (1991) 'Tourist destination images of the Wet Tropical rainforests of North Queensland', *Australian Psychologist*, 26(3): 153–7.

Rossiter, D. and Wood, P. (2005) 'Fantastic topographies: neo-liberal responses to Aboriginal land claims in British Columbia,' *The Canadian Geographer*, 49(4): 352–66.

Ruhanen, L. (2004) 'Strategic planning for local tourism destinations: an analysis of tourism plans', *Tourism and Hospitality Planning and Development*, 1(3): 239–53.

Ruskin, J. (1989) *The Seven Lamps of Architecture*, Dover, New York.

Rutherford, L. (1994) 'Protecting World Heritage sites: Coal Contractors Limited v Secretary of State for the Environment and Northumberland County Council', *Journal of Environmental Law*, 6(2): 369–84.

Ryan, C. (2002) 'Equity, management, power sharing and sustainability – issues of the "new tourism"', *Tourism Management*, 23: 17–26.

Ryan, C. and Montgomery, D. (1994) 'The attitudes of Bakewell residents to tourism and issues in community responsive tourism', *Tourism Management*, 15(5): 358–70.

Rydin, Y. (2007) 'Re-examining the role of knowledge within planning theory', *Planning Theory*, 6(1): 52–68.

Rypkema, D. (1992) 'Making renovation feasible', *Architectural Record*, January: 27.

Sabatier, P.A., (1986) 'Top-down and bottom-up approaches to implementation research: a critical analysis and suggested synthesis', *Journal of Public Policy*, 6(1): 21–48.

Sabatier, P.A. (1987) 'Knowledge, policy oriented learning, and policy change', *Knowledge: Creation, Diffusion, Utilization*, 8(4): 649–92.

Sachs, W. (ed.) (1993) *Global Ecology: A New Arena of Political Conflict*, Fernwood Publications, Halifax.

Sadler, D. (1993) 'Place-marketing, competitive places and the construction of hegemony in Britain in the 1980s', in G. Kearns and C. Philo (eds), *Selling Places: The City as Cultural Capital, Past and Present*, Pergamon Press, Oxford, 175–92.

Saetren, H. (2005) 'Facts and myths about research on public-policy implementation: out-of-fashion, allegedly dead, but still very much alive and relevant', *Policy Studies Journal*, 33(4): 559–82.

Sager, T. (1994) *Communicative Planning Theory*, Avebury, Aldershot.

Sagoff, M. (1988) *The Economy of the Earth*, Cambridge University Press, Cambridge.

Saul, J.R. (1995) *The Unconscious Civilization*, Anansi, Concord.

Sautter, E.T. and Leisen, B. (1999) 'Managing stakeholders: a tourism planning model', *Annals of Tourism Research*, 26(2): 312–28.

Schattsneider, E. (1960) *Semi-sovereign People: A Realist's View of Democracy in America*, Holt, Rinehart & Wilson, New York.

Schiffman, I. (1995) *Alternative Techniques for Managing Growth*, Institute of Government Studies, University of California at Berkeley, Berkeley.

Schofield, J. (2001) 'Time for a revival? Public policy implementation: a review of the literature and an agenda for future research', *International Journal of Management Reviews*, 3(3): 245–63.

Scholte, J.A. (2000) *Globalization: A Critical Introduction*, St. Martins, New York.

Schrecker, T. (1991) 'Resisting environmental regulations', in R. Paehlke and D. Torgerson (eds), *Managing Leviathan*, Belhaven, London, 165–99.

Schusler, T.M., Decker, D.J. and Pfeffer, M.J. (2003) 'Social learning for collaborative natural resource management', *Society and Natural Resources*, 16(4): 309–26.

Scoullos, M.J. (2003) Impact of anthropogenic activities in the Coastal Region of the Mediterranean Sea, paper presented at the *International Conference on the Sustainable Development of the Mediterranean and Black Sea Environment*, Thessaloniki, Greece, May.

Selin, S. (1993) 'Collaborative alliances: new interorganizational forms in tourism', *Journal of Travel and Tourism Marketing*, 2(2/3): 217–27.

Selin, S. (1998) 'The promise and pitfalls of collaborating', *Trends*, 35(1): 9–13.

Selin, S. (1999) 'Developing a typology of sustainable tourism partnerships', *Journal of Sustainable Tourism*, 7(3/4): 260–73.

Selin, S. and Beason, K. (1991) 'Interorganizational relations in tourism', *Annals of Tourism Research*, 18: 639–52.

Selin, S. and Chavez, D. (1994) 'Characteristics of successful tourism partnerships: a multiple case study design', *Journal of Park and Recreation Administration*, 12(2): 51–62.

Selin, S. and Chavez, D. (1995) 'Developing a collaborative model for environmental planning and management', *Environmental Management*, 19(2): 189–96.

Selin, S. and Myers, N. (1995) 'Correlates of partnership effectiveness: the coalition for unified recreation in the Eastern Sierra', *Journal of Park and Recreation Administration*, 13(4): 38–47.

Selin, S. and Myers, N. (1998) 'Tourism marketing alliances: member satisfaction and effectiveness attributes of a regional initiative', *Journal of Travel and Tourism Marketing*, 7(3): 79–94.

Selin, S., Schuett, M. and Carr, D. (1997) 'Has collaborative planning taken root in the National Forests?', *Journal of Forestry*, 95(5): 25–8.

Selman, P. (1992) *Environmental Planning: The Conservation and Development of Biophysical Resources*, Paul Chapman, London.

Senate Standing Committee on Environment, Recreation and the Arts (1992) *The Australian Environment and Tourism Report*, Senate Standing Committee on Environment, Recreation and the Arts, The Parliament of the Commonwealth of Australia, AGPS, Canberra.

Senbel, M., McDaniels, T. and Dowlatabadi, H. (2003) 'The ecological footprint: a non-monetary metric of consumption applied to North America', *Global Environmental Change*, 13: 83–100.

Sewell, W.R.D. and Phillips, S.D. (1979) 'Models for the evaluation of public participation programmes', *Natural Resources Journal*, 19(2): 337–58.

Shackley, M. (1998) 'Introduction: world cultural heritage sites', in M. Shackley (ed.), *Visitor Management: Case Studies from World Heritage Sites*, Butterworth-Heinemann, Oxford, 1–9.

Sharpley, R. and Telfer, D. (eds) (2002) *Tourism and Development: Concepts and Issues*, Channel View Publications, Clevedon.

Shaw, G. and Williams, A.M. (2004) *Tourism and Tourism Spaces*, Sage, London.

Simeon, R. (1976) 'Studying public policy', *Canadian Journal of Political Science*, 9(4): 558–80.

Simmons, D. (1994) 'Community participation in tourism planning', *Tourism Management*, 15(2): 98–108.

Simpson, K. (2001) 'Strategic planning and community involvement as contributors to sustainable tourism development', *Current Issues in Tourism*, 4(1): 3–41.

Sinclair, T.A.P. (2006) 'Previewing policy sciences: multiple lenses and segmented visions', *Politics and Policy*, 34(3): 481–504.

Singh, S., Timothy, D. and R. Dowling (eds) (2003) *Tourism in Destination Communities*, CABI, Wallingford.

Slatyer, R.O. (1983) 'The origin and evolution of the World Heritage Convention', *Ambio*, 12(3–4): 138–9.

Slatyer, R.O. (1984) 'The World Heritage Convention: introduction comments', in J.A. McNeely and K.R. Miller (eds), *National Parks, Conservation and Development: The Role of Protected Areas in Sustaining Society*, Proceedings of the World Congress on National Parks, Bali, Indonesia, 11–12 October 1982, Smithsonian Institution Press, Washington, 734.

Smith, L.G. (1992) 'From condescension to conflict resolution: adjusting to the changing role of the public in impact assessment', in *Proceedings of an International Symposium on Hazardous Materials/Waste: Social Aspects of Facility Planning and Management*, Institute for Social Impact Assessment, Toronto, 96–101.

Smith, S.L.J. (1995) *Tourism Analysis: A Handbook*, 2nd edn, Longman, Harlow.

Smith, V. (ed.) (1977) *Hosts and Guests: The Anthropology of Tourism*, University of Pennsylvania Press, Philadelphia.

Smith, V.L. (ed.) (1989a) *Hosts and Guests: The Anthropology of Tourism*, 2nd edn, University of Pennsylvania Press, Pennsylvania.

Smith, V.L. (1989b) 'Preface', in V. Smith (ed.), *Hosts and Guests: The Anthropology of Tourism*, 2nd edn, University of Pennsylvania Press, Philadelphia, ix–xi.

Smith, V.L. and Eadington, W.R. (eds) (1992) *Tourism Alternatives: Potentials and Problems in the Development of Tourism*, 2nd edn, University of Pennsylvania Press, Pennsylvania.

Smyth, H. (1994) *Marketing the City: The Role of Flagship Developments in Urban Regeneration*, E & FN Spon, London.

Soldatos, P. (1993) 'Cascading subnational paradiplomacy in an interdependent and transnational world', in D.M. Brown and E.H. Fry (eds), *States and Provinces in the International Economy*, Institute of Governmental Studies Press, Berkeley.

Soterlou, E.C. and Roberts, C. (1998) 'The strategic planning process in national tourism organizations', *Journal of Travel Research*, 37(1): 21–9.

Spann, R.N. (1979) *Government Administration in Australia*, George Allen & Unwin, Sydney.

Stein, J.M. (ed.) (1993) *Growth Management: The Planning Challenge of the 1990s*, Sage, Newbury Park.

Stein, S.M. and Harper, T.L. (2003) 'Power, trust, and planning', *Journal of Planning Education and Research*, 23(2): 125–39.

Stephen, N. (1991) 'The growth of international environmental law', *Environmental and Planning Law Journal*, 8(3): 183–9.

Stoddart, D.R. (1965) 'Geography and the ecological approach: the ecosystem as a geographic principle and method', *Geography*, 49: 369–76.

Stoddart, D.R. (1967) 'Organism and ecosystem as geographical models', in R.J. Chorley and P.J. Haggett (eds), *Models In Geography*, Methuen, London, 511–48.

Stoddart, D.R. (1972) 'Geography and the ecological approach: the ecosystem as a geographic principle and method', in P.W. English and R.C. Mayfield (eds), *Man, Space and Environment: Concepts in Contemporary Human Geography*, Oxford University Press, New York, 156–64.

Storper, M. (1997) *The Regional World*, Guilford Press, New York.

Stout, R.J., Cannon-Bowers, J.A., Salas, E. and Milanovich, D.M. (1999) 'Planning, shared mental models, and coordinated performance: an empirical link is established', *Human Factors*, 41: 61–71.

Strohschneider, S. and Güss, D. (1999) 'The fate of the Moros: a cross-cultural exploration of strategies in complex and dynamic decision making', *International Journal of Pyschology*, 34(4): 235–52.

Sunley, P. (1999) 'Space for stakeholding? Stakeholder capitalism and economic geography', *Environment and Planning A*, 31(12): 2189–205.

Susskind, L. and Madigan, D. (1984) 'New approaches to solving disputes in the public sector', *Justice System Journal*, 9(2): 179–203.

Suter, K.D. (1991) 'The UNESCO World Heritage Convention', *Environmental and Planning Law Journal*, 8(1): 4–15.

Swart, K. (2005) 'Strategic planning: implications for the bidding of sport events in South Africa', *Journal of Sport and Tourism*, 10(1): 37–46.

Swedish Environmental Protection Agency [Naturvårdsverket] (2003) *Natura 2000: Safeguarding EU Biodiversity*, Swedish Environmental Protection Agency, Stockholm.

Talen, E. (2000) 'The problem with community planning', *Journal of Planning Literature*, 15(2): 171–83.

Tansley, A.G. (1935) 'The use and abuse of vegetational concepts and terms', *Ecology*, 16: 284–307.

Testoni, L. (2001) 'Planning for sustainable tourism', *Pacific Tourism Review*, 4: 191–9.

Timothy, D.J. (1999) 'Participatory planning: a view of tourism in Indonesia', *Annals of Tourism Research*, 26(2): 371–91.

Timothy, D.J. (2003) 'Supranationalist alliances and tourism: insights from ASEAN and SAARC', *Current Issues in Tourism*, 6(3): 250–66.

Timothy, D. and Tosun, C. (2003) 'Appropriate planning for tourism in destination communities: participation, incremental growth and collaboration', in S. Singh, D. Timothy and R.K. Dowling (eds), *Tourism in Destination Communities*, CABI, Wallingford, 181–204.

Torres, R.M. and Momsen, J.D. (2005) 'Gringolandia: the construction of a new tourist space in Mexico', *Annals of the Association of American Geographers*, 95(2): 314–35.

Tourism South Australia (1990) *Planning for Tourism: A Handbook for South Australia*, Tourism South Australia, Adelaide.

Tourism South Australia (1991) *Making South Australia Special: South Australian Tourism Plan 1991–1993*, Tourism South Australia, Adelaide.

Treuren, G. and Lane, D. (2003) 'The tourism planning process in the context of organized interests, industry structure, state capacity, accumulation and sustainability', *Current Issues in Tourism*, 6(1): 1–22.

Tuan, Y.-F. (1974) 'Space and place: humanistic perspectives', *Progress in Geography*, 6: 211–52.

Turner, A. (2001) *Just Capital: The Liberal Economy*, Macmillan, London.

Turner, B.L., Clark, W.C., Kates, R.W., Richards, J.F., Mathews, J.Y. and Meyer, W.B. (eds) (1990), *The Earth as Transformed by Human Action*, Cambridge University Press, Cambridge.

Tyler, D. and Dinan, C. (2001) 'The role of interested groups in England's emerging tourism policy network', *Current Issues in Tourism*, 4(2–4): 210–52.

Umemoto, K. (2001) 'Walking in another's shoes: epistemological challenges in participatory planning', *Journal of Planning Education and Research*, 21(1): 17–31.

Umemoto, K. and Suryanata, K. (2006) 'Technology, culture and environmental uncertainty: considering social contracts in adaptive management', *Journal of Planning Education and Research*, 25(3): 264–74.

Ungar, D.G. (1994) *The USDA Forest Service Perspective on Ecosystem Management*, Symposium on Ecosystem Management and Northeastern Area Association of State Foresters Meeting, 18 July, Burlington, Vermont.

United Nations (1992a) *Agenda 21: Earth Summit – The United Nations Plan of Action from Rio*, United Nations, New York.

United Nations (1992b) *Report of The United Nations Conference on Environment and Development, (Rio de Janeiro, 3–14 June 1992) Annex I, Rio Declaration on Environment and Development*, A/CONF.151/26 (Vol. I), United Nations, New York.

United Nations (1994) *Recommendations on Tourism Statistics, Statistical Papers, Series M. No. 83*, United Nations, New York.

United Nations (2000) *United Nations Millennium Declaration, Resolution 55/2, September 18*, United Nations, New York.

United Nations (2002a) *Johannesburg Declaration on Sustainable Development*, United Nations, New York.

United Nations (2002b) *Johannesburg Plan of Implementation*, United Nations, New York.

United Nations (2006) *The Millennium Development Goals Report 2006*, United Nations, New York.

United Nations Educational, Scientific and Cultural Organization (UNESCO) (1972) *Convention Concerning the Protection of the World Cultural and Natural Heritage, Operational Guidelines for the Implementation of the World Heritage Convention*, UNESCO, Paris, http://www.unesco.org:80//whc/opgutoc.htm [accessed 11 January 1999].

United Nations Educational, Scientific and Cultural Organization (UNESCO) Intergovernmental Committee for the Protection of the World's Cultural and Natural Heritage (1999) *Operational Guidelines for the Implementation of the World Heritage Convention*, UNESCO, Paris, UNESCO.http://www.unesco.org/whc/toc/mainf8.htm.

United Nations Environment Programme (UNEP) (2004) *UNEP/SETAC Life-cycle Initiative*, UNEP, Paris.

United Nations Environment Programme, Mediterranean Action Plan, Priority Actions Programme (UNEP/MAP/PAP) (2001) *White Paper: Coastal Zone Management in the Mediterranean*, Priority Actions Programme, Split.

United Nations, Conference on International Travel and Tourism (1963) *Recommendations on International Travel and Tourism*, United Nations, Rome.

van der Aa, B.J.M. (2005) *Preserving the Heritage of Humanity? Obtaining World Heritage Status and the Impacts of Listing*, doctoral thesis, Faculty of Spatial Sciences, University of Groningen, Groningen.

van der Aa, B.J.M., Groote, P.D. and Huigen, P.P.P. (2004) 'World heritage as NIMBY: the case of the Dutch part of the Wadden Sea', *Current Issues in Tourism*, 7(4–5): 291–302.

van der Haar, D. (2002) A positive change, http://appreciativeinquiry.case.edu/research/ bibCompletedDissertationsDetail.cfm?coid= 2473 [accessed 7 July 2006].

van der Haar, D. and Hosking, D. (2004) 'Evaluating appreciative inquiry: a relational constructionist perspective', *Human Relations*, 57: 1017–36.

Van Meter, D. and Van Horn, C. (1975) 'The policy implementation process', *Administration and Society*, 6(4): 445–88.

Vargo, S.L. and Lusch, R.F. (2004) 'The four service marketing myths: remnants of a goods-based, manufacturing model', *Journal of Service Research*, 6(4): 324–35.

Vickers, G. (1980) *Responsibility: Its Sources and Limits*, Intersystems, Seaside.

Visnovsky, E. and Bianchi, G. (2005) 'Editorial', *Human Affairs* 15/2005, http://www. humanaffairs.sk/editorial.htm [Accessed 15 April 2006].

von Droste, B. (1995) *World Heritage Newsletter*, No. 9, December.

Vukonic, B. (1997) 'Selective tourism growth: targeted tourism destinations', in S. Wahab and J. Pigrim (eds), *Tourism, Development and Growth: The Challenge of Sustainability*, Routledge, London, 95–108.

Waddock, S.A. and Bannister, B.D. (1991) 'Correlates of effectiveness and partner satisfaction in social partnerships', *Journal of Organizational Change Management*, 4(2): 74–89.

Wainwright, G.J. (2000) 'The Stonehenge we deserve', *Antiquity*, 74: 334–42.

Waits, M.J. (2000) 'The added value of the industry cluster approach to economic analysis, strategy development, and service delivery', *Economic Development Quarterly*, 14: 35–50.

Wall, G. and Mathieson, A. (2005) *Tourism: Change, Impacts, Opportunities*, Pearson, Harlow.

Wall, S. (2004) 'Protected areas as tourist attractions', paper presented at 'Tourism Crossroads: Global Influences, Local Responses', 13th Nordic Symposium in Tourism and Hospitality Research, 4–7 November, Aalborg.

Warner, K. and Molotch, H. (2000) *Building Rules: How Local Controls Shape Community Environments and Economies*, Westview Press, Boulder.

Warnken, J. and Buckley, R. (2000) 'Monitoring diffuse impacts: Australian tourism developments', *Environmental Management*, 25(4): 453–61.

Weber, E.U. and Hsee, C.K. (2000) 'Culture and individual judgment and decision making', *Applied Psychology: An International Review*, 49: 32–61.

Wettenhall, R. (2003) 'The rhetoric and reality of public–private partnerships', *Public Organization Review*, 3(1): 77–107.

Wheeller, B. (1993) 'Sustaining the ego', *Journal of Sustainable Tourism*, 1(2): 121–29.

White, G. (1972) 'Geography and public policy', *Professional Geographer*, 24: 101–4.

Whitford, M., Bell, B. and Watkins, M. (2001) 'Indigenous tourism policy in Australia: 25 years of rhetoric and economic rationalism', *Current Issues in Tourism*, 4(2–4): 151–81.

Whitney, D. and Trosten-Bloom, A. (2003) *The Power of Appreciative Inquiry: A Practical Guide to Positive Change*, Berrett-Koehler, San Francisco.

Wight, P.A. (1998) 'Tools for sustainability analysis in planning and managing tourism and recreation in the destination', in C.M. Hall and A. Lew (eds), *Sustainable Tourism Development: A Geographical Perspective*, Addison Wesley Longman, London, 75–91.

Wildavsky, A. (1987) *Speaking Truth to Power: The Art and Craft of Policy Analysis*, 2nd edn, Transaction, New Brunswick.

Williams, A.M. and Shaw, G. (1988) 'Tourism policies in a changing economic environment', in A.M. Williams and G. Shaw (eds), *Tourism and Economic Development: Western European Experiences*, Belhaven Press, London, 230–39.

Williams, P.W. and Gill, A. (1994) 'Tourism carrying capacity management issues', in W. Theobold (ed.), *Global Tourism: The Next Decade*, Butterworth-Heinemann, Oxford, 174–87.

Williams, R. (1997) *Marxism and Literature*, Oxford University Press, Oxford.

Wilson, A.G.W. (1986) 'System', in R.J. Johnston, D. Gregory and D.M. Smith (eds), *Dictionary of Human Geography*, 2nd edn, Blackwell, Oxford, 476–7.

Wingspread Journal (1996) 'Fostering sustainable community', *Wingspread Journal*, Spring, (www.johnsonfdn.org/jspring96.html) (accessed 17/3/97).

Wood, D.J. and Gray, B. (1991) 'Toward a comprehensive theory of collaboration', *Journal of Applied Behavioral Science*, 27(2): 139–62.

World Commission on Environment and Development (WCED) (the Brundtland Report) (1987) *Our Common Future*, Oxford University Press, London.

World Economic Forum (WEF) (2007) *The Travel and Tourism Competitiveness Report 2007: Furthering the Process of Economic Development*, World Economic Forum, Geneva.

World Heritage Committee (UNESCO, Intergovernmental Committee for the Protection of the World Cultural and Natural Heritage) (1984) *Operational Guidelines for the Implementation of the World Heritage Convention*, WHC/2 Revised, UNESCO, Paris.

World Tourism Organization (1970) *Statutes of the World Tourism Organization*, Text adopted by the Extraordinary General Assembly of IUOTO held at Mexico City, from 17–28 September.

World Tourism Organization (1991) *Resolutions of International Conference on Travel and Tourism*, Ottawa, Canada, World Tourism Organization, Madrid.

World Tourism Organization (1993) *Indicators for the Sustainable Management of Tourism: Report of the International Working Group on Indicators of Sustainable Tourism to the Environment Committee, World Tourism Organization*, World Tourism Organization, Madrid.

World Tourism Organization (1997) *Tourism 2020 Vision*, World Tourism Organization, Madrid.

World Tourism Organization (1998a) 'Asia warned about too much red tape', *WTO News*, September/October.

World Tourism Organization (1998b) 'Education seminar: unleashing tourism's job potential', *WTO News*, April/March.

World Tourism Organization (1998c) 'Governments' role in tourism', *WTO News*, September/October.

World Tourism Organization (1998d) 'Public–private partnerships', *WTO News*, May/June.

World Tourism Organization (1998e) 'Public–private strategy group formed', *WTO News*, May/June.

World Tourism Organization (1998f) 'European Tourism Forum: SG calls for European tourism strategy', *WTO News*, September/October.

World Tourism Organization (1998g) 'Austria streamlines its national tourism organization', *WTO News*, January/February.

World Tourism Organization (1998h) 'Baltic Sea destinations posed for tourism growth', *WTO News*, September/October.

World Tourism Organization (1999) http://www.world-tourism.org/.

World Tourism Organization (2001) *Tourism 2020 Vision: Global Forecasts and Profiles of Market Segments*, World Tourism Organization, Madrid.

World Tourism Organization (2006a) *International Tourist Arrivals, Tourism Market Trends, 2006 Edition – Annex*, United Nations World Tourism Organization, Madrid.

World Tourism Organization (2006b) *Tourism Highlights 2006*, United Nations World Tourism Organization, Madrid.

World Tourism Organization (UNWTO) (2007a) *About the WTO*, http://www.unwto.org/aboutwto/eng/menu.html [accessed 1 April 2007].

World Tourism Organization (UNWTO) (2007b) Tourism will contribute to solutions for global climate change and poverty challenges, press release, UNWTO Press and Communications Department, 8 March, Berlin/ Madrid.

World Tourism Organization (UNWTO) (2007c) *Why Join the UNWTO Affiliate Members?*, http://www.unwto.org/aboutwto/eng/menu.html [accessed 1 April 2007].

World Tourism Organization (UNWTO) (2007d) *Affiliate Members* (application brochure), UNWTO, Madrid.

World Travel and Tourism Council (1990) *Environmental Impact Assessment and Audit Guidelines*, World Travel and Tourism Council, Brussels.

World Travel and Tourism Council (2003) *Blueprint for New Tourism*, World Travel and Tourism Council, London.

Worpole, K. (1991) 'Trading places: the city workshop', in M. Fisher and U. Owen (eds), *Whose Cities?*, Penguin, Harmondsworth.

Worster, D. (1977) *Nature's Economy: A History of Ecological Ideas*, Cambridge University Press, Cambridge.

Yeoman, I., Brass, D. and McMahon-Beattie, U. (2007) 'Current issue in tourism: the authentic tourist', *Tourism Management*, 28(4): 1128–38.

Yuksel, F., Bramwell, B. and Yuksel, A. (1999) 'Stakeholder interviews and tourism planning at Pamukkale, Turkey', *Tourism Management*, 20(3): 351–60.

Zhang, Q.H., Chong, K. and Jenkins, C. (2002) 'Tourism policy implementation in mainland China: an enterprise perspective', *International Journal of Contemporary Hospitality Management*, 14(1): 38–42.

Zimmermann, E.W. (1951) *World Resources and Industries*, rev. edn, Harper & Brothers, New York.

Index

Aboriginal people 252, 253–4
Acropolis, Athens 155
action-research 85, 86
action sets 216
action statements 116
activity audits 129
adaptive planning 9
adaptive systems 230–1,
    233, 267
administrative coordination
    119
air pollution 148
Antarctic Treaty 138
appreciative inquiry (AI)
    85–91
Appreciative Participatory
    Planning and Action
    (APPA) 88
architecture, vernacular 233–4,
    239, 240
argument, dialectical
    analysis 98
argumentative planning
    theory 84
Asia Pacific Economic
    Cooperation (APEC)
    157, 183
Assembleia das Regioes
    Europeias Viticolas
    (AREV) 215
associate audits 128–9
Association of South East
    Asian Nations (ASEAN)
    144, 148, 157
Athens 155
audits 121–3, 127–9
Australia
    Aboriginal people 252
    Closer Economic Relations
        agreement 144
    community-oriented
        approach to planning 59
    Crown Casino,
        Melbourne 196
    Darling Harbour, Sydney 194
    economic approach to
        development 55–6
    environmental impact of
        tourism 35–6

Franklin Dam 149, 150,
    156, 246
government role 164, 165,
    168, 176, 183, 184
Hyatt Coolum, Queensland 4
Noosa, Queensland 2–4
Northern Territory 183, 252
OECD 144
Sister City relationships 185
South Australia 102–3
statistics, provision of 167
tourism policy 10, 11
Wet Tropics 153
wine tourism 215
World Heritage Convention
    150, 153, 156, 246–8, 249
World Tourism
    Organization 145
Austria 176, 188
Austrian National Tourism
    Organization (ANTO) 188
authenticity 230, 241

BACIP sampling 35–6
Baltic Sea Tourism
    Commission 157
baseline information 35
Birds Directive 110
Bohm, David 75
boosterism 15, 51, 52, 65
bottom-up approach to
    implementation
    255–6, 257–8
boundaries, system 72–3
Brazil 267
British Columbia 60, 202,
    204, 253–4
Brundtland Report 20, 62, 146
Bureau of Industry Economics
    (BIE) 211, 215–16

Canada
    Aboriginal people
        252, 253–4
    appreciative inquiry 88
    British Columbia 60, 202,
        204, 253–4
    First Nations Society, British
        Columbia 253–4

government role 165, 176,
    183, 184, 188
Granville Island, Vancouver
    233, 234, 235
growth management
    202, 204
NAFTA 144
OECD 144
statistics, provision of 167
tourism policy 10, 11
Vancouver 233, 234,
    235, 253
Whistler, British Columbia
    202, 204, 253
Winter Olympics 253
World Heritage
    Convention 156
World Tourism
    Organization 145
Canterbury, England 57,
    58, 77, 80
capital 26–7, 166
change, hierarchies of 231–3
Childwise 157
China 148, 185
Christchurch,
    New Zealand 240
Clarke Quay, Singapore 199
Cliff Palace, Mesa Verde
    National Park,
    Colorado 154
climate change 41, 140, 144
Closer Economic Relations
    agreement 144
clusters 56, 217–18
Cohesion Fund, EU 159
collaboration 120–5, 216, 218,
    263–4, 267
collective action 93
communicative planning
    theory 84
community management-based
    indicators of tourism
    impact 204–6
community-oriented approach
    to planning 51, 53, 59–62,
    65, 66, 67, 88, 204, 206
competitiveness 171–5,
    197, 198–200

compliance audits 128
conference centres 184, 196,
    200, 237, 239
conflict resolution 218–20, 221
connectedness 228
'conscious consumption' 64
conservation legislation and
    regulation 138, 147–56,
    160, 161
constituent diplomacy 183
constituent policy 223, 224
consumer awareness 64
contradiction, dialectical
    analysis 98
control systems, co-operative
    and integrated 63
Convention for the
    Preservation of Wild
    Animals, Birds and Fish in
    Africa 149
Convention on Biological
    Diversity 110, 138, 140
Convention on International
    Trade in Endangered
    Species of Wild Fauna and
    Flora (CITES) 140
Convention on Nature
    Protection and Wildlife
    Preservation in the
    Western Hemisphere 149
cooperation 119
coordination mechanisms 63,
    118–25, 164–5, 216
Copenhagen, Denmark 198
corporate audits 128
corporate planning 74
corporatisation of tourism 48
corporatist mentality 94
creativity, dialectical
    analysis 98
Crown Casino, Melbourne 196
Cuba 159
Customs Cooperation Council
    (CCC) 141–2

Darling Harbour, Sydney 194
decision-making 21, 61, 64,
    107–13
Denmark 198

deregulation 47–8, 143, 144, 160, 196, 197
Derwentside, UK 170
descriptive approaches to tourism planning 71
destination planning 114, 141, 142, 191–226
destinations 76, 77, 78, 79–80, 191–2, 193–202
devalorisation of capital 166
developmental planning 9
dialectical analysis 95–9
differentiation of destinations 31–2
direction setting 120
Disneyfication 229
distributive policy 223, 224
diversity 228, 238–9
Docklands, London 195
Dublin, Ireland 197
dyadic linkages 216

ecological approach to development 25–6, 58, 227–43, 262
ecological footprint analysis 39–40, 228
ecology
    ergodic hypothesis 34–5
    principles 228–9
economic analysis 73
economic approach to development 26, 51, 52, 55–6
economic dimension of tourism 27–30, 31–2, 35, 36, 41
economic planning 9
ecosystems
    concept of 73–4
    ecosystem services 26, 27
    human impact on 23–5, 37–41, 148
ecotourism 10, 19, 59
    planning 108–9
    regulation of 110, 112, 124–5
eduction, dialectical analysis 98–9
End Child Prostitution in Asian Tourism (ECPAT) 157
energy use 41
entrepreneurial role of government 166–7
environmental auditing 127–9
environmental capital 26, 27
environmental impact statements 57–8, 128
environmental impact of tourism 19, 23–5, 27–30, 31, 33, 35–41
    and land-use planning 58

life cycle assessment 234, 236–7
environmental issues, internationalisation of 110, 111–12
environmental legislation and regulation 93, 110, 112, 138, 147–56, 161, 166
environmental planning 10, 16, 58–9
ergodic hypothesis 34–5
Europäische Weinstrassen 215
European Community (EC) 143, 144, 147, 215
European Council of Wine Regions 215
European Council of Wine Routes 215
European Investment Bank (EIB) 159
European Regional Development Fund (ERDF) 159
European Union (EU) 157–60, 164, 183
    governance 135
    nature conservation 110, 112
    'welfare' tourism 7
European Year of Tourism 158
evaluation 88, 125–31
excursionists 5
exhibition centres 184
explicate order 75
'exploitative' rules 149
export industry, tourism as 55

feedback relations in systems 72
Finland 110, 112, 252
First Nations Society, British Columbia 253–4
flagship developments 237–8
forced migration 6–7
Forest Service, US 120, 124–5, 188
fragmentation of research 36, 49–50
Frangialli, Francesco 147
Franklin Dam, Tasmania 149, 150, 156, 246
freerider problem 168
'future preservation' 239

General Agreement on Tariffs and Trade (GATT) 136, 143
General Agreement on Trade in Services (GATS) 136, 143
generating region 76, 77
geographic scale 32–4
'geographical marketing' 193
Germany 31–2

global environmental change (GEC) 37, 41, 44, 139
global impact of tourism 37–41
Global Relief and Development Organisation (GRDO) 88
globalisation 163, 193–4
goals 115, 116, 117, 130
governance 134–6, 137–41
    implementation model 255–6
government role 10–11, 12–13, 14, 44–5, 47–9, 157, 163–89
    conflict resolution 221
    planning 61, 63, 64, 92, 119, 165
    regulation 65, 135, 143–4, 165–6
Granville Island, Vancouver 233, 234, 235
Greece 155
growth management 202, 203–4, 206–10, 264
Gujarat Tourism Corporation 166–7

Habitats Directive 110
Hadrian's Wall, UK 248
'hard' and 'soft' international law 137–40, 146, 156, 160
heritage attractions 56–7, 58, 241
'high-road' policies 200–2
Hong Kong 148
Hotels, Restaurants and Cafés in Europe (HOTREC) 157–8
human rights 1, 166
Hyatt Coolum, Queensland 4

Iceland 110
implementation
    approaches to 254–9
    definitions 244–5
    planning and policy instruments 249–54
    problem of 245–9
implicate order 75
India 166–7, 237, 267
indicators 118, 129–31, 204–6
Indonesia 148
industrialisation, partial 80, 216
infrastructure provision 49, 57, 164, 166, 196, 200–2
integrated tourism planning process 16, 17, 36–7, 101–33
interactional approach to implementation 255–6, 258–9

interest groups 121
International Air Transport Association (IATA) 171
International Bureau of Social Tourism 169
International Center for Conservation in Rome (ICCROM) 151, 152
International Civil Aviation Organization (ICAO) 141, 145, 171
International Council for Monuments and Sites (ICOMOS) 151, 152
International Expositions 184, 233, 235
international level of planning 134–61, 183
International Maritime Organization (IMO) 141
International Monetary Fund (IMF) 141
International Union for Conservation of Nature and Natural Resources (IUCN) 139, 151, 152
International Union of Official Travel Organizations (IUOTO) 48, 145, 164
International Union of Official Travel Publicity Organizations 145
interpretative planning theory 84
interviews 88, 90–1
Ireland 197
Israel 165
issue attention cycle 46–7
issues audits 128

Japan 148, 185

Kyoto Protocol 148, 237

land-use planning 13, 50, 146–7
    physical/spatial approach to planning 51, 53, 56–9, 65
Law of the Sea 110
legislation
    conservation 138, 147–56, 160, 161
    government role 165–6
    'hard' and 'soft' international 137–40, 146, 156, 160
    see also deregulation; environmental legislation and regulation; regulation
life cycle assessment (LCA) 234, 236–7
Lillehammer, Norway 240

linkages 216, 229–30, 263
literary tourism 170
local tourism planning process
102–3, 140, 141,
142, 188
London 195
'low-road' policies
200–2, 239

McDonaldisation 229
Malaysia 148
Man and the Biosphere
Programme 138
marine tourism 56, 110
market failure 48, 49
market imperfection 48, 49
marketing 48, 55, 167–8
place marketing 193–202
markets 49, 92
Mesa Verde National Park,
Colorado 154
Mexico 144
Migratory Species
Convention 140
millennium development goals
(UN) 21, 22
Millennium Ecosystem
Assessment (MEA) 21,
23–5, 26
mission statements 116, 117
monitoring effects of tourism
35–6, 204–6
Monterey, USA 229
Mount Cook National Park,
New Zealand 153
multipliers, tourist 73

national level 163–89
national parks 55, 56, 64, 149,
153, 188
Natura 2000 (EU) 110, 112
neoliberalism 196–7
networks 56, 210–18
implementation model
255–6, 258–9
New Zealand
Aboriginal people 252
Christchurch 240
Closer Economic Relations
agreement 144
government role,
institutional arrangements
for 175–6, 177–82
Mount Cook National
Park 153
OECD 144
Rogernomics 193
Sister City relationships
185–7
South Westland 153, 156
statistics, provision of 167
wine tourism 213–15

World Heritage Convention
156
World Tourism
Organization 145
non-tariff barriers 144
Noosa, Queensland 2–4
North American Free Trade
Agreement (NAFTA)
144, 156–7
North Korea 148
Northern Territory, Australia
183, 252
Norway 110, 155, 240, 252

objectives 115, 117, 130
obstacles to tourism 144
Olympic Games 55, 137, 184,
237, 239, 253
organisation change 88
organisation sets 216
organisations
characteristics of 74–5
planning and 113
Organization for Economic
Cooperation and
Development (OECD)
141, 143–4, 147
Organization of American
States (OAS) 142, 147,
149, 157, 159–60

Pacific Asia Tourism
Association 157
Pacific islands 165
Pan American Union 149
paradiplomacy 183
parallel relations in systems 72
partial industrialisation
80, 216
Participatory Learning and
Action (PLA) 88
performance monitoring
125–31
physical approach to planning
51, 53, 56–9, 65
place marketing 193–202
planning
approaches to 50–67,
70, 71
changing dimensions
of 44–50
definitions 8–9, 17
implementation instruments
249–54
international level
134–61, 183
national level 163–89
planning orientations 266–7
role of planning theory
12–13
sub-national level 134,
136–7, 164, 183–8

supranational level 110,
111–12, 134, 135, 140,
141–2, 147, 156–61
as theory 69–70, 84, 262
for tourism 10–15
policy
classifying 223–4
coordination 119
definitions 9–10
evaluation 125–6
implementation instruments
249–54
integration 107–13
'low-road' versus 'high-road'
200–2, 239
study of 10
as theory 69–70
prescriptive approaches to
tourism planning 71
preservation movements
233–4, 239, 241
private sector
coordination 164–5
deregulation 196, 197
entrepreneurial role of
government 166–7
partnership with
government 48
public interest
protection 170
supranational organisations
157, 160
World Tourism
Organization 145–6, 147
privatisation of tourism 48
problem definition 36
problem setting 120
producer awareness 64
project planning 206
promotion 48, 55, 166, 167–8
'protective' rules 149
public good 93–4, 168, 196–7
public interest 94, 169–70, 175
public participation 60–1, 63,
65, 66, 67, 94–5, 222,
253–4, 267
public policy 9–10, 14, 69–70,
107–13, 223–4

Ramsar Convention 110
Reaganism 47, 193
redistributive policy 223, 224
regional development 56
regional tourism planning
process 102–3, 104–6,
140, 141, 142, 165,
184, 188
regulation 65, 135,
143–4, 165–6
ecotourism 110, 112, 124–5
see also deregulation;
legislation

regulative policy 223, 224
'reimaging strategies' 193
relational effects of
tourism 35
relational psychology 75
relationships 210–18, 230
research 36, 49–50, 167
resources, controlling use of
25–6, 56–9
Rogernomics 193
Roros, Norway 155

San José Declaration 160
scale analysis 32–4, 81–2,
108–10, 111–12
series relations in
systems 72
Singapore 148, 199
Sister City
relationships 185–7
site audits 128
smart growth 204
social capital 26, 218
social dimension of tourism
27–30, 31, 36, 41, 49
and land-use planning
58, 146
social justice 166
social tourism 169
'soft' international law see
'hard' and 'soft'
international law
South Australia 102–3
South Korea 148, 185
South Westland, New Zealand
153, 156
space in dialectical analysis 97
spatial approach to planning
51, 53, 56–9, 65
sports stadia 184, 196, 200,
237, 239
stakeholders 120, 164–5, 219,
263–4, 267
audit 121–3
standpoint issue 82–4, 91–2
stimulation of tourism 167
strategic place marketing
194–5, 197
strategic tourism planning
64–5, 113–32, 195
structuration theory 98
sub-national level 134, 136–7,
164, 183–8
subsumption architecture 242
supranational level 110,
111–12, 134, 135, 140,
141–2, 147, 156–61
sustainable development
19–27, 36, 50, 264
indicators 129–31
and land-use planning
58, 65

sustainable tourism 20, 27–30, 33–4, 227–43, 262–7
  indicators 130–1
  planning 11, 44, 51, 53, 62–7, 92, 118, 147
  systems approach 92–5
Sweden 31–2, 110, 112, 170, 252
Sydney 194
synergistic approach to planning 102
systems approach to planning 16, 69–99, 96, 101

Taiwan 185
targets 117
tariff barriers 144
Tasmania, Franklin Dam 149, 150, 156, 246
temporal scale 32–4
Thatcherism 47, 193
theory, planning and policy as 69–70
time in dialectical analysis 97
top-down approach to implementation 254–7, 258
tourism
  definitions 1, 5–8, 30–1
  planning for 10–15
  relational effects of 35
  statistics and forecasts 1, 2, 5, 143, 167, 171–5
  see also sustainable tourism
Tourism Canada 188
Tourism Council of the South Pacific (TCSP) 142
tourism planning insights
  air pollution 148
  appreciative inquiry 85–91
  authenticity 230
  classifying policy 223–4
  ecological footprint analysis 39–40
  First Nations in British Columbia 253–4
  issue attention cycle 46–7

life cycle assessment 236–7
national travel and tourism competitiveness 171–5
prescriptive and descriptive approaches to tourism planning 71
role of planning theory 12–13
stakeholder audit 121–3
Tourism Program of the Organization of American States 142
Tourism South Australia 102, 103
tourism systems 76–81
Tourism Unit, OAS 160
trade agreements 141–7
'Tragedy of the Commons' 93
transit region/route 76, 77
travel, reasons for 5–7
Travel and Tourism Competitiveness Index (TTCI) 171–5
trust 220–2

uncertainty avoidance 266–7
United Kingdom
  appreciative inquiry 88
  Canterbury 57, 58, 77, 80
  'democratic deficit' 170
  Derwentside 170
  Docklands, London 195
  government role 183
  Hadrian's Wall 248
  Thatcherism 47, 193
  World Heritage Convention 248–9
United Nations 5, 21, 22, 144, 145
United Nations Conference on Environment and Development 20–1, 23, 138, 139
United Nations Conference on International Travel and Tourism 142

United Nations Development Programme (UNDP) 145, 147
United Nations Educational, Scientific and Cultural Organization (UNESCO) 145, 150–1, 152, 153, 156, 171, 246, 249
United Nations Environment Programme Mediterranean Action Plan Priority Actions Programme (UNEP/MAP/PAP) 41
United States
  Aboriginal people 252
  appreciative inquiry 88
  boosterism 55
  Cliff Palace, Colorado 154
  collaboration 120, 124–5
  government role 183, 184, 188
  growth management 204
  life cycle assessment 237
  Monterey 229
  NAFTA 144
  national parks 55, 188
  Reaganism 47, 193
  Sister City relationships 185
  statistics, provision of 167
  tourism policy 10, 11, 147
  uncertainty avoidance 267
  wilderness areas 149
  World Tourism Organization 145
United States Forest Service 120, 124–5, 188
United States Wilderness Act 149
Universal Declaration of Human Rights 1

Vancouver 233, 234, 235, 253
vernacular architecture 233–4, 239, 240
vision 115, 117

water consumption 41
waterfront redevelopments 194, 195, 196, 197, 198, 199, 237
Western Hemisphere Convention 149
Wet Tropics, Australia 153
Wetlands Convention 140
Whistler, British Columbia 202, 204, 253
wilderness areas 149
wine tourism 212–16
World Commission on Environment and Development (WCED) 20, 62
World Conservation Strategy (WCS) 138, 139, 140
World Economic Forum (WEF) 171–5
World Health Organization (WHO) 145
World Heritage Convention (WHC) 110, 138, 139–40, 149, 150–6
  implementing 245–9
World Heritage Fund 150, 151
World Heritage in Danger List 150, 152
World Heritage List (WHL) 150, 151–4, 156, 246, 247, 248
World Summit on Sustainable Development 21, 23
World Tourism Organization (WTO) 5, 136, 141, 143, 144–7, 171
  role 48, 56, 160
  tourism forecasts 1, 2
World Trade Organization (WTO) 136, 141, 143, 144
World Travel and Tourism Council (WTTC) 48, 56, 144, 147, 171